OSGi in Depth

OSGi in Depth

ALEXANDRE DE CASTRO ALVES

MANNING

SHELTER ISLAND

Manning Publications Co.
20 Baldwin Road
PO Box 261
Shelter Island, NY 11964

Development editor:	Sebastian Stirling
Copyeditor:	Linda Recktenwald
Poofreader:	Andy Carroll
Typesetter:	Marija Tudor
Cover designer:	Marija Tudor

ISBN: 9781935182177
Printed in the United States of America
1 2 3 4 5 6 7 8 9 10 – MAL – 17 16 15 14 13 12 11

brief contents

contents

foreword

After many years in ClassPath-land, the Java industry at large is finally starting to see the need for modularity in software development and deployment. There are many reasons for this. Maybe you just want to get out of the *Jar Hell*, where you're not quite sure anymore where a particular class comes from in your deployment. Other use cases for modularity center around providing isolation in a multi-tenancy context.

But there are more reasons. A modular approach makes developing software more scalable as modules tend to be highly focused with a clear demarcation of responsibility. A module's internals are inaccessible to the outside, which means that a modular approach tends to lead to well-defined APIs that better allow for concurrent development. It enables structuring of development teams such that parallel development of modules, which together form the application, is achievable.

The OSGi specifications provide a very mature, stable, and comprehensive modularity solution. The OSGi Core specification defines the OSGi framework, addressing modularity, lifecycle, services, and security aspects. Together these enable a dynamic system where *bundles*, the OSGi name for modules, are often remarkably reusable, properly encapsulated, and loosely coupled. The OSGi service registry enables an elegant plug-in model where consumers don't need to be preconfigured with any expected service provider implementation. The OSGi service model allows for services to be changed dynamically at runtime without the need to modify their consumers.

In this age of cloud computing, a system needs to be dynamically adaptable, highly manageable, and easily maintainable. OSGi technology facilitates all this alongside what is generally an extremely light infrastructure footprint. Runtime metadata and framework management is available through a standard API or via JMX, if enabled, and because bundles generally have clearly defined purposes, maintenance is easier and more localized—there's no more *big ball of mud* that needs to be dealt with.

OSGi is the only standards-based solution to modularity today, and given that it has been around since the late 1990s, it's a well-matured and very stable technology. A number of highly popular open source projects provide OSGi framework implementations today, and a number of commercial implementations are also available. OSGi is being used in contexts from embedded, residential, and mobile devices to highly scalable and performant server systems. Additionally, it is the infrastructure behind many rich client applications, of which the Eclipse IDE is probably the most well-known.

In this book, Alex Alves looks in detail at many of the OSGi Core concepts while also elaborating on a number of vital technologies from the OSGi Compendium and Enterprise specifications. As cochair of the Enterprise Expert Group, I'm particularly pleased to see a number of Enterprise OSGi technologies covered. You'll find chapters about OSGi remote services (note a very interesting cloud computing section in this chapter), JDBC and JPA, transactions, JNDI integration, and JMX support, while the Configuration Admin and Event Admin services are also covered. Last but not least, you'll find coverage of OSGi Blueprint, a specification inspired by the Spring Framework aimed at using and creating OSGi services in a simple and user-friendly way.

This is a book that both covers the high-level big-picture architecture topics as well as the details involved in getting things working on a practical level. It will give you a deep understanding of OSGi and will provide you with the knowledge you need to utilize OSGi to the full.

DAVID BOSSCHAERT
PRINCIPAL SOFTWARE ENGINEER, JBOSS BY RED HAT
OSGi ENTERPRISE EXPERT GROUP COCHAIR

preface

Ah, to build, to build! That is the noblest art of all the arts. Painting and sculpture are but images, are merely shadows cast by outward things on stone or canvas, having in themselves no separate existence. Architecture, existing in itself, and not in seeming a something it is not, surpasses them as substance shadow.

—Henry Wadsworth Longfellow (1807–1882)

Technology does not drive change—it enables change.

—Unknown source

I started working with OSGi in about 2006. This was back in the days of BEA and Web-Logic. Our goal was a very ambitious one: to create a new application server profiled for a particular vertical market—financial front offices.

The journey has been a long one. But as they say, it is not just about reaching the destination, but rather about the journey. I've learned more than I expected along the way. I've learned how to better develop reusable software, how to architect service-oriented implementations, and how to conceptualize software that is both maintainable and extensible.

The success of our project at BEA and now at Oracle is to a large extent a positive testimonial to the advantages of using OSGi. Relating my experience using OSGi and the advantages I've learned are the focus of this book.

acknowledgments

As it is the case with any large project, success is largely based upon the collective work of numerous people.

I would like to thank Manning for the opportunity—in particular Michael Stephens, my acquisitions editor, and the production team of Maureen Spencer, Karen Tegtmeyer, Mary Piergies, Linda Recktenwald, Andy Carroll, and my technical proofreader Ivan Kirkpatrick, who went over and beyond the call of duty in checking the code and providing many helpful suggestions for improving the manuscript. I would also like to express special thanks to my development editor Sebastian Stirling, for his excellent insight and feedback on my day-to-day work.

I would like to thank the following reviewers for reading the manuscript at various stages during its development and for providing invaluable feedback: Norman Richards, Adam Taft, Mykel Alvis, Mike Keith, Chad Wilson, Peter Kriens, Richard S. Hall, Rick Wagner, Pratik Patel, Jeff Davis, Mirko Jahn, Sivakumar Thyagarajan, Dru Sellers, Frank Kieviet, Gabor Paller, Jeremy Flowers, Denys Kurylenko, Steve Gutz, Janardhanan Vembunarayana, and Benjamin Muschko.

I would like to thank David Bosschaert of Red Hat for reviewing the final manuscript and writing an insightful foreword to my book.

I would like to thank the Oracle CEP team, for giving me the experience needed to write this book.

I would like to thank my father, Duarte, and my mother, Ana, for giving me the support I needed to continue my work regardless of all the other problems that life throws at you. Also, I would like to thank my brother, Rodrigo, for always being help-ful, and my sister, Larissa, for being the enthusiastic and loving person she is.

I would like to thank my sons, Gabriel and Lucas, for providing fun-filled book-writing breaks, and understanding when I was in the book-writing no-breaks mode (as they saw it).

Finally, I would like to thank Juliana, my wife-to-be, for her unyielding support, her caring, and for her lifelong understanding. For you, it's all worth it! Words put into a book last forever, and so will our love.

about this book

In this book, I show how the OSGi technology can be used to write better software, and in particular, how OSGi can be used to write better platforms for the development of better software.

Most importantly, I focus on real problems and on how OSGi can be used to solve them. Instead of just explaining OSGi's API for modularization, I first show you the problems that arise due to the lack of modularization. Instead of simply giving you OSGi's transaction API, I show you why and when you need to use transactions, and what the implications are of using transactions in a modularized service-oriented fashion in OSGi. As you read this book, you'll acquire in-depth knowledge of OSGi, and learn how to create containers that can manage transactions and persistence for applications!

Several years ago, it was inconceivable for a developer to write their own enterprise-grade development container or platform. OSGi has drastically changed this; it allows you to create your own domain-specific platform. OSGi is to domain-specific platforms what yacc is to domain-specific languages (DSLs).

Finally, in this book, I tackle some basic problems, but I don't shy away from the complex ones. You'll learn OSGi *in depth*. You won't just be looking at OSGi's API, but rather at the reason why the API is what it is, how you can best use it, and when not to use it. You'll even learn about open OSGi issues and what can be expected to change.

OSGi is an extraordinary technology. More than that, it's a game changer in the way large software is developed. To fully understand the reason for this, you need to understand OSGi *in depth*.

Who should read this book?

First and foremost, this book is aimed at developers, especially Java developers, who are interested in learning how to write better maintainable and extensible software.

The book will be of particular interest to enterprise-level developers and architects who are learning better ways of putting their software together, reusing components from different vendors, and extending the usable life of their systems, while decreasing their costs. Enterprise developers and architects will learn how to seamlessly leverage enterprise services, such as persistence, transactions, and remote communication from different vendors.

Finally, the book is aimed at experienced developers and architects who have either built or want to learn how to build their own development platforms and software frameworks.

The book is not targeted to a particular OSGi implementation or vendor, but it does use Apache Felix and, to a lesser extent, Eclipse Equinox for the examples in the book.

The book is based upon OSGi Service Platform 4.2 and some aspects of the recently published 4.3 version.

Ultimately, I like to think this is a book for programmers and architects who wish to learn how to build better systems.

Roadmap

The book can be divided into two main parts. Chapters 1 to 4 focus on the OSGi framework. Chapters 5 to 13 focus on OSGi services.

Chapter 1 provides a high-level description of OSGi and a rationale for using it. It also highlights the state of the art in terms of players and vendors in the market.

Chapter 2 provides a quick but complete primer on the OSGi framework.

In chapter 3, you explore a case study for a real OSGi application. At the end of this chapter, several shortcomings are highlighted, such as the lack of persistence, which you'll learn how to solve throughout the book.

In chapter 4, you take an in-depth look at advanced features of the OSGi framework.

In chapter 5, you learn how to configure OSGi applications.

In chapter 6, you learn how to send and receive OSGi events.

In chapter 7, you learn about persistence bundles.

In chapter 8, you take your first steps toward learning how to write your own containers by developing a container-managed transaction bundle.

In chapter 9, you learn how to use JNDI to integrate OSGi and JEE.

In chapter 10, you learn about remote services and how OSGi can be used for cloud computing.

In chapter 11, you learn how to use JMX to manage in-production OSGi applications.

In chapter 12, you learn about start levels, and how to abstract OSGi from end users.

Finally, in chapter 13, you take your second step towards learning how to write containers by extending the Blueprint service. Here you revisit the application from chapter 3, improving it by putting together everything you've learned in the book.

For reference, appendix A describes all the OSGi manifest headers used in this book.

Code conventions and downloads

All code in the book is presented in a `fixed-width font like this` to separate it from ordinary text. Code annotations accompany many of the listings, highlighting important concepts. In some cases, numbered bullets link to explanations that follow the listing.

You will find the full code for all the examples in the book available for download from the publisher's website at www.manning.com/OSGinDepth.

Author Online

The purchase of *OSGi in Depth* includes free access to a private forum run by Manning Publications where you can make comments about the book, ask technical questions, and receive help from the author and other users. You can access and subscribe to the forum at www.manning.com/OSGiinDepth. This page provides information on how to get on the forum once you're registered, what kind of help is available, and the rules of conduct in the forum.

Manning's commitment to our readers is to provide a venue where a meaningful dialogue between individual readers and between readers and the author can take place. It isn't a commitment to any specific amount of participation on the part of the author, whose contributions to the book's forum remain voluntary (and unpaid). We suggest you try asking the author some challenging questions, lest his interest stray!

The Author Online forum and the archives of previous discussions will be accessible from the publisher's website as long as the book is in print.

about the cover illustration

On the cover of *OSGi in Depth* is "A man from Kastela," a village in the Dalmatian region of Croatia. The illustration is taken from a reproduction of an album of Croatian traditional costumes from the mid-nineteenth century by Nikola Arsenovic, published by the Ethnographic Museum in Split, Croatia, in 2003. The illustrations were obtained from a helpful librarian at the Ethnographic Museum in Split, itself situated in the Roman core of the medieval center of the town: the ruins of Emperor Diocletian's retirement palace from around AD 304. The book includes finely colored illustrations of figures from different regions of Croatia, accompanied by descriptions of the costumes and of everyday life.

Kastela is comprised of a series of seven towns in central Dalmatia, located northwest of Split. Once an ancient Greek port, a stopover point for the Roman army, and a summer place for Croatian kings, Kastela today is a vibrant tourist resort, with long sandy beaches, beautiful terraces, tennis courts, and other sports venues, surrounded by the lush greenery of pine and tamaris trees. The figure on the cover wears a costume typical for this region of Croatia—blue woolen trousers and jacket, decorated with fancy embroidery, and a red pillbox cap called a *crvenkapa*.

Dress codes and lifestyles have changed over the last 200 years, and the diversity by region, so rich at the time, has faded away. It is now hard to tell apart the inhabitants of different continents, let alone of different hamlets or towns separated by only a few miles. Perhaps we have traded cultural diversity for a more varied personal life—certainly for a more varied and fast-paced technological life.

Manning celebrates the inventiveness and initiative of the computer business with book covers based on the rich diversity of regional life of two centuries ago, brought back to life by illustrations from old books and collections like this one.

OSGi as a new platform for application development

This chapter covers

- Underlying concepts of development platforms
- OSGi technology, including the framework and the enterprise services
- The benefits of using OSGi for the development of enterprise-grade applications
- The relation of Enterprise OSGi to Java Standard Edition and Java Enterprise Edition
- The current OSGi players in the market

We've all used development platforms in the past, such as Java Enterprise Edition (JEE), and even though there have been great advances in this industry, we're still building large complex systems, which are hard to develop, maintain, and extend.

OSGi provides a new development platform, based on modular decoupled components and a pluggable dynamic service model. In this book, you'll learn that OSGi is the ideal platform for the development of full-fledged, enterprise-grade, maintainable applications. Furthermore, we'll look in depth at how OSGi applications can use a plethora of carrier-grade infrastructure services, such as HTTP, configuration, deployment, event handling, transactions, persistence, RMI, naming and directory services, and management.

We'll start this chapter by exploring development platforms and the benefits of using such platforms to develop software. We'll then discuss the requirements of a platform intended for the development of enterprise-grade applications. Next, we'll focus on the OSGi technology, expanding into its core pieces, called the OSGi framework, and its enterprise services. Finally, you'll learn why OSGi is a good fit as a development platform, particularly in light of existing solutions, such as JEE. Let's start by examining the basics.

1.1   *What are development platforms and application frameworks?*

In the context of software development, a *development platform* is a set of software libraries and tools that aid in the development of software components, and the corresponding runtime environment that can host these developed components, as shown in figure 1.1.

The *runtime environment* may consist of the hardware, operating system (OS), and supporting runtime libraries. One example of a runtime environment is the Java Runtime Environment (JRE), which includes the Java virtual machine (JVM) that isolates the developer from the details of the underlying OS and hardware.

Software frameworks are specialized types of a development platform's libraries and tools. Wikipedia defines a software framework as an "abstraction providing generic functionality that can be selectively specialized to provide specific functionality."

Particularly interesting to us are application frameworks. An application framework is a type of software framework whose purpose is to provide a structure for the creation of software applications. Applications are programs that allow users to perform related tasks together. Examples of software applications are document editors and antivirus software.

Putting it all together, a development platform allows a developer to create applications and to host these applications so that end users can use them. Throughout this book, it's important to keep these two players in mind: the developer (you) and

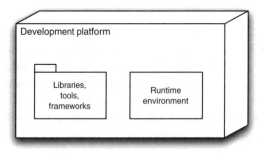

Figure 1.1   **A development platform consists of a software framework and its supporting runtime environment.**

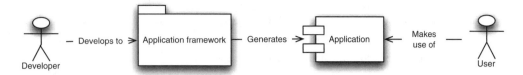

Figure 1.2 A developer creates an application, which is used by a user, and develops to a framework.

the end user, as illustrated in figure 1.2. Software development platforms are also called toolkits or SDKs (software development kits).

Historically, development platforms have always played an import role in software. The Java platform, also known as Java Standard Edition (JSE), is one example. In this case, the Java development kit (JDK) provides the software framework, and the Java Runtime Environment (JRE) provides the runtime environment. The OSGi Service Platform, which is the subject of this book, is another example of a development platform. The OSGi Service Platform uses the JRE as its runtime environment. In addition, it provides an application framework layered on top of the JDK. We'll look into its details throughout this book, but first let's see why it's important to use a development platform to begin with.

1.1.1 Why use a development platform?

Consider the following definition of the word *framework*:

> *"an essential supporting structure of a building, vehicle, or object"*

Why is the supporting structure of a vehicle important? It clearly sounds like it's important, but let's see if I can articulate why that's the case. I can think of two main reasons:

- It guarantees that I'm sitting on top of something that's solid—something that has been designed properly, implemented suitably, and tested thoroughly. A framework helps to decrease defects. This is a runtime characteristic.
- It gives the manufacturer an opportunity to reuse the frame for different vehicles. A framework helps to improve productivity through reuse. This is a design-time characteristic.

It's no different for development platforms. Development frameworks allow the creation of new applications in a form that's both efficient and has a high degree of quality.

1.1.2 Enterprise platforms

Enterprise platforms are development platforms that support the creation of enterprise applications—applications that implement business processes, business logic, or business integration to an enterprise. Examples of enterprise applications are a loan-approval application, an order-processing application, a customer relationship management (CRM) application, and a travel management application.

The following two aspects characterize enterprise platforms:

- Enterprise platforms provide a collection of infrastructure-level utilities and services common to many businesses and industries, such as management, directory service, monitoring, and distribution.
- Enterprise platforms must scale, perform efficiently, and be robust and fault tolerant.

Following up on our previous example, Java also has an enterprise version, which is called Java Enterprise Edition (JEE). Other examples of enterprise platforms are Microsoft's .NET Framework, SpringSource's tc Server Development Edition, and to some extent, Google's Web Toolkit. Recently, a new enterprise platform has been developed, the OSGi Service Platform Enterprise Specification.

As you can see by the number of players, enterprise technology is quite mature, so why is there a need for a new platform, such as the one being provided by OSGi? We'll address this question in section 1.3, but before we can do that, you need to understand OSGi a bit better.

1.2   *The OSGi technology*

The Open Service Gateway initiative (OSGi) was formed in March 1999 by a consortium of leading technology companies with the mission to define a *universal integration platform for the interoperability of applications and services.*

When I first read their mission, it gave me the impression of being both overly complex and somewhat outdated. Hadn't people already created a universal platform for applications? As you'll learn, no one has been able to do it successfully.

1.2.1   *The problem domain*

First, let's investigate the underlying problem that these companies were facing. The initial members of the OSGi alliance were in a large part telecommunication equipment manufacturers and service providers. They were interested in deploying software applications on small-memory devices. For example, consider a mobile phone as the device and a location-tracking application and an advertisement application as the software applications being deployed to the mobile phone. The location-tracking application uses the mobile phone to verify the current location of the subscriber and informs the advertisement application of the location. The app then retrieves selected advertisements that are suitable to the current location of the subscriber, such as promotions from nearby restaurants, as shown in figure 1.3.

This seemingly simple interaction caused the equipment and service providers several interesting problems. First, the devices tend to have different hardware and thus different programming APIs. Hence, each vendor had to program its applications to a specific device and then port to other devices. Second, not only do the various hardware devices use different programming APIs, but there's also a large variation in their functions and capabilities. Some have more memory than others; some have a disk whereas others are completely diskless; some have GPS and some do not. Third, the

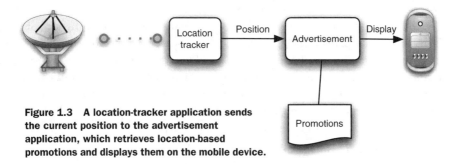

Figure 1.3 A location-tracker application sends the current position to the advertisement application, which retrieves location-based promotions and displays them on the mobile device.

lifetime of these devices is generally between one to two years, which means that new applications are likely to be created during this period, partly because of changing market demands. These new applications need to be dynamically deployed to the devices and join the existing collaborating applications that are currently running in the devices. And finally, because of the scarcity of the resources, these applications needed to closely cooperate with each other in a concise and, more important, light-weight manner.

This is no simple matter after all. Is there an existing universal platform that could help us, or does one need to be created?

Again, let's go through the problems.

PROBLEM: COPING WITH DIVERSE PROGRAMMING APIS

The first problem is portability. We need a single programming platform that abstracts the application from the underlying operating system and the hardware. In other words, we need a virtual machine. Does anything come to your mind? Yes, of course. Let's use Java to solve our first problem.

PROBLEM: VARYING DEVICE CAPABILITY

The second problem is subtler. Let's consider a specific case. The advertisement application can retrieve the available promotions from different sources. If the device has ample bandwidth, the data source could be remote. If the device doesn't have enough bandwidth but has a disk, then the promotions could be retrieved in the background and cached in the local disk as the subscriber enters a location, as shown in figure 1.4.

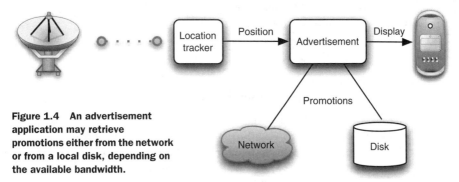

Figure 1.4 An advertisement application may retrieve promotions either from the network or from a local disk, depending on the available bandwidth.

There's a clear service contract between the advertisement application and the data source, but the implementation of this contract will vary depending on the device. This universal platform must make it easy for applications to decouple service contracts from the service implementation. The Standard Edition of Java (JSE) doesn't have a service registry or a service management framework that could help us with this. Hence, this facility either needs to be implemented from scratch, or we could try to borrow something from the Enterprise Edition (JEE) of Java. Let's hold on to this thought and tackle it after going through the other problems.

PROBLEM: SUPPORTING DYNAMIC CHANGES

The third problem can be summarized by the following requirement: the platform must allow the dynamic deployment and undeployment of applications in a secure form. Does JSE have support for this? Not really. You could try to solve this with the Java class loaders, but it wouldn't be easy, and there's no simple way of unloading classes after they've been loaded, not to mention that there's no concept of an application deployment unit. The closest concept to an application deployment unit is the idea of JARs (Java Archives), but JARs by themselves don't provide all the metadata that's needed, such as a unique naming schema for the applications.

As with the previous problem, we can implement our own solution for dynamic deployment of applications or try to leverage something from JEE. For example, web servers do have the concept of web applications, which are defined as part of a WAR (Web Archive) deployment unit file.

PROBLEM: PROVIDING A LIGHTWEIGHT SYSTEM

This brings us to the last problem. Whatever solution we pick, it must be lightweight. Yes, we could try to leverage a directory service such as JNDI from JEE or leverage the architecture from web servers, but these solutions would fail to consider the size and memory constraints enforced by the devices onto the platform, making it less suitable for embedded solutions and not a viable option.

1.2.2 *The solution: a dynamic module system for Java*

Java addresses some of the problems we've discussed, such as portability, but not all of them. For instance, it lacks proper support for dynamic service management.

Enter the OSGi Service Platform. In its most succinct definition, the OSGi Service Platform, or OSGi platform for short, is a dynamic module system for Java. In OSGi terminology, a Java module is called a *bundle*.

The OSGi Service Platform is composed of two main components, the OSGi framework and the OSGi services, as shown in figure 1.5.

THE OSGI FRAMEWORK

The OSGi framework provides its users with all the pieces that we discussed in the previous section:

- A portable and secure execution environment based on Java
- A service management system, which can be used to register and share services across bundles and decouple service providers from service consumers

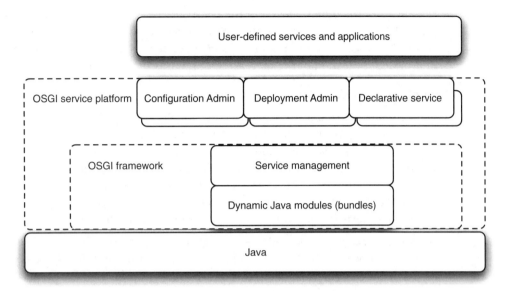

Figure 1.5   The OSGi Service Platform comprises the OSGi framework and the OSGi services.

- A dynamic module system, which can be used to dynamically install and uninstall Java modules, which OSGi calls bundles
- A lightweight and scalable solution

The OSGi framework is the core structure of the OSGi Service Platform. It can be seen as a backplane that hosts bundles, possibly containing services. If you consider that a bundle can be an application, then the definition of the OSGi framework is in accordance with our definition of application frameworks. That is to say, the OSGi framework is an example of an application framework.

Right now, we'll leave the definition of the OSGi framework somewhat loose. Let's not worry about what exactly bundles and services are. We'll discuss the framework, its concepts, and its APIs in detail in the next chapters.

THE OSGI SERVICES

Alongside the OSGI framework, the OSGI Service Platform includes several general-purpose services. You can think of these services as native applications of the OSGi Service Platform.

Some of these services are horizontal functions that are mostly always needed, such as a logging service and a configuration service.

Some are protocol related, such as an HTTP service, which could be used by a web-based application.

And finally, some services are intrinsically tied to the framework, which won't work without them. Examples of these are the bundle wiring, which manages the dynamic module system itself, and the start-level service, which manages the bootstrap process of the framework.

The focus of the initial releases of the OSGi Service Platform had been on the OSGi framework, but gradually we see the OSGi services playing a more prominent role. This trend toward other components, such as services, built on top of the core OSGi framework is a reflection of the increasing popularity of the technology.

1.2.3   *The Enterprise OSGi*

As can be deduced from its history, OSGi was initially employed in the embedded market. But with its growing popularity and maturity, OSGi is moving to the enterprise market. To address this requirement, the OSGi Enterprise Expert Group (EEG) created the OSGi Service Platform Enterprise Specification (Enterprise OSGi).

This specification combines OSGi services that can selectively be used to provide enterprise functionality. These services can be grouped into enterprise features. Examples of enterprise features, as shown in figure 1.6, are the following:

- *Management and configuration*—This group includes the Configuration Admin service as well as the JMX Management Model service and the Metatype service.
- *Distribution*—This feature allows the communication of end points between remote instances of OSGi framework instances. Some of the services in this group are the Remote Service and the SCA Configuration Type.
- *Data access*—This feature includes support for JDBC, JPA, and JTA and allows the manipulation of persisted objects.

Before getting into the details of the OSGi technology itself, you should understand the high-level benefits of using OSGi as your development platform. We address this topic in the next section.

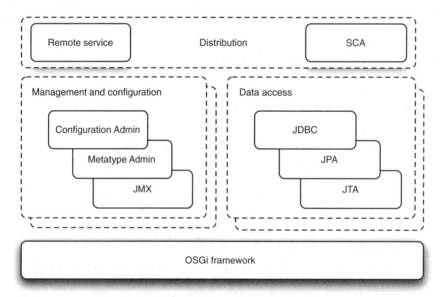

Figure 1.6   Enterprise OSGi consists of the OSGi framework and several OSGi services; together they provide enterprise features.

1.3 Benefits of using the OSGi platform

Why is the OSGi technology a good development platform for Java applications? Even further to the point, why or when is it better than the existing platforms on the market? To answer this question, we need to consider the problems we face when we develop full-fledged carrier-grade applications today.

For simplification, we can categorize these problems into two groups: problems intrinsic to the development of complex applications and problems related to existing development platforms. The problems intrinsic to applications include the following:

- As applications become larger and more complex, they become harder to maintain, sometimes exponentially so!
- Applications are difficult to extend without causing their erosion.

The problems related to existing platforms include these:

- Existing platforms are large, heavyweight systems and thus are complex to learn and use.
- There's a lack of portability among software vendors, making it difficult to reuse or share vendor components, even at the API level.

We'll explore each of these problems individually in the next sections. If the OSGi technology is able to help us address the problems of both of these categories, then not only is it suitable for the development of applications, but it's also a better tool for doing so.

1.3.1 OSGi manages the complexity of large systems

As developers, we've one time or another all faced the problem of complexity. Things are good when we're working by ourselves, on a separate, isolated piece of code. But as the team grows, from one person to ten, and the code grows from a few thousand lines to several hundred thousand, so does the complexity of working with the code and the team, and the bad news is that the increase isn't linear.

I'm positive all of the following will sound familiar:

- A simple change to the implementation of one component causes breakages throughout the application, at apparently dissociated locations.
- No one on the development team knows with certainty whether an interface can be changed without breaking existing clients.
- There are several closely related versions of the same utility functions in the application's source code.

How is the problem of managing large systems related to enterprise applications? Enterprise applications are by their very nature complex systems because of the following two factors:

- Business processes and business logic are inherently complex.

- Enterprise applications need to deal with complex issues such as resilience, management, and distribution.

How can OSGi help you manage the complexity of large systems? OSGi decreases complexity by allowing you to efficiently modularize your code and thus deal with smaller problems one at a time. By designing your code as independent modules that interact collectively to achieve the application's goal, rather than as a single mono-lithic structure, you're able to apply the millennia-old strategy of *divide and conquer* to your solutions.

Remember that the OSGi framework allows you to define Java modules, or bun-dles. These bundles have formal versioned interfaces, which must be explicitly refer-enced by any consuming client. In fact, by defining formal contracts between producers and consumers of code, you're able to decrease the likelihood of experi-encing the three problems raised in the preceding paragraphs.

For example, let's look at the first problem again in detail. Consider bundle B, which con-tains three packages: p, q, and r. Packages p and q contain only implementation classes and don't need to be public, whereas r contains public user interfaces, as shown in figure 1.7. There's a bug in class C of package p (p.C) that needs to be fixed. If you were using the OSGi framework, you could have specified that the packages p and q of bundle B are not public. This means that the

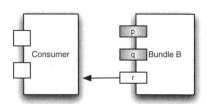

Figure 1.7   Bundle B with private packages p and q and public package r, which is being used by a consumer

only code that has visibility to these packages would be within the bundle itself, which would allow you to restrict testing to the bundle and to any consumers of the public package r when p.C is changed. By modularizing your code, you have better control over it and know what the impact will be when something changes.

In this particular case, could you have achieved the same results by meticulously coding and making sure that all Java classes are final, using the least open accessibility modifier (for example, private members), and so on? Perhaps, but would it be effi-cient or even possible to do these tasks on a large scale, involving several people and thousands of lines of code? Most certainly, it would not.

Furthermore, keep in mind that in OSGi the contract between producers and con-sumers is specified declaratively, that is, not in Java. This gives you enormous potential for tooling. For example, you could find out the transitive closure of all classes that should be tested when a class is changed.

Nevertheless, as brilliantly stated by Fred Brooks in 1986, there are no silver bul-lets. It's still the developer's responsibility to design adequately. For example, there'd be no point in using the OSGi framework to achieve modularization and then make everything public. We'll address modularity in the following chapters, so don't worry if the details aren't clear yet. The main point to understand is that the OSGi framework improves modularity, which in turn decreases the complexity of managing large proj-ects and increases reuse.

1.3.2   *OSGi provides extensibility without eroding the system*

Successful applications commonly need to be extended throughout their lifecycle; this is largely driven by changes to business requirements in today's fast-paced markets.

The problem with extensions is that they open up your system. Extensions are like public APIs, but they're more problematic because people have greater flexibility with extensions than with public APIs. You'll find that people sometimes do the unexpected with extensions.

Extending a system slowly helps erode it.

This is similar to software maintenance. As software ages, fixing bugs becomes harder and harder. Every code change takes longer to make and has a greater potential of causing other problems in the software. The reason for this erosion is that both when adding extensions and fixing bugs you're incorporating new code that wasn't made by the original authors of the software.

How can you restrain the erosion? You have to bind and control the new code. How can OSGi help you with binding and controlling extensions? As you've seen, OSGi defines the concepts of services, service consumers, and service providers.

A service consists of an interface and an implementation. The service consumer only sees and uses the service interfaces, whereas the service provider supplies the service implementations and doesn't interact directly with the consumers.

Generally, extensions of an application framework play the role of service providers, and the actual framework plays the role of the service consumer, as shown in figure 1.8. The service interface defines the contract of the extension; in other words, it's the extension point.

In this case the extension hooks into the lifecycle of the framework, and the framework calls back into the extension when appropriate. One example is an extension that wants to be notified when events of a certain type are received by the framework.

Sometimes extensions also act as the service consumers. The framework still defines the service interface, but it also provides the service implementation, which is then used by extensions.

Regardless of the approach, by keeping the extensions decoupled from the framework as separate service providers or consumers and by having a formal extension contract, you're able to isolate the extension code and thus decrease the overall erosion of the system.

Furthermore, OSGi allows you to dynamically manage the service providers. For example, OSGi supports the shutdown of a service provider that might be misbehaving without impacting the rest of the system.

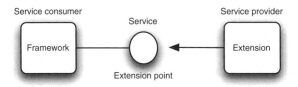

Figure 1.8   Extensions provide services through extension points. The framework consumes the services.

1.3.3   *OSGi is lightweight and customizable*

As you've seen, the applications you develop can become quite complex. This complexity has historically also been reflected in the development platforms. To support the complexity of full-fledged applications, the development platforms comprise collections of features, APIs, and tools and therefore have become heavyweight and complex themselves. They try to be a one-size-fits-all solution to all the requirements of all businesses.

For example, a loan-approval application may need to interact with a credit-checking system using web services, whereas an order-processing application interacts with its partner using some messaging middleware, such as JMS. Regardless of these different requirements, the existing development platforms include both web services and JMS technologies for both applications' runtimes. Even though the order-processing application uses only JMS, its runtime also ends up paying the price of a web services stack.

This may seem inconsequential initially, but consider that there are dozens of different enterprise technologies, as you've seen in the OSGi services section, and thus a simple hello world application may end up having a runtime that takes megabytes of memory and seconds to minutes to start. No matter what, this complexity leaks out to us developers in different forms. Our iterative development lifecycle becomes slow, we must learn more APIs than we need to use, the programming model becomes complex, and so on. We can all relate to how complicated it is to deploy the simplest of applications to any enterprise platform today.

The OSGi platform addresses this by providing a bare-bones framework, the OSGi framework, to which services can be added a la carte. For example, if you need a web services stack, you can install it; otherwise, it's not present. The OSGi platform can be customized to be as lightweight or as complex as needed. Furthermore, this flexibility shows in different ways; for example, being able to install features dynamically means that the lifecycle of new features provided by software vendors can be shortened. You don't need to wait a year or two for the next version of your application servers; instead, you can download and install new enterprise features by themselves as soon as they become available.

1.3.4   *OSGi allows for portability*

Java Enterprise Edition and some of the other enterprise platforms are standardized. This means that in theory you should be able to move a JEE application from one JEE application server to another, albeit hinging on the fact that you must use only standard APIs and no vendor extensions. This capability of being able to host an application on a different vendor's application server is called *application portability*.

Yet, there's another level of portability, not always mentioned, which is that of vendors' features themselves. For example, wouldn't it be nice to be able to use a vendor's JMS implementation with another vendor's web services stack in a single container? Why would you want to do this? Among other reasons, here are the three main ones:

- It allows you to pick and choose the best-of-breed implementations of different features across all vendors. For example, one vendor might be known for its messaging implementation, whereas another might have more experience with persistence service.
- It allows you to make use of new features that may be available only from certain vendors.
- Being able to move a particular feature to a different container means that you can use vendor extensions and still achieve application portability, because you can migrate the container's features alongside the application.

So, whereas most enterprise platforms try to standardize their entire APIs as a single unit, OSGi standardizes the APIs piecemeal, in modules, allowing the vendors to provide smaller pieces and the developers to select and reuse the pieces they find to be better.

OSGi also has another major advantage over other standards such as the JEE specification: simplicity. As you'll see, you can create an OSGi-compliant Java module by adding a few lines to a Java's MANIFEST.MF file. Conversely, a JEE-compliant module needs several JEE configuration files, annotations, and Java classes that implement technology-specific Java interfaces. Simplicity plays well with standardization. Vendors are more apt to invest in standardization if the cost isn't prohibitive. Take a look at the Apache Software Foundation projects at http://www.apache.org/. You'll notice that several projects, such as Derby, have already been made into OSGi modules. Would this have happened if the process of making a library into an OSGi module was costly? I doubt it.

So far we've looked at four benefits of using OSGi. In the next section, we'll sum these up in one practical example.

1.4 Building blocks: the essence of OSGi

Let's reconsider the location-specific advertisement application of section 1.2.1. There are several features or services you could add to it:

- You could persist the selections of the promotions preferred by the mobile client, which later could be used for data mining.
- You could inform the correspondent of the promotion (for example, the store) that the mobile client has received the promotion and spent more than some considerable amount of time looking at it, perhaps through the use of an event-dispatching service.
- You could provide a mechanism that allows configuring of the application.

Figure 1.9 depicts the advertisement application and the services it uses.

Put simply, the most important thing to learn in this chapter is that the OSGi platform provides you with the means to quickly, efficiently, and easily build applications just by putting together *building blocks*. OSGi allows you to use and integrate building blocks that are being provided by different vendors, unknown to them. As you'll see,

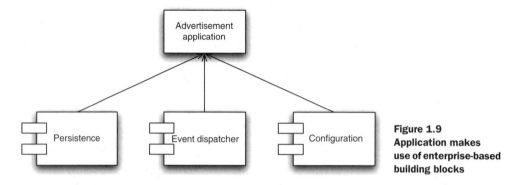

**Figure 1.9
Application makes
use of enterprise-based
building blocks**

you can even replace a building block dynamically, if a newer, better version is available from the same vendor or from a different vendor.

In this book, you'll learn how to use OSGi to create modular enterprise-grade applications by reusing infrastructure-based building blocks. You'll also learn how to perform the role of a building block vendor, providing your own reusable infrastructure services.

Collectively, all of these benefits have triggered the dissemination of public libraries of features—repositories of OSGi modules. We'll go through a list of such repositories in the next section.

1.5   *Players*

A multitude of vendors have implemented some aspect of the OSGi Service Platform, be it just the framework or selected services. This is no doubt a testament to OSGi's simplicity and its modularization.

Some of the most commonly used implementations of OSGi frameworks are these:

- Eclipse Equinox: http://www.eclipse.org/equinox/
- Apache Felix: http://felix.apache.org/site/index.html
- Knopflerfish: http://www.knopflerfish.org/

Most of these framework vendors also publish a public repository of services. For example, the following URLs point to these different vendors' repositories:

- Felix Repository: http://felix.apache.org/obr/releases.xml
- Knopflerfish Repository: http://www.knopflerfish.org/repo/repository.xml

In addition, several new projects have been created to tackle the implementation of the Enterprise OSGi. The goal is to allow developers to build enterprise applications using standard Enterprise OSGi services and the framework implementation of their choosing. Following are two projects that are working on implementing the Enterprise OSGi:

- Eclipse Gemini: http://www.eclipse.org/proposals/gemini/
- Apache Aries: http://incubator.apache.org/aries/

Finally, diverse development platforms, which have distinct goals, are using OSGi internally to implement their solutions. Some of these completely hide OSGi, whereas some do actually expose OSGi in some form or other. For example, a common exposure is to treat the OSGi module as the deployment unit of their platforms. Regardless, here are some examples of development platforms that are OSGi based:

- IBM WebSphere Application Server
- Oracle (formerly Sun) GlassFish Application Server
- Eclipse Virgo (SpringSource dm Server)
- JBoss Application Server
- Apache Camel
- Apache Sling
- Apache ServiceMix
- Apache Karaf

This is a reasonable number, especially if you consider that OSGi is still an emerging technology. Furthermore, because you can mix and match the components from different vendors, the overall gains are even larger! For example, you can use the Felix OSGi framework with the Eclipse service implementations and perhaps implement a few services of your own along the way.

By now, you're probably convinced and excited to use OSGi, but does this mean you need to start from scratch? We'll tackle this issue in the next section.

1.6   Are we starting from scratch?

If you're going to develop to the OSGi platform, does it mean that you need to drop your existing development platforms, such as JEE, and learn a new technology from scratch yet again? Or, even more important, can you leverage code from any of your existing enterprise applications?

Fortunately, the OSGi platform builds heavily upon JEE. As you'll see, there'll be several cases where we use, in some form or other, existing specifications defined by JEE, just in a slightly more modularized and isolated manner. This means that you're able to use the skill sets you learned in the past.

In addition, because existing JEE applications have been coded to APIs that also exist in the OSGi platform, you can move over some of the code from JEE containers to OSGi containers; however, this isn't always possible, and even when it is possible, some rewriting may be needed.

Finally, the reverse is also true; you should be able to migrate OSGi applications to JEE in some form. Furthermore, there's an even more appealing option in this case, where OSGi applications can be hosted in existing JEE application servers. This is done by hosting the full OSGi framework on top of JEE, and it's possible because OSGi is, after all, lightweight and modular.

As you'll see, the benefits of using OSGi are numerous, but in the end it all hinges on the fact that OSGi allows you to modularize both the static as well as the dynamic structure of a program in a productive and efficient form. You may point out that the concept of modularization has been used in software engineering for decades, so why is this any different now? The difference is that OSGi allows you to apply modularization in a systematic form to software systems at their very foundation, which was never attempted before.

1.7   Summary

Development platforms consist of an application framework and a supporting runtime environment. The Java platform, with the JDK and JRE, is one example of a development platform. Enterprise platforms, such as Java Enterprise Edition (JEE), add enterprise features to the platform.

The OSGi Service Platform provides a dynamic Java module system for Java. It allows Java code to be modularized and to be managed as services. The OSGi Service Platform consists of the OSGi framework and the OSGi services. The OSGi Service Platform Enterprise Specification (Enterprise OSGi) was created to support enterprise use cases. It defines a collection of OSGi services that can be used together for enterprise features.

OSGi provides the means to achieve modularization, which helps decrease and manage the complexity of large systems. OSGi provides a native extensibility mechanism through the use of services. Finally, a consortium of several large companies is driving the OSGi specifications, hence aiding with its adoption as a standard.

In the next chapter, we'll drill down into the OSGi framework in detail. In chapter 3, we'll employ what you've learned so far to build your first OSGi-powered application. But this application will lack several useful features, such as persistence. Following up on this, we'll take an in-depth look into how we can use configuration, event handling, persistence, RMI, transactions, naming and directory services, and management to develop full-fledged carrier-grade OSGi solutions.

Finally, you must keep in mind that the main purpose of OSGi is to provide you with an efficient framework for creating and integrating software building blocks.

An OSGi framework primer

2

This chapter covers

- Creating and sharing OSGi bundles
- Importing and exporting bundle packages
- Running bundles in an OSGi framework
- Defining and retrieving OSGi services
- Understanding the OSGi service registry

In this chapter you'll expand your knowledge of the OSGi framework. I'll describe two of the most important concepts related to OSGi: bundles and services. Bundles and services are the cornerstone of OSGi, and we'll keep revisiting these two concepts throughout this book.

We'll also cover the OSGi service registry and several less common, albeit still essential, APIs of the framework, such as the event listener interfaces.

As tradition dictates, to learn the basics, we'll use an OSGi-powered hello world application. This will allow us to demonstrate the OSGi concepts in the scope of a single simplistic application. It'll also allow us to compare the OSGi technology to other programming environments that, without doubt, are part of your background. Let's start by creating a simple OSGi module.

2.1   *Modules and information hiding*

The unit of modularization in OSGi is called a bundle. Bundles allow us to enforce the principles of information hiding. As was brilliantly stated by D. Parnas as early as 1972, information hiding helps us achieve the following benefits:

- Changeability
- Comprehensibility
- Independent development

Through the use of bundles, and by applying the principles of information hiding, we're better able to cope with the complexity of large systems.

This all seems complicated and abstract, but a bundle is easily defined in OSGi by adhering to the following two simple steps:

- Package the module as a JAR file.
- Include a manifest file with the mandatory manifest header `Bundle-Symbolic-Name`. This header provides an identifier for the bundle.

As defined by Java's manifest format specification, a JAR manifest file exists within the JAR file with the name of META-INF/MANIFEST.MF.

Here's a sample manifest file:

```
Manifest-Version: 1.0
Bundle-SymbolicName: helloworld
```

The `Bundle-SymbolicName` header specifies a name of `helloworld` for this bundle. Strictly speaking, that's all you need to create a bundle. But as a best practice, you should also specify the version of the OSGi specification being used. The manifest header `Bundle-ManifestVersion`, which defaults to 1, is used for this purpose. In this book, we use OSGi Platform Version 4.2, which maps to

```
Bundle-ManifestVersion: 2
```

In summary, a bundle encapsulates a collection of Java classes that are highly cohesive. This means we're achieving information hiding by using the technique of encapsulation.

The next step is to create some useful piece of code in the bundle that can be reused. Let's code a simple `Printer` class that outputs to standard `out`, à la hello world.

```
package manning.osgi.helloworld;

public class Printer {

    public void print(String message) {
        System.out.println(message);
    }

}
```

Don't worry about the triviality of the code being used; our goal for the time being is to implement a hello world application using OSGi.

Let's share this code with other Java clients. Create a `PrinterClient` class that imports the `Printer` class and invokes it:

```
package manning.osgi.helloworld.client;

import manning.osgi.helloworld.Printer;

public class PrinterClient {

    public void printMyMessage() {
        new Printer().print("Hello World");
    }
}
```

Figure 2.1 demonstrates this interaction.

Figure 2.1 The `PrinterClient` class invokes the method `print` in the `Printer` class.

NOTE This book attempts to be goal oriented. Rather than presenting the technology for the technology's sake, the discussion of a topic is driven by first introducing a problem to be solved. I hope this makes the book more enjoyable to read and more useful.

We've created the simplest possible bundle. Can OSGi help us improve anything in this simple interaction between the `Printer` and the `PrinterClient` classes? Yes. After all, we haven't achieved any form of information hiding so far. Consider the case where you want to prohibit the usage of `PrinterClient` by any other class. Applications can reuse the `Printer` class, but the client application code can't be reused. Another way of looking at this is that you'd like to "hide" the `PrinterClient` module. This is a reasonable requirement; you wouldn't want someone else printing your unique "Hello World" message, would you? How do you go about fulfilling this requirement in OSGi?

2.1.1 Establishing a formal import/export contract

First, you should keep the `Printer` and the `PrinterClient` classes in separate bundles. This is just good engineering, because it's likely that these classes are provided by different developers and should be decoupled.

Next, you'd like a mechanism whereby you can formally specify the dependencies between bundles. Using this mechanism, you can grant permission for bundles to use the `Printer` class and conversely restrict bundles from using the `PrinterClient` class, as illustrated in figure 2.2.

Figure 2.2 Other classes are restricted from invoking the `printMyMessage` method in the `PrinterClient` class.

In OSGi, you accomplish this by having the provider bundle export the Java packages that are meant to be shared, and then have the consumer bundle import the Java packages that it needs.

To export Java packages, a bundle uses the manifest header `Export-Package`:

```
Manifest-Version: 1.0
Bundle-ManifestVersion: 2
Bundle-SymbolicName: helloworld
Export-Package: manning.osgi.helloworld
```

In this case, the bundle `helloworld` is exporting all of its public classes located in the package `manning.osgi.helloworld`.

To import a Java package, a bundle uses the manifest header `Import-Package`:

```
Manifest-Version: 1.0
Bundle-ManifestVersion: 2
Bundle-SymbolicName: manning.osgi.client
Import-Package: manning.osgi.helloworld
```

The bundle `helloworld.client` is importing all public classes in the package `manning.osgi.helloworld`.

As should be clear, we have two bundles, `helloworld` and `helloworld.client`, as shown in figure 2.3. The bundle `hello-world` includes the `Printer` class. The bundle `helloworld.client` includes the `Printer-Client` class, which makes use of the `Printer` class.

Figure 2.3 The bundle `helloworld` includes the `Printer` class. The bundle `helloworld.client` includes the `PrinterClient` class.

Have we solved our initial problem? That is, have we prohibited other classes from using the `PrinterClient` class? Yes, by not exporting the package `manning.osgi.helloworld.client`, we make sure that no other class outside the `helloworld.client` bundle can use it.

Couldn't we have simply made `PrinterClient` private? Not really; we need to keep in mind that `PrinterClient` can't be completely inaccessible because it needs to be invoked or bootstrapped at some time. For example, it may need to be invoked by the application's `main` method.

What if we moved the `main` method to the `PrinterClient` class itself and kept its other methods private? If we did this, we'd be coupling together some application logic code with the JVM's bootstrap method, which isn't a good practice; for example, it would prevent us from creating JUnit test cases to test the `PrinterClient` class because its constructor would be private. In addition, we'd be leaving the `main` method open for access.

What if we made the `PrinterClient` package protected and included both the `main` method and the JUnit test cases in the same package? That might work, if we're willing to always have a single package for our application, which clearly isn't a good practice either. Of course, we could also cheat by using our package name when creating our classes.

The conclusion is that even though we may be able to devise some clever way of achieving similar results, OSGi provides a simple, elegant, and standard approach to the issue. OSGi allows us to scale, both in terms of code complexity and in terms of working with larger teams. Furthermore, OSGi achieves this through a metadata-driven approach. OSGi doesn't impose changes on either the `Printer` or `Printer-Client` classes; only the manifest files are impacted.

By having separate bundles for the provider and the consumer of the code and explicitly establishing their interdependencies, we've increased the modularity of our hello world application.

Next, we should run and test our hello world OSGi application. But before we do that, we need to code how the bundles get bootstrapped.

2.1.2 *Activating a bundle*

How do you control the start of a regular Java SE application? As touched on in the previous section, you have to implement the `main` native method:

```
package manning.osgi.helloworld.client;

public class PrinterClientMain {

    public static void main(String args[]) {
        new PrinterClient().printMyMessage();
    }
}
```

The JVM invokes the `main` method, which takes care of starting the application in JSE.

What's the equivalent of a `main` method in OSGi? The `BundleActivator` class.

In OSGi, an application is made of potentially several bundles, so you need a way of individually starting the bundles. You can start a bundle by including a `Bundle-Activator` class in the bundle's JAR file. You have to follow these steps:

1 Create a class that implements the interface `org.osgi.framework.Bundle-Activator`.

2 Provide an empty constructor that can be instantiated with `Class.new-Instance()`.

3 Add the manifest header `Bundle-Activator` to the bundle's manifest file, as shown in the following listing. The value of this header must be the fully qualified class name of the class defined in step 1.

Listing 2.1   `BundleActivator` for `helloworld.client` bundle

```
package manning.osgi.helloworld.client;

import org.osgi.framework.BundleActivator;
import org.osgi.framework.BundleContext;
```

```
public class PrinterClientActivator implements BundleActivator {

    public void start(BundleContext context)
        throws Exception {
        new PrinterClient().printMyMessage();
    }

    public void stop(BundleContext context)
        throws Exception {

    }
}
```

Called-back before bundle is started

Called-back before bundle is stopped

A bundle activator not only allows you to control the starting of the bundle but also allows you to control the stopping of the bundle. In the stop(BundleContext) method, you can release allocated resources and perform other general cleanups. We'll discuss the BundleContext class in detail in chapter 4. Note that, conversely, the method start(BundleContext) can be used to acquire resources, as you'll see in several examples throughout this book.

Finally, you must not forget to update the manifest file to include the Bundle-Activator header:

```
Manifest-Version: 1.0
Bundle-SymbolicName: helloworld.client
Import-Package: manning.osgi.helloworld
Bundle-Activator: manning.osgi.helloworld.client.PrinterClientActivator
```

The Bundle-Activator header references the class name of a class that implements the BundleActivator interface within the bundle's JAR file.

Now you have everything you need to run the OSGi-powered hello world application.

2.2 *Running and testing OSGi*

To run a standard Java application, you have to execute the JVM program with the application's JAR files in the JVM's CLASSPATH. For example, to run our hello world example, you could archive the classes Printer, PrinterClient, and PrinterMain in a helloworld.jar and then execute the JVM with the following configuration:

```
java -jar helloworld.jar manning.osgi.helloworld.client.PrinterClientMain
```

To run an OSGi bundle, you have to first run an OSGi framework and then install the bundle into the framework. Which OSGi framework should we use to test our OSGi-powered hello world application?

We'll use the Apache Felix product, which is an open source implementation of the OSGi framework. You can download Felix from http://felix.apache.org/site/index.html.

2.2.1 *Apache Felix, the open source OSGi framework*

As a first step, install Felix in your machine. For the purpose of the examples in this book, we'll be using Felix 3.0.6.

Open a shell, and change directory to Felix's installation home. You can run Felix with the following command:

```
felix-framework-3.0.6$ java -jar bin/felix.jar
```
```
Welcome to Apache Felix Gogo
```
```
g!
```

> ### Conventions
>
> Before we continue, here are some assumptions and conventions you should know:
>
> - We'll assume that the Java program is in your shell's path. This is generally the case.
> - We'll be using JDK 1.5.0_16 to run the examples.
> - We'll be using UNIX commands, as executed in a bash shell, as the convention. Thanks to Java, we're mostly isolated from the operating system, except for a few file-related commands.
> - If you're using Windows, you may have to replace the forward slash (/) with a backward slash (\) in file-related commands. As an example, this command,
>
> ```
> java -jar bin/felix.jar
> ```
>
> should be changed to the following in a Windows environment:
>
> ```
> java -jar bin\felix.jar
> ```

You've started the OSGi framework. When Felix starts, it presents its own text-based shell, called Gogo. Gogo uses g! as its prompt.

> **WARNING** There's no standard for the shell commands for OSGi. Therefore, some of the commands used in this book, such as install, start, and uninstall, may be subject to change.

You can use Felix's shell to install the bundles into the framework and perform other bundle- and framework-related tasks. For a list of all the commands, type help at the prompt.

2.2.2 Building OSGi bundles

As you saw in section 2.1, a bundle is built as a standard JAR file, whose manifest file contains OSGi-related entries. Hence, you can use your Java build tool of choice. In particular, Maven has added support for packaging OSGi bundles and even generating a MANIFEST.MF file with the appropriate OSGi header entries.

But to keep things simple and most importantly transparent, we'll use Ant to compile and build the `helloworld` bundle. First, let's start by defining an Ant macro, as shown in the following listing.

Listing 2.2   Bundle-up ANT macro

```
<macrodef name="bundle-up">
  <attribute name="name" />                         ❶ Bundle's
  <sequential>                                          name
    <mkdir dir="modules/@{name}/target" />
    <mkdir dir="dist" />

    <javac destdir="modules/@{name}/target"
 srcdir="modules/@{name}/src/main/java" debug="true">
      <classpath>
        <fileset dir="dist" includes="*.jar" />
        <fileset dir="../lib" includes="*.jar" />
        <fileset dir="${osgi.install.dir}/bin"      ❷ OSGi framework
          includes="*.jar" />                            location
        <fileset dir="${osgi.install.dir}/bundle" includes="*.jar" />
      </classpath>
    </javac>

    <jar destfile="dist/@{name}.jar"
      basedir="modules/@{name}/target"
 manifest="modules/@{name}/src/main/resources/META-INF/MANIFEST.MF" />
    </sequential>
</macrodef>
```

The `bundle-up` macro takes one argument: the name of the bundle ❶. In addition, it references the `osgi.install.dir` property, which should point to the location of the OSGi framework installation directory ❷. It then assumes that the bundle's source files and manifest file are positioned using the Maven convention:

```
${basedir}/
    modules/
        ${name}/
            src/main/java/
            src/main/resources/META-INF/
```

`${basedir}` points to the directory that invokes the `bundle-up` Ant macro, and `${name}` maps to the attribute name used in the macro. In the case of the `helloworld` bundle, first make sure all sources are lined up using this convention:

```
build.xml
modules/
    helloworld/
        src/main/java/
                  manning/osgi/helloworld/Printer.java
        src/main/resources/
                  META-INF/
                      MANIFEST.MF
```

Then invoke `bundle-up` as follows:

```
<bundle-up name="helloworld" />
```

Keep in mind that you need to set the `osgi.install.dir` property to point to the directory where you've installed Felix, therefore ensuring that the bin/felix.jar file is in the class path. The output bundle file helloworld.jar, which is used in the next section, is placed in this directory:

```
${basedir}/dist
```

2.2.3 Installing bundles into Felix

Next, you need to install the `helloworld` and `helloworld.client` bundles into the framework.

We have two bundles, or JAR files: helloworld.jar and helloworld.client.jar. The archived content of the helloworld.jar bundle is

```
META-INF/MANIFEST.MF
manning/osgi/helloworld/Printer.class
```

And for the helloworld.client.jar, it's

```
META-INF/MANIFEST.MF
manning/osgi/helloworld/client/PrinterClient.class
manning/osgi/helloworld/client/PrinterClientActivator.class
```

Copy helloworld.jar and helloworld.client.jar to the Felix installation to make it easier to reference the files. Create a dist directory underneath the install directory, and place the JAR files there.

> **NOTE** Don't place the hello world bundles in the bundle directory, because this directory is by default configured as Felix's autodeploy directory, a feature that we'll talk about in later chapters.

Now, you can install these bundles with the `install` command typed in the Felix shell:

```
g! felix:install file:dist/helloworld.jar
Bundle ID: 5
g! felix:install file:dist/helloworld.client.jar
Bundle ID: 6
```

Each time you install a bundle, Felix provides a unique bundle ID, which is needed later by the other commands.

> **NOTE** The `Gogo` shell commands, such as `felix:install`, can be specified without the prefix (that is, `felix`, `obr`, `gogo`) if they're unique. But generally it's good to keep the prefix because it helps with backward compatibility for future versions of Felix.

Did you expect to see "Hello World" printed? We're almost there.

The installation of a bundle copies the binary image of the bundle, that is, its JAR file content, into the framework. It does not, however, actually start the bundle.

2.2.4   *Starting the bundles in Felix*

To start a bundle, you must use the `start` command in the Felix shell. As expected, the `start` command triggers the `BundleActivator.start()` callback. Let's try it out:

```
g! felix:start 4
g! felix:start 5
```

Note that you must use the ID returned by the `install` command.

You should get a stack trace and still no "Hello World" message, which probably isn't what you expected. If you go down the stack, you'll eventually notice the following message:

```
Caused by: java.lang.NoClassDefFoundError: org/osgi/framework/BundleActivator
```

The class `PrinterClientActivator` inherits from `BundleActivator`, which is in the package `org.osgi.framework`, so you must add this package to the `Import-Package` header in the bundle's manifest file:

```
Manifest-Version: 1.0
Bundle-SymbolicName: helloworld.client
Import-Package: manning.osgi.helloworld,
 org.osgi.framework
Bundle-Activator: manning.osgi.helloworld.client.PrinterClientActivator
```

> **TIP** You must explicitly import the packages of all classes being used. A bundle must even explicitly import the OSGi framework's own APIs, such as the `org.osgi.framework` package. As you'll see later, this can be quite tricky to get right when dealing with classes that are loaded using reflection.

Update the MANIFEST.MF file, re-archive helloworld.client.jar, and copy it to the bundle directory in the Felix installation. Then uninstall the offending bundle from Felix, reinstall the fixed one, and start it over again.

```
g! felix:uninstall 5
g! felix:install file:dist/helloworld.client.jar
Bundle ID: 6
g! felix:start 6
Hello World
```

Congratulations, you got your hard-earned "Hello World" message!

Looking back at section 2.2, have we actually solved the problem of restricting access to the `PrinterClient` class? There's no way of being completely sure without testing it. Let's create another bundle, helloworld.client2.jar, as shown in the following listing.

> **Listing 2.3   `PrinterClientActivator2` tries to invoke non-exported `PrinterClient`**

```
package manning.osgi.helloworld.client2;

import org.osgi.framework.BundleActivator;
import org.osgi.framework.BundleContext;
```

```
import manning.osgi.helloworld.anotherclient.PrinterClient;

public class PrinterClientActivator2 implements BundleActivator {

    public void start(BundleContext context) throws Exception {
        new PrinterClient().printMyMessage();
    }

    public void stop(BundleContext context) throws Exception {
        // NOP
    }
}
```

❶ Instantiating non-exported PrinterClient

In the `PrinterClientActivator2` class, we try to invoke the `PrinterClient` class ❶. We'll even add `manning.osgi.helloworld.client` to the `Import-Package` header in the bundle's manifest file:

```
Manifest-Version: 1.0
Bundle-SymbolicName: helloworld.client2
Import-Package: manning.osgi.helloworld.client,
org.osgi.framework
Bundle-Activator: manning.osgi.helloworld.client2.PrinterClientActivator2
```

The `helloworld.client2` JAR has only two files: the `PrinterClientActivator2` class and the MANIFEST.MF file.

You're now ready. Copy the helloworld.client2.jar file to Felix's bundle directory, install and start the bundle in Felix, and see what happens:

```
g! felix:install file:dist/helloworld.client2.jar
Bundle ID: 7
g! felix:start 7
org.osgi.framework.BundleException: Unresolved constraint in bundle 7:
➥ package; (package=manning.osgi.helloworld.client)
```

The `helloworld.client2` bundle isn't able to import the package `manning.osgi .helloworld.client`. You'll get an exception when you try to use a class whose package hasn't been exported, even though you try to import it. Thus, we can validate that the code is indeed restricted.

In chapter 4, we'll look in detail at the process that OSGi goes through to match the imported packages with exported packages, which in the OSGi nomenclature is known as resolving package constraints.

2.2.5 *Can we cheat using reflection?*

Before we move on, there's another test worth pursuing. Could we cheat the OSGi framework by trying to use the `PrinterClient` class through reflection? There are cases in other frameworks, including application servers, where you can create "backdoors" through reflection. Is this the case for the OSGi framework?

Let's test and see. In the following listing, the `PrinterClientIntrospector-Activator` class uses reflection to access the `PrinterClient` class.

Listing 2.4 Using reflection to attempt to invoke a non-exported package

```
package manning.osgi.helloworld.introspector;

import java.lang.reflect.Method;

import org.osgi.framework.BundleActivator;
import org.osgi.framework.BundleContext;

public class PrinterIntrospectorActivator implements BundleActivator {

    public void start(BundleContext context) throws Exception {
        Class<?> printerClientClass =
            Class.forName("manning.osgi.helloworld.client.PrinterClient");
        Object printerClientInstance =
            printerClientClass.newInstance();
        Method printMethod =
            printerClientClass.getMethod("printMyMessage");
        printMethod.invoke(printerClientInstance);
    }

    public void stop(BundleContext context) throws Exception {
        // NOP
    }
}
```

The `helloworld.introspector` bundle includes the `PrinterClientIntrospector-Activator` class. As you've learned, you must also not forget to import the package `manning.osgi.helloworld.client` in the bundle's manifest file:

```
Manifest-Version: 1.0
Bundle-ManifestVersion: 2
Bundle-SymbolicName: helloworld.introspector
Import-Package: manning.osgi.helloworld.client,
org.osgi.framework
Bundle-Activator:
➥ manning.osgi.helloworld.introspector.PrinterIntrospectorActivator
```

Install the bundle in Felix and start it. Again, as desired, you'll get a `BundleException`:

```
g! felix:install file:dist/helloworld.introspector.jar
Bundle ID: 19
g! felix:start 19
org.osgi.framework.BundleException: Unresolved constraint in bundle 19:
➥ package; (package=manning.osgi.helloworld.client)
```

We'll be using the OSGi framework to build enterprise-grade solutions, so we must make sure it's robust.

2.2.6   *Eclipse Equinox*

Eclipse Equinox is another open source OSGi framework implementation. Although we're generally using Felix in this book, any OSGi framework implementation will do. One reason for opting for Equinox would be if you need to interact with or leverage Eclipse IDE plug-ins in some form.

You can download the Equinox OSGi framework implementation from the following URL: http://download.eclipse.org/equinox/. You can choose to download just the Equinox JAR file, which at the time of writing is named org.eclipse.osgi_3.6.2.R36 x_v20110210.jar, or you can download the full SDK, containing the Equinox JAR file and several other infrastructure bundles.

You can start Equinox by typing the following command in the current directory where the Equinox JAR file exists:

```
java -jar org.eclipse.osgi_3.6.2.R36x_v20110210.jar -console
```

Equinox provides you with this prompt:

```
osgi>
```

You can type `help` to get a list of all console commands, which should look similar to what you've used so far with Felix. For example, the following commands install our `helloworld` bundles and start them as expected:

```
osgi> install file:helloworld.jar
Bundle id is 1

osgi> install file:helloworld.client.jar
Bundle id is 2

osgi> start 1 2
Hello World
```

When needed, I'll point out the differences between Felix and Equinox in upcoming chapters.

2.3   *Coping with changes to a module*

Consider the scenario where you've decided that always printing "Hello World" to the standard output is a bit inflexible; instead, you want to allow the user of the `Printer` class to specify the location where the message should be printed. In addition, you've noticed a mistake in your current interface; the interface is named `print`, but it actually prints and adds a new line, so a more suitable name would have been `println`. Changing the interface of a module is a common scenario, which we'll explore next.

2.3.1   *Changing a bundle's interface*

Following up with our example, let's say you want to replace the existing interface, `public void print(String message)`, with `public void println(PrintStream stream, String message)`.

This presents a problem. If you do this, you'll have to modify and recompile all client code that uses the `Printer` class, which may be unacceptable. For example, if you're on a production system, you can't just stop the system. Or, quite frequently, you may not own the client code and hence have no way of changing it.

Here are two valid reasons for changing the interface:

- The interface name is wrong and you want to correct it.
- The interface is inflexible and you want to add parameters to it.

But because of a series of constraints, such as backward compatibility, you can't simply fix the existing code. What's the solution?

One solution is to create a new class, say the `Printer2` class, which has the new interface, and keep the old one untouched. That's an option that is commonly employed today, but it has plenty of problems:

- It isn't clear to the user which class to use. Should the user look for `Printer3`, `Printer4`, ...? What if you had called it `NewPrinter`; would you call the next one `NewerPrinter`? In other words, there's no clear convention on how to name a class to represent versioning.
- Encoding the version into the class name binds the client to a specific version. What if the client wanted to always use the latest version? This wouldn't be possible.

Next, you'll learn how OSGi addresses this problem.

2.3.2 *Versioning bundles*

OSGi provides native support for bundle versioning. With OSGi, a bundle can specify a version for each package being exported, and conversely a bundle can specify version ranges when importing packages. OSGi defines a version as a value of four parts: major, minor, micro, and qualifier, as shown in figure 2.4.

For now, let's not worry about this. You just need to know that by default 0.0.0 is used, and that any time a part isn't specified, it takes the value 0, or an empty string in the case of the qualifier. For example, version 1.1 is equal to and is actually converted to 1.1.0. The full definition of versions and version ranges is provided in chapter 4.

Let's look at how to do this with the `helloworld` bundle and the `Printer` class.

First, we'll create a new version of the `helloworld` bundle. We'll do this by creating a new bundle JAR file, which we'll name helloworld_1.1.0.jar. Note that the bundle JAR filename has no implications at runtime and doesn't need to have a version number. Bundle helloworld_1.1.0.jar has the same bundle symbolic name of `helloworld` as bundle helloworld.jar. But, in addition, the bundle helloworld_1.1.0.jar must use

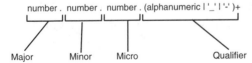

Major   Minor   Micro   Qualifier

Figure 2.4 OSGi defines a version as a value of four parts: major, minor, micro, and qualifier. The first three take numeric values. The last part takes alphanumeric digits, or _, or -. By default, zero is used for the first three parts.

the manifest header `Bundle-Version`. In our case, we'll set `Bundle-Version` with the value 1.1. In reality, it's the conjunction of the `Bundle-Version` header and the `Bundle-SymbolicName` header that uniquely identifies a bundle. If we had tried to install helloworld_1.1.0.jar without using the `Bundle-Version` header, we'd have gotten a `BundleException` informing us that our bundle isn't unique:

```
org.osgi.framework.BundleException: Bundle symbolic name and
➥ version are  not unique: helloworld:0.0.0
```

`Bundle-Version` takes care of versioning the bundle, but it doesn't version the packages being exported by the bundle. In other words, we still need to version the package being exported so that we don't create a non-backward change to the `Printer` class.

To do this, append the tag `version` to each exported package listed in the `Export-Package` header. The MANFIEST.MF file for version 1.1 of `helloworld` is as follows:

```
Manifest-Version: 1.0
Bundle-ManifestVersion: 2
Bundle-SymbolicName: helloworld
Bundle-Version: 1.1
Export-Package: manning.osgi.helloworld;version=1.1
```

We keep the same bundle symbolic name of `helloworld`, but we change the bundle version to 1.1 and also export the package `manning.osgi.helloworld` with version 1.1. Note, as explained previously, that we don't necessarily need to use the same version of the bundle for the packages being exported.

What would have happened if we hadn't versioned the exported package `manning.osgi.helloworld` in the bundle helloworld_1.1.0.jar? It would have meant that both helloworld.jar and helloworld_1.1.0.jar are exporting version 0.0.0 of the package `manning.osgi.helloworld`. OSGi calls this a split package, and it's decidedly not something you want to do. We'll investigate this matter further in chapter 4.

TIP Do not export the same package (of the same version) in more than one bundle.

Next, we need to implement the new version of the `Printer` class and include it in the bundle helloworld_1.1.0.jar:

```
package manning.osgi.helloworld;

import java.io.PrintStream;

public class Printer {

    public void println(PrintStream stream, String message) {
        stream.println(message);
    }
}
```

Now we have two hello world bundles: helloworld.jar, which is technically version 0.0.0, and helloworld_1.1.0.jar, which contains the new interface for the `Printer` class.

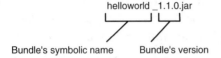

helloworld _1.1.0.jar

Bundle's symbolic name   Bundle's version

Figure 2.5   The convention is to name a bundle's JAR file using the bundle's symbolic name, appended with _ and the bundle's version.

In hindsight, we should have named helloworld.jar as helloworld_1.0.0.jar, and we should have set its Bundle-Version manifest header with the value 1.0.0. It's considered good practice to name the bundle JAR file with the following pattern: bundle-SymbolicName + _ + bundleVersion + .jar, as shown in figure 2.5. As you've noticed, that convention is used in this book.

We've finished the provider side of the equation. On the client side, let's create a new client class that makes use of version 1.1 of the Printer class. We'll name it the PrinterAnotherClient class:

```
package manning.osgi.helloworld.anotherclient;

import manning.osgi.helloworld.Printer;

public class PrinterAnotherClient {

    public void printAnotherMessage() {
        new Printer().println(System.out, "Another Hello World");
    }
}
```

This class needn't be a new version of the PrinterClient class. In practice, it may be just as common that the first user of a new version is a new client rather than an existing client that changes working code to use the new version. To our advantage, there's no binding of a version number in the Java code.

We'll create a new bundle JAR file called helloworld.anotherclient_1.0.0.jar, which contains the PrinterAnotherClient class. Bundle helloworld.anotherclient must import helloworld version 1.1 in its Import-Package manifest header:

```
Manifest-Version: 1.0
Bundle-ManifestVersion: 2
Bundle-SymbolicName: manning.osgi.anotherclient
Bundle-Version: 1.0.0
Import-Package: manning.osgi.helloworld;version="[1.1,1.1.9]",
  org.osgi.framework
Bundle-Activator:
➥ manning.osgi.helloworld.anotherclient.PrinterAnotherClientActivator
```

Note how we use a version range for the Import-Package manifest header. In this case, we're specifying that the package to be imported must be of version 1.1.0 (inclusive) up to version 1.1.9 (inclusive).

> **TIP**   When specifying version ranges in the Import-Package manifest header, you must enclose the version range in double quotes. The reason is that version ranges include a comma, which is used to delimit the packages being imported.

Archive hellworld_1.1.0.jar and helloworld.anotherclient_1.0.0.jar, and copy them to the bundle directory in Felix. Make sure Felix is running. You're now ready to run the bundles.

RUNNING MULTIPLE VERSIONS OF A BUNDLE

Before you install the new bundles, let's double-check which bundles you've installed and started so far.

In the Felix shell prompt, type the command lb (list bundles):

```
g! felix:lb
START LEVEL 1
   ID|State      |Level|Name
    0|Active     |    0|System Bundle (3.0.6)
    1|Active     |    1|Apache Felix Bundle Repository (1.6.2)
    2|Active     |    1|Apache Felix Gogo Command (0.6.1)
    3|Active     |    1|Apache Felix Gogo Runtime (0.6.1)
    4|Active     |    1|Apache Felix Gogo Shell (0.6.1)
    5|Active     |    1|helloworld (0.0.0)
    6|Active     |    1|helloworld.client (0.0.0)
    7|Installed  |    1|helloworld.client2 (0.0.0)
```

You should see a list of all installed bundles, which should include our first version of helloworld, and two helloworld client bundles, namely helloworld.client and helloworld.client2. The latter has the state of "Installed" instead of "Active" as the other bundles have. If you remember in section 2.2.4, the bundle hellworld.client2 attempted to import a package that wasn't being exported and therefore failed to start. We'll study bundle states and actions, namely install, resolve, start, stop, and uninstall, in chapter 4.

> **Equinox**
>
> In Equinox, you can get a list of all bundles by typing the following command:
>
> ```
> osgi> ss
> Framework is launched.
> id  State       Bundle
> 0   ACTIVE      org.eclipse.osgi_3.6.2.R36x_v20110210
> ```

Even if you shut down and restart Felix, the list of installed bundles remains the same. Let's do some cleanup. We obviously don't need helloworld.client2, so let's uninstall it.

```
g! felix:uninstall 7
```

Now, let's install and start version 1.1 of helloworld—the helloworld_1.1.0.jar bundle JAR. (By the way, don't worry if the bundle ID associated with your bundle is different from what's being shown in the code.)

```
g! felix:install file:dist/helloworld_1.1.0.jar
Bundle ID: 10
```

```
g! felix:start 10
g! felix:lb
START LEVEL 1
   ID|State          |Level|Name
    0|Active         |    0|System Bundle (3.0.6)
    1|Active         |    1|Apache Felix Bundle Repository (1.6.2)
    2|Active         |    1|Apache Felix Gogo Command (0.6.1)
    3|Active         |    1|Apache Felix Gogo Runtime (0.6.1)
    4|Active         |    1|Apache Felix Gogo Shell (0.6.1)
    5|Active         |    1|helloworld (0.0.0)
    6|Active         |    1|helloworld.client (1.0.0)
    7|Active         |    1|helloworld (1.1.0)
```

The bundle named `helloworld` (1.1.0) represents version 1.1 of the bundle `hello-world`.

In spite of having started a new non-backward-compatible version of the `Printer` class, you'll notice that this didn't break the running `helloworld.client` bundle. If you want to double-check, stop and restart the `helloworld.client` bundle, and it should still print the "Hello World" message:

```
g! felix:stop 6
g! felix:start 6
Hello World
```

Finally, install and start bundle `helloworld.anotherclient`:

```
g! felix:install file:dist/helloworld.anotherclient_1.0.0.jar
Bundle ID: 11
g! felix:start 11
Another Hello World
```

If we hadn't imported version 1.1 of `manning.osgi.helloworld`, we'd have gotten the following exception when we tried to start the bundle `helloworld.anotherclient`:

```
java.lang.NoSuchMethodError:
➡ manning.osgi.helloworld.Printer.println(Ljava/io/PrintStream;
➡ Ljava/lang/String;)V
```

There you have it. We're able to run two versions of the same application concurrently within the same JVM. Regardless of it being a simple hello world application, this isn't to be taken lightly and generally isn't supported by most application frameworks.

TESTING BUNDLE VERSIONING

Let's make matters more interesting by quickly creating a version 1.2.0 of `helloworld`:

```
Manifest-Version: 1.0
Bundle-ManifestVersion: 2
Bundle-SymbolicName: helloworld
Bundle-Version: 1.2
Export-Package: manning.osgi.helloworld;version=1.2
```

Version 1.2 adds a `Date` parameter to the `println` method in the `Printer` class:

```
package manning.osgi.helloworld;
```

```
import java.io.PrintStream;
import java.util.Date;

public class Printer {

    public void println(PrintStream stream, String message,
Date dateOfMessage) {
        stream.println(dateOfMessage.toString() + ':' + message);
    }
}
```

As usual, archive helloworld_1.2.0.jar, and then install and start it in Felix. You'll get no exceptions. If you stop and restart the `helloworld.client` bundle, you'll again get the correct "Hello World" message:

```
g! felix:stop 6
g! felix:start 6
Hello World
```

Isn't this a bit strange? After all, you installed an incompatible version of the `Printer` class. Try uninstalling and then reinstalling the `helloworld.client` bundle. As you'll see when you reinstall the bundle, the OSGi framework raises a `NoSuchMethodError` exception:

```
java.lang.NoSuchMethodError:
manning.osgi.helloworld.Printer.println(Ljava/lang/String;)V
```

The bundle `helloworld.client` was unable to find the method `Printer.println (String message)`, which corresponds to version 0.0.0 of the bundle `helloworld`. First of all, why was it that we got different behavior when we reinstalled a bundle as opposed to when we restarted the bundle? The reason is that the OSGi framework won't attempt to change the packages being imported by a bundle after the packages have already been selected, even if you install new versions of these packages or stop and restart the importing bundle. If you need to renegotiate the packages being imported, a process called *resolve*, you must reinstall the bundle. To be precise, you could also update the bundle, but we'll examine bundle updates in chapter 4.

Now that you understand when the packages get resolved, and you've taken the correct measures to have a clean sheet, let's try to make sense of the versioning model:

- Bundle `helloworld` version 0.0.0 exports `manning.osgi.helloworld` version 0.0.0.
- Bundle `helloworld` version 1.1.0 exports `manning.osgi.helloworld` version 1.1.0.
- Bundle `helloworld` version 1.2.0 exports `manning.osgi.helloworld` version 1.2.0.
- Bundle `helloworld.client` doesn't specify a version when importing package `manning.osgi.helloworld`, which means that it's specifying the version range starting at 0.0.0 and up to infinity, that is, $[0.0.0, \infty)$.

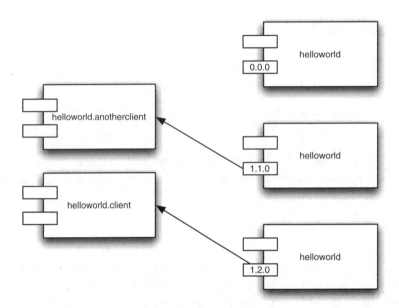

Figure 2.6   Bundle `helloworld.client` resolves to package `helloworld` version 1.2.0; bundle `helloworld.anotherclient` resolves to package `helloworld` version 1.1.0.

- Bundle `helloworld.anotherclient` specifies the version range [1.1.0,1.1.9] when importing `manning.osgi.helloworld`, which maps to the version range starting at 1.1.0 and going up to 1.1.9.

The OSGi framework resolves `helloworld.client` to version 1.2.0 of package `manning.osgi.helloworld`, and it resolves `helloworld.anotherclient` to version 1.1.0 of package `manning.osgi.helloworld`, as shown in figure 2.6. No bundle is bound to version 0.0.0 of package `manning.osgi.helloworld`.

The bundle `helloworld.client` specifies a version range of [0.0.0,∞), which potentially means versions 0.0.0, 1.1.0, and 1.2.0 of `manning.osgi.helloworld`. But the highest available package version of 1.2.0 is the one being selected. The bundle `helloworld.anotherclient` is also bound to the highest available package version that is allowed by the constraint of its version range of 1.1.0 to 1.1.9, which in this case is package version 1.1.0.

> **TIP**   The OSGi framework resolves an imported package to the highest available package version that meets its constraints.

This seemingly simple but somewhat counterintuitive rule is important. You could argue that a better policy would be to select the lowest available package version, because it would avoid incompatibility problems caused by new installed bundle versions, such as those we ran into at the beginning of this section. But as you've seen, this isn't such a good idea. The OSGi framework correctly resolves the packages of a bundle only once per installation (or, more precisely, per update), so new installed bundles won't break existing bundles that have already been installed. In addition, if a bundle does need to be sure that it always resolves to a single specific version, it can always use a range that includes only that version, such as version=`"[1.0.0,1.0.0]"`.

2.3.3 Changing a module's implementation

Previously, we ran into a scenario where we needed to change the interface of a bundle. Life isn't always so dramatic, and most commonly you may need to change the implementation of a bundle and not its exposed interface.

Let's look again at our first version of the `Printer` class, from section 2.1. We'd like to change it, as shown in the following listing, so that each printed message gets timestamped with the current time.

Listing 2.5 The `Printer` service implementation

```
package manning.osgi.helloworld;

import java.text.DateFormat;
import java.util.Date;

public class Printer {

    private static final String SEPARATOR = ": ";

    public void print(String message) {
        System.out.println(getCurrentTime() + SEPARATOR + message);
    }

    private String getCurrentTime() {
        return DateFormat.getTimeInstance(DateFormat.LONG).
format(new Date());
    }
}
```

You know the drill. Create a new version of bundle `helloworld`, and then as usual provision it in Felix. Here's where it starts getting interesting. When would the existing client bundles pick up this new version? For bundle `helloworld.client` to be able to use version 1.3 of bundle `helloworld`, which includes the timestamp in the printed message, you'll have to uninstall and reinstall the `helloworld.client` bundle, as we proved in section 2.3.2.

Doesn't it feel wrong that you need to reinstall bundle `helloworld.client` in this case? After all, you're just changing the implementation of a method in an imported class, and not its interface. You don't need to recompile the client code, so why do you need to reinstall it?

The problem is that the contract, as it stands with the current solution between the `helloworld.client` bundle and the `helloworld` bundle, is the `Printer` class in its entirety.

To break this contract, the client bundle needs to reestablish the packages and classes it imports, a process known as resolving package dependencies. As you'll see in

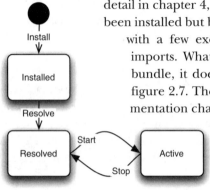

detail in chapter 4, package resolving happens after the bundle has been installed but before the bundle has been commanded to start, with a few exceptions, such as when dealing with dynamic imports. What this means is that when you start and stop a bundle, it doesn't change its resolved packages, as shown in figure 2.7. Therefore, new versions of packages or class implementation changes won't be picked up.

Figure 2.7   Starting and stopping a bundle changes the state of the bundle between active and resolved, which means that the bundle's package won't be resolved again during this process.

TIP   Starting and stopping a bundle won't change the list of classes that a bundle has access to.

You can easily test this. Start Felix with a clean sheet. You can do this by uninstalling all the bundles you've installed so far. Create helloworld_1.3.0.jar with the new `print` method implementation you saw in the beginning of this section. The MANFIEST.MF file for bundle helloworld_1.3.0.jar is as follows:

```
Manifest-Version: 1.0
Bundle-ManifestVersion: 2
Bundle-SymbolicName: helloworld
Bundle-Version: 1.3
Export-Package: manning.osgi.helloworld;version=1.3.0
```

Here are the steps:

1   Install the bundles helloworld.jar and helloworld.client.jar. Start them. As expected, you'll get your "Hello World" message.

2   Install helloworld_1.3.0.jar. Stop and restart helloworld.client.jar. You'll notice that again the "Hello World" message *without* the timestamp is printed, which indicates that the `helloworld.client` bundle is still using the first version of the `helloworld` bundle, even though a more recent version is available.

3   Try shutting down and restarting Felix. The bundle `helloworld.client` still prints the old message. The OSGi framework persists the state of the bundle and doesn't change it even during a shutdown.

TIP   The OSGi framework persists the state of the bundles when the framework is shut down and restarted without changes. But during a restart, the OSGi framework may remove old packages that have been uninstalled, a process called *refresh*.

4   Uninstall and reinstall helloworld.client.jar. Start it, and this time you'll get a message *with* the timestamp, something similar to "08:03:00 AM PST: Hello World."

OSGi does provide another option for dealing with this problem. You can tell OSGi to update a bundle. In this case, OSGI stops the bundle, changes the bundle state to installed, and refreshes the resolved packages, in the process picking up new versions and implementations. Although you're not uninstalling a bundle, it's almost as if you were. You're essentially reinstalling a bundle from already-read bits. We'll discuss update and refresh in chapter 4.

This isn't optimal; could we do better?

Yes, the heart of the problem is that we're coupling two bundles on a class that contains implementation code. What we should be doing is sharing an interface between the bundles, therefore keeping the interface's implementation hidden within the providing bundle. To do this right, we rely on OSGi's service layer, as you'll see next.

2.4 Services and loose coupling

Our objective is to be able to change the implementation of a class, such as the `Printer` class, without having to reinstall the bundles, such as the `helloworld.client` bundle, that use this class. To accomplish this, we need to define the `Printer` class as a service.

With the popularity of Service Oriented Architecture (SOA), the term *service* has become somewhat overused. In OSGi, a service has three parts:

- *An interface*—An OSGi service interface is a conjunction of Java class (`java.lang.Class`) names. These Java classes don't have to extend or implement any particular OSGi API, or follow any particular conventions, such as that of JavaBeans.

  TIP Remember that `java.lang.Class` represents classes, interfaces, enums, and annotations.

- *An implementation*—An OSGi service implementation is a Java object. This Java object must be an instance of all the classes whose names were used to define the service interface.
- *Service properties*—A map of key-value pairs that can be used to provide metadata to the service is optional.

> **Technology-agnostic services**
>
> One of the advantages of OSGi is that it doesn't dictate that the service objects implement any technology-specific interfaces. This technology-agnostic behavior is a good quality of a framework. It allows user code to move freely from one framework to another.

The OSGi service registry manages the OSGi services. The OSGi service registry has two main roles:

- It allows services to be registered and deregistered by the service provider bundle.
- It allows services to be retrieved and released by the service requestor bundle.

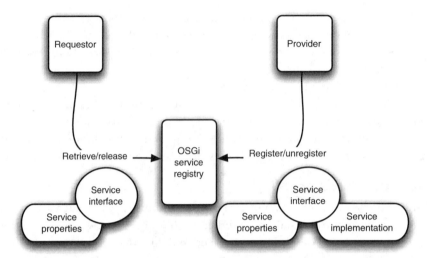

Figure 2.8   **The service provider bundle registers the service interface, service properties, and service implementation into the OSGi service registry. The service requestor bundle retrieves the service interface and the service properties from the OSGi service registry.**

In these roles, the OSGi service registry acts as the mediator, isolating the provider from the requestor. The service provider bundle owns the service interface, service properties, and service implementation. The service requestor bundle uses the service interface and service properties, but it can't access the service implementation. A diagram of the OSGi service registry is shown in figure 2.8.

Returning to our example, what do we need to do to change the Printer class into a Printer service?

2.4.1 The Printer service

First, we must create a service interface for the Printer service. OSGi makes this a simple task. We'll just create a Java interface for the Printer class:

```
package manning.osgi.helloworld;

public interface Printer {

    public void print(String message);

}
```

The Printer service interface is defined by a Java interface with a single println method. No implementation is needed to define the service interface. Technically, we could use a Java class rather than a Java interface to define the OSGi service interface. In this case, the service implementation would extend the Java class instead of implementing the Java interface. But using a Java interface is cleaner, is easier to understand, and keeps coupling between the service provider and the service requestor to a minimum.

Next, we need a Java object to serve as the service implementation. Version 1.3 of the `Printer` class is almost good enough; we just need to change it so that it implements the service interface, as shown here.

Listing 2.6 Upgraded `Printer` service implementation

```
package manning.osgi.helloworld.impl;

import java.text.DateFormat;
import java.util.Date;

import manning.osgi.helloworld.Printer;

public class PrinterImpl implements Printer {

    private static final String SEPARATOR = ": ";

    public void print(String message) {
        System.out.println(getCurrentTime() + SEPARATOR + message);
    }

    private String getCurrentTime() {
        return DateFormat.getTimeInstance(DateFormat.LONG).
format(new Date());
    }
}
```

First, the service implementation must implement (or extend) the service interface. Second, it's important to use a different Java package for the implementation than what is used for the interface. The package used by the interface needs to be exported, whereas we don't want to export the package used by the implementation. Otherwise, we might not be able to change the implementation easily without reinstalling the clients.

> **TIP** Use different packages for the service interface and service implementation, and export the package for the service interface. Don't export the package for the service implementation.

Those are all the changes needed to make the `Printer` class into an OSGi service. Observe how we didn't have to change the class to use any of the OSGi framework APIs; we just had to refactor it to adhere to software engineering practices that would have made sense regardless of OSGi.

Now that we have a service, we must register it in the OSGi service registry.

2.4.2 *Registering a service in the OSGi service registry*

We register a service into the OSGi service registry by using the `BundleContext` class provided in the `BundleActivator`, as shown in the following listing. We should register the `Printer` service when the `helloworld` bundle is started and unregister the service when the bundle is stopped.

Listing 2.7   Registering the `Printer` service in the OSGi service registry

```
package manning.osgi.helloworld.impl;

import org.osgi.framework.BundleActivator;
import org.osgi.framework.BundleContext;
import org.osgi.framework.ServiceRegistration;

import manning.osgi.helloworld.Printer;

public class PrinterActivator implements BundleActivator {

    private ServiceRegistration serviceRegistration;

    public void start(BundleContext bundleContext) throws Exception {
        serviceRegistration =
            bundleContext.registerService(
                    Printer.class.getName(),            ❶ Printer service
                    new PrinterImpl(),                     interface
                    null);                              ❷ Printer service
    }                                                      implementation

    public void stop(BundleContext bundleContext) throws Exception {
        serviceRegistration.unregister();              ❸ Unregister
    }                                                      service

}
```

You can archive the `Printer` interface, the `Printer` implementation, and the `PrinterActivator` classes into version 1.4.0 of the `helloworld` bundle:

```
Manifest-Version: 1.0
Bundle-ManifestVersion: 2
Bundle-SymbolicName: helloworld
Bundle-Version: 1.4
Export-Package: manning.osgi.helloworld;version=1.4.0
Import-Package: org.osgi.framework
Bundle-Activator: manning.osgi.helloworld.impl.PrinterActivator
```

In the `start` method, you instantiate the service by specifying its interface ❶ and implementation ❷, and you register it in the service registry using the `bundle-Context.registerService()` method. This method returns a `serviceRegistration` object, which represents the registered service.

Next, you use the `serviceRegistration` object in the `stop()` method to unregister the service ❸. This is done by invoking the `ServiceRegistration.unregister()` method.

NOTE   The OSGi framework automatically unregisters all services registered by a bundle when the bundle in question is stopped. Strictly speaking, it's unnecessary to explicitly invoke `unregister()` as we've done previously. But for completeness' sake, you generally include the unregistration of a service to highlight its proper usage and role. Furthermore, if you pass along the ownership of your serviceReference to another bundle, it then becomes that bundle's responsibility to unregister the service. Therefore, to avoid having to worry about who owns a service reference, it's better to always unregister it when it's no longer needed.

We've finished with the provider side of the Printer service. Next we need to work on the client side, which is more commonly referenced as the service requestor side, of the Printer service.

Let's start with the PrinterClient class. Instead of printing a single message, let's print a message every couple of seconds, as shown in the following listing. Printing multiple messages should make it easier for you to see the dynamic behavior of the OSGi services.

Listing 2.8 RunnablePrinterClient class

```
package manning.osgi.helloworld.client;

import manning.osgi.helloworld.Printer;

public class RunnablePrinterClient implements Runnable {

    private static final int TWO_SECS = 2000;

    private boolean stop;

    private Printer printer;

    void start() {
        stop = false;
        new Thread(this).start();
    }

    void stop() {
        stop = true;
    }

    public void run() {
        while (!stop) {

            printer.print("Hello...");

            try {
                Thread.sleep(TWO_SECS);
            } catch (InterruptedException e) {
                stop = true;
            }
        }
    }

    void setPrinterService(Printer printer) {
        this.printer = printer;
    }
}
```

Annotations:
- **Invoke service in separate thread** ← (points to `new Thread(this).start();`)
- **Stop the running thread** ← (points to `void stop() {`)

Again, you can observe that the RunnablePrinterClient class doesn't import any OSGi framework API. The only interface it depends on is the Printer service interface. In particular, it doesn't depend on the Printer service implementation anywhere.

The last piece to this puzzle is the PrinterClientActivator class. The main purpose of this class is to look up the Printer service in the OSGi service registry, which it then sets into the RunnablePrinterClient.

2.4.3　*Looking up a service from the OSGi service registry*

The lookup of a service is done through BundleContext, using the getService-Reference method, which takes a service interface as the key for the lookup. The get-ServiceReference method returns a service reference instead of the actual service object.

> **WARNING**　The method getServiceReference() returns null if no reference is found for the requested service.

The reason for this indirection is that the service reference includes the service properties. These properties can provide additional metadata to help you determine if the service you've requested is the correct one before fully retrieving it from the registry.

If you do decide to go on, you can get to the service object by using the method BundleContext.getService(ServiceReference). This method returns an object that can be safely cast to the Java class defined as the service interface.

> **TIP**　A service retrieved from the OSGi service registry can be safely cast to its service interface.

Generics

Why weren't generics used to implement the service layer in OSGi version 4.2? The simple answer is that the OSGi Alliance didn't want to impose usage of JDK 5.0 and above. This has since been relaxed in version 4.3, and it avoids the cast of the service objects returned from BundleContext.getService(ServiceReference).

But because OSGi version 4.3 is barely out at the time of writing, I've generally used version 4.2 throughout the book.

As part of retrieving a service from the service registry, a client must also release the when the service is no longer needed or when the service is no longer available. The release of a service is done through BundleContext, using the method ungetService, which takes the service reference that we retrieved previously.

You need to release the service when your client bundle stops. In addition, you should register a service listener with the OSGi framework, so that it can inform you when the service you're using is no longer available, in which case you should also release it. We'll discuss service listeners in following chapters.

NOTE Strictly speaking, the OSGi framework will also *unget* a service for you when it's unregistered, even if you forget to do it. But by doing it yourself, you're likely improving memory management and most importantly allowing service factories to work properly, a subject that we'll discuss in chapter 4.

There are a lot of details and caveats related to dealing with services. These will be dealt with in detail in chapter 4. You'll also learn a way of using services by using a declarative language instead of Java, which will greatly simplify things. In the following listing, we stick to the basics.

Listing 2.9 `BundleActivator` for `Printer` service requestor

```
package manning.osgi.helloworld.client;

import org.osgi.framework.*;

import manning.osgi.helloworld.Printer;

public class PrinterClientActivator implements
BundleActivator, ServiceListener {

    private RunnablePrinterClient runnablePrinterClient =
        new RunnablePrinterClient();
    private BundleContext bundleContext;
    private ServiceReference serviceReference;

    public void start(BundleContext bundleContext) throws Exception {
        this.bundleContext = bundleContext;

        serviceReference =
            bundleContext.getServiceReference(          ⟵  Retrieve reference
                Printer.class.getName());                    using interface

        if (serviceReference != null) {
            Printer printer = (Printer)                      Retrieve object
                bundleContext.getService(serviceReference); ⟵ using reference

            if (printer != null) {
                runnablePrinterClient.setPrinterService(printer);
                runnablePrinterClient.start();       ⟵⊟   Start client and return
            }                                         ❶   immediately
        }

        bundleContext.addServiceListener(this,
            "(objectClass=" +
            Printer.class.getName() + ")");      ⟵⊟   Register listener for
    }                                             ❷   service changes
```

```
public void stop(BundleContext bundleContext) throws Exception {
    if (serviceReference != null) {
        bundleContext.ungetService(serviceReference);          Release
    }                                                          reference

    bundleContext.removeServiceListener(this);          Remove listener
}                                                       from OSGi

public void serviceChanged(ServiceEvent serviceEvent) {
    switch (serviceEvent.getType()) {
        case ServiceEvent.UNREGISTERING: {                Service is being
            bundleContext.ungetService(                   unregistered
                serviceEvent.getServiceReference());
            break;
        }
        case ServiceEvent.REGISTERED: {                   Service is being
            Printer printer = (Printer)                   registered
                bundleContext.getService(
                    serviceEvent.getServiceReference());

            if (printer != null) {
                runnablePrinterClient.setPrinterService(printer);
                runnablePrinterClient.start();
            }
            break;
        }
    }
}
}
```

We have self-contained all of the OSGi-related usage in the `PrinterClientActivator` class. This is a good design pattern. If you ever need to move to a different framework, you just need to replace this class.

> **TIP** Avoid using OSGI framework APIs in the classes that implement the application logic. Keep them contained in a single location, the `Bundle-Activator` class being a good choice.

The filter syntax used in the registration of the service event listener in ❷ is based on LDAP (Lightweight Directory Access Protocol) and is used extensively by the OSGi framework. We'll study it in detail in chapter 4. For the purpose of this chapter, it suffices to know that it selects only events related to the `Printer` service.

By now, you've surely noticed that your `BundleActivator` class is invoked on a thread provided by the OSGi framework. In other words, you don't have to spawn any thread or implement `java.lang.Runnable` to be called back when the bundle starts or stops. But if that's the case, why did we spawn a different thread to execute the logic of the `RunnablePrinterClient` class in ❶? Couldn't we just have called the `Printer` service in a loop in the `start` method of the `PrinterClientActivator` class?

No, we couldn't have. The OSGi framework invokes all of the `BundleActivators` sequentially and dictates that the `BundleActivators` must return quickly in their implementation of the start and stop methods. If we were to hold on to the start method, not only would our bundle not activate, but we could likely be holding on to other bundles waiting to be activated.

> **TIP** A BundleActivator implementation must return quickly in the implementation of its start and stop methods. As you'll learn in later examples, spawning new threads can accomplish this.

To finalize, let's archive PrinterClientActivator and the RunnablePrinterClient classes in version 1.1.0 of the helloworld.client bundle:

```
Manifest-Version: 1.0
Bundle-ManifestVersion: 2
Bundle-SymbolicName: helloworld.client
Bundle-Version: 1.1.0
Import-Package: manning.osgi.helloworld;version=1.4.0,
 org.osgi.framework
Bundle-Activator: manning.osgi.helloworld.client.PrinterClientActivator
```

Figure 2.9 shows the interaction among the Printer service, its implementation, its client, and the activators.

Now we're finished with both the service provider and the service requestor, and we're ready to test.

2.4.4 *Running OSGi service-oriented applications*

Starting fresh, let's install and then start the bundles helloworld_1.4.0 and helloworld.client_1.1.0 in Felix.

The first test is to stop the bundle helloworld. When stopped, helloworld unregisters the Printer service. The OSGi framework then sends an unregistering service

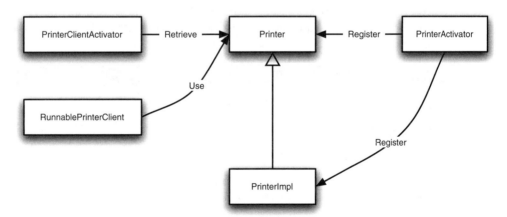

Figure 2.9 The PrinterActivator class registers the Printer and the PrinterImpl classes in the OSGi registry. The PrinterClientActivator class retrieves the Printer service and provides it to the RunnablePrinterClient, which invokes the Printer methods.

event to the bundle `helloworld.client`, which should then stop using the `Printer` service:

```
g! felix:install file:dist/helloworld_1.4.0.jar
Bundle ID: 63
g! felix:start 63
g! felix:install file:dist/helloworld.client_1.1.0.jar
Bundle ID: 64
g! felix:start 64
g! 11:06:38 PM PST: Hello...
11:06:40 PM PST: Hello...
g! felix:stop 64
g! 11:06:42 PM PST: Hello...
11:06:44 PM PST: Hello...
```

If you try this out, you'll notice that nothing happens. You'll still see the "Hello..." messages being printed out. Let's uninstall the `helloworld.client` bundle. This surely will stop the messages from being printed:

```
g! felix:uninstall 64
g! 11:06:46 PM PST: Hello...
11:06:48 PM PST: Hello...
```

Guess again; nothing changed. OK, so let's give it a final try. Let's use the `refresh` command; this worked the last time, so it must work now.

```
g! felix:update
g! 11:06:50 PM PST: Hello...
11:06:52 PM PST: Hello...
```

The problem is a simple but crucial one. We forgot to stop the `RunnablePrinter-Client` thread when the `Printer` service was unregistered. We'll do so now in listing 2.10.

> **TIP** Remember to release all resources when a bundle is stopped. This is generally done in the implementation of the `BundleActivator.stop` method.

Listing 2.10 `BundleActivator` must release resources when stopped

```
package manning.osgi.helloworld.client;

import org.osgi.framework.*;

import manning.osgi.helloworld.Printer;

public class PrinterClientActivator implements
  BundleActivator, ServiceListener {

    private RunnablePrinterClient runnablePrinterClient =
      new RunnablePrinterClient();
    private BundleContext bundleContext;
    private ServiceReference serviceReference;
```

```
public void start(BundleContext bundleContext) throws Exception {
    this.bundleContext = bundleContext;

    serviceReference =
        bundleContext.getServiceReference(Printer.class.getName());

    if (serviceReference != null) {
        Printer printer = (Printer)
            bundleContext.getService(serviceReference);

        if (printer != null) {
            runnablePrinterClient.setPrinterService(printer);
            runnablePrinterClient.start();
        }
    }

    bundleContext.addServiceListener(this,
            "(objectClass=" + Printer.class.getName() + ")");
}

public void stop(BundleContext bundleContext) throws Exception {
    runnablePrinterClient.stop();                          ⟵┐  Stop
    if (serviceReference != null) {                        │  runnablePrinterClient
        bundleContext.ungetService(serviceReference);    ⟵─┘
    }

    bundleContext.removeServiceListener(this);
}

public void serviceChanged(ServiceEvent serviceEvent) {
    switch (serviceEvent.getType()) {
        case ServiceEvent.UNREGISTERING: {
            runnablePrinterClient.stop();                  ⟵
            bundleContext.ungetService(
                serviceEvent.getServiceReference());       ⟵  Release service
            break;                                             when finished
        }
        case ServiceEvent.REGISTERED: {
            Printer printer = (Printer)
            bundleContext.getService(
                serviceEvent.getServiceReference());

            if (printer != null) {
                runnablePrinterClient.setPrinterService(printer);
                runnablePrinterClient.start();
            }
            break;
        }
    }
}
}
```

Stop runnable-
PrinterClient
when
unregistered

TIP Thread management is tricky in Java and particularly hard to get right when dealing with frameworks. In this example, no matter what we did, the JVM and OSGi weren't able to stop a running thread. The only predictable way to stop a running thread in Java is to let its run method return.

We're almost there. Fix the code and reinstall helloworld.client_1.1.0.jar in Felix. Start both helloworld_1.4.0.jar and helloworld.client_1.1.0.jar. Stop `helloworld`, and `helloworld.client` also ceases to print the "Hello..." message. Start `helloworld`, and `helloworld.client` resumes printing the message.

All seems fine. Let's get back to our original problem. What we want is to change the implementation of the `Printer` service and have the `Printer` service client bundle pick up the new implementation without us having to do anything, such as refreshing or reinstalling the client bundle. Let's see if we're able to solve the problem. Uninstall `helloworld`. Change the `SEPARATOR` field of the `PrinterImpl` class:

```
private static final String SEPARATOR = "-> ";
```

Reinstall and start the `helloworld` bundle:

```
g! felix:install file:dist/helloworld_1.4.0.jar
Bundle ID: 70
g! felix:start 70
g! 11:06:54 PM PST: Hello...
```

And the problem is still there. But in this case, if you refresh the `helloworld.client` bundle, which is something you won't like to do, you'll get the right message.

The issue is that the `PrinterImpl` class is located in the same bundle as the `Printer` service interface. When you uninstall the `PrinterImpl` class, you're also uninstalling the `Printer` class, which is used in the contract with the `helloworld.client` bundle. Because the packages can't be changed without refreshing the bundle, what happens is that the OSGi framework keeps around an old version of the `helloworld` bundle associated with the `helloworld.client` bundle and will only pick up the new version of `helloworld` when the packages are resolved again. This behavior is vendor specific, which makes it an even bigger problem.

What you need to do to avoid all the confusion is to move the `PrinterImpl` class to another bundle separate from the bundle that includes the service interface. You do this by creating a third bundle named helloworld.impl_1.4.0.jar, which includes the `PrinterImpl` and `PrinterActivator` classes, as shown in figure 2.10.

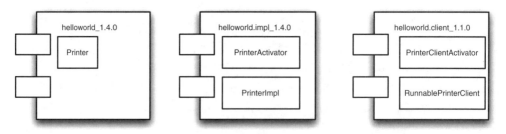

Figure 2.10   Bundle `helloworld` version 1.4 includes the `Printer` class. Bundle `helloworld.impl` version 1.4 includes the `PrinterActivator` and `PrinterImpl` classes. Bundle `helloworld.client` version 1.1 includes the `PrinterClientActivator` and `RunnablePrinterClient` classes.

The bundle `helloworld.impl` needs to import the package `manning.osgi.` `helloworld`, but it doesn't need to export any packages. The MANIFEST.MF file for helloworld.impl_1.4.0.jar is shown here:

```
Manifest-Version: 1.0
Bundle-ManifestVersion: 2
Bundle-SymbolicName: helloworld.impl
Bundle-Version: 1.4
Import-Package: manning.osgi.helloworld;version=1.4.0,org.osgi.framework
Bundle-Activator: manning.osgi.helloworld.impl.PrinterActivator
```

In the helloworld_1.4.0.jar bundle, we keep only the `Printer` class, and we no longer need to import the `org.osgi.framework` package:

```
Manifest-Version: 1.0
Bundle-ManifestVersion: 2
Bundle-SymbolicName: helloworld
Bundle-Version: 1.4
Export-Package: manning.osgi.helloworld;version=1.4.0
```

Let's retest:

```
g! felix:lb
START LEVEL 1
   ID|State       |Level|Name
    0|Active      |    0|System Bundle (3.0.6)
    1|Active      |    1|Apache Felix Bundle Repository (1.6.2)
    2|Active      |    1|Apache Felix Gogo Command (0.6.1)
    3|Active      |    1|Apache Felix Gogo Runtime (0.6.1)
    4|Active      |    1|Apache Felix Gogo Shell (0.6.1)
g! felix:install file:dist/helloworld_1.4.0.jar
Bundle ID: 63
g! felix:start 63
g! felix:install file:dist/helloworld.impl_1.4.0.jar
Bundle ID: 64
g! felix:start 64
g! felix:install file:dist/helloworld.client_1.1.0.jar
Bundle ID: 65
g! felix:start 65
g! 11:06:38 PM PST: Hello...
11:06:40 PM PST: Hello...
g! felix:uninstall 64
g! felix:install file:dist/helloworld.impl_1.4.0.jar
Bundle ID: 66
g! felix:start 66
g! 11:06:42 PM PST-> Hello...
11:06:44 PM PST-> Hello...
```

Install bundle `helloworld` version 1.4, which contains the `Printer` service interface. Install bundle `helloworld.impl` version 1.4, which contains the `Printer` service implementation. Install bundle `helloworld.client` version 1.1, which contains the client that retrieves the `Printer` service and prints the "Hello ..." messages. Next, uninstall `helloworld.impl` and install a new implementation for the `Printer` service, replacing the `SEPARATOR` constant : with ->. The `helloworld.client` continues to function normally, but now it uses the new `Printer` service implementation. Congratulations, you changed the implementation of a running application!

This simple hello world application allowed us to investigate several important features from OSGi, ranging from versioning, to package restriction and accessibility, to service management. In the next section, we'll discuss the role of these features in the overall architecture of the OSGi framework.

2.5   *The OSGi layered architecture*

The OSGi framework is implemented using a layered architecture, depicted in figure 2.11.

The bottom layer is the execution environment. Even though the OSGi framework is running on top of a JVM, the JVM itself can have different versions and profiles. For instance, there's a Java Micro Edition of the JVM, which is named Java ME; there's also a Java Standard Edition and a Java Enterprise Edition. On top of that, each edition may have several versions, such as Java SE 1.5 and 1.6. Because the developer can be using bundles provided by different vendors, it's important that each bundle be annotated with the execution

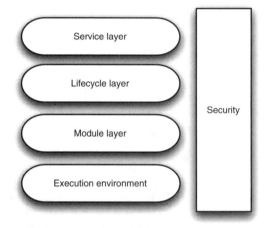

Figure 2.11   OSGi's layered architecture is composed of four layers: the execution environment, the module layer, the lifecycle layer, and the service layer. In addition, all layers make use of security.

environment it supports, which is done though the manifest header `Bundle-RequiredExecutionEnvironment`. This allows the developer to select only bundles that are known to execute on the environment that the developer is using. For instance, if you're running the OSGi framework on top of Java 1.3, then you don't want to install a bundle that uses enumerations. Unfortunately, in practice, it's seldom the case that people take the time to annotate the bundle's execution environment.

The module layer takes care of OSGi's modularity. The module layer manages the import and export of packages, through the use of a class loader delegation model, which is explained in chapter 4.

The lifecycle layer allows the developer to install, uninstall, start, stop, and update the bundles. This layer manages the bundle's lifecycle.

The last layer is the service layer, which allows the user to register and retrieve service objects through the use of the OSGi service registry. All layers are secured by an extension to Java security architecture.

From an architectural perspective, we've touched on all of the main features of the OSGi framework. In the next chapter, we'll look further into the details of the OSGi framework, but with an eye to techniques and OSGi features that are important for building complex full-fledged applications.

2.6 *Summary*

Bundles and services are the cornerstone of OSGi. Bundles help us achieve the principles of information hiding, whereas services allow us to create loosely coupled modules.

Bundles are Java modules. A bundle is a regular JAR file that contains OSGi-related manifest header entries. The `Bundle-SymbolicName` and `Bundle-Version` headers uniquely define a bundle.

Bundles are used to improve the modularity of an application. They do so by allowing the developer to control access to code. The manifest headers `Import-Package` and `Export-Package` are used for this purpose.

In addition, bundles can be versioned. Versioning a bundle allows the developer to change interfaces without impacting existing clients. Developers can version bundles by specifying a version tag in the packages referenced in the `Import-Package` and `Export-Package` manifest headers.

Services are regular Java objects that are managed individually by the OSGi service layer. A service has a service interface, a service implementation, and service properties.

Developers can use services to further decouple bundles that provide code to bundles that consume code. Using services, the developer can dynamically change a service implementation without impacting the bundles that use the service.

In the next chapter, we'll employ what you've learned so far and author a full-fledged application using OSGi.

The auction application: an OSGi case study

This chapter covers

- Modularization and extension as application requirements
- Service properties
- Development of a full-fledged OSGi application consisting of several decoupled bundles

Having explored the concepts behind development platforms in chapter 1 and working through the OSGi framework primer in chapter 2, we're ready to implement our first unabridged OSGi application: an auction system where buyers and sellers can trade goods through bids and ask offers.

The chapter starts by describing the auction use case. We'll consider a traditional approach for implementing the use case and investigate its shortcomings. We'll then look at a solution using OSGi where we develop a modular and extensible solution, thus improving maintainability. We'll prove its modularity by easily replacing the initial test bidder with a web-based bidder, and we'll make use of its extensibility to allow different brokering strategies to be developed as plug-ins.

Finally, we'll determine what's missing from the auction application to make it into a full-fledged enterprise-grade application, and we'll highlight how this can be achieved using standard OSGi services.

We'll start, as is usual in the development of any software, by establishing the requirements of the system.

3.1 Establishing the requirements for an auction system

In an auction, sellers offer goods by asking a price. Conversely, buyers bid for these goods, offering their own prices that they're willing to pay. The sellers and buyers of an action are called the *auction participants.* The institution that performs the auction is the *auctioneer.*

In an *English auction,* buyers can see the bids from other buyers and thus provide additional bids themselves, perhaps increasing their original offer. After some stipulated time, or when buyers cease to make bids, the buyer with the highest bid, which must be at least as high as the asking price, pays the seller for the item. In a *sealed-first-price auction,* each buyer can make only one bid, which is kept secret. The highest bid gets the item. There are dozens of variations on this. It's clear that if we want to build an auction system, the system must be easily extensible to support different auction styles. This is our first requirement.

Auctions are audited. This is necessary so that we can make sure that the auctioneer is not cheating the buyers and sellers. For example, consider the stock market, which is a type of auction. The exchange market—the auctioneer—matches bids from buyers with the asking price of sellers of equities, such as stocks. You, as a buyer or seller of an equity, want to make sure that you're paying or getting the best price you can. What you don't want is the exchange market to select a buyer who is paying less for your equity than other buyers are willing to pay, just because the buyer happens to be an important client of the exchange—not that this would ever happen in the real world, or would it? This brings us to our second requirement: our system must allow the pluggability of different auditing applications. Figure 3.1 shows the entities of the auction system and their relationships.

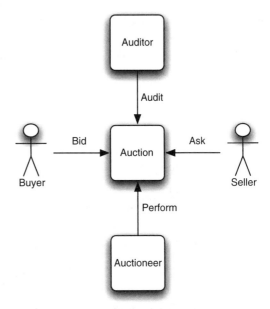

Figure 3.1 In an auction system, sellers ask a price for goods and buyers bid for them. Auditors monitor the overall auction activity.

In addition, it's very likely that the developer (or team of developers) who wrote the auction subsystem isn't the same one who wrote the auditing subsystem. Even further, these subsystems don't share the same lifecycle. An auction system may be initially deployed without any auditors because it may sell only goods that are under $100, but as the number of users grows, or the goods become expensive, or the type of good is one that demands it, we may need to support different types of auditors. Thus, our third requirement is that the auctions and auditors must be completely decoupled from each other and collaborate through some transparent form.

Finally, let's consider the end users of such an auction system. The end users are the buyers and sellers of goods. Some end users may want to interact with the auction system via a web interface, whereas others may prefer to use a rich-client interface. Finally, there's even the case where the buyers and sellers are computer systems themselves, implementing some algorithmic trading, and therefore will interact via a web service with the auction system. It's thus important that the seller and buyer components are modular and can be easily replaced or changed without impacting the overall system.

Next, we'll look at how to implement such modularity.

3.2 *Modularization and extensibility as application requirements*

Let's list the requirements from the previous section, so that we can select the proper architecture for implementing the solution:

- We must be able to replace or add different sellers and buyers.
- We must be able to extend the system with different auction policies.
- We must be able to extend the system with different auditing policies.
- Sellers, buyers, auctions, and auditors must not be aware of each other; that is, they must be completely decoupled and modular because they're likely to be implemented by different development teams.

From these requirements, it's clear that we need to implement a system that's modular and extensible.

The auction system implementation is therefore composed of four logical entities, or modules:

- The buyer module
- The seller module
- The auction (extension) module
- The auditor (extension) module

In addition, we need an implementation module that serves as the mediator and integrates the previously listed modules. We'll call it

- The auction manager module

The modules are represented in figure 3.2.

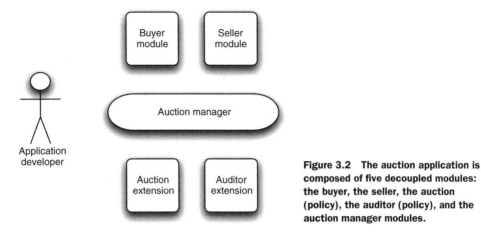

Figure 3.2 **The auction application is composed of five decoupled modules: the buyer, the seller, the auction (policy), the auditor (policy), and the auction manager modules.**

From this initial analysis, one characteristic that jumps out is that our auction application will be composed of several modules, or more precisely, OSGi bundles.

> **TIP** One common approach to achieving modularity with OSGi is to organize an application as separate collaborating bundles.

As you'll see, using the OSGi framework, we're able to support all of these requirements in a natural form.

The first step in implementing this modularity is defining the interfaces between bundles.

3.3 *Defining the interfaces*

We'll start the implementation of our auction application by focusing on the interfaces between the bundles. In the same way that test-driven development dictates that we should develop the tests for an application before we implement the actual application, when developing modular OSGi applications, it's best to start by defining the intermodule interfaces.

The main class of the auction application is the `Auction` class:

```
package manning.osgi.auction;

public interface Auction {

    Float ask(String item, float price, Participant seller)
throws InvalidOfferException;

    Float bid(String item, float price, Participant buyer)
throws InvalidOfferException;

}
```

A seller invokes the `ask` method to inform the participants that the seller wishes to sell `item` for the given `price`. The return value depends on the type of the auction. If it's an open auction, the ask method returns the highest available bid for the item being asked or null if no bidders for this item exist or if it's a sealed auction.

NOTE You may want to opt for BigDecimal when representing currency. Here, however, I used a simple float for its readability and simplicity.

Conversely, a buyer invokes the bid method to inform the participants that the buyer wishes to buy item with the given price. If it's an open auction, the method returns the highest available bid for the item or null otherwise. Note that if no other bidders exist, but an ask price is available, the ask price is returned if the auction is open.

Both methods take a callback reference to the class Participant:

```
package manning.osgi.auction;

public interface Participant {

    String getName();

    void onAcceptance(Auction auction, String item, float price);

    void onRejection(Auction auction, String item, float bestBid);

}
```

The implementation invokes the method onAcceptance to inform the seller that the seller's bid was awarded the item. The method includes the item being awarded, the price that must be paid, and the auction in which the item was auctioned. Likewise, the implementation invokes this same method on the buyer's object reference to inform the buyer that the item being asked for was sold for the price included as a parameter in the onAcceptance method. If the transaction doesn't go through, then the sellers and buyers are called back using the method onRejection, which would include the auction, the item that wasn't sold, and the best bid provided. The best bid may be the asking price if no other bids exist.

Finally, we define an exception in case the bid or ask is invalid, such as if the item isn't an exchangeable item or if the price is non-positive.

Because these interfaces are all end-user facing, we place them in an application programming interface (API) bundle called auction.api_1.0.0:

```
Manifest-Version: 1.0
Bundle-ManifestVersion: 2
Bundle-SymbolicName: manning.osgi.auction.api
Bundle-Version: 1.0.0
Export-Package: manning.osgi.auction;version=1.0.0
```

So far the interfaces are quite simple: the buyer and seller get hold of an auction reference and then bid on or ask for items, providing a reference back to themselves so they're informed of the results. But how does the buyer or seller find an auction reference? The buyer and seller not only need to find an auction, but they also need to find one with the proper terms, such as the right type, duration, and the like.

3.3.1   *Using service properties*

One way to look at the Auction class is to consider it as a service. This makes sense, because an auction is an important concept in our system, and we want to manage it closely. Remember from chapter 2 that the following triplet defines a service: a service interface, a service implementation, and service properties. We've already discussed the first two; let's take a look at the last item, service properties.

> **Service properties**
>
> Service properties are key-value pairs that are associated with service objects to act as metadata. The metadata is generally used to find a service of interest in the OSGi service registry. A common example of a service property is a text description of the service.

We can use the service properties to describe the terms of the auction. The buyers and sellers can then search the OSGi service registry for the auction service object whose service properties meet the criteria of terms desired.

Let's define two auction terms, the auction type and the auction duration, and model these terms as service properties. OSGi service property keys must be of Java String type. The service property value can be any Java object, but it's advisable to only use Java primitive or standard types, such as the Collection classes in the java.util package.

> **WARNING**   The OSGi framework doesn't manage dependencies between bundles created by the exchange of objects in the service properties; hence, you should use only primitive and standard types as service property values. We'll look into dependencies in detail in chapter 4.

In our example, we'll define the auction type property as a String, for which valid examples are "English" and "Sealed-First-Price". The auction duration property is defined as an integer. Normally, the duration of an auction is defined in terms of a number of hours, but to keep it practical for us to test in this book, we're defining the auction duration as the maximum number of bids that an auction may have.

Because the service requester may use the service properties, we should include their definition in the service interface:

```
package manning.osgi.auction;

public interface Auction {

    /**
     * Value: String
     */
    String TYPE = "auction-type";
```

```
/**
 * Value: Integer
 */
String DURATION = "auction-duration";

// Service Methods

Float ask(String item, float price, Seller seller) throws
➡ InvalidOfferException;

Float bid(String item, float price, Buyer buyer) throws
➡ InvalidOfferException;

}
```

Having defined the auction service properties, how do we use them when searching for an auction service? First, let's implement a participant that finds any available auction service:

```
serviceReference =
    bundleContext.getServiceReference(Auction.class.getName());

if (serviceReference != null) {
    Auction auction = (Auction)
        bundleContext.getService(serviceReference);
    // Use service...
}
```

In this case, had there been more than one `Auction` service object, the OSGi framework would have returned to us the service with the highest ranking. As you'll see in chapter 5, the OSGi framework has a set of predefined service properties, one of which is the `SERVICE_RANKING`. When a service provider registers a service, the provider can specify any arbitrary service ranking number, which is then used to disambiguate services during a lookup. If more than one service has the same service ranking, the one that was registered first is returned.

> **NOTE** Use the predefined service property `org.osgi.framework.Constants.`
> `SERVICE_RANKING` to prioritize service objects that have the same service interface during their lookup in the OSGi service registry. We'll look at service ranking in depth in the next chapter.

Next, let's change the code to search for auctions that follow the English auction style and whose duration is a maximum of 50 bids:

```
ServiceReference[] serviceReferences =
    bundleContext.getServiceReferences(
        Auction.class.getName(),
        "(&(auction-type=English)(auction-duration=50))");
```

The second argument of the method `getServiceReferences()` is a `String`, which is used as a filter for the service properties. As mentioned in chapter 2, the filter expression is based on the LDAP syntax. Let's dissect the one used in this example.

The filter expression uses a prefix format (also known as the Polish notation), which makes it a bit confusing to developers used to traditional imperative languages like Java and C, which use the infix format for their expressions. Let's change the expression to infix and replace the & operator by a more descriptive AND, as shown in figure 3.3.

Hopefully it looks less puzzling now. The filter expression searches for service objects that have a service property named auction-type whose value must be equal

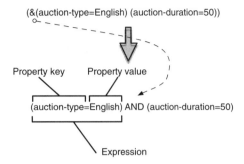

Figure 3.3 An OSGi LDAP filter that uses service properties reformatted to infix format and uses the descriptive AND instead of &

to the string "English" and a service property auction-duration whose value must be equal to the number 50. The comparison of the service property name is case insensitive, but the comparison of their values is dependent on their type. As a general rule of thumb, the comparison of the service property values relies on the equal method of the value's Java class. We'll discuss OSGi's filter expression in detail in chapter 5.

Comparison of the service property values

It's important to select the proper type for the service property values; otherwise, you may get some unexpected behavior. For example, if you define a service property PRICE to be of type String, then the following two expressions have different results:

```
"(PRICE=10)"
"(PRICE=10.0)"
```

But if you define PRICE to be of type float, then both previous expressions are equal. Even though this may seem obvious, it's a common mistake for people to define a service property unnecessarily as being of type String, even when their values are numbers.

The method getServiceReferences returns an array of all services that meet these criteria, or null instead of an empty array if none are found. In our case, if it returns more than one service reference, we'll arbitrarily pick the first one.

3.3.2 Implementing the seller module

Let's put it all together. First, we implement a bundle activator that searches for a sealed-first-price auction, as shown in the following listing.

Listing 3.1 BundleActivator for auction seller

```
package manning.osgi.auction.seller.simple;

import org.osgi.framework.*;

import manning.osgi.auction.Auction;
```

```
public class SellerActivator implements BundleActivator, ServiceListener {

    private BundleContext bundleContext;
    private Seller seller = new Seller("Seller 1");

    public void start(BundleContext bundleContext) throws Exception {

        this.bundleContext = bundleContext;

        String filter =
            "(&(objectClass="
            + Auction.class.getName()
            + ")(" + Auction.TYPE
            + "=Sealed-First-Price))";

        ServiceReference[] serviceReferences =
            bundleContext.getServiceReferences(null,
            filter);

        if (serviceReferences != null) {
            ask(serviceReferences[0]);
        }
    }

    public void stop(BundleContext bundleContext) throws Exception {
    }

    private void ask(ServiceReference serviceReference) {
        Auction auction = (Auction)
        bundleContext.getService(serviceReference);

        if (auction != null) {
            seller.ask(auction);
            bundleContext.
                ungetService(serviceReference);
        }
    }
}
```

❶ **Filter uses predefined objectClass property**

❷ **Look up service using properties as filter criteria**

❸ **Release service after single usage**

The OSGi framework predefines several service properties, one of which is object-Class. The objectClass property can be used to specify the service interface name as a filter expression ❶. If you do this, you don't have to specify the service interface name when using the getServiceReference() method ❷, and you can instead can use null as the first argument to this method.

In listing 3.2 we implement the seller. Because the seller is making a single offering, we immediately release the Auction service object after invoking the ask method by *ungetting* its service reference in listing 3.1 ❸. Because we aren't keeping a reference to the service, the SellerActivator class is simpler than the PrinterClient-Activator defined in listing 2.9, which had to register a service listener to receive changes made to the service it was holding.

> **WARNING**   Because OSGi provides a dynamic environment, anytime you keep a reference to a service object beyond the BundleActivator.start method,

you must register a service listener to make sure the service hasn't been unregistered.

Listing 3.2 Implementation class for auction seller

```
package manning.osgi.auction.seller.simple;

import manning.osgi.auction.Auction;
import manning.osgi.auction.InvalidOfferException;
import manning.osgi.auction.Participant;

public class Seller implements Participant, Runnable {

    private final String name;
    private Auction auction;

    public Seller(String name) {
        this.name = name;
    }

    public String getName() {
        return this.name;
    }

    public void ask(Auction auction) {
        this.auction = auction;
        new Thread(this).start();
    }

    public void run() {
        try {
            auction.ask("bicycle", 24.0f, this);
        } catch (InvalidOfferException e) {
            e.printStackTrace();
        }
        auction = null;
    }

    public void onAcceptance(Auction auction, String item,
        float price) {
        System.out.println(this.name + " sold " + item + " for " + price);
    }

    public void onRejection(Auction auction, String item,
        float bestBid) {
        System.out.println("No bidders accepted asked price for " + item
+ ", best bid was " + bestBid);
    }
}
```

❶ **Runs in new thread**

Use action service to sell item

Callback if offered price is accepted

Callback if offered price is rejected

You may ask why we need to start a new thread ❶ if we're only performing a single ask and immediately returning in the run method. The answer is that we don't know how long it will take for the implementation of the ask method to return and therefore shouldn't risk blocking the `BundleActivator`'s `start` method, which started the whole process.

> **NOTE** Generally speaking, you wouldn't invoke printouts from your Java code, but we do it here for succinctness.

We've finished implementing this sample seller. Let's place both the `SellerActivator` and `Seller` classes into an auction.seller.simple_1.0.0.jar bundle, whose manifest file is shown here:

```
Manifest-Version: 1.0
Bundle-ManifestVersion: 2
Bundle-SymbolicName: manning.osgi.auction.seller.simple
Bundle-Version: 1.0.0
Import-Package: manning.osgi.auction;version=1.0.0,
 org.osgi.framework
Bundle-Activator: manning.osgi.auction.seller.simple.SellerActivator
```

The buyer code is overall very similar to the seller code. We'll discuss it later in this chapter when we test the auction application itself. But it's important to point out that even though buyers and sellers interact through the auction service, they remain decoupled from each other. For example, buyer objects have no references to any seller objects and vice versa. In addition, the auction will proceed even if a buyer bids before the seller has offered an item. This is the case of a buyer who wants to inform potential sellers of the desire for a particular item.

3.3.3 *Avoiding temporal cohesion between bundles*

The OSGi framework provides a dynamic environment; services may come and go, so it's important that service requesters are implemented in a way that they're able to cope with this dynamism. It's easy to overlook this. Let's look again at listing 3.1, which implements the bundle activator for the seller application. The activator retrieves an auction and then issues an ask offer. What's wrong with this implementation?

This implementation assumes that an auction has already been registered. What if the auctioneer bundle is started immediately after the seller bundle? The seller would have found no auction and then would have done no work. There's a temporal cohesion between the seller bundle and the auctioneer bundle, where the latter must be started before the former. The correct implementation for the seller's bundle activator is shown in the following listing.

> **Listing 3.3 Cohesion-free implementation of the `SellerActivator` class**

```
package manning.enterprise.auction.seller.simple;

import org.osgi.framework.*;

import manning.osgi.auction.Auction;

public class SellerActivator implements BundleActivator, ServiceListener {
```

```
private BundleContext bundleContext;
private Seller seller = new Seller("Seller 1");

public void start(BundleContext bundleContext) throws Exception {

    this.bundleContext = bundleContext;

    String filter =
        "(&(objectClass=" + Auction.class.getName()
        + ")(" + Auction.TYPE
        + "=Sealed-First-Price))";

    ServiceReference[] serviceReferences =
        bundleContext.getServiceReferences(null,
            filter);

    if (serviceReferences != null) {
        ask(serviceReferences[0]);
    } else {
        bundleContext.addServiceListener(this,
            filter);
    }
}

public void serviceChanged(ServiceEvent
        serviceEvent) {
    switch (serviceEvent.getType()) {
        case ServiceEvent.REGISTERED: {
            ask(serviceEvent.getServiceReference());
            break;
        }
        default:
            // do nothing
    }
}

private void ask(ServiceReference serviceReference) {
    Auction auction = (Auction)
        bundleContext.getService(serviceReference);

    if (auction != null) {
        seller.ask(auction);
        bundleContext.
            ungetService(serviceReference);
    }
}

public void stop(BundleContext bundleContext) throws Exception {
    bundleContext.removeServiceListener(this);
}
}
```

Common filter to retrieve and listen for services

1 Retrieve existing services

2 Listen for future services

3 Manage changes to services

4 Release service

5 Remove listener

As usual, we retrieve the Auction service from the OSGi service registry **1**. But if the service isn't yet available, we also register a listener so that we're notified when it does become available **2**. The notification is done through the invocation of the method serviceChanged ❸. In the implementation of this method, we handle the registered service event by getting the auction service and invoking the method ask(). Because we immediately release the auction service after its usage ❹, we don't need to handle the unregistered service event. Finally, we must not forget to remove the service listener ❺ when we stop the bundle; otherwise, we may cause memory leakage.

> **TIP**   Avoid temporal cohesion between a service provider bundle and a service requester bundle by having the service requester bundle pull for the services in the start method as well as listen for them using a service listener.

SERVICE TRACKERS

As you saw in listing 3.3, ServiceListeners can be used to avoid temporal cohesion. However, there is a reasonable amount of boilerplate code that needs to be written to accomplish this. One alternative to the ServiceListener is the ServiceTracker.

To use a ServiceTracker, you first register your intent of usage, that is, the services that you wish to track. The ServiceTracker then does what you have learned about in this section; it registers a ServiceListener and handles the ServiceChange events appropriately for you. For example, the following code creates a service tracker to track the Auction service as in listing 3.3:

```
String filter =
  "(&(objectClass=" + Auction.class.getName()
  + ")(" + Auction.TYPE + "=Sealed-First-Price))";

ServiceTracker tracker =
  new ServiceTracker(bundleContext, filter, null);

tracker.open();

Auction auction = (Auction) tracker.waitForService(0);
```

When you invoke the ServiceTracker.waitForService(long) method, the tracker checks if a service already exists for the filter used in the constructor, and if a service doesn't exist, it waits until a ServiceChange event is received indicating that the service is now available, and it returns the corresponding service object. The parameter to the waitForService() method indicates how long the tracker should wait in milliseconds, and a value of 0 means it waits indefinitely.

> **WARNING**   Avoid calling waitForService() within a BundleActivator, as you should not be blocking a bundle activator's execution for a long period of time.

When you no longer wish to track a service, you can call the ServiceTracker.close() method.

ServiceTrackers are easier to use, and they remove some of the boilerplate code, so they're a preferable option to using ServiceListeners. However, sometimes you need greater flexibility, and in that case you can always rely on the ServiceListener directly. In chapter 13, you'll learn yet another approach to managing services through the Blueprint service.

> **NOTE** The examples in this book sometimes omit the complete use of the `ServiceListener` or `ServiceTracker` for brevity.

3.3.4 *The registry design pattern*

We've finished with our auction API. If you look back at the classes `SellerActivator` and `Seller`, you can see that end users only have to deal with concepts that are relevant to their tasks. For example, they don't even have to know about other entities we've discussed, such as auditors.

> **NOTE** Modular systems are composed of modules that yield simple, highly cohesive interfaces.

Furthermore, we're able to leverage the OSGi service layer; we had to implement only a few lines of code to retrieve an auction service that had the proper terms, such as the proper style and duration.

Albeit being somewhat obvious, we can use the OSGi service registry as a general registry of application services and thus implement a common design pattern known as the *registry design pattern*, shown in figure 3.4.

Registry design pattern

Intent—Allows a consumer to find a service by knowing only its name or some attribute of the service

Participants—Consuming bundle, Registry service, Provider bundle

Structure—Consuming bundle searches the registry using a name or attributes for a particular service that has been registered by a provider bundle

Consequences—Consuming bundle doesn't know who provides the services or care how

Known uses—Data source service (see chapter 8)

Related patterns—Whiteboard pattern

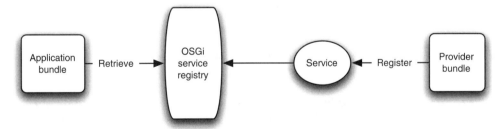

Figure 3.4 In the registry design pattern, the application bundle retrieves the application service from the OSGi service registry, and the providing bundle registers the service objects.

The following steps define the collaboration for this pattern:

1 Define the application service interfaces. In the case of the seller application, it's the Auction class.

2 Retrieve the service references using the service interfaces and any other service properties needed for filtering.

3 Register a listener to changes to the retrieved service references.

4 Handle registered, unregistered, and modified service events for the retrieved service references in step 2. In the case of the seller application, we manage only registered service events.

5 Release the service references when finished using them.

6 Remove the service change listener when stopping the bundle.

There's one drawback to this approach: the BundleActivator class, which is part of the end-user application, is tied to the OSGi framework API. One of your aims when defining an API should be to keep it agnostic to any particular technology. Throughout the book, we'll look into other approaches that avoid the problem of coupling our end users to a particular technology.

Next, we'll look at the interfaces needed for the auction and auditor extension modules, or plug-ins.

3.4   *Defining the extension points*

As you've seen, OSGi helps us achieve application extensibility. One approach for doing so is to define special interfaces to be implemented by the plug-ins, or extensions. These interfaces are often called extension points, or service provider interfaces (SPIs). Contrary to the API, the SPI is generally not seen by the end users.

The auction application extension points consist of two interfaces, the Auctioneer and the Auditor interfaces. Let's start with the Auctioneer interface:

```
package manning.osgi.auction.spi;

import java.util.Dictionary;

import manning.osgi.auction.Auction;

public interface Auctioneer {

    Auction getAuction();

    Dictionary<String, Object> getAuctionProperties();

}
```

Vendors that would like to plug a new auction type into the auction application must implement this class. The method getAuction() must return the auction service object that will be used by the sellers and buyers. This method shouldn't behave as a factory but rather just provide a single object instance of the auction service. This means that if a vendor would like to provide several different auctions, the vendor

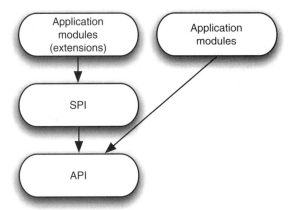

Figure 3.5 A layered architecture for bundle dependencies: extensions depend on the SPI, and the SPI and applications depend on the API.

must provide different `Auctioneer` classes. The method `getAuctionProperties()` must return the service properties that are associated with the auction service object; in other words, the auction terms supported by the auctioneer, such as the auction duration and the auction type.

Interestingly, the `Auctioneer` class makes use of the `Auction` class, which is defined in the API and not part of the SPI. It's common and perfectly reasonable for an SPI to reference a class of the API, but the opposite shouldn't happen: classes of the API shouldn't reference classes of the SPI. The way to rationalize this is to consider module dependencies as a layered architecture whose dependencies must flow in only one direction, as shown in figure 3.5.

WARNING   The API should be self-contained as much as possible and not reference classes of the SPI.

Next, let's look at the `Auditor` class:

```
package manning.osgi.auction.spi;

import manning.osgi.auction.Participant;

public interface Auditor {

    void onAcceptance(Auctioneer auctioneer, Participant participant,
            String item, float ask,
            float acceptedBid, Float [] bids);

    void onRejection(Auctioneer auctioneer, Participant participant,
            String item, float ask,
            Float [] rejectedBids);

}
```

The method `onAcceptance()` is called back by the implementation every time an auction's transaction is completed successfully; for every item that's sold, the auction system implementation calls back all available auditors with interesting data, such as the item that was sold, the selling price, the asked price, and all non-accepted bids. This provides the auditors with enough information to audit the auctions. Similarly, the method onRejection() is called when a transaction completes unsuccessfully, such as when there are no bids for an offered item.

Doesn't it feel like we're missing something? This can't be everything; don't we need some AuctionFrameworkService class to bootstrap the whole thing? How do auctions, auctioneers, and auditors get registered into the OSGi framework? Well, again, we'll be leveraging the OSGi service layer, but in a slightly different way that complements the previous usage of the OSGi service registry by the buyers and sellers discussed in section 3.3.3, as you'll see next.

3.4.1 Developing our first auction extension

To fully explain the SPI, in the following listing we'll implement an Auctioneer that provides a sealed-first-price type of auction.

Listing 3.4 Sealed-auction auctioneer service implementation

```
package manning.osgi.auction.auctioneer.sealed;

import java.util.*;

import manning.osgi.auction.Auction;
import manning.osgi.auction.spi.Auctioneer;

public class SealedFirstPriceAuctioneer implements Auctioneer {

    private static final String SEALED_FIRST_PRICE = "Sealed-First-Price";
    private final int DURATION = 3;

    private final Dictionary<String, Object> properties =
        new Hashtable<String, Object>();

    private final Auction auction;

    public SealedFirstPriceAuctioneer() {                    ❶ Auction service
        properties.put(Auction.TYPE, SEALED_FIRST_PRICE);       properties
        properties.put(Auction.DURATION, DURATION);
        auction = new SealedFirstPriceAuction(DURATION);
    }

    public Auction getAuction() {
        return auction;
    }

    public Dictionary<String, Object> getAuctionProperties() {
        return properties;
    }
}
```

The SealedFirstPriceAuctioneer class is simple. First, it creates a dictionary with the proper terms to be used for the auction ❶, and then it instantiates a Sealed-FirstPriceAuction object.

Next, let's look at the `SealedFirstPriceAuction` class, which does the bulk of the work, as shown in the following listing.

Listing 3.5 Sealed-auction implementation

```
package manning.osgi.auction.auctioneer.sealed;

import java.util.*;

import manning.osgi.auction.Auction;
import manning.osgi.auction.InvalidOfferException;
import manning.osgi.auction.Participant;

public class SealedFirstPriceAuction implements Auction {

    private class Book {
        float ask;
        Participant seller;
        float highestBid;
        Participant highestBidder;
        int numberOfBids;
    }

    private Map<String, Book> openTransactions;
    private final int maxAllowedBids;

    public SealedFirstPriceAuction(int duration) {          ❶ Initialize from
        maxAllowedBids = duration;                            service property
        openTransactions = new HashMap<String, Book>();
    }

    public Float ask(String item, float price, Participant seller)
            throws InvalidOfferException {
        if (price <= 0.0f) {
            throw new InvalidOfferException("Ask must be greater than
            ➥ zero.");
        }
                                                            ❷ Get transaction
        Book book = openTransactions.get(item);               for item

        if (book == null) {
            book = new Book();
            openTransactions.put(item, book);
        }
                                                            ❸ Check if item is
        if (book.seller != null) {                            already being sold
            throw new InvalidOfferException("Item [" + item + "] has
            ➥ already being auctioned.");
        }

        book.ask = price;
        book.seller = seller;

        System.out.println(seller.getName() + " offering item "
            + item + " for the asking price of " + price);

        return price;
    }
```

```
public Float bid(String item, float price, Participant buyer)
    throws InvalidOfferException {
    if (price <= 0.0f) {
        throw new InvalidOfferException("Bid must be greater than
        ➥ zero.");
    }

    Book book = openTransactions.get(item);

    if (book == null) {
        book = new Book();
        openTransactions.put(item, book);
    }

    assert book.numberOfBids < maxAllowedBids;

    if (price > book.highestBid) {
        book.highestBid = price;
        book.highestBidder = buyer;
    }

    if ((++book.numberOfBids) == maxAllowedBids) {
        if (book.seller != null) {
            if (book.highestBid >= book.ask) {
                book.seller.onAcceptance(this, item,
                    book.highestBid);
                book.highestBidder.onAcceptance(this, item,
                    book.highestBid);
            } else {
                book.seller.onRejection(this, item, book.highestBid);
                book.highestBidder.onRejection(this, item,
                    book.highestBid);
            }
        } else {
            book.highestBidder.onRejection(this, item,
                book.highestBid);
        }

        openTransactions.remove(item);
    } else {
        System.out.println(buyer.getName() + " bidding for item "
            + item);
    }

    return null;
}
}
```

4 **Check if current bid is highest**

5 **Check if bids have reached maximum**

6 **Check if there's an existing seller**

7 **Notify seller and buyer of acceptance**

8 **Conceal bid price**

In the constructor, we set the duration of the auction **1**. The duration of an auction is immutable and can't be changed after an auction has been initiated. In **2**, the seller has invoked the method ask, and we check for any existing transactions or bookings for the item being offered. If there are no open books, or if there's an open transaction for the item, but there are no sellers yet **3**, just bids, we proceed. The bid method also retrieves the open transaction for the item or creates a new transaction if there are none yet. In ❹, it checks to see if the current bid is greater than the highest bid so far, and if it is, it becomes the new highest bid. In ❺, we check if we've reached the maximum number of bids. If we have and there's an available seller ❻, we check if the highest bid seen so far is greater than or equal to the asking price, in which case we call back the onAcceptance method of the seller and the highest bidder ❼; otherwise we call back the onRejection methods. Because this is a sealed auction, it returns null ❽.

The last class for our extension is the SealedAuctioneerActivator class, as shown in the following listing.

Listing 3.6   Bundle activator for sealed-actions auctioneer

```
package manning.osgi.auction.auctioneer.sealed;

import org.osgi.framework.*;

import manning.osgi.auction.spi.Auctioneer;

public class SealedFirstPriceAuctioneerActivator
⮕ implements BundleActivator {

    private ServiceRegistration serviceRegistration;

    public void start(BundleContext bundleContext) throws Exception {
        SealedFirstPriceAuctioneer auctioneer =
            new SealedFirstPriceAuctioneer();

        serviceRegistration =                              ❶ Register service
            bundleContext.registerService(          ◁——┘     when started
                    Auctioneer.class.getName(),
                    auctioneer, auctioneer.getAuctionProperties());
    }

    public void stop(BundleContext bundleContext) throws Exception {
        serviceRegistration.unregister();              ◁——┐ Unregister service
    }                                                  ❷   when stopped
}
```

Note how the only real work we have to do is to register the SealedFirstPrice-Auctioneer service object in the OSGi service registry ❶. Contrast this to the bundle activator in listing 3.3. In listing 3.3, the activator is employing the registry design pattern, whereas the SealedAuctioneerActivator uses what's commonly referred to as the whiteboard design pattern.

3.4.2   *Whiteboard design pattern*

In the whiteboard design pattern, a bundle interacts with the OSGi framework by registering a service object that implements some well-known shared service interface. The framework then invokes or calls back the bundle by using the registered services. It's a pull mechanism; the client bundle is passive and waits to be called back. The framework or invoker bundle does this by retrieving the service objects from the OSGi service registry, using the established shared service interface. The invoker bundle is the one that employs the registry design pattern in this case. The whiteboard design pattern and the registry design pattern complement each other; generally whenever there's a bundle employing one of these design patterns, there's another one using its complement.

Whiteboard design pattern

Intent—Allows a client to be called back when needed by an invoker bundle

Participants—Client bundle, registry, service, invoker bundle

Structure—Client bundle registers a shared service in the registry and waits to be called back by the invoker bundle as needed

Consequences—Client bundle is indifferent to the details of how and when it's going to be called back; it's concerned only with implementing the callback interface

Known uses—Extender pattern

Related patterns—Registry pattern

As you saw in listing 3.6, the whiteboard design pattern is easy to implement. You only have to do the following:

1. Define the shared service interfaces. In this case, the shared interface is the SPI's `Auctioneer` class.
2. Register a service object using the service interface in the OSGi service registry. This is done in ❶ (see listing 3.6).
3. Unregister the service object when the bundle stops. This is done in ❷ (see listing 3.6).

The whiteboard design pattern is illustrated in figure 3.6.

The OSGi framework, or more precisely the invoker bundle, will do the rest. In the case of the auction application, as you'll see in section 3.5, a core bundle retrieves the

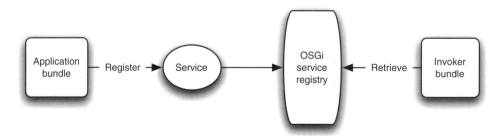

Figure 3.6 In the whiteboard design pattern, the application bundle registers the service object, and the invoker bundle retrieves it from the OSGi service registry.

auctioneer services registered by all auction extensions and manages them by mediating the auctioneer services with the auditor services and the seller and buyer applications. As several examples will illustrate, the whiteboard design pattern tends to have a granularity of one to many; a single invoker bundle retrieves the services of several extension bundles.

Compare this approach to that of the registry design pattern as described in section 3.3.4. In the registry design pattern, not only do you have to retrieve the proper service object, but you must also cope with the fact that the service objects may go away at any time. This latter fact is what makes it more difficult.

Because it's harder to implement the registry design pattern, the application developer should use it in the implementation of the application and thus allow the application extensions to rely on the whiteboard design pattern, which is simpler. In other words, we take the onus of complexity upon ourselves and let our clients relish the simplicity.

It isn't always possible to use the whiteboard pattern. There are cases where the bundle needs to be in an active mode; the bundle needs to drive the interaction rather than be pulled back. This is the case for the buyer and seller applications. It's more natural for the buyer and seller to actively issue bids and ask prices than for the auction application implementation to prompt them for bids or ask prices periodically. For example, as an eBay customer, you log into the eBay website when you want to sell or buy an item, rather than waiting for eBay to contact you to inform you when a new item is being sold. In general, the whiteboard design pattern is more suitable for extension bundles than application bundles. We'll look into other design patterns in future chapters.

3.4.3 *Keeping service properties immutable*

It so happens that the `auction type` and `auction duration` service properties are immutable in nature—you shouldn't change the duration or the type of an auction after the auction has been initiated. But what if you were dealing with some auction term that's changeable, let's say the currency. An auction may deal in one currency for one item and then use another currency for a different item that originates from a different country. Should you also model changeable properties as service properties?

No, generally you should avoid changing service properties. For starters, changing the `Dictionary` object, which contains the service property, after the service has been registered has no effect. To improve the service lookup, OSGi framework implementations tend to create indexes using the property's values, which won't be updated if the original `Dictionary` object is changed. Instead, if you wish to change a service property, you have to use the method `ServiceRegistration.setProperty(Dictionary properties)`. This method is part of the `ServiceRegistration` class, whose objects are returned when you register a service. You also have to make sure that the service requester bundles are able to cope with service property changes, which isn't always the case. To handle service property changes, a service requester bundle should listen to service events of the type `ServiceEvent.MODIFIED`. In addition, some of the pre-defined service properties are indeed immutable, such as the `objectClass` property, which you saw earlier in this chapter.

> **WARNING** Avoid changing service properties. If you do need to change a service property, use the method `ServiceRegistration.setProperty-(Dictionary properties)` instead of changing the original `Dictionary` object.

All in all, it's best to avoid changing service properties. You'll learn a better mechanism for dealing with these types of service configuration changes in chapter 5.

3.4.4 Developing the auditor extension

Our second extension to the auction application is the creation of an auditor. In a sealed-first-price auction, the bids aren't disclosed. The `SealedFirstPriceAuditor` class checks to see if two consecutive bids have prices within 1.0 of each other, as shown in the following listing, which signals that a possible disclosure may have happened between the buyers in the auction.

Listing 3.7 Sealed-auction auditor

```
package manning.osgi.auction.auditor.sealed;

import manning.osgi.auction.Auction;
import manning.osgi.auction.Participant;
import manning.osgi.auction.spi.Auctioneer;
import manning.osgi.auction.spi.Auditor;

public class SealedFirstPriceAuditor implements Auditor {

    public void onAcceptance(Auctioneer auctioneer, Participant participant,
            String item, float ask,
            float acceptedBid, Float[] bids) {         Auction transaction
        verify(auctioneer, participant, bids);         accepted callback
    }

    public void onRejection(Auctioneer auctioneer, Participant participant,
        String item, float ask, Float[] rejectedBids) {     Auction transaction
        verify(auctioneer, participant, rejectedBids);       rejected callback
    }

    private void verify(Auctioneer auctioneer, Participant participant,
            Float[] bids) {
        if ("Sealed-First-Price".equals(
                                                            Checks type
                                                            of auction
                auctioneer.getAuctionProperties().get(Auction.TYPE))) {
            for (int i = 0; i < bids.length - 1; i++) {
                if ((bids[i + 1] - bids[i]) <= 1.0) {       Checks if consecutive
                    System.out.println("Warning to '" +     bids are close
                        participant.getName()               together
                        + "': bids (" + bids[i] + ", "
```

```
                                    + bids[i+1] + ") are too close together,
                              ➥ possible disclosure may have happened");
                    }
                }
            }
        }
}
```

Similar to the auction extension, the auditor extension also makes use of the white-board pattern, as the next listing shows.

Listing 3.8 Bundle activator for sealed-auction auditor

```
package manning.osgi.auction.auditor.sealed;

import org.osgi.framework.*;

import manning.osgi.auction.spi.Auditor;

public class SealedFirstPriceAuditorActivator implements BundleActivator {

    private ServiceRegistration serviceRegistration;

    public void start(BundleContext bundleContext) throws Exception {
        serviceRegistration =
            bundleContext.registerService(            ◁──┐ Register auditor service
                    Auditor.class.getName(),              │ when started
new SealedFirstPriceAuditor(), null);
    }

    public void stop(BundleContext bundleContext)
      throws Exception {                               ◁──┐ Unregister auditor
        serviceRegistration.unregister();                 │ service when stopped
    }
}
```

The class `SealedFirstPriceAuditorActivator` is even simpler than the `Sealed-FirstPriceAuctioneerActivator` class, because the former doesn't even need to use service properties.

We package the auditor and the activator classes into the bundle auction.auditor.sealed_1.0.0.jar, using the following MANIFEST.MF file:

```
Manifest-Version: 1.0
Bundle-ManifestVersion: 2
Bundle-SymbolicName: manning.osgi.auction.auditor.sealed
Bundle-Version: 1.0.0
Import-Package: manning.osgi.auction;version=1.0.0,
 manning.osgi.auction.spi;version=1.0.0,
 org.osgi.framework
Bundle-Activator: manning.osgi.auction.auditor.sealed.SealedFirstPriceAuditor
```

Note how we import both the `manning.osgi.auction.spi` package from the `auction.spi` bundle and the `manning.osgi.auction` package from the `auction.api` bundle. Considering that the `auction.spi` bundle already imports the package `manning.osgi.auction` from the `auction.api` bundle, could we have simplified our

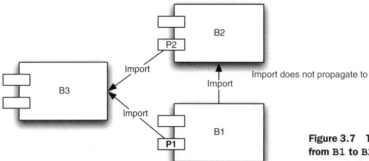

Figure 3.7   The import of package P1 from B1 to B2 doesn't automatically propagate to bundle B3.

MANIFEST.MF file by only importing the `manning.osgi.auction.spi` package from the `auction.spi` bundle? No, we must import both packages.

> **WARNING**   Importing and exporting packages in OSGi bundles are not transitive operations.

In figure 3.7, if bundle B3 is using package P1 from bundle B1 and package P2 from bundle B2, it doesn't matter if bundle B2 is also importing package P1 from bundle B1; bundle B3 must import both P1 and P2. There are also other ways of importing packages, which we'll study in chapter 4.

We're finished with both the auctioneer and the auditor extensions. Next, let's look at the implementation of the last remaining piece, the auction manager itself.

3.5   *Putting it all together*

In section 3.3, we implemented the seller application bundle. In section 3.4, we implemented two extension bundles: one for the sealed-first-price auctioneer and one for the sealed-first-price auditor. In this section, we'll implement the last component, the auction manager. The buyers, sellers, auctioneers, and auditors all interact among themselves to achieve a common goal, always through the auction manager, even though they're not aware of this.

Let's name the auction implementation bundle `auction.manager_1.0.0`. The main class is `AuctionManagerActivator`, as shown in the following listing.

Listing 3.9   Bundle activator for auction implementation

```
package manning.osgi.auction.manager;

import java.util.HashMap;
import java.util.Map;

import org.osgi.framework.*;

import manning.osgi.auction.Auction;
import manning.osgi.auction.spi.Auctioneer;
import manning.osgi.auction.spi.Auditor;

public class AuctionManagerActivator implements BundleActivator,
```

```
ServiceListener {

    private BundleContext bundleContext;
    private Map<ServiceReference, ServiceRegistration> registeredAuctions =
        new HashMap<ServiceReference, ServiceRegistration>();
    private Map<ServiceReference, Auditor> registeredAuditors =
        new HashMap<ServiceReference, Auditor>();

    public void start(BundleContext bundleContext) throws Exception {
        this.bundleContext = bundleContext;

        String auctionOrAuctioneerFilter =
            "(|" +
                "(objectClass=" + Auctioneer.class.getName() + ")" +
                "(objectClass=" + Auditor.class.getName() + ")" +
            ")";                                              ◄———  ❶ Filter includes auctioneer
                                                                      and auditors
        ServiceReference [] references =
            bundleContext.getServiceReferences(null,
            auctionOrAuctioneerFilter);
        if (references != null) {
            for (ServiceReference serviceReference : references) {
                registerService(serviceReference);   ◄———  ❷ Get all auctioneer and
            }                                                   auditor services
        }

        bundleContext.addServiceListener(this,
auctionOrAuctioneerFilter);                           ◄———  ❸ Register listener for register
    }                                                            and unregister events

    public void stop(BundleContext bundleContext) throws Exception {
        bundleContext.removeServiceListener(this);
    }

    public void serviceChanged(ServiceEvent serviceEvent) {
        ServiceReference serviceReference =
serviceEvent.getServiceReference();

        switch (serviceEvent.getType()) {
            case ServiceEvent.REGISTERED: {
                registerService(serviceReference);
                break;
            }
            case ServiceEvent.UNREGISTERING: {        ❹ Check service
                String [] serviceInterfaces =   ◄———     reference's property
                    (String[]) serviceReference.getProperty("objectClass");
                if (Auctioneer.class.getName().
                    equals(serviceInterfaces[0])) {
                    unregisterAuctioneer(serviceReference);
                } else {
                    unregisterAuditor(serviceReference);
                }
                bundleContext.ungetService(serviceReference);
                break;
            }
            default:
                // do nothing
```

```
        }
    }

    private void registerService(ServiceReference serviceReference) {
        Object serviceObject =
            bundleContext.getService(serviceReference);

        if (serviceObject instanceof Auctioneer) {
            registerAuctioneer(serviceReference, (Auctioneer)
                serviceObject);
        } else {
            registerAuditor(serviceReference, (Auditor) serviceObject);
        }
    }

    private void registerAuditor(ServiceReference auditorServiceReference,
    ➡ Auditor auditor) {
        registeredAuditors.put(auditorServiceReference,
            auditor);                                    ◁──┐  Store reference
    }                                                    ❺    to all auditors

    private void registerAuctioneer(ServiceReference
            auctioneerServiceReference, Auctioneer auctioneer) {
        Auction auction =                          ◁──┐    Wrap original
            new AuctionWrapper(auctioneer,         ❻    auction object
                registeredAuditors.values());
                                                   ❼  Register auction
        ServiceRegistration auctionServiceRegistration =  ◁──┘   using wrapper
            bundleContext.registerService(Auction.class.getName(),
                auction, auctioneer.getAuctionProperties());

        registeredAuctions.put(auctioneerServiceReference,  ◁──┐  Store auction
            auctionServiceRegistration);                    ❽  registration
    }

    private void unregisterAuditor(ServiceReference serviceReference) {
        registeredAuditors.remove(serviceReference);
    }

    private void unregisterAuctioneer(ServiceReference
    ➡ auctioneerServiceReference) {
        ServiceRegistration auctionServiceRegistration =
            registeredAuctions.remove(auctioneerServiceReference);

        if (auctionServiceRegistration != null) {
            auctionServiceRegistration.unregister();   ◁──┐  Unregister auction
        }                                                     when auctioneer
    }                                                    ❾  is stopped
}
```

The `AuctionManagerActivator` class has two main roles:

- It acts as a mediator between auctioneers and auditors, using the registry design pattern. Every time an auction's transaction from any registered auctioneer is accepted or rejected, the auction manager notifies all registered auditors.
- It registers auctions as service objects in the OSGi service registry for all registered auctioneers.

First, we create a filter that includes both auditors and auctioneer service objects ❶. As you learned in section 3.3.3, we use the filter to retrieve existing services ❷ and to register a listener to manage `registered` and `unregistering` events ❸. When handling the `unregistering` events, we avoid getting the service object; instead, we use the service reference directly by getting its `objectClass` service property ❹ to determine if the reference is related to the auctioneer or the auditor service.

> **TIP** The `objectClass` service property is defined as an array of `Strings`, instead of a plain `String`, because the service interface is composed of several Java classes. It's a common mistake to assume that the `objectClass` service property is a single `String`.

When we receive an auditor service object, we add it to a `registeredAuditors` map ❺. This map, which uses the auction service reference as the key, keeps track of all existing auditors that need to be notified of all auction transaction acceptances and rejections.

Service references and service registration

All service references related to the same service registration are equal. But this doesn't hold across different service registrations, even if the service registrations are related to the same service object.

For example, consider the following scenario: Bundle `B1` registers service `S`. Bundle `B2` gets service reference `R1` for `S`. Bundle `B3` gets service reference `R2` for `S`. `R1` and `R2` are equal, that is, `R1.equals(R2)` returns `true`. Next, `B1` unregisters `S` and re-registers the same service `S`. Bundle `B4` gets service reference `R3` for `S`. `R3` is not equal to `R1` and `R2` (and `R1` and `R2` are no longer valid, although that's immaterial to the discussion).

When we receive an auctioneer service object, we wrap this service object with the `AuctionWrapper` class, passing along a reference to the registered auditors ❻ retrieved in ❺. Next, we register the auction service object retrieved from the auctioneer service object in the OSGi service registry ❼. Doing this allows the buyer and seller bundles to proceed and retrieve the auction services themselves. Finally, similarly to the auditor services, we add the auctioneer service reference and the auction service registration to a map ❽. This map is used later when an auctioneer service is unregistered. In this case, we need to likewise unregister its auction service from the OSGi registry ❾.

You may ask, why don't we just register the auction service object directly instead of relying on the `Auctioneer` class? The reason we need to go through this indirection is to be able to wrap #6 the auction object so that we can notify all the auditors of the auction's activities. If the auction service objects were registered directly by the extension bundles, then we wouldn't be able to intercept its methods. Can you think of a problem with this approach? Today, there's nothing preventing a bundle from directly registering an auction service object in the OSGi service registry, and by doing so bypassing the auction manager.

The `AuctionWrapper` class does the wrapping of the auction class, as shown in the following listing.

Listing 3.10   The `AuctionWrapper` class

```
package manning.osgi.auction.core;

import java.util.*;

import manning.osgi.auction.*;
import manning.osgi.auction.spi.*;

public class AuctionWrapper implements Auction {

    private Collection<Auditor> auditors;
    private Auctioneer delegate;
    private Map<String,List<Float>> bidsPerItem =
        new HashMap<String,List<Float>>();
    private Float ask;

    class ParticipantWrapper implements Participant {

      private Participant delegate;

      public ParticipantWrapper(Participant delegate) {
          this.delegate = delegate;
      }

      public String getName() {
          return delegate.getName();
      }

      public void onAcceptance(Auction auction, String item, float price) {
          delegate.onAcceptance(auction, item, price);

          Float [] bids = bidsPerItem.get(item).toArray(new Float [0]);
          for (Auditor auditor : auditors) {
             auditor.onAcceptance(AuctionWrapper.this.delegate,
               delegate,
                  item, ask, price, bids);
          }
      }

        public void onRejection(Auction auction, String item,
              float bestBid) {
           delegate.onRejection(auction, item, bestBid);

           Float [] bids = bidsPerItem.get(item).toArray(new Float [0]);
           for (Auditor auditor : auditors) {
               auditor.onRejection(AuctionWrapper.this.delegate,
                  delegate, item, ask, bids);
           }
```

Delegate onAcceptance to participant ❶

```
        }
    }

    public AuctionWrapper(Auctioneer delegate, Collection<Auditor>
 ➡ auditors) {
        this.delegate = delegate;
        this.auditors = auditors;
    }

    public Float ask(String item, float price, Participant seller)
            throws InvalidOfferException {
        ask = price;
        return delegate.getAuction().ask(item, price,
                new ParticipantWrapper(seller));
    }

    public Float bid(String item, float price, Participant buyer)
            throws InvalidOfferException {
        List<Float> bids = bidsPerItem.get(item);
        if (bids == null) {
            bids = new LinkedList<Float>();
            bidsPerItem.put(item, bids);
        }
        bids.add(price);

        return delegate.getAuction().bid(item, price,
                new ParticipantWrapper(buyer));
    }
}
```

The `AuctionWrapper` class implements the standard wrapper design pattern (http://en.wikipedia.org/wiki/Adapter_pattern), delegating all method invocations to the original auction and participant object instance ❶. In addition, while delegating, it keeps enough information to provide to the registered auditors when the auction's transactions are closed.

This all that's needed to implement the `auction.manager_1.0.0` bundle, which uses the following MANIFEST.MF file:

```
Manifest-Version: 1.0
Bundle-ManifestVersion: 2
Bundle-SymbolicName: manning.osgi.auction.manager
Bundle-Version: 1.0.0
Import-Package: manning.osgi.auction;version=1.0.0,
 manning.osgi.auction.spi;version=1.0.0,
 org.osgi.framework
Bundle-Activator: manning.osgi.auction.manager.AuctionManagerActivator
```

3.5.1 *Semantic versioning*

Remember from section 2.3.2 that OSGi defines a version as a value consisting of four parts: major, minor, micro, and qualifier. Let's explore the meaning of each of these parts and look at the semantic interpretation of OSGi versioning.

- Major number—A change to this number indicates that the versioned package is not backward compatible with clients that *use* classes of the previous version of this package.

- Minor number—A change to the minor number indicates that the versioned package is not backward compatible with clients that *implement* classes (interfaces) of the previous version of this package. Later in this section, you'll learn the difference between using a class and implementing a class.
- Micro and qualifier numbers—These numbers have no specific semantic meaning. They can be used by developers to identify particular bug fixes or builds of the package.

For example, the `Seller` class is a user of the `Auction` class, which is in the `auction.api` bundle. If this bundle changes from version 1.0 to 2.0, it means that it is no longer backward compatible for users of the 1.0 version. In practice, this means that a method or field in the `Auction` class was changed or removed, and that the `Seller` needs to be changed and recompiled to be able to use this new version. However, if only a new method was added to the `Auction` class, we could keep the major number the same and increase the minor version from 1.0 to 1.1, indicating that the `Auction` class is still backward compatible with the `Seller` class version 1.0.

Similarly, the `SealedFirstPriceAuditor` class is an implementer (or implementation provider) of the `Auditor` interface located in the `auction.spi` bundle. This means that if the `auction.spi` bundle changes from 1.0 to 1.1, it is no longer backward compatible with version 1.0 of the `SealedFirstPriceAuditor` class. This makes sense, because any changes to the `Auditor` interface, even the addition of a new method, would break a class that implements it.

What should you take away from this? The rule of thumb is that if you're importing a class for use, you should protect yourself by specifying a range up to but excluding the next major number, as in the following example:

```
version="[1,2)"
```

But if you are importing an interface to implement it, you should specify a range up to but excluding the next minor number, as follows:

```
version="[1,1.1)"
```

Finally, if you are exporting a package, make sure you follow the semantic rules presented in this section.

We're almost finished with the implementation of the pieces of the auction application. Let's look at the remaining piece, the buyer module, and finally test our solution.

3.6   *The OSGi HTTP service*

Our next task is to test our auction system. Let's consider the details. So far we've created six bundles:

- `auction.api_1.0.0` and `auction.spi_1.0.0` define the interfaces for the auction application.
- `auction.manager_1.0.0` provides the auction manager implementation.

- `auction.auctioneer.sealed_1.0.0` and `auction.auditor.sealed_1.0.0` provide extensions for a sealed-first-price type of auction.
- `auction.seller.simple_1.0.0` provides a simple seller client.

We're missing a buyer module. Because our implementation is modular and decoupled, we have the flexibility to implement our buyer module in different forms. To be able to better test our solution, we'll implement a web-based buyer module. The web-based buyer module allows a buyer end user to send bids through a web browser.

3.6.1 Developing an HTTP buyer

A web browser is a great testing tool for sending remote commands. HTTP is simple and text based, and you can pretty much encode anything on a URL. Furthermore, Enterprise OSGi already defines an OSGi HTTP service that facilitates the usage of the Java servlet technology (http://java.sun.com/products/servlet/index.html).

First, let's look at the implementation of a simple servlet that uses the URL parameters to place bids on an item, as shown in the following listing.

Listing 3.11 Bidder servlet

```
package manning.osgi.auction.buyer.http;

import java.io.IOException;
import java.io.PrintWriter;

import javax.servlet.*;

import manning.osgi.auction.*;

public class BidderServlet implements Servlet,
    Participant {                                    ⟵─┐ Implement Servlet
                                                        │ interface
    private Auction auction;
    private String name;
    private PrintWriter writer;

    public BidderServlet(String name) {
        this.name = name;
    }

    public String getName() {
        return this.name;
    }

    public void setAuction(Auction auction) {
        this.auction = auction;
    }

    public void destroy() {
    }

    public ServletConfig getServletConfig() {
        return null;
    }
```

```
public String getServletInfo() {
    return null;
}

public void init(ServletConfig config) throws ServletException {
}

public void service(ServletRequest req,
  ServletResponse resp) throws ServletException,
    IOException {                                        ◁──┐   HTTP request
                                                        ❶   callback
        String bidValue =
            req.getParameter("bid");                ◁──┐   Retrieve parameter
                                                    ❷   from URL
        String item =
            req.getParameter("item");

        try {
            if (bidValue == null || item == null) {
                throw new IllegalArgumentException("Invalid bid");
            } else {
                writer = resp.getWriter();
                Float price = new Float(bidValue);
                auction.bid(item, price, this);       ◁──┐   Bid using
                                                      ❸   parameter values
                writer.println("Accepted bid of "
                        + bidValue + " for item " + item);
            }
        } catch (Exception e) {
            throw new ServletException(e);
        }
    }

public void onAcceptance(Auction auction, String item, float price) {
    writer.println(this.name + " was awarded "
        + item + " for " + price);                ◁──┐   Write HTTP
}                                                 │   response

public void onRejection(Auction auction, String item, float bestBid) {
    writer.println("Bid for " + item + " from " + name
        + " was rejected");
    }
}
```

Most of the implementation follows the same pattern as the Seller class in listing 3.2. The main difference is in how we receive the customer input. In this case, we receive the customer input by means of HTTP requests (for example, HTTP GET), so we must implement the Servlet API, which abstracts the handling of HTTP requests and responses. Every time an HTTP client, such as a web browser, connects to our URL, our Servlet is called back on its service() method ❶. Our work is mostly cut out for us; we just need to retrieve the customer information, consisting of the bid price and the item, from the HTTP request parameters ❷ and use those values to do the actual bidding ❸. Finally, if the bid is valid, we write the result to the HTTP response and send it back to the web client.

Next, we need to register our `Servlet` in the OSGi HTTP service, which is shown in the following listing.

Listing 3.12 Bundle activator for HTTP `Servlet`

```
package manning.osgi.auction.buyer.http;

import javax.servlet.ServletException;

import org.osgi.framework.*;
import org.osgi.service.http.*;

import manning.osgi.auction.Auction;

public class BuyerServletActivator implements BundleActivator,
  ServiceListener {

    private BundleContext bundleContext;
    private BidderServlet bidderServlet =
      new BidderServlet("Http Bidder");                    ◁─┐ Create
    private HttpService httpService;                          │ Servlet

    public void start(BundleContext bundleContext) throws Exception {

        this.bundleContext = bundleContext;

        String filter =
            "(&(objectClass=" + Auction.class.getName()
            + ")(" + Auction.TYPE + "=Sealed-First-Price))";

        ServiceReference[] serviceReferences =
            bundleContext.getServiceReferences(null,
              filter);                                       ◁─┐ Get auction to be
                                                               │ set in servlet
        if (serviceReferences != null) {
            start(serviceReferences[0]);
        } else {
            bundleContext.addServiceListener(this, filter);
        }
    }

    public void stop(BundleContext bundleContext) throws Exception {
        bundleContext.removeServiceListener(this);
        if (httpService != null) {
            httpService.unregister("/bidder");
        }
    }

    public void serviceChanged(ServiceEvent serviceEvent) {
        try {
            switch (serviceEvent.getType()) {
                case ServiceEvent.REGISTERED: {
                    start(serviceEvent.getServiceReference());
                    break;
                }
```

```
                case ServiceEvent.UNREGISTERING: {
                    stop(bundleContext);
                    break;
                }
                default:
                    // do nothing
            }
        } catch (Exception e) {
            e.printStackTrace();
        }
    }

    private void start(ServiceReference serviceReference)
    throws ServletException, NamespaceException {
        Auction auction = (Auction)
            bundleContext.getService(serviceReference);

        if (auction != null) {
            bidderServlet.setAuction(auction);

            ServiceReference ref =
                bundleContext.getServiceReference(                ❶ Get HTTP service
                    HttpService.class.getName());              ◄──┘

            httpService =
                (HttpService) bundleContext.getService(ref);
              httpService.registerServlet("/bidder", bidderServlet,
              null, null);                                   ◄──┐  Register Servlet
        }                                                       ❷ in HTTP service
    }
}
```

The `BuyerServletActivator` class is also similar to the `SellerActivator` class. The main difference is that it retrieves the `HttpService` ❶ and then uses it to register the bidder servlet using the context `"/bidder"` ❷.

Finally, here's the MANIFEST.MF file for the bundle auction.buyer.http_1.0.0.jar:

```
Manifest-Version: 1.0
Bundle-ManifestVersion: 2
Bundle-SymbolicName: manning.osgi.auction.buyer.http
Bundle-Version: 1.0.0
Import-Package: manning.osgi.auction;version=1.0.0,
 org.osgi.framework, javax.servlet,
 org.osgi.service.http
Bundle-Activator: manning.osgi.auction.buyer.http.BuyerServletActivator
```

We're finally ready to test the auction application.

3.6.2 *Testing the auction application*

Obviously, we'll need to install all of the seven bundles we developed in Felix, which are shown in figure 3.8. But before we do so, we also need to install the OSGi HTTP Service and its implementation.

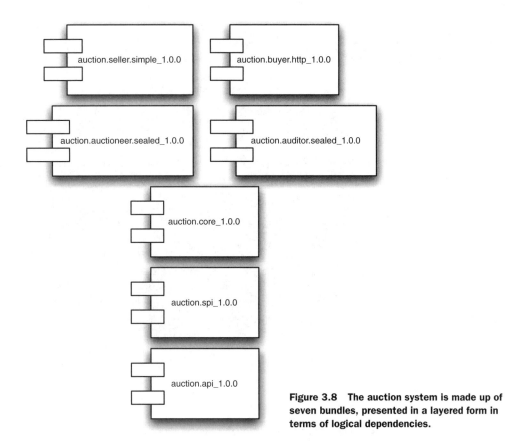

Figure 3.8 The auction system is made up of seven bundles, presented in a layered form in terms of logical dependencies.

As of this writing, Felix organizes its OSGi HTTP Service implementation, which is based on Jetty, into four separate bundles, as follows:

- org.apache.felix.http.api-2.0.4.jar
- org.apache.felix.http.base-2.0.4.jar
- org.apache.felix.http.bundle-2.0.4.jar
- org.apache.felix.http.jetty-2.0.4.jar

These can all be found in Felix's HTTP Service project, http://felix.apache.org/site/apache-felix-http-service.html, and should be downloaded, installed, and started in your OSGi framework instance.

Next, we're back to our auction-application bundles. You can install them in any particular order. Finally, we'll start the bundles, but now we need to consider the dependencies. First, start the interfaces `auction.api` and `auction.spi`. You might think that you'd need to install the auction manager implementation first (`auction.manager`), then the extensions (`auction.auctioneer.sealed` and `auction.auditor.sealed`), and then the client bundles (`auction.buyer.http` and `auction.seller.simple`). This is actually not the case. Because we've taken care of avoiding the temporal cohesion

Figure 3.9   Use a web browser to make bids on the auction application.

problem as described in section 3.3.3, you can start the services in any order and the implementation will do the proper thing. But you do need to have everything started before you get to the next step, which is to send bids through the web browser.

Open your favorite web browser, such as Firefox, and then type the following URL: `http://localhost:8080/bidder?bid=100&item=bicycle`. You should see an output on the shell running Felix, informing you that a buyer has sent a bid of 100 to the auction, and the outcome of `accepted` in the web browser, as shown in figure 3.9.

Jetty

By default, Jetty listens to port 8080, so make sure this port is available before activating the Jetty bundle. You can change this configuration by editing the file conf/config.properties that exists in the Felix install home and setting the property `org.osgi.service.http.port`.

For example, the following line changes the Jetty port to 9090:

`org.osgi.service.http.port=9090`

You can keep sending additional bids, but you may need to restart the seller bundle to sell additional items. You can try starting and stopping the different bundles, such as the auditor and auctioneer bundles, to see how the system behaves. For example, if the auditor bundle is stopped, you won't get the warning message even if the bids are within 1.0 of each other.

Participants are not services

What happens if you stop the buyer or seller bundle without stopping the auctioneer bundle? The auctioneer will have a reference to a participant object that's no longer available. You saw this problem in chapter 2. Ideally, the participant class should also be an OSGi service, which would allow the auction class to know when bundles are no longer available.

The OSGi HTTP Service is a handy abstraction on top of HTTP and servlets, and it can be used for many things, testing being just one example. Next, we'll look at what other services OSGi has that can be used to further improve our auction application.

3.7 Improving the auction application to enterprise grade

We've successfully implemented our first application using the OSGi technology. Have we met all of our requirements as stated in section 3.2? Yes; the application is both modular and extensible. Nonetheless, we still have a lot of room for improvements.

First, the auction application doesn't manage its configuration adequately. Currently, it deals only with immutable service properties, such as the auction type and the auction duration. But we're not able to handle simple configuration changes, such as changing the buyer's server port. Chapter 5 tackles the issue of application configuration.

Second, what would happen if the system were to be shut down? We would lose all the data, such as open offers. We'll look at the issue of persisting application data in chapter 7.

Next, how do you make sure all application bundles are installed correctly, and then how do you manage their operations at runtime? These issues are explored in chapters 11 and 12.

Finally, after having coded several bundle activators, it's clear that we could avoid a lot of boilerplate code, particularly when coding for the service registration and service retrieval from the OSGi service registry. In addition, we'd like an approach that doesn't tie the application code to the OSGi framework API. In chapter 13, we'll investigate a declarative approach for using OSGi that helps remove most of the boilerplate code.

3.8 Summary

In this chapter we implemented an auction application that supports the collaboration of buyers, sellers, auctioneers, and auditors to trade goods. Through the use of

OSGi, we implemented a solution that's both modular and extensible. The solution is composed of several cohesive but decoupled modules: buyer, seller, auction (policies), auditor (policies), and auction manager.

OSGi service properties are key-value pairs that can be associated with a service object. Service requesters can then specify the service properties as filtering criteria when retrieving the services from the OSGi service registry. Although a developer can change a service property by invoking the method `BundleContext.setProperties()`, a better design pattern is to have the providing bundle treat the service properties as immutable.

In the registry design pattern, the application bundle retrieves application services from the OSGi service registry. The application bundle must be careful to handle changes to the application service, such as the service being unregistered. In addition, the bundle must not assume that the application service has already been registered, a situation that could create a temporal cohesion with the service provider bundle.

Conversely, in the whiteboard design pattern, the application bundle registers a service in the OSGi service registry. Invoker bundles retrieve the services from all application bundles and call back the applications when needed. The whiteboard design pattern is easier to implement than the registry design channel and is therefore preferable when it's an option.

The auction application meets our established goals, but there's room for improvement in configuration, management, and monitoring. In addition, the auction application is tightly coupled with the OSGi framework APIs, which we should try to minimize. In the next chapter, we'll take an in-depth look at OSGi bundles and services, such as the details of OSGi class loading, to help us build better enterprise-grade software.

In-depth look at
bundles and services

This chapter covers

- Keeping bundle packages private to decrease exposure
- Making bundle packages optional to improve flexibility
- The wiring API
- Understanding class loading in a bundle
- Advanced use of service filtering
- Service prioritization
- Service factories
- Unit testing and integration testing for robustness

In chapter 3, we developed our first OSGi-based application employing two important OSGi features: bundles and services. As you've seen, bundles allow you to modularize your code, which lends to better reuse of code. Likewise, services improve the decoupling between the bundles, which yields a more resilient and flexible system architecture.

In this chapter we'll take an in-depth look into several patterns and techniques that will help us develop better decoupled, flexible, and extensible bundles and services for our OSGi applications. We'll start our discussion by looking into how to minimize the dependencies between the bundles we create and use.

4.1 *Restricting a bundle's export contract*

In object-oriented programming, you learn that you should keep the signature of a class as restrictive as possible. This is done, for example, by first annotating a method of a class as private, and if that's not possible, making it protected, and only if absolutely necessary making it public.

The same guideline applies to bundles. To begin with, make your bundle as restrictive as possible by not exporting any of its packages. If that's not possible, the second step is to check to see if you can embed the dependency within the bundle itself; these are known as private packages.

4.1.1 *Keeping packages private*

If only a single bundle—the keyword being *single*—needs to import a class, you can embed the class, or library, in the consumer bundle itself and keep it private, rather than creating a new bundle that exports this class. This way the bundle is still able to use the class, but the class doesn't need to be exported and thus made visible to any other bundle. Such a class is part of the bundle's class path and is named the bundle's private package.

For example, consider a bundle B1 that wants to use classes within the JAR file mylegacy.jar. First, archive the legacy JAR file within the bundle JAR file. The general convention is to place the legacy JAR under a lib directory. Thus, the contents of the bundle JAR file are

```
META-INF/MANIFEST.MF
lib/mylegacy.jar
manning/osgi/MyClass.class
```

Second, you need to use the manifest header `Bundle-Classpath` to specify the internal class path of the bundle. By default, it points to the dot (.), but in our case we need to add the lib directory to it:

```
Bundle-ClassPath: .,lib
```

In this example, the bundle's class path comprises all resources (for example, classes, JAR files) at the root of the bundle's JAR and within its lib directory.

> **TIP**   You can load a bundle resource from its class path by using the method `Bundle.getResource(String resourceName)`.

Next, we'll consider the case where other bundles need to access the package.

4.1.2 *Excluding classes from an exported package*

If more than one bundle needs to use a class, then the proper solution is indeed to create a bundle and export it. But you don't need to export the full package where the class resides; instead, you can pick and choose which classes are to be exported from a package. This is done using the include and exclude parameters of the Export-Package manifest header.

By default, the include parameter is set to *, meaning that all classes of the package are included, and the exclude parameter is set to an empty string, meaning that no class is excluded. Irrespective of which one is defined first, a class is exported only if it's part of the include list and not part of the exclude list.

For example, if the package being exported has several classes, and you'd like to export only a single class, say class APublicClass, then the best approach is to use the include parameter:

```
Export-Package: manning.osgi.test; include:=APublicClass
```

Conversely, if you'd like to export all classes except for one, then it's easier to use the exclude parameter:

```
Export-Package: manning.osgi.test; exclude:=APrivateClass
```

You can list several packages in the include and exclude parameters by using the comma character (,). For example, consider the following entry:

```
Export-Package: manning.osgi.test; include:="Foo*, Bar"; exclude:=FooImpl
```

As illustrated in figure 4.1, the exclude parameter takes precedence, hence the class FooImpl is excluded in spite of being included by the include parameter. The class BarImpl is also not included because it isn't part of the include parameter.

Figure 4.1   Inclusion and exclusion of classes in an exported package

Export-Package syntax

Anytime a parameter, such as include, exclude, version, or uses for an OSGi entry (Export-Package), uses a comma (,) to enumerate its component values, you'll need to specify this parameter in double quotes. This is necessary because the clauses of an OSGi entry already use commas to separate their values.

Consider the following OSGi entry:

```
Export-Package: manning.osgi.foo; include="Foo1, Foo2",
manning.osgi.bar; version="[1,2]"
```

In this example, note how a comma (,) is used to separate both the items Foo1 and Foo2 and the manning.osgi.bar item, hence the former need to be in quotes.

Note that the package specification (manning.osgi.foo) is separated from the include, exclude, version, and uses parameters with a semi-colon (;).

4.1.3   *Avoiding split packages*

As you've learned, the `Import-Package` and `Export-Package` manifest headers work (intuitively) at the granularity of Java packages. The `Require-Bundle` manifest header is another mechanism for establishing code dependency, but in this case it's at the granularity of a bundle. A bundle that specifies `Require-Bundle` is able to see all the exported packages of the required bundle. In addition, the requiring bundle can even be configured to transitively inherit all of the imported packages of the required bundle.

For example, consider a bundle B2 that exports packages p and q and imports package r from bundle B3. Now, consider a bundle B1 with the following manifest:

```
Bundle-SymbolicName: B1
Require-Bundle: B2; visibility:=reexport
```

Notably, bundle B1 has no `Import-Package` header, only a `Require-Bundle` package with the `visibility` parameter set to reexport. As a result, bundle B1 is able to see packages p, q, and r, as shown in figure 4.2. If the `visibility` parameter is removed or set to `private`, then B1 sees only packages p and q.

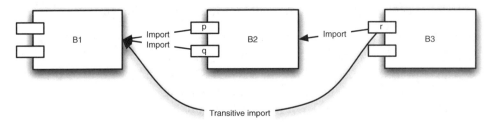

Figure 4.2   Bundle B1 specifies bundle B2 as a required bundle. B1 imports B2's exported packages and B2's imported packages from bundle B3.

What did we gain by using the `Require-Bundle` header? We avoided having to explicitly list three separate packages to be imported. This is a good thing, right?

Well, not really. There's a host of problems created because of `Require-Bundle`. The most serious issue is that when you use `Require-Bundle`, a package may be split between the requiring and the required bundles, as shown in figure 4.3.

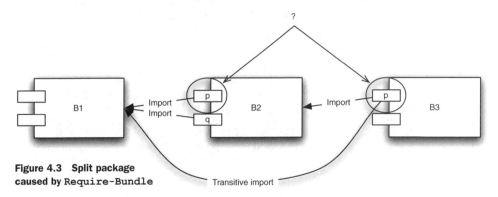

Figure 4.3   Split package caused by `Require-Bundle`

This means that the same class could exist in both locations, which is very confusing, makes the ordering of Require-Bundle significant, and hinders the runtime performance of the OSGi framework.

> **NOTE** Split packages can only happen when the Require-Bundle header is used. None of the other mechanisms, such as fragment bundles, which you'll see later, can cause split packages.

Another problem is that the requiring bundle is coupled with the symbolic name of the required bundle, which leads to a poor contract. The required bundle can be refactored and its packages changed, but this incompatibility doesn't show in the contract. There are several other problems as well, such as class shadowing and unexpected signature changes.

What's the solution? The solution is simple: don't use the Require-Bundle header. You can restrict yourself to using only the Import-Package and Export-Package headers and still accomplish the same goals but without any of these mishaps. I've implemented a fair share of bundles and systems, and to this date I haven't had to use Require-Bundle, so avoid it!

Now that you understand how to keep a bundle's signature to a minimum, the next issue that the developer frequently runs into is dealing with Java reflection as a mechanism of creating generic code. We'll tackle this issue in the next section.

4.2 Expanding a bundle's export contract

We seldom work in isolation when developing new applications; it's common that we need to integrate and communicate with legacy systems. One way of achieving this is by keeping the solution open and generic. In Java, this sometimes translates to the use of reflection.

Let's consider the example of a federated database system. A federated database allows an application to write a single query that, in a transparent manner, may scope several distributed sources, some of which may be other databases.

One way of implementing this is to break the query into separate clauses that are individually forwarded to the different sources. For example, consider the following SQL query:

```
SELECT *
FROM Sale sale, Customer customer
WHERE sale.customer = customer.name
    AND sale.price > 100 AND customer.location = "CA"
```

This query finds all sale transactions that are higher than $100 and where the customer resides in California (CA). Now, consider that the Sale table is located in a Derby database running on one machine, and the Customer table is located in a MySQL database running on another machine. The goal is to have a client issue a single query to a central database, which is responsible for breaking it up, dispatching to the proper remote servers, and putting their responses back together into a single return to the client, as shown in figure 4.4.

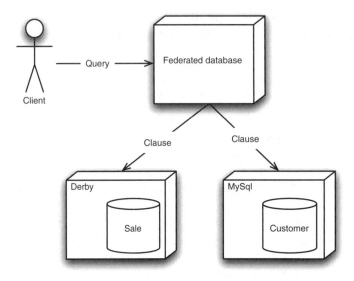

Figure 4.4   The client issues a query to a federated database, which breaks it into separate clauses to be executed remotely in a Derby database and a MySQL database.

A federated database could take the following approach to servicing the query in the example. First, it retrieves all sale records from the remote Derby instance whose price is higher than $100. Second, it retrieves all customers residing in CA from the remote MySQL instance, and finally it locally joins together these records brought from the distributed sources.

If the source is another database, as it is in this example, then the federated database can communicate with the source database using JDBC.

> **NOTE**   JDBC is a standard Java API for communicating with databases. If you haven't used JDBC yet, don't despair; we'll cover JDBC in detail in chapter 7.

To load a JDBC driver manager, the common approach is to use reflection. For example, here's the command to load the Apache Derby JDBC driver:

```
Class.forName("org.apache.derby.jdbc.EmbeddedDriver");
```

Let's say you'd like to implement a federated database so that you can dynamically load new database sources into the federated database without having to shut it down. In other words, these are the requirements:

- You must be able to dynamically install database drivers.
- You must be able to dynamically start (for example, load) the drivers using some generic mechanism, such as reflection.

The first issue is easily addressed by using OSGi to dynamically install bundles. But can OSGi handle the second issue? The problem is that OSGi's import and export package specification is static. At compilation time, the federated database OSGi bundle doesn't know in advance which JDBC drivers need to be loaded; hence the bundle can't be authored with the proper `Import-Package` manifest header that's needed so that `Class.forName` would work. For example, to load the Derby driver, you need the following import to be present in the federated database bundle's MANIFEST file:

```
Import-Package: org.apache.derby.jdbc
```

Does OSGi have a solution to this problem? Yes, through the use of dynamic imports.

4.2.1 Dynamic imports

The OSGi framework defines the manifest header `DynamicImport-Package`, which can be used to specify Java packages that can be dynamically searched at runtime to load Java classes. In our case, we should specify the following manifest header:

```
DynamicImport-Package: org.apache.derby.jdbc
```

The OSGi framework uses `DynamicImport-Package` as a last resort. OSGi first attempts to resolve a class through the normal means of wiring `Import-Packages` to `Export-Packages`. Only if the class isn't found when needed will the OSGi framework search the packages specified in the `DynamicImport-Package` header. If the class is then found, its location is fixed and can't be changed.

> **NOTE** You can use * when specifying dynamic imports, which makes the command very powerful. For example, `DynamicImport-Package: org.apache.*` imports all classes under the package `org.apache`.

`DynamicImport-Package` is convenient and flexible, so why shouldn't you always use it? First, if you only use `DynamicImport-Package`, then you'd be by all practical means not really taking advantage of OSGi to achieve modularization. You'd lose the power of the contract established by `Import-Package` and `Export-Package`. Second, because `DynamicImport-Package` is searched when a class is needed, rather than when the bundle is resolved, there's a higher performance cost and less-predictable behavior at runtime.

4.2.2 Optional packages

Consider a variation of the previous scenario; instead of arbitrarily loading any database source, let's say that the federated database system supports only a set of well-known database sources, which may or may not be present at runtime. This is a more likely scenario, because to make sure that the federated database really works, it has to be tested with the drivers, so it's unlikely that it would support an unknown and thus untested driver. But this list of supported drivers could be extensive, numbering in the dozens, so it's also likely that in a particular instance of the environment, only a subset of these would be present.

The OSGi framework has a different and somewhat better solution for this case. In OSGi, you can specify a package that's being imported as optional. This means that the framework will attempt to wire this class during the resolve process, as the bundle is being installed, but it won't consider it an error if the package isn't found. If some bundle is exporting the package, then it will be imported normally; if no exported package is found, then the import of the package is ignored.

This can be done in the following manner in our case:

```
Import-Package: org.apache.derby.jdbc;resolution:=optional
```

What happens in the case where the package isn't imported, and the bundle still tries to use it? As expected, the bundle will get a `NoClassDefFoundError` or a `ClassNotFoundException`. This means that anytime you define a package as optional, you have to be prepared to handle these situations. In the case of our federated database system, we could simply ignore those drivers that aren't found at runtime by doing the following:

```
try {
    Class.forName("org.apache.derby.jdbc.EmbeddedDriver");
} catch (ClassNotFoundException e) {
    // log
}
```

Let's take a step back and consider the overall solution we have so far, as shown in figure 4.5. We, the framework developers, are providing a federated database bundle, which through either optional packages or dynamic imports can generically load different drivers. The database vendors, such as Derby or MySQL, provide their own drivers, which are wrapped as OSGi bundles and export their respective driver manager classes. The remaining role is that of the federated database client, who has to develop an OSGi application that uses the federated database bundle, for example, by issuing the SQL query that's to be distributed.

If the database vendor has to provide a new bundle containing the driver, couldn't the vendor also somehow extend the behavior of the federated database bundle in

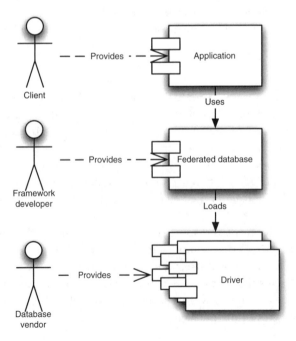

Figure 4.5   The client provides an application bundle, the framework developer provides a federated database bundle, and the database vendors provide the driver bundles.

such a way that it's able to see the driver? Yes, OSGi allows this to be done using fragment bundles.

4.2.3 *Fragment bundles*

Fragment bundles are degenerated bundles that need to attach to a host bundle in order to function. A fragment bundle doesn't work by itself; it logically merges with its host bundle as if both bundles were a single bundle and, most important, with a single class loader.

For example, we could have each driver vendor provide a fragment bundle that attaches to the federated database bundle and in doing so augments the federated database bundle's internal class path, as shown in figure 4.6. Therefore, the federated database bundle would have visibility to the driver's class and would be able to do a `Class.forName()` without having to import its package.

> **WARNING** At runtime, the OSGi framework first searches the class path of the host bundle and only then searches that of its fragment bundles, in ascending order of bundle IDs.

To do this, each vendor fragment bundle must add the following manifest header that references the federated database bundle:

`Fragment-Host: manning.osgi.federated-database`

In this case, we assume that the symbolic name of the federated database bundle is `manning.osgi.federated-database`. Also, we assume that the driver manager class is part of the content of the driver's bundle.

> **WARNING** A fragment bundle can't specify a bundle activator class.

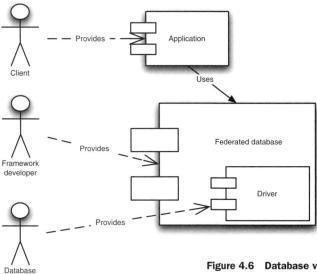

Figure 4.6 Database vendors provide driver bundle fragments, which attach to the federated database bundle.

At face value, fragment bundles would seem like the best approach we've investigated so far for solving our problem of implementing a generic bundle, but they also have their problems and limitations. Fragment bundles must be installed before their host bundle; in other words, a host bundle after it's resolved ignores any other fragment bundles. In our example, this means that we wouldn't be able to dynamically load new drivers after the system is started. The other drawback is that fragment bundles create a tight coupling with their host bundles. Again, citing our example, the driver fragment bundle and the federated database bundle share an implicit contract that a driver manager class is contained within the fragment.

Nonetheless, fragment bundles are well suited for cases when the fragment complements a well-established aspect of the host bundles, and their assembly can be done ahead of time. Localization is the perfect case. For example, you could place the localization files for English in one fragment, for French in another fragment, and so on. Then you could install the internationalized host bundle and the localized fragment bundles all together, and the host bundle would be able to see all the localization files and select the proper one to use. In this scenario, it's unlikely that you'd need to support a new localization without being able to redeploy the host bundle or restart the platform.

Augmenting a bundle's manifest

A fragment bundle can not only augment the internal class path of its host bundle but also extend its manifest header entries. For example, the fragment bundle can specify an `Import-Package` header, which is associated with the host bundle, thus increasing the number of packages being imported.

The use of reflection to dynamically load features is a common pattern for the development of enterprise applications. We've investigated three approaches for accomplishing this in OSGi. These are summarized in table 4.1.

Table 4.1 Different approaches to supporting generic bundles in OSGi

Approach	When	Advantage	Disadvantage
Dynamic imports	After resolve, at runtime	Most dynamic	Decreases modularity, predictability
Optional packages	During package resolve	Similar to standard `Import-Package`	Optional packages must be known at design time
Fragment bundles	During package resolve of host bundle	Allows host bundle's class path to be augmented with new resources	Coupling of fragment and host bundles

Reflection is a great tool, but it comes with a price: applications that use reflection have a greater chance of causing class-loading-related exceptions, like the `ClassNot-FoundException`. Later on in this chapter, we'll take a look at several approaches for avoiding this type of problem. But before we do that, let's take a final look at the concept of a bundle's exported and imported packages.

4.3   *Packages as requirements and capabilities*

As you've seen, a bundle's exported packages define the bundle's modularization signature; another way of looking at this is to consider the exported packages as the capabilities of a bundle and the imported packages as the requirements of a bundle.

> **SNEAK PREVIEW** The wiring API is new in version 4.3, and at the time of this writing there were no existing framework implementations for it. Nonetheless, this is a central change in the specification, so we'll look at the basic concepts here.

Version 4.3 of the OSGi specification takes this approach and provides a generic mechanism—the `org.osgi.framework.wiring` API—for specifying a bundle's capabilities and requirements. This mechanism is then used to represent the relationship of a bundle's exported and imported packages. Let's try to understand this API by looking at simple example. Consider a provider bundle and requirer bundle, each respectively defining the following MANIFEST files:

```
Manifest-Version: 1.0
Bundle-ManifestVersion: 2
Bundle-SymbolicName: provider
Bundle-Version: 1.0.0
Export-Package: manning.osgi.mypackage;version=1.0.0

Manifest-Version: 1.0
Bundle-ManifestVersion: 2
Bundle-SymbolicName: requirer
Bundle-Version: 1.0.0
Import-Package: manning.osgi.mypackage;version=1.0.0
```

In this case, the provider bundle is declaring its capability of being a provider of the `manning.osgi.mypackage` package. This capability declaration can be introspected using the `BundleRevision` API as follows.

Listing 4.1   Retrieving a bundle's declared capabilities

```
Bundle bundle =
    bundleContext.getBundle();

BundleRevision revision =
    bundle.adapt(BundleRevision.class);                    ◁──┐  Get bundle
                                                           ❶  revision
List<BundleCapability> capabilities =
    revision.getDeclaredCapabilities(
```

```
        BundleRevision.PACKAGE_NAMESPACE);                          Get
                                                                 ❷ capabilities
for (BundleCapability capability : capabilities) {
    Map<String, Object> attributes =
        capability.getAttributes();                              Get capability
    System.out.println("Package name = " +                    ❸ attributes
        attributes.get("osgi.wiring.package"));
    System.out.println("Package version = " + attributes.get("version"));
}
```

Version 4.3 of the specification introduces a `Bundle.adapt()` method ❶, which allows
you to adapt a bundle object to a `BundleRevision`. The `BundleRevision` object represents the latest revision of the bundle and contains its declared metadata, such as its
capabilities. The capabilities are grouped into namespaces. In particular, you can
retrieve the `export` package capability by specifying the `PACKAGE_NAMESPACE` ❷.
Finally, a capability is organized as a set of attributes ❸ and directives, corresponding
to the package name and version attributes and the uses and resolution directives.

Next, let's retrieve the declared requirements for the requirer bundle:

```
Bundle bundle =
    bundleContext.getBundle();

BundleRevision revision =
    bundle.adapt(BundleRevision.class);

List<BundleRequirement> requirements =
    revision.getDeclaredRequirements(BundleRevision.PACKAGE_NAMESPACE);

for (BundleRequirement requirement : requirements) {
    Map<String, Object> attributes = requirement.getAttributes();
    System.out.println("Package name = " +
        attributes.get("osgi.wiring.package"));
    System.out.println("Package version = " + attributes.get("version"));
}
```

In this case, the only difference is that you retrieve a list of requirements.

The OSGi framework defines not only the package namespace but also a bundle
namespace to manage bundle-related metadata, such as a bundle's symbolic name,
and a host namespace, which takes care of fragments. But most important, it also
allows you to define your own namespace to manage user-defined resources within a
bundle. For example, in the federated database scenario, you could create a schema
namespace, which an application bundle would use to indicate the table schema it
either defines or depends on. Later, in subsequent chapters, we'll explore this further
and look at an example where you define your own namespace to manage the dependencies between remote bundles.

One other noteworthy feature of the `wiring` API is that it also allows you to introspect the runtime live association between the requirements and capabilities. For
example, should you install both the provider and requirer bundles, during their
resolve process a wire would be created between these two bundles, indicating that
the provider's declared capability has been resolved and therefore wired to the

requirer's declared requirements. The following listing illustrates how to navigate this relationship.

Listing 4.2   Navigating a bundle's wire

```
// Of the provider bundle
BundleRevision revision =
    bundle.adapt(BundleRevision.class);

List<BundleWire> providedWires =                          ❶ Get provider's
    revision.getWiring().                                    wiring
    getProvidedWires(BundleRevision.PACKAGE_NAMESPACE);   ❷ Get provider's
                                                             wires
for (BundleWire bundleWire : providedWires) {
    Bundle requirerBundle =
        bundleWire.getRequirerWiring().getBundle();       ❸ Get requirer's
                                                             wiring
    System.out.println("Requirer's bundle symbolic name = "
            + requirerBundle.getSymbolicName());
}
```

Starting from the provider bundle, you retrieve its latest revision and then retrieve its bundle wiring ❶. Bundle wiring holds the runtime live wires that connect to other bundle wirings. Using the wiring, you retrieve all the provided wires for the package namespace ❷. Then you traverse the wire by retrieving the requirer endpoint ❸, which can be used to retrieve the requirer bundle.

The wiring API is powerful. As you've seen, it provides a BundleRevision object for the current bundle. Furthermore, the framework also keeps a BundleRevision object for each previous revision of a bundle that hasn't been refreshed yet, that is, for revisions that are waiting to be removed. This information allows a user to consider among other things the cost of a bundle update.

Now that you understand how to declare and use a bundle's package, let's look at how to avoid runtime problems because of class loading.

4.4   Avoiding the dreaded class-hell problem

The OSGi framework achieves much of its power through its class-loading architecture, which is more complex than the usual class loading of a standard Java application. Thus, it should come as no surprise that class-loading problems, popularly known as *class hell*, can be more prevalent. In the next few sections, we'll go through some of the possible problems you may run into and see how they can be addressed.

4.4.1   Don't forget to import the package!

The first problem you're likely to run into is a ClassNotFoundException as a result of having forgotten to import its package using the Import-Package header. This is the most common problem you'll run into in OSGi. The good news is that it's easily spotted and corrected. But can you avoid it? Yes, you could automate the generation of the MANIFEST file of a bundle. The tool would have to introspect the Java code within the bundle, checking for all the import class statements. Then, the tool would need to generate an `Import-Package` for each package whose class is being imported.

This is what Peter Kriens does with his popular `bnd` tool, which can be found at http://www.aqute.biz/Code/Bnd. You can use his tool, which has several interesting configurations, or create your own custom tool for the job.

4.4.2   *Keeping class space consistency*

Being able to create a system that relies on multiple bundles is beneficial, because it means that you're maximizing reuse. Yet, there's one negative side effect: it increases the likelihood of creating class space inconsistency between the bundles. Class space inconsistency has the annoying attribute of causing seemly random class-cast exceptions at runtime. To understand the reason for this, we must first look into the class-loading architecture in Java.

In Java, a class isn't really defined by its full class name, such as `frameworks.Test-Class`, as intuitively expected, but rather by the combination of its full class name and the `ClassLoader` instance that loaded the class.

What this means is that class `A` loaded by class loader `L1`, henceforth identified as `L1.A`, and the same class loaded by class loader `L2` are considered different classes at runtime by the JVM.

```
Object instanceOfClassA =
Class.forName("A", true, firstClassLoader);
Object anotherInstanceOfClassA =
Class.forName("A", true, secondClassLoader);
assert !instanceOfClassA.getClass().equals(
anotherInstanceOfClassA.getClass());
```

Thus, if you try to cast `L1.A` to `L2.A` or vice versa, you'll get a cast exception. This can be quite tricky to debug, because it wasn't caused by an application logic error or by a mistake in some algorithm, but rather it's an infrastructure error.

The good news is that in a standard Java application you're unlikely to run into this type of class cast exception because by default the class-loader architecture is simple. There's a system class loader, which loads the JRE classes, and it has a child class loader, which is used to load the application classes, as shown in figure 4.7. The child class loader inherits all classes from its parent class loader, avoiding the problem of the same class being loaded by different loaders.

Things are less simple in OSGi. As you've seen, each OSGi bundle has a unique visibility of the classes it can use, which is determined by the `Import-Package` specifications in its MANIFEST.MF file. This scoping of classes can be achieved by each bundle having its own class loader, which delegates to the class loader of the bundle whose packages

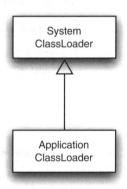

Figure 4.7   Hierarchical class-loader architecture for standard Java applications

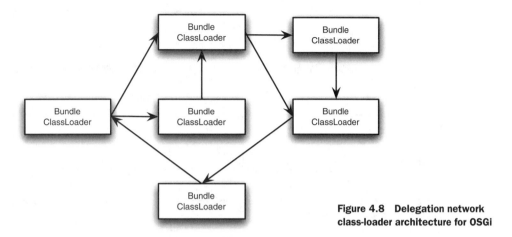

Figure 4.8   Delegation network class-loader architecture for OSGi

it's importing. Because each bundle may import packages from different bundles, which may also then import from other bundles, the class-loading delegation mechanism forms a network (graph) of connections. In other words, whereas a regular Java application has a hierarchical class-loader architecture, OSGi uses a network-based class-loader architecture, as shown in figure 4.8.

Summing it up, there's an abundance of class loaders in OSGi, which means that the likelihood of a class being loaded by different class loaders has greatly increased.

NOTE The OSGi delegation network class-loader architecture even allows for cycles. This cyclic behavior surfaced a race condition in several JVM implementations in JSE 6.0, which is addressed in the next release of JSE.

You may ask, "What if I just avoid casting altogether? Would this solve the problem?" Unfortunately, the story gets a bit more complicated. When a bundle `B1` imports a class `MyClass`, the bundle needs to know the complete signature of the class, which includes the types it extends and the types of the parameters of its methods, as shown in figure 4.9.

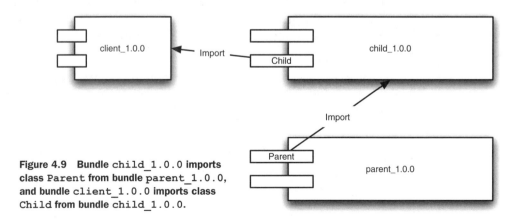

Figure 4.9   Bundle `child_1.0.0` imports class `Parent` from bundle `parent_1.0.0`, and bundle `client_1.0.0` imports class `Child` from bundle `child_1.0.0`.

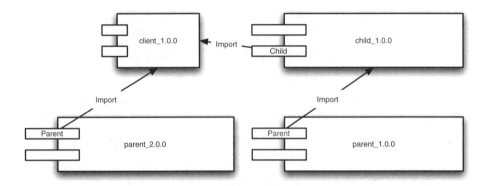

Figure 4.10   Bundle `client_1.0.0` gets the same class `Parent` from two different bundles and thus likely causes an exception.

> **TIP**   This is another reason why it's so important to export interfaces instead of classes. An interface has a much smaller "surface area" for dependencies.

For example, if bundle `client_1.0.0` imports class `Child`, which extends class `Parent`, then bundle `client_1.0.0` must not only load class `Child` but also load class `Parent`. Well, class `Parent` is similar to any other class, and we need to find the bundle that's exporting it.

So far, so good. Now consider that bundle `child_1.0.0` is exporting class `Child` and importing class `Parent` from bundle `parent_1.0.0`. You've learned that each bundle has a different class loader, so this means that bundle `child_1.0.0` uses `Parent` from class loader `parent_1.0.0`. Here's where we get into trouble. Assume that bundle `parent_2.0.0` exports a different version of class `Parent`. Also assume that bundle `client_1.0.0`, in addition to importing the class `Child` from bundle `child_1.0.0`, is also importing `Parent` from bundle `parent_2.0.0`. In this scenario, bundle `client_1.0.0` is using a different class loader for class `Parent`. When bundle `client_1.0.0` gets hold of the class `Child`, it will also see the class `Parent` owned by the class loader of `parent_1.0.0`, which it may try to cast to `Parent` as if it were owned by the class loader of `parent_2.0.0`, and, alas, will find it incompatible! See figure 4.10.

Let's take a closer look at the source code and MANIFEST files for this scenario. First, let's consider version 1 of the `Parent` class and its corresponding MANIFEST file, as shown in the following listing.

Listing 4.3   `Parent` class version 1 and its MANIFEST

```
package manning.osgi.parent;

public class Parent {

    public Parent() {
        System.out.println("Parent (v1)");
    }
}
```

```
Manifest-Version: 1.0
Bundle-ManifestVersion: 2
Bundle-SymbolicName: parent
Bundle-Version: 1.0.0
Export-Package: manning.osgi.parent;version=1.0.0
```

The class is simple enough; its main purpose is to allow us to understand OSGi's class-loading implications. In the next listing is version 2 of this same class and its MANIFEST file.

```
package manning.osgi.parent;

public class Parent {

    public Parent() {
        System.out.println("Parent (v2)");
    }

    public void newMethod() {
        System.out.println("new method");
    }
}

Manifest-Version: 1.0
Bundle-ManifestVersion: 2
Bundle-SymbolicName: parent
Bundle-Version: 2.0.0
Export-Package: manning.osgi.parent;version=2.0.0
```

Now that you've seen the parent classes, let's look at the `Child` and `Client` classes and their MANIFEST files, as shown in the following listings.

```
package manning.osgi.child;

import frameworks.parent.Parent;

public class Child extends Parent {

    public Child() {
        System.out.println("Child");
    }
}

Manifest-Version: 1.0
Bundle-ManifestVersion: 2
Bundle-SymbolicName: child
Bundle-Version: 1.0.0
Import-Package: manning.osgi.parent;version="[1,1]"      ➊ Import
Export-Package: manning.osgi.child;version=1.0.0              version I
```

Notably, this version of the Child class imports version 1 of the Parent class ❶. The next listing shows the second version of the Client class.

Listing 4.6   Client class and its MANIFEST

```
package manning.osgi.client;

import org.osgi.framework.BundleActivator;
import org.osgi.framework.BundleContext;

import frameworks.child.Child;
import frameworks.parent.Parent;

public class ClientBundleActivator implements BundleActivator {

    public void start(BundleContext arg0) throws Exception {
        Parent parent = new Child();
        parent.newMethod();                      ⟵——  ❶ Invalid
    }                                                    invocation

    public void stop(BundleContext arg0) throws Exception {
    }
}

Manifest-Version: 1.0
Bundle-ManifestVersion: 2
Bundle-SymbolicName: client
Bundle-Version: 1.0.0
Bundle-Activator: manning.osgi.client.ClientBundleActivator
Import-Package: org.osgi.framework,
  manning.osgi.parent;version=2.0.0,      ⟵——  ❷ Import
  frameworks.child                                 version 2
```

Version 2 of the Client class imports version 2 of the Parent class ❷. There is a clear indication that something is amiss, because you're invoking the method newMethod ❶, which you know isn't present in the class Child. Nonetheless, compilation will go through successfully because it assumes you're using version 2 of Parent.

When you install and start these bundles in Felix, you'll get the following exception:

```
java.lang.VerifyError: (class: frameworks/client/ClientBundleActivator,
  method: start signature: (Lorg/osgi/framework/BundleContext;)V)
 Incompatible object argument for function call
```

To say the least, this can be brutal. This is a simple example and the error message wasn't too enigmatic, but how would you be able to handle the case when there are dozens or hundreds of bundles? It would be hard to find the closure of their dependencies.

Fortunately, OSGi has a simple solution to this problem. The idea is to specify which packages are being used by the package that's being exported and thus group them together. This is done with the uses parameter. In this case, only the child bundle needs to be corrected:

```
Manifest-Version: 1.0
Bundle-ManifestVersion: 2
Bundle-SymbolicName: child
```

```
Bundle-Version: 1.0.0
Import-Package: manning.osgi.parent;version="[1,1]"
Export-Package: manning.osgi.child;version=1.0.0;uses:= manning.osgi.parent
```

TIP Note how the uses fragment is followed by := instead of just = as the version parameter.

Reinstall this bundle, refresh, and restart the client bundle. Now you'll get a different error message:

```
org.osgi.framework.BundleException: Unable to resolve due to constraint
violation.
```

This looks a little better. The OSGi framework is telling you that the client bundle can't be resolved because it has a constraint that can't be fulfilled. In other words, the child bundle, through the uses parameter, is stating that if a bundle imports its exported package of manning.osgi.child, this bundle must also import version 1 of the package manning.osgi.parent. The client bundle doesn't fulfill this constraint, hence the OSGi framework exception.

Ultimately, to make this example work, you either have to change the client bundle to import and use version 1 of the package manning.osgi.parent or change the child bundle to import version 2 of this same package.

Method implementation

As you've seen, when you import a class, you also need to import all classes referenced by any public signatures of the imported class. Why is it that you don't need to import the classes used in the implementation of the methods of the imported class?

The reason you don't is that when you instantiate class B within a method of class A, it's equivalent to loading class B using the class loader of class A, so the importing bundle doesn't need to use its own class loader for the task.

```
class A {
    void method() {
        new B();
    }
}
```

is equivalent to

```
class A {
    void method() {
    try {
        A.class.getClassLoader().
            loadClass(B.class.getName());
    } catch (ClassNotFoundException e) {
            // ...
        }
    }
}
```

4.4.3 Package export race condition

This last problem isn't related to class loading but rather it's a race condition between bundles, which can be just as painful to debug.

Consider a bundle that initializes some static field during its startup—when the framework invokes the bundle's activator `start` method. Furthermore, the class that provides access to the static field is being exported through an `Export-Package` header.

A bundle that imports this class through an `Import-Package` header and accesses the static field may get an uninitialized value. The reason for this is that the `Export-Package` takes effect immediately after the bundle is resolved but before the bundle has been started.

The lesson here is to be careful when exporting a package and not assume that the bundle activator will be executed before the package is made available to clients. And yes, please avoid static members.

Having looked at several class path–related issues, we'll look next at OSGi's class-loading architecture itself.

4.5 *Understanding OSGi's class loading*

So far you've learned different mechanisms for importing a class in OSGi. A bundle may import the class from another bundle by using the `Import-Package` header or the `DynamicImport-Package` header; a bundle may also rely on its own class path (a private package) or use fragments. This process of searching for a class, or more precisely for any resource, as you've probably guessed, isn't a simple one.

First, it's useful to model the entire searchable space of a bundle as a four-layer architecture, as shown in figure 4.11. At the top level is the boot class loader, which is the parent class loader for all the bundles' class loaders. Below it are all the packages that are imported from a separate bundle. Next is the bundle's own internal class path, as specified by the `Bundle-Classpath` header. And finally comes the class path of any attached fragments.

This model provides a rather simple but mostly accurate class space for a bundle, where the top layers have precedence over the lower layers. When a bundle attempts to load a class (or resource), the OSGi framework uses the following algorithm:

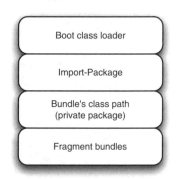

Figure 4.11   Class space for a bundle in order of precedence, starting at the top

1 If the class is in the `java.*` package, then the OSGi framework searches for the class definition at the top layer, that is, at the boot class loader. If it isn't found, then the process fails.

2 Next, the framework checks to see if the class is in a package that's being imported using the `Import-Package` header. If it is, then there must be some

bundle that's exporting this package, in which case the importer and exporter are wired together and the process stops. If no exporter is found, the process fails. If the class isn't in a package that's being imported using the `Import-Package` header, then the framework continues to the next step.

3 Next, the framework searches for the class in the bundle's own internal class path.

4 If the class is not found, the framework searches for the class in the attached fragment bundles in ascending order of bundle IDs.

5 If the class is still not found, the framework checks to see if a `DynamicImport-Package` header is defined and it may then attempt to dynamically load the class. If it succeeds, the class is wired to the exporter, and this wiring isn't changed afterward.

I've omitted two details in this algorithm. First, I've assumed that the `Require-Bundle` header isn't being used. As explained in section 4.2.3, `Require-Bundle` should be avoided, and you simplify the process by omitting it. Second, I've omitted the parent delegation list. In reality, step 1 should also check to see if the class is in a package that's included in the parent delegation list and should stop if it's found or continue to step 2 if it's not found.

> ### Parent delegation
>
> Standard Java applications have a hierarchical class-loader architecture, which delegates to the parent class loader first. It's sometimes necessary in OSGi to explicitly force certain classes to be delegated to the boot (parent) class loader. This can be done using the system property `org.osgi.framework.bootdelegation`.
>
> For example, the following configuration forces the OSGi framework to always delegate the loading of all `sun.*` classes to the parent class loader:
>
> ```
> org.osgi.framework.bootdelegation=sun.*
> ```

What happens if a bundle has a package within its class path and also tries to import it using an `Import-Package` header? Figure 4.7 tells us that `Import-Package` has precedence; hence, an exporter for the package must be present. If no exporter is found, then the resolve fails, in spite of the class being present in the bundle's class path. If you consider that the class in the private package has no version, this makes sense, because the importer always needs a versioned package.

Let's try a harder question: what if a bundle imports and exports the same package? In this case, the resolve process is successful because the bundle ends up importing the class from its own exporter.

By the way, why would someone import and export the same package? Although it may seem counterintuitive, this is a useful pattern in OSGi. This pattern allows the bundle to first try to find a package that's being provided by some other bundle, and if no exporter is found, it falls back to its own version of the package within its class path.

> **TIP** Generally, it's a good idea to always import a package that you're exporting. Although not necessary, because the class is found in the private package, it makes for more flexible bundles.

You've learned how to develop robust bundles, minimizing their exposure. Next, we'll look at how to further improve our architecture by making good use of OSGi services.

4.6   *Decoupling bundles using services*

One of the intrinsic qualities of easy-to-maintain applications is that you can change the implementation of a particular application's features without impacting the other features and subsystems that together form the application. This is in great part achieved by the correct use of the OSGi service layer. Clients must interact solely through defined service interfaces, thus allowing the application framework to swap and improve service implementations transparently. In chapter 2, we changed the implementation of the printer service without impacting existing clients. In chapter 3, we went through another more elaborate example, where buyers and sellers who participate in auctions are shielded from the details of the auction and auditor policies being used.

Albeit being simple and intuitive, this is the most important pattern to be followed when building applications using OSGi. Strive to keep interactions between bundles strictly through service interfaces, as shown in figure 4.12. Your bundle shouldn't import packages that contain implementation classes from other bundles.

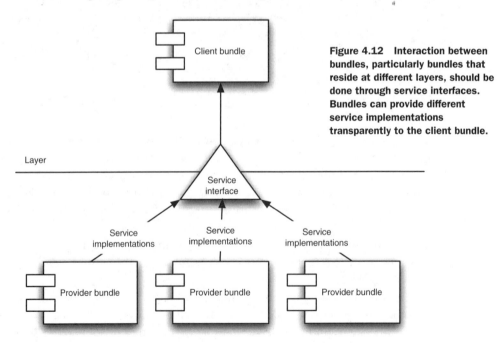

Figure 4.12 **Interaction between bundles, particularly bundles that reside at different layers, should be done through service interfaces. Bundles can provide different service implementations transparently to the client bundle.**

Even more to the point, you should generally import only Java interfaces and not any Java classes, and you should likewise avoid exporting packages that contain anything but Java interfaces.

As you start using services more frequently, there are other important aspects that you need to learn; namely, how to author advanced service filters, how to prioritize a service, how to uniquely identify a service, and the concept of service factories. Let's begin by tackling services filters.

4.6.1 Advanced service filtering

If there's one feature that the OSGi developer must master, it's the authoring of service reference filters. As you've seen, service reference filters allow bundles to find services provided by other bundles through a declarative mechanism, yielding more robust and flexible systems. In section 3.3.1, we skimmed over this. Let's go over filters now in detail.

Instead of providing a BNF (Backus-Naur Form) to describe the syntax used for specifying filters, we'll use a series of parse trees, each one describing a useful instance of a filter scenario. Collectively these should allow you to understand fully the "language" of OSGi filters.

An OSGi filter is a collection of operations. An operation is defined by the following three elements: attribute, comparison operator, and value. An attribute is a string representing a service property key. The comparison operators are equals (=), greater than or equals (>=), less than or equals (<=), approximate (~=), and exists (=*). A value is a string representing a service property value.

COMPARISON OPERATORS

The simplest case of an OSGi service filter is an equality comparison of an attribute to a value, such as `"(attribute=value)"`, as shown in figure 4.13.

Attributes aren't case sensitive and may contain white spaces, but the leading and trailing spaces are stripped during comparison. Conversely, values are case sensitive, and leading and trailing white spaces aren't stripped.

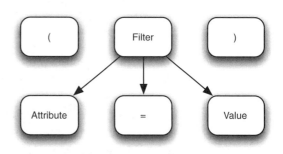

Figure 4.13 Parse tree for the filter expression `"(attribute=value)"`

For example, the following expressions are similar:

```
" myAttr =myvalue"
"myattr=myvalue"
```

But that's not the case of the following expressions, none of which match:

```
"my attr=myvalue"
"myattr=myvalue"
"myattr= myvalue"
```

As you've seen, the exact semantic of the comparison operators depends on the type of the value. Here are the rules:

- The equals (=) operator maps to `Object.equal` if the service property value is a Java object instance that can be instantiated using a constructor that takes a single `String` object as its argument. In other words, this is applicable to all primitive type wrappers, such as `Integer`, `Char`, and `Long`. If the value is a collection or an array of objects, then the comparison is true if at least one of the elements of the collection or of the array compares successfully with the rules outlined here.

  For example, the service property value [a,b,c] representing an array of characters matches with the following service property values:

  `"a"`

  `"b"`

  But it doesn't match with

  `"ab"`

Collection matches

Doesn't it strike you as odd that the OSGi filter matches even if only one of the values of a collection or array matches, instead of all the values? The reason for this seemingly counterintuitive rule is that this approach is consistent with the handling of OSGi service interfaces. Remember that a service interface is actually an array of Java classes, and that you need to match with only one of them to be able to retrieve the service object and cast it to the matched Java class. This makes even more sense if you consider that a service interface is really a service property whose key is `objectClass` and whose value is an array of `String`s.

- The exists (=*) operator returns `true` if the service property key is present in the service reference, so in this case the value and its type are irrelevant.
- If the value is of type `String`, or a collection or array of `String`s, you can use wildcards to perform substring equality matches. This is done using the * character, and it can be used multiple times in the value.

  For example, the value *a*b*c matches with the following service property values:

  `"aabbcc"`

  `"1a2b3c"`

  But this same value of *a*b*c doesn't match with the following property values:

  `"abc"`

  `"abbccd"`

- The operators >= and <= use the same rules as the equals operator, except that they map to `Comparable.compareTo()`. In other words, the value must be a Java object that implements `Comparable` and can be constructed from a `String`.

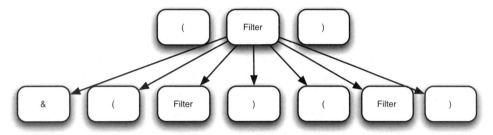

Figure 4.14 Parse tree for the filter expression `"(&(attribute=value)(attribute=value))"`

- The approximate (~=) operator is implementation-specific, but it must at least ignore case and white space differences in the value.

EXPRESSION OPERATORS

The OSGi filter operations themselves can be combined with three logical operators: the conjunction (and) operator (&), the disjunction (or) operator (|), and the negation (not) operator (!). The first two operators, contrary to the norm, aren't exclusively binary and are specified in prefix form, so you can associate any number of operations with them. The last operator is unary as expected; that is, it modifies a single operation.

The parse tree shown in figure 4.14 describes an OSGi filter that verifies if all the conditions are met.

You can associate several operations together using a single expression operator. For example, consider the following Java expression:

```
if ((attr1 == value1) && (attr2 == value2) && (attr3 == value3)) { … }
```

This can be expressed using the following OSGi filter:

```
(&(attr1=value1)(attr2=value2)(attr3=value3))
```

Also, the slightly more complicated Java expression,

```
if ((attr1 == value1) && ((attr2 == value2) || (attr3 == value3))) { … }
```

can be expressed using the following OSGi filter:

```
(&(attr1=value1)(|(attr2=value2)(attr3=value3)))
```

So there you have it; you're now an expert on the OSGi filter syntax. Don't feel bad though if you still prefer the infix style, such as that used in Java, instead of the prefix style used here. You're not alone.

In the next section, we'll look at how to distinguish services that share the same interface.

4.6.2   *Prioritizing services*

Sometimes there's a need to prioritize which OSGi service is retrieved from the OSGi registry. Consider the scenario where a user wants to check the integrity of messages being exchanged with other parties. A user can do this by fingerprinting, or hashing, the message.

Hash functions used for this purpose have the property that no pair of input messages that differ will have the same hash value. This means that a user can send a message and its hash value to a receiver, which can then apply the same hash function to the received message. The generated hash value will match the received hash value only if the message has not been altered.

We can define our fingerprint service as follows:

```
public interface FingerprintService {

    byte [] hash(String input);

}
```

There are several implementations of hash functions; in particular, there are the MD4 and MD5 algorithms, both invented by Rivest. MD4 is quicker, but there are known attacks for it, whereas MD5 is slower but safer. Most users don't really care about these differences; they just want to get some default implementation, which should probably be MD5. When dealing with security, we always want to be conservative. But other users who may be more educated on the subject would like to pick a particular algorithm. How do you solve this problem in the OSGi framework?

First of all, you should register these two different service implementations, providing some additional service property that highlights their differences. For example, you can define a PERFORMANCE property whose value is set to SLOW and FAST respectively for the MD4 and MD5 service implementations:

```
Dictionary<String, Object> md4Properties =
    new Hashtable<String, Object>();

md4Properties.put("PERFORMANCE", "FAST");

registration = bundleContext.registerService(
        FingerprintService.class.getName(),
        MD4FingerprintServiceImpl,
        md4Properties
);
```

A user who wants the FAST fingerprint service indicates so by setting the PERFORMANCE property to FAST when retrieving the service from the OSGi service registry:

```
String filter =
    "(&(objectClass=" + FingerprintService.class.getName() + ")" +
    "(PERFORMANCE=FAST))";

ServiceReference[] serviceReferences =
    bundleContext.getServiceReferences(null, filter);
```

But in the typical case, where the user doesn't care to specify the PERFORMANCE property, which service would you get? You could get either; it's largely nondeterministic which service the framework would hand back to you.

In this case, you want to avoid this nondeterminism; you'd like the MD5 service implementation to have priority over the MD4 implementation. This can be done through the use of the predefined SERVICE_RANKING property, whose value is of type Integer. When multiple qualifying service implementations exist, the OSGi framework selects the one with the highest SERVICE_RANKING property, as shown in the following listing.

Listing 4.7 Service rankings for the fingerprint service

```
Dictionary<String, Object> md5Properties =
    new Hashtable<String, Object>();

md5Properties.put("PERFORMANCE", "SLOW");
md5Properties.put("ALGORITHM", "MD5");
md5Properties.put("SECURITY_LEVEL", "HIGH");
md5Properties.put(Constants.SERVICE_RANKING, 10);          ❶  Higher service
                                                               priority
registration = bundleContext.registerService(
        FingerprintService.class.getName(),
        MD5FingerprintServiceImpl,
        md5Properties
);

Dictionary<String, Object> md4Properties =
    new Hashtable<String, Object>();

md4Properties.put("PERFORMANCE", "FAST");
md4Properties.put("ALGORITHM", "MD4");
md4Properties.put("SECURITY_LEVEL", "MEDIUM");
md4Properties.put(Constants.SERVICE_RANKING, 5);           ❷  Lower service
                                                               priority
registration = bundleContext.registerService(
        FingerprintService.class.getName(),
        MD4FingerprintServiceImpl,
        md4Properties
);
```

The MD5 service implementation has a service ranking of 10 ❶, whereas the MD4 service implementation has a ranking of 5 ❷. Thus the OSGi framework selects the MD5 service if no other service property is specified to further differentiate the services.

> **NOTE** In this example, if you specify any other service property, such as the PERFORMANCE, ALGORITHM, or SECURITY_LEVEL, then the ranking won't be used because the additional service property alone is able to differentiate between the MD4 and MD5 implementations.

Next, let's look at when and how you can uniquely identify a service, even after the OSGi framework is restarted.

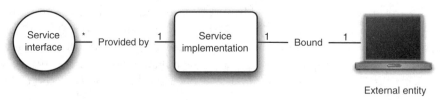

External entity

Figure 4.15   A service representing a single external entity

4.6.3   *Uniquely identifying services*

There are several cases where it's useful to uniquely identify a service. One such a case is when the service represents some external entity. For example, a service may represent a machine in the network, as shown in figure 4.15. Generally, networked machines are referenced through their TCP/IP addresses. Wouldn't it be ideal if you could use the IP address as the service identification? By doing so, you'd allow a client bundle to retrieve the service that represents the machine by using its IP address, which is generally a well-known and understood concept. Can you solve this problem of creating identifiers for services in the OSGi framework?

In the previous examples, you may have noticed that all services have a special service property called SERVICE_ID. The OSGi framework sets this service property automatically when a service implementation is registered. The value of the SERVICE_ID property is transient; the framework sets a new value every time the service or the framework is restarted. The only guarantee is that for an instance of the framework, that is, for each launch of the framework, no two services have the same SERVICE_ID.

Could you associate the IP address to the SERVICE_ID property? No, you can't. Not only is the OSGi framework responsible for assigning a value to the SERVICE_ID property, but it changes at every restart of the framework.

Instead, the OSGi framework defines another built-in property: the SERVICE_PID. You can assign your own value to the SERVICE_PID property, providing it's kept unique and persistent. This means that you should only register a single service with the same SERVICE_PID, and you must keep using the same value across restarts of this service. Client bundles are then guaranteed that they're always getting the same service.

Bundle identification

The SERVICE_PID property uniquely and durably identifies a service. What's the equivalent for a bundle?

The most obvious persistent identification for a bundle is the combination of a bundle's symbolic name (Bundle-SymbolicName) and its bundle version (Bundle-Version). This pair not only is unique within an OSGi framework instance but also will survive restarts of the platform. But it's too long an identification to be used effectively in day-to-day operations such as installs, updates, and uninstalls. Therefore, there's also the bundle identification.

(continued)

The bundle identification (or bundle ID) is the long value returned when you invoke an install command in the Gogo shell. As you recall, this ID can later be used to identify a bundle through its lifecycle. The bundle ID is guaranteed to be unique and likewise is the same if you restart the OSGi framework and don't change the current bundles installed. In other words, it's dependent on the order of installation of the bundles. This means that if you uninstall a bundle and reinstall it, the bundle ID will change. This is different from the bundle's symbolic name, which wouldn't necessarily change after a reinstall.

Finally, there's a third option, which is the bundle's location. The bundle location is a name assigned to a bundle during its installation. It is generally a URL to the bundle's JAR file, but it could be anything. The bundle location is the identification of choice for operators, because they generally wouldn't have access to a bundle's symbolic name and most likely do know the location of the bundle's JAR file to be installed. The bundle location is unique and persists across OSGi framework restarts.

In summary, these are the three options for identifying a bundle and the roles for which they're most adequate:

- Bundle symbolic name, bundle version (used by application developers)
- Bundle identifier (shorthand for operators)
- Bundle location (initial handle for operators)

In our example, the provider registers the service by setting the SERVICE_PID property:

```
Dictionary<String, Object> properties =
        new Hashtable<String, Object>();

properties.put(Constants.SERVICE_PID, "10.0.0.1");

registration = bundleContext.registerService(
        NetworkMachine.class.getName(),
        machineImpl,
        properties);
```

Then the client bundle specifies the IP value of the machine it wants to manage:

```
String filter =
    "(Constants.SERVICE_PID + "=10.0.0.1)";

ServiceReference[] serviceReferences =
    bundleContext.getServiceReferences(null, filter);
```

SERVICE_PID

Because the `SERVICE_PID` is enough to identify a service, you don't even need to specify the service interface in this case. But if you're going to eventually cast the service object to its service interface, it's generally a good practice to specify it as the first argument to `getServiceReferences()`:

```
String filter = "(" + Constants.SERVICE_PID + "=10.0.0.1)";
ServiceReference[] serviceReferences =
    bundleContext.getServiceReferences(
    NetworkMachineService.class.getName(), filter);
    NetworkMachineService service =
    (NetworkMachineService)
    bundleContext.getService(serviceReferences[0]);
```

Why not just define your own service property called MACHINE_IP and use this property instead of the predefined SERVICE_PID? There are two reasons for this. The first is that by defining a fixed property, the framework can make sure that all of its invariants are kept, that is, that no two services have the same SERVICE_PID and that it's persistent. The framework wouldn't be able to do this if the property was being defined by the application.

> **WARNING**   Unfortunately, as of this writing, neither Apache Felix (3.0.2) nor Eclipse Equinox (3.5.0) actually performs any validation on the SERVICE_PID property. In other words, two services could be registered with the same SERVICE_PID and the framework wouldn't flag it.

The second reason is that we're able to coordinate and link together several services using this one common property. We'll explain this in detail in chapter 5.

4.6.4   *Service factories*

So far, through all of our previous examples, the service implementations (service objects) have had a one-to-one association with their services or, more precisely, with their service references, as shown in figure 4.16. In other words, any time a client bundle retrieves a service reference and uses the reference to get to a service, it's getting

Figure 4.16   Typically, there's a one-to-one association between a service reference and its service implementation (object).

the same service implementation object instance, which is the instance used by the providing bundle in the call to registerService().

> **NOTE** In this context, a service reference is the logical entity that represents the handle to a service and not the actual Java object instance. There may be several object instances pointing to the same service reference. These are all considered the same service reference.

In most cases, this one-to-one mapping makes sense. For example, consider the machine management scenario we used in the previous section. There's a single entity, represented by its state, being managed; hence you can keep the state within a single object instance. This pattern is commonly referenced as the *singleton pattern* for object creation.

There are cases, however, when this style doesn't fit the application logic. For example, consider a Telnet service:

```
public interface TelnetService {

    void open(InetAddress target, int port);

    void close();

    String send(String text);

}
```

A Telnet service allows a client to connect to a remote machine and send and receive text commands.

A client bundle that retrieves the Telnet service and uses it to connect to a machine must be kept isolated from a different client bundle that may also be using the Telnet service. Each client bundle needs a separate instance of the Telnet session. In this case, there's a one-to-many association between a service reference and the service implementation, as shown in figure 4.17. This pattern is commonly referred as the *prototype pattern* for object creation.

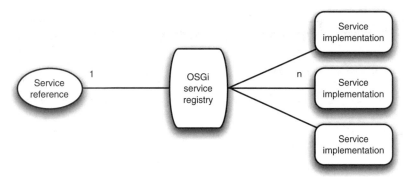

Figure 4.17   One-to-many associations between a service reference and its service implementations can be achieved through the use of a `ServiceFactory`.

Fortunately, the OSGi framework does support this scenario. To accomplish this, the service implementation must implement the `ServiceFactory` interface, as shown in the following listing.

Listing 4.8   Telnet service factory

```
import org.osgi.framework.ServiceFactory;

public class TelnetServiceFactory implements ServiceFactory {

    public Object getService(Bundle bundle,
ServiceRegistration registration) {
        return new TelnetImpl();
    }

    public void ungetService(Bundle bundle,
ServiceRegistration registration,
        Object serviceImplementation) {
        // NO-OP
    }
}
```

❶ Create service callback

❷ Delete service callback

The `getService()` method ❶ is called back by the framework when a client bundle first invokes the method `BundleContext.getService()` using a service reference whose service object implements the interface `ServiceFactory`, as shown in figure 4.18.

> **WARNING** The object returned from the `ServiceFactory.getService()` method must be an instance of the service interface classes used during registration. In our case, this means that `TelnetImpl` must implement the interface `TelnetService`.

Likewise, `ungetService()` ❷ is called back when a bundle invokes the method `BundleContext.ungetService()` for such a service reference.

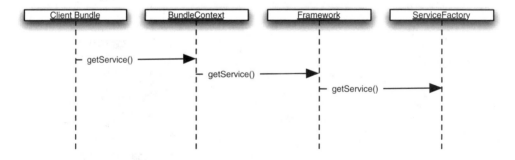

Figure 4.18   Client bundle invokes `BundleContext.getService()`, which causes the method `ServiceFactory.getService()` to be called back by the OSGi framework.

In our example, the Telnet service factory is quite simple; it creates a new object instance each time a service is needed by a client bundle. By doing so, each Telnet service has a separate object implementation holding its state.

Service management

Don't we need to manage the `TelnetImpl` object instance somehow? No, in most cases, nothing needs to be done. The `TelnetImpl` becomes a OSGi service and therefore has its lifecycle managed by the OSGi framework.

Shouldn't we do something in the `ungetService()` method? Again, in the typical case, the OSGi framework will take care of managing the service implementation lifecycle, and hence nothing special needs to be done.

The registration remains as expected; you keep the `TelnetService` as the service interface, but you use the `TelnetServiceFactory` object as the service implementation:

```
registration = bundleContext.registerService(
    TelnetService.class.getName(),
    new TelnetServiceFactory(), null);
```

This allows the client bundle to work through the `TelnetService` interface, and it's thus shielded from having to know about factories at all:

```
ServiceReference serviceReference =
    bundleContext.getServiceReference(
    TelnetService.class.getName());

TelnetService telnetService =
    (TelnetService) bundleContext.getService(serviceReference);
```

Note how the previous code fragment used by a client to retrieve a service doesn't have any coupling to service factories, in spite of the fact that the service provider is using a service factory.

SERVICE CACHE

What happens if the same bundle calls `getService()` twice on the `TelnetService` service reference? Interestingly enough, the framework returns the same service implementation used in the first call to `getService()`.The `TelnetServiceFactory` isn't invoked in this case; instead, a cached service implementation is returned. What this means is that a service created using a service factory is associated with the requester (client) bundle.

At first, this may seem strange; shouldn't a new service be created every time? Why cache it per bundle? The reason for this behavior is that the OSGi framework assumes that if the same bundle tries to get the same service twice, its intent is to use the same exact service. This makes sense in some cases. For example, to avoid keeping references to a stale service, a bundle may decide to get the same service over and over again from the OSGi registry as needed, rather then holding on to it in some field variable.

But there are cases when this doesn't apply. For example, consider the case where a single bundle wants to open different Telnet sessions. This isn't possible today, because all the `TelnetService` services retrieved by this bundle would point to a single `TelnetImpl` object instance. In my opinion, this behavior should be made configurable, perhaps through the specification of some new predefined service property, so as to follow the same pattern initiated by `SERVICE_RANKING` and the other predefined properties. In the end, this is a result of overloading the function `getService()` to both indicate the retrieval of a service as well as the creation of a service when using a `ServiceFactory`. Therefore, perhaps another option would have been to define a `createService()` method in the `BundleContext`.

We've looked into several advanced features of OSGi services that help us improve decoupling. Next, you'll learn how to test your applications.

4.7   *Improve robustness by testing your applications*

In the previous sections, we went through several issues pertaining to developing OSGi bundles and services. One final issue related to the process of developing OSGi applications remains: how do you test OSGi bundles effectively?

4.7.1   *Unit tests*

It's a good idea to start by testing a bundle at the unit level. You want to make sure that the bundle, which generally is defined by a well-established contract or interfaces, works in isolation. For a standard library or module, this is generally done by creating JUnit test cases. The good news is that you can continue using JUnit to test your OSGi bundle. This is so because OSGi avoids imposing any of its technology-specific interfaces on the application. This allows developers to test their classes as they normally would.

Let's look into an actual example. Recall our auction framework from chapter 3? How could we test the `SealedFirstPriceAuction` class of the `auction.auctioneer.sealed` bundle, which is where the most complex application logic resides in the case of the auction application?

Because we were careful to isolate the OSGi-related code to a single class called `SealedFirstPriceAuctioneerActivator`, you can instantiate the class `SealedFirstPriceAuction` in isolation within a JUnit `Testcase` class without having to worry about the OSGi environment, as shown in the following listing.

> **Listing 4.9   A unit test for the `SealedFirstPriceAuction` class**

```
public class TestSealedFirstPriceAuction extends TestCase {

    static class MockParticipant implements Participant {

        int numberOfAcceptances = 0;

        public String getName() {
            return "participant";
        }
    }
```

```
        public void onAccepted(Auction auction, String item, Float price) {
            numberOfAcceptances+=1;                                         ┌── Count
        }                                                            ❶  acceptances

        public void onRejected(Auction auction, String item, Float bestBid)
        {
            fail("Rejected");
        }
    }

    public void testSingleBidAsk() throws InvalidOfferException {

        SealedFirstPriceAuction auction =            ❷ Class to be
            new SealedFirstPriceAuction(1);             tested

        MockParticipant participant =        ❸ Mock
            new MockParticipant();             class

        auction.ask("book", new Float(50.0), participant);
        auction.bid("book", new Float(50.0), participant);

        assertEquals(2, participant.numberOfAcceptances);  ┌── Check
    }                                                   ❹ results
}
```

In ❷, you instantiate the test subject as a regular Java class, which in fact it is. You create a mock participant ❸, which only counts the number of accepted callbacks that were invoked ❶. Finally, you test the auction by sending a single bid and ask that match, and you assert the results ❹.

To run this test, which you can do through the command line or in some IDE such as Eclipse, you need to make sure the following JARs are in the class path: the JUnit library, the auction bundle, and the OSGi framework API (in our case, felix.jar will do). The latter is needed only because of the `SealedFirstPriceAuctioneer-Activator` class. Remember that our test is a JUnit test case, so the easiest option is to run it using a JUnit runner, which is provided in the JUnit library itself.

What if we hadn't been so careful and had polluted our application logic with OSGi-related interfaces? Or what if you just wanted to unit test the bundle activator class itself?

In this case, there are two options: you could either run the unit test within the OSGi platform itself, or you could emulate (that is, mock) an OSGi environment for the unit test. Fortunately, the Spring Framework provides an OSGi mock library, making the latter approach an attractive one. Continuing with our example, let's unit test the `SealedFirstPriceAuctioneerActivator` class, as shown in the following listing.

Listing 4.10   Unit test for `SealedFirstPriceAuctioneerActivator` class

```
public void testAuctionnerActivator() throws Exception {

    MockBundleContext mockContext = new                ❶ Mock
        MockBundleContext();                    ┌──      BundleContext
```

```
SealedFirstPriceAuctioneerActivator activator =
    new SealedFirstPriceAuctioneerActivator();
```
2 Activator to be tested

```
activator.start(mockContext);
```
3 Start using mock context

```
ServiceReference reference =
    mockContext.getServiceReference(Auctioneer.class.getName());
```
4 Validate activator

```
assertNotNull(reference);
}
```

In **2**, you create a bundle activator instance outside the OSGi environment. Then you create Spring's mock bundle context **1** and use it to start the activator **3**, as if the activator was being started by the OSGi platform. Then you validate the activator by making sure that it has registered a service reference for the auction service **4**.

> **The Spring Framework**
>
> The Spring Framework is known for the popular dependency-injection library provided by the company SpringSource, among other things. SpringSource has adopted the OSGi platform and is providing several tools, libraries, and its own OSGi application server!

You can also run this test in isolation similarly to the previous case, but you must remember to add the Spring OSGi mock library to the class path.

NOTE Spring OSGi libraries, also called Spring DM, can be found at http://www.springsource.org/osgi.

After having unit tested all of our bundles, the next step is to make sure the bundles are able to talk to each other within the OSGi platform itself. This process is called *integration testing*.

4.7.2 Integration tests

To execute integration tests for our bundles, you'll need to run the bundles and the tests within an actual OSGi platform. And obviously, because you want to automate the execution of the tests, you'll want to do this through scripts or the command line. In essence, you need to do the following:

1 Start the OSGi platform.
2 Install all the bundles that need to be tested and their dependencies.
3 Install the test itself; this can be in the form of another bundle.
4 Trigger the execution of the test by invoking an MBean from a script or by having the test bundle include a bundle activator that starts the execution of the test.
5 Store the verdict (that is, pass or fail) of the test; writing the result to a file can do this.
6 Shut down the OSGi platform, and repeat the process if other tests are needed.

Fortunately, Spring DM also provides a facility for helping you doing this. Simply have your test extend the JUnit abstract class `AbstractConfigurableBundleCreatorTests`. This base class will take care of starting the OSGi platform, creating a test bundle, executing it, and shutting down the platform, as shown in the following listing.

Listing 4.11   Integration test for the auction framework

```
import org.osgi.framework.ServiceReference;
import org.springframework.osgi.test.AbstractConfigurableBundleCreatorTests;
import org.springframework.osgi.test.platform.Platforms;

import manning.osgi.auction.spi.Auctioneer;

public class IntegrationTestAuction extends                    ❶ Extend test
        AbstractConfigurableBundleCreatorTests {                   framework class

    public void testSealedFirstPriceAuction() {
        ServiceReference reference =
            bundleContext.getServiceReference(                  ❷ Use service
Auctioneer.class.getName());                                       as usual

        Auction auction =
            (Auction) bundleContext.getService(reference);

        // Place bids, asks...
    }
                                                                ❸ Specify OSGi
    protected String getPlatformName() {                          framework
        return Platforms.FELIX;
    }
}
```

To test the auction framework, you create a JUnit class `IntegrationTestAuction`, which extends the Spring DM helper class `AbstractConfigurableBundleCreator-Tests` ❶. This class is run as a bundle, so it has access to a `bundleContext`. With the `bundleContext`, you retrieve the Auction service ❷ and perform the actual test by placing bids and asks as you did previously, but now the whole interaction is done through the OSGi framework.

You can test the JUnit test case using a JUnit runner. But you need to include several JARs in its class path this time: the JUnit library, the Spring DM libraries and their dependencies, and the OSGi platform libraries, which in our case is felix.jar. You should run the test from the Felix home directory, so that the test helper class is able to start Felix correctly. You also need to tell the helper class that you want to use Felix and not some other OSGi platform, such as Equinox. This is done at ❸. And finally, don't forget to install all the necessary bundles, such as all of the auction application bundles, in Felix before running the test; otherwise they won't be found. It still seems a fair amount of work, but it's simpler than doing all these tasks manually.

4.8   *Summary*

In this chapter, we explored several advanced OSGi bundle and service features that allow you to develop flexible, extensible, and robust OSGi applications.

The OSGi framework provides several options for minimizing bundle dependencies. You can restrict a resource to be within a private package and thus not visible to any other bundle. You can also choose to export only a subset of the classes residing in a package, thus reducing the number of classes that make up the exported package contract. Finally, you learned that you should avoid creating bundle dependencies using the `Bundle-Required` header, because it can cause split packages and cause other problems.

We looked into three OSGi features that facilitate the creation of generic bundles. Dynamic imports provide a way out of the explicit import and export package contract, because they allow classes to be searched as needed. Optional packages are regular import packages that aren't considered an error if they're not resolved. And finally, fragment bundles are degenerated bundles that attach and merge with a host bundle, possibly extending its class path.

When a bundle loads a resource, this resource is searched through the bundle's class space, starting at the boot class loader, then at any `Import-Package` header, next at the bundle's private package, and finally at any fragment bundles attached to the bundle.

You learned how to specify complex service reference filters. OSGi service filters follow a prefix form, which can be non-intuitive but allows several operations to be grouped together on a single conjunction or disjunction.

You can use the predefined `SERVICE_RANKING` property to prioritize which service is used if multiple services meet a criterion when being retrieved from the OSGi service registry. This is useful when you need to specify which service among many should be the default one.

The predefined `SERVICE_PID` property is used to uniquely identify a service. This is useful when a service represents a real-world entity. No two services should be registered with the same `SERVICE_PID`, and the `SERVICE_PID` must be persisted; that is, the same value must be used when a service is restarted.

Generally, a service reference maps to a single service implementation object instance. But if each service must have its own state, then multiple service implementation object instances must be created for the same service reference. To do this, a service implementation object must implement the interface `ServiceFactory`.

The OSGi framework imposes very few vendor interfaces into the application classes, so it's generally easy to unit test a bundle by treating it as a regular Java class. Spring DM provides several mock classes for the OSGi framework API. Spring DM also allows you to perform integration tests. It has helper classes that start an OSGi platform, install bundles, and allow you to test their integration.

In the next chapter, we'll look at how to configure these decoupled bundles in a way that's consistent for the entire application.

Configuring OSGi *5* applications

This chapter covers

- The reasons for configuration
- The advantages of handling configuration through the Configuration Admin service
- Validation of configuration data
- Transaction-ability of configuration changes

As you'll see, most applications need some form of configuration. This configuration includes not only IT-related configuration, such as server names and TCP/IP ports, but also business-related configuration, such as custom or localized labels.

The OSGi platform provides several services, including the Configuration Admin service, the OSGi Log service, and the OSGi Metatype service, that collectively can be used as a configuration framework for OSGi applications.

In this chapter, we'll look into these services and see how they can be used collectively to configure an application. We'll start by confronting the configuration problem systematically.

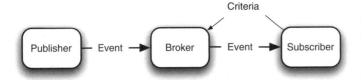

Figure 5.1 The notification publisher dispatches events to the broker, which dispatches them to the subscriber if criteria are met.

5.1 The configuration problem

Before we look into how to configure a service in OSGi, you should understand why and when configuration is needed. To do this, we'll use an example—the Notification Broker service.

5.1.1 The Notification Broker service

A notification system allows an application to send events of interest to another application. Such a system typically consists of three main components or services: a publisher, a broker, and a subscriber. The notification subscriber registers filters in the notification broker; these filters are sometimes called event criteria. The notification publisher sends events to the notification broker, which dispatches those events that match the criteria to the registered subscribers, as shown in figure 5.1.

In summary, this is similar to any other messaging infrastructure, such as the popular Java Messaging Service (JMS). The service interfaces for the Notification Broker service are shown in the following listing.

Listing 5.1   The Notification Broker service

```
package manning.osgi.notification;

public interface NotificationBroker {

    void sendEvent(Object event);

    int subscribe(String criteria, NotificationSubscriber subscriber);

    void unsubscribe(int susbcriberId);

}
```

The publisher sends an event, which is a plain Java object, to the service by invoking sendEvent(). A subscriber registers its filter and a callback object by invoking subscribe() and unregisters by invoking unsubscribe().

```
package manning.osgi.notification;

public interface NotificationSubscriber {
    void onEvent(Object event);
}
```

When a criterion that has been registered is met, the onEvent() callback on the subscriber is invoked.

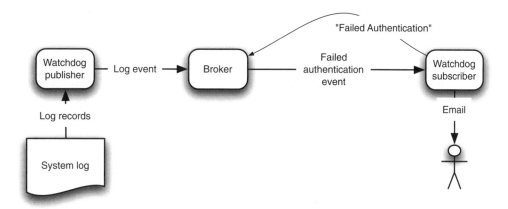

Figure 5.2 The watchdog publisher dispatches log events to a broker, which dispatches them to a watchdog subscriber if the log events contain a "Failed Authentication" message.

One example of an application that can be built on top of this service is a security watchdog. A security watchdog application consists of a publisher that reads, or more precisely tails, the system log file of a machine, sending every log record to the notification broker. The watchdog application also provides a subscriber, which registers to the broker with the following criteria: the presence of the phrase "Failed Authentication." When the broker receives an event that contains this phrase, the broker sends an event to the watchdog subscriber, which finally sends an email to the machine's administrator, as shown in figure 5.2.

> **Remote publishing**
>
> Remote publishers are important because it's more efficient to keep the publishers close to the source of the events. By doing so, you can optimize by discarding events at the source itself. without sending them to the network, thus decreasing event processing time and network traffic.
>
> It's less important to support remote subscribers because generally the number of events that match the criteria and reach the subscribers is an order of magnitude less.

The Notification Broker service is central to the notification system. One important feature of a notification broker is supporting remote publishers—publishers that reside in a different machine than that of the broker and subscriber. In the next section, we'll consider how this feature can be implemented in a configurable manner.

5.1.2 *Configuring the port of the notification broker*

To support remote publishers, the notification broker needs to provide a transport address to its clients, for example, a TCP/IP port. But what port should you use? You can't just hardcode a port into the broker, because you may need a different port depending on the machine that's being used as the host. For example, a port may be free on one machine but taken on another one. In addition, you may need to select a port that's open in the network's firewall.

The solution is to allow the port to be configured. There are several ways of doing this, one being by adding a `setPort(int port)` method in the Notification Broker service:

```
public interface NotificationBroker {

    // ...

    void setPort(int port);

}
```

This solution is extremely simple, but consider the implications of this approach:

- It isn't clear who should be invoking this method. Should it be the subscriber or the publisher? In reality, it's neither. As you've seen, the IT administrator should configure the port. Ideally, you want a mechanism whereby it's clear that setting the port is part of the configuration of the application and not part of the application's logic; the configuration shouldn't be done by the application's client, such as the subscriber or consumer.

- You'd like to avoid polluting the service interface with configuration-related interfaces. In this particular case, you have a single configuration item, the port number, but what if you had dozens of configuration data, which isn't that uncommon? The Notification Broker service interface would become unreadable. Furthermore, any changes to the configuration model of an application would also imply changes to the service interfaces of the application.

- Because the configuration needs to survive the restart of the application, it needs to be persisted. This means that every service that has some configuration needs to have a persistent storage mechanism. Instead of having each service implement its own storage, you'd like to get some help from the platform and have the platform manage the persistence of configuration data.

- You'd like to restrict access to configuration changes; that is, only certain personas, such as the IT manager, should be allowed to change the port configuration.

- Finally, it's sometimes helpful to use the configuration data as part of the identification of a service. For example, a subscriber may want to subscribe only to the notification broker that's associated with a specific port.

By now, it should be clear that adding a `setPort()` method to the Notification Broker service isn't such a good idea after all. What's the alternative? Thankfully, as you've seen, the OSGi platform provides not only a framework but also a set of compendium services, one of which is the Configuration Admin service, which addresses all the shortcomings we've discussed so far.

Figure 5.3   A configuring bundle provides configuration information to the Configuration Admin, which sends it to the target services.

5.2   *The Configuration Admin service*

Let's start our evaluation of the Configuration Admin by considering how it could be used to configure the port of the notification broker. Three components collaborate to implement this use case, as shown in figure 5.3: a configuring bundle provides the port information, the Notification Broker service receives and uses the port information, and the Configuration Admin serves as a mediator.

The next sections examine each of these components and their roles.

5.2.1   *The target service*

The Notification Broker service acts in the role of a configuration target; that is, it receives configuration data in the form of a configuration object.

> **DEFINITION** A configuration object is defined as a dictionary of configuration properties and a configuration PID.

To allow the Notification Broker service to receive configuration objects, you need to indicate to the platform that the notification broker is a configurable service. You can do this by implementing the interface org.osgi.service.cm.ManagedService.

But should you have the Notification Broker service implement this interface? If you do that, the service will be bound to an OSGi API, which, as you've seen in previous chapters, is something to avoid. In addition, you need the port configuration before you can start the Notification Broker service; hence having an instance of a Notification Broker service receive this configuration is somewhat of a lifecycle mismatch. Because of these reasons, we'll have the notification broker activator class implement the ManagedService interface.

Listing 5.2   Manageable notification broker activator

```
package manning.osgi.notification.impl;

import java.util.Dictionary;

import org.osgi.framework.BundleActivator;
import org.osgi.framework.BundleContext;
import org.osgi.service.cm.ConfigurationException;
import org.osgi.service.cm.ManagedService;

public class NotificationBrokerActivator
implements BundleActivator, ManagedService {
```

```
// ...

@SuppressWarnings("unchecked")
public void updated(Dictionary configuration) throws
 ConfigurationException {
    // ...
}
}
```

We'll look into the details later on; for now we're interested in the `ManagedService` interface, which has a single `update()` method.

> **NOTE** As you've seen, the OSGi framework API for the Core Specification version 4.2 doesn't use generics. Hence, if you're using JSE 5.0 or above, you'll find the annotation `@SupressWarnings("unchecked")` surprisingly handy.

Next, you need to associate a unique identification with the Notification Broker service. The configuring clients use this identification to link the configuration object to a managed service. We'll use the service's persistent identifier (PID), as defined in chapter 4, for this purpose. Remember that the PID is associated with a service through service properties during the service registration in the OSGi service registry, as shown in the following listing.

Listing 5.3   Registration of the target service's PID

```
public class NotificationBrokerActivator implements BundleActivator,
    ManagedService {

    public void start(BundleContext bundleContext) throws Exception {
        // ...

        Dictionary<String, Object> properties =
            new Hashtable<String, Object>();

        properties.put(Constants.SERVICE_PID,              ❶ Target service
            "manning.osgi.notification.broker");              PID

        registration = bundleContext.registerService(
                ManagedService.class.getName(),
                this,
                properties
        );
    }
```

In this case, the PID for the Notification Broker service is `"manning.osgi. notification.broker"` ❶. For the reasons pointed out previously, you register the activator itself as the target service for the notification broker. Notice how you only specify the `ManagedService` interface in the call to register and not the `NotificationBroker` interface. This means that a consuming bundle that retrieves this service can't cast it to the `NotificationBroker` interface. In other words, this service can only be used to configure the `NotificationBroker` and not to actually send events or subscribe to events. The separation of the configuration interface from the service interface is a useful one and is one of the advantages we discussed of using the Configuration Admin service.

> **WARNING** In the Enterprise Specification 4.2, every managed service must have a unique PID. If more than one service has the same PID, these services may be ignored and may end up not receiving the configuration. Unfortunately, this behavior is rather confusing. It would have been clearer if the framework would raise an exception when the duplicate PID is registered; to avoid the problem, make sure the PID is unique. Using the reverse domain name schema as we do here is generally a good approach to achieving this.

Finally, you must handle the updated(Dictionary configurationProperties) callback method in the NotificationBrokerActivator class. This callback is invoked by the platform when a configuration that has been targeted for this service is created, changed, or deleted, as shown in the next listing.

Listing 5.4 ManagedService's update callback

```
@SuppressWarnings("unchecked")
public void updated(Dictionary configuration)
throws ConfigurationException {
    if (configuration != null) {
        Integer port =
            (Integer) configuration.get("port");        ◁──┐   Get port from
                                                           ❶   configuration property
        if (port != null) {
            // TODO

            updateBrokerService(port);
        }

    } else {
        // TODO
    }
}

@SuppressWarnings("unchecked")
private void updateBrokerService(int port) {
    broker = new NotificationBrokerImpl(port);

    Dictionary serviceProperties =
        new Hashtable();                            ❷   Set port into
    serviceProperties.put("port", port);        ◁──┘   service property

    brokerRegistration = context.registerService(
            NotificationBroker.class.getName(),
            broker,
            serviceProperties
    );
}
```

In this example, first you retrieve the port information from the configuration properties ❶. Having the port configuration, you can now create the actual Notification-Broker service implementation and make it available in the OSGi service registry. Note

Figure 5.4   Configuration properties are transformed into service properties and are then used as filters by service consumer bundles.

that now you do use the `NotificationBroker` interface in the call to register. In addition, notice how you don't specify a PID for this service, because its activator class is already managing its configuration. If you had to register a PID, you'd have to use a different one than the one being used for the configuration.

Finally, you should include the configuration properties as part of the service properties for the Notification Broker service ❷. In chapter 3, remember how the service properties were used as filtering criteria? By updating the service properties with the port configuration, a service consumer bundle can use the port information as part of the OSGi service filter:

```
String filter =
    "(&(objectClass=" + NotificationBroker.class.getName()
    + ")(port=" + port + "))";

ServiceReference[] serviceReferences =
    bundleContext.getServiceReferences(null, filter);
```

This is a useful feature; it closes the loop around configuration properties and service properties, whereby the configuration properties become the service properties of the managed bundle. After this point, these service properties become visible to the managed bundle's service consumers, as shown in figure 5.4.

> **WARNING**   The `updated()` callback is invoked asynchronously by the Configuration Admin, so you must take care to synchronize it if needed.

By default, all configuration properties include the `service.pid` property, whose value is the configuration object's PID, that is, the PID used when registering the managed service.

Aside from a few tasks left to do, which we'll look into later, you're mostly finished with the managed service. Next, let's look at the bundle that's providing the configuration—the configuring bundle.

5.2.2   *The configuring bundle*

A configuring bundle has to do the following to provide configuration objects when using the Configuration Admin service:

First, it has to retrieve a reference to the Configuration Admin service. The Configuration Admin service is no different than any other OSGi service; you can retrieve it normally from the OSGi service registry as we've done previously:

```
ServiceReference serviceReference =
    bundleContext.getServiceReference(ConfigurationAdmin.class.getName());
```

```
ConfigurationAdmin configAdmin =
        (ConfigurationAdmin)
            bundleContext.getService(serviceReference);
```

Next, create a `Configuration` object. Somewhat counterintuitively, this is done using the `getConfiguration(String targetServicePID)` method, as shown in the following listing. This method returns a new `Configuration` object if one doesn't exist or returns an existing `Configuration` object associated with the target service PID specified as the input parameter.

Listing 5.5   Creating a `Configuration` object

```
Configuration configuration =
    configAdmin.getConfiguration(
        "manning.osgi.notification.broker");       ◁──┐
                                                        ❶ Target PID
Dictionary<String, Object> configProperties =
    new Hashtable<String, Object>();

configProperties.put("port", 8080);                        ❷ Updates Configuration
                                                              object
configuration.update(configProperties);        ◁──┘
```

You use the Notification Broker service PID of `"manning.osgi.notificationservice.broker"` to associate the `Configuration` object to the Notification Broker service ❶. Now you can set the port information in the configuration object. This is done by creating a dictionary object, adding the port to it, and invoking the method `update(Dictionary configurationProperty)` ❷. When this is done, the Configuration Admin service takes care of finding the target service—the Notification Broker service in this case—and invoking its `updated()` callback.

> **NOTE** The creation of a `Configuration` object doesn't cause any callbacks to be invoked in the target bundles. Only when the configuration properties themselves are set into the `Configuration` object through the `update` call will the `updated` callback be invoked.

What if the Notification Broker service itself hasn't been created yet; do we lose the configuration objects? No, the Configuration Admin persists the configuration, making sure that the configuration isn't lost even after the framework restarts. That's one reason for having a separate Configuration Admin service functioning as a mediator instead of just having the configuring bundle interacting directly with the target bundle.

Felix's persistence strategy

Felix's implementation of the Configuration Admin service allows users to plug in their own persistence manager implementation. By default, Felix provides a filesystem-based implementation, but users can provide their own configuration persistence strategy by registering an OSGi service that implements the interface `org.apache.felix.cm.PersistenceManager`. The one with the highest `service.ranking` order is selected.

Next, let's look at the details of the Configuration Admin service.

5.2.3   *The Configuration Admin: a mediator of configuration*

The Configuration Admin provides several infrastructure services. First, it mediates the configuring bundles and the target services. A configuring bundle can create configuration objects to target services that don't yet exist. When the target service is eventually registered, it will receive the configuration properties.

It also handles the durability of the configuration. When a configuring bundle updates the configuration in the Admin through the `org.osgi.service.cm.` `Configuration` interface, the Admin first persists the configuration properties and only then returns from the call. This means that the configuration isn't lost if the platform is shut down before the configuration is handed over to the target services. Furthermore, during the start of the platform, all the target services are updated with the latest configuration; the target services themselves don't need to worry about persisting their configuration.

5.2.4   *Finding the Configuration service using bundle repositories*

We've gone through the implementation of both the configuring bundle and the notification broker managed service bundle, albeit having glossed over the implementation details of the notification broker that weren't related to its configuration. What next? How do you test this? As you may have noticed, the Felix framework distribution doesn't include an implementation of the Configuration Admin service. Fortunately, there's an Apache Felix subproject for the Configuration Admin, which you can download and use.

Let's take a step back and consider this. The Configuration Admin service is a standard OSGi platform service; in other words, the OSGI consortium defines and provides its Java service interface. So do you really need to use Felix's implementation of this standard service? You shouldn't have to; as you've learned so far, one of the greatest strengths of the OSGi service platform is the decoupling of service interfaces from service implementations.

Let's search for a different vendor implementation of the Configuration Admin service. We could search the web for it, but there's a better solution. The OSGi consortium not only defines the services, but it also provides a repository for service implementations in the form of bundles. We'll discuss bundle repositories, which are another standard platform service, in chapter 11. For the time being, let's just use it to find a Configuration Admin implementation.

As of this writing, these are the well-known bundle repositories:

- SpringSource Repository: http://ebr.springsource.com/repository/app/
- OSGi Alliance Repository: http://www.osgi.org/Repository/HomePage
- Oscar Bundle Repository: http://oscar-osgi.sourceforge.net/
- Eclipse Repository: http://eclipse.org/equinox/bundles/

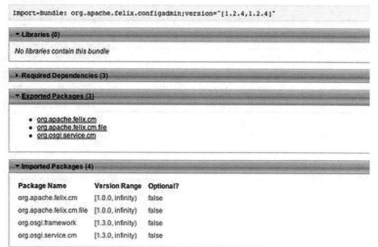

**Figure 5.5
Bundle details for
Configuration
Admin service
implementation**

Point your web browser of choice to any of these and type `ConfigurationAdmin` in the search box. For example, going through the SpringSource repository, I got the information shown in figure 5.5.

Make sure you download all the needed dependencies, as stated in the Required Dependencies section. For example, some Configuration Admin implementations don't include the compendium interfaces, which define the `org.osgi.service.cm` package, so you may need to download them separately. To do so, you can search for the `osgi.compendium` bundle.

Felix OBR client

Felix by default also includes a Bundle Repository client; therefore, you can also download the Configuration Admin through Felix's Gogo shell. This is done with the following commands:

```
g! obr:deploy "Apache Felix Configuration Admin Service"
Target resource(s):
-------------------
   Apache Felix Configuration Admin Service (1.2.4)
Optional resource(s):
---------------------
   Apache Felix Log Service (1.0.0)
Deploying...done.
g! lb
START LEVEL 1
   ID|State      |Level|Name
    0|Active     |    0|System Bundle (3.0.6)
    1|Active     |    1|Apache Felix Bundle Repository (1.6.2)
    2|Active     |    1|Apache Felix Gogo Command (0.6.1)
    3|Active     |    1|Apache Felix Gogo Runtime (0.6.1)
```

(continued)

```
     4|Active    |     1|Apache Felix Gogo Shell (0.6.1)
    23|Installed |     1|Apache Felix Configuration Admin Service (1.2.4)
    24|Installed |     1|Apache Felix Log Service (1.0.0)
g!
```

As it happens, Felix's OSGI Bundle Repository (OBR) automatically brings in a bundle's dependency. For example, in this case it automatically deployed the Log service, which is a dependency for the Felix Configuration Admin service. You'll learn more about Felix OBR in the following chapters.

Download all the bundles to your Felix home directory. Now you have all the pieces you need to test the scenario, which we'll do next.

5.2.5 *Running the Configuration Admin service*

Start Felix, and install the `osgi.compendium` bundle, the Configuration Admin bundle implementation of your choosing, the bundle containing the notification bundle's managed service from section 5.2.1, and finally the configuring bundle from section 5.2.2. Start these bundles, and you'll get a Notification Broker service registered with the correctly configured port.

You can check this by listing the service properties of the notification framework bundle. To do so, enter the following commands at the Felix prompt:

```
g! sr = serviceReference "manning.osgi.notification.NotificationBroker"
...
g! $sr property "port"
8080
```

The shell commands retrieve the service reference for the service implementing the `NotificationBroker` interface and then get the value of the property service `port` property, which yields the configured data.

There you have it; you're configuring an OSGI bundle in Felix using some other vendor's Configuration Admin implementation. Software engineering has been promising large-scale software reuse for decades. I hope you can relate to the simplicity, resilience, and power of being able to use a variety of vendors for a set of common services.

Next, we'll expand our scenario to consider complex data types instead of just simple types, as has been the case so far.

5.3 *Configuring using complex data types*

In our previous example, we used a simple integer type for configuring the port of the notification broker. What other types are supported by the Configuration Admin service?

Somewhat regrettably, only the Java simple types, and vectors or arrays of these, are supported. For example, the following are valid properties:

```
Integer intProperty = ...
String stringProperty = ...
```

```
Long longProperty = ...
Vector<Integer> intVectorProperty = ...
String [] stringArray = ...
```

But the following are *not* supported:

```
MyClass myClassProperty = ...
int primitiveIntProperty = ...
long primitiveLongProperty = ...
```

> **Arrays in configuration properties**
>
> Arrays of primitives are also supported for properties, even though plain primitives are not. The reason is that the `Dictionary` class can only take objects as input, and a plain primitive isn't an object, whereas an array of primitives is still an object.
>
> With Java's 5.0 autoboxing feature, the distinction is blurred, and the following would work:
>
> ```
> dictionary.add("intProperty", 10);
> ```
>
> The reason this works is that the compiler converts `10` to `new Integer(10)` as part of the autoboxing process.

Why the lack of support for user-defined types? Remember how configuration properties eventually become service properties, which can be queried using the OSGi filters? Well, an OSGi filter is based on the LDAP language, which doesn't define support for complex types. In summary, support for any arbitrary type would overly complicate querying, which is intrinsic to the OSGi service layer, so it's not supported.

Is there any workaround or alternatives? Yes, you must encode your class into one of the supported types. This seems a bit complicated, doesn't it? Fortunately, there's a simple solution: use XML. You can serialize the user-defined type into a `String` using some object-to-XML technology, such as Java Architecture for XML Binding (JAXB), insert it into the configuration object, and then deserialize the `String` back into a Java object in the managed service. But one drawback is that the OSGi filter would still treat this property as a `String` and not as a complex type. For example, this means that the filter predicate won't be able to contain references to nested properties; you'll be able to perform only simple `String` comparisons.

So far, you've learned how to add configuration. In the next section, we'll look into how to delete configuration.

5.4 Deleting configuration

You've seen how the configuring bundle sets the port configuration for the Notification Broker service by creating a new configuration object. What if you'd like to change the port?

From the perspective of the configuring client, this scenario is just like creating a new configuration property. The one thing to keep in mind is that updating the former Dictionary object used during the creation of the configuration object won't have any effect. This is because the Configuration Admin service copies the values of the dictionary used as an argument, instead of keeping a reference to it. This means that you need to always create a new Dictionary object when invoking the update() method, regardless of whether it's for creating a new configuration object or for updating an existing one.

What about deletion? How does the configuring bundle delete a configuration object? Intuitively, this is done by invoking the method delete() on the configuration object in the configuring bundle. Non-intuitively, the invocation of the delete() method causes the callback of the updated() method with a null parameter in the target service, as shown in the following listing.

> **Listing 5.6   Managed service supporting update and delete of configuration**

```
@SuppressWarnings("unchecked")
public void updated(Dictionary configuration)
        throws ConfigurationException {
    if (configuration != null) {
        Integer port =
            (Integer) configuration.get("port");

        if (port != null) {                          ❶ Restart with
            stopBrokerService();                         new port

            updateBrokerService(port);
        }

    } else {                                         ❷ Unbind port
        stopBrokerService();                             if null
    }
}

private void stopBrokerService() {
    if (broker != null) {
        broker.shutdown();
    }

    if (brokerRegistration != null) {
        brokerRegistration.unregister();
    }
}
```

This means that the Notification Broker service should unbind its port when it receives a null configuration object ❷. Furthermore, you must make sure that you handle updates to the port configuration by shutting down the former port and starting a new service using the new port ❶.

Isn't it a bit odd that you can only support a single notification broker at a time? This is a reflection of the ManagedService interface. If you were to create a new notification service for each port configuration update, you wouldn't know which one to delete when you received the updated() method with a null argument. The alternative of predefining a set of PIDs for the Notification Broker services is still too limiting and, to say the least, too draconian. The solution is to use managed service factories, as you'll see next.

5.5   *Configuring multiple services*

Managed service factories allow you to create multiple services from the same configuration schema. For example, they allow you to create a different Notification Broker service for each configured port, rather than changing the port of a single Notification Broker service multiple times.

The main difference between a ManagedServiceFactory and a ManagedService is that in the case of the former, the Configuration Admin creates a unique PID for each new configuration that's associated with the registered PID of the managed service factory, as you'll see next.

5.5.1   *Configuring bundle for configuration factories*

Let's look at the changes done at the configuring bundle from listing 5.5 to support managed factories. This is shown in the following listing.

Listing 5.7   Configuration of two Notification Broker services

```
ServiceReference serviceReference =
    bundleContext.getServiceReference(ConfigurationAdmin.class.getName());

ConfigurationAdmin configAdmin =
            (ConfigurationAdmin) bundleContext.getService(serviceReference);

Configuration configuration =
    configAdmin.createFactoryConfiguration(
"manning.osgi.notification.broker");

Dictionary<String, Object> configProperties =
    new Hashtable<String, Object>();

configProperties.put("port", 8080);

configuration.update(configProperties);

configuration =
        configAdmin.createFactoryConfiguration(
        "manning.osgi.notification.broker",
    null);

configProperties =
    new Hashtable<String, Object>();

configProperties.put("port", 8081);

configuration.update(configProperties);
```

① Creates managed factory

② Sets config property

③ Creates new configuration

In the case of managed service factories, you use the method createFactory-
Configuration() instead of getConfiguration() ❶. Regardless, the PID doesn't
need to change and is kept with the value of "manning.osgi.notification.broker".

> **NOTE** You could change the PID to "manning.osgi.notification.broker-
> factory". But in essence, you're still configuring the Notification Broker ser-
> vice; the fact that it happens to be a factory is really an implementation
> detail. Hence, as a convention, don't include the term factory in the PID.

You set the port configuration as usual in the configuration object ❷. But if you'd like
to create a new configuration with a managed service factory, you can again invoke the
createFactoryConfiguration() method ❸. By doing so, you can configure a new
Notification Broker service. This saves you from having to create a new dictionary and
update the existing configuration object as you did previously. Finally, you set the port
value in the new configuration object and invoke update as usual.

> **NOTE** To delete a configuration, you invoke the delete() method in the con-
> figuration object for both managed services and managed service factories.

Next, let's look at the changes needed in the target service to support managed service factories.

5.5.2 *Managed service factories*

Superficially, the changes to a target service to support managed service factories may
seem considerable, but it boils down to handling a new argument provided to the
updated() method callback, representing a container-generated PID, as shown in the
following listing.

Listing 5.8 Managed service factory for the Notification Broker service

```
public class NotificationBrokerFactoryActivator
    implements BundleActivator, ManagedServiceFactory {        Implement
                                                               ManagedService-
    private ServiceRegistration registration;              ❶  Factory interface
    private BundleContext context;
    private Map<String, NotificationBrokerImpl> brokers =
        new HashMap<String, NotificationBrokerImpl>();
    private Map<String, ServiceRegistration> brokerRegistrations =
        new HashMap<String, ServiceRegistration>();

    public void start(BundleContext bundleContext) throws Exception {
        this.context = bundleContext;

        Dictionary<String, Object> properties =
            new Hashtable<String, Object>();

        properties.put(Constants.SERVICE_PID,
            "manning.osgi.notification.broker");
```

```
    registration = bundleContext.registerService(
            ManagedServiceFactory.class.getName(),
            this,
            properties
    );
}

@SuppressWarnings("unchecked")
public synchronized void updated(String pid,
    Dictionary configuration)
        throws ConfigurationException {
    Integer port =
        (Integer) configuration.get("port");

    if (port == null) {
        throw new ConfigurationException("port",
                "Port configuration property is missing");
    }

    if (brokers.get(pid) == null) {
        startBrokerService(pid, port);
    } else {
        throw new ConfigurationException("port",
                "Update to existing service not allowed");
    }
}

public synchronized void deleted(String pid) {
    stopBrokerService(pid);
}

@SuppressWarnings("unchecked")
private void startBrokerService(String pid, int port) {
    NotificationBrokerImpl broker =
        new NotificationBrokerImpl(port);

    Dictionary serviceProperties =
        new Hashtable();
    serviceProperties.put("port", port);

    ServiceRegistration registration =
        context.registerService(
            NotificationBroker.class.getName(),
            broker,
            serviceProperties
    );

    brokerRegistrations.put(pid, registration);
    brokers.put(pid, broker);
}

private void stopBrokerService(String pid) {
    NotificationBrokerImpl broker = brokers.remove(pid);

    if (broker != null) {
```

② Configuration-updated callback

③ Configuration-deleted callback

④ Register new managed service

⑤ Store registration for deletion

```
            broker.shutdown();
            brokerRegistrations.remove(pid).unregister();
        }
    }

    public String getName() {
        return "Notification Broker Managed Service Factory";
    }
}
```

As expected, the target service class must implement the ManagedServiceFactory interface ❶. You register the target service as usual, with the one difference that you specify the ManagedServiceFactory interface as the service interface. When a new configuration is created or an existing configuration is updated, the updated() method is called back asynchronously ❷. The updated() method has one additional parameter: a PID. As mentioned, this PID is generated by the Configuration Admin service based on the original PID used to identify the managed service factory, which in our case is "manning.osgi.notification.broker", and it's appended with some generated suffix. This PID is then used to identify a new configuration object. In other words, every time you get a new PID that you haven't seen before, you should create a new service object ❸. You do this by creating a new NotificationBrokerImpl object and then registering it as an OSGi service as usual. Finally, you store the PID in a map, so that you can manage its deletion later ❺. You may also be informed of a configuration deletion ❹, in which case you should unregister the service.

> **NOTE** A common usage pattern for the ManagedServiceFactory interface is to implement service factories, where each new configuration triggers the creation of a new service. This is a great way of managing services, because the contract for creating and deleting a service is tied to the creation and deletion of its configuration and it's therefore very clear. Contrast this with the ServiceFactory interface, which instead creates new service objects for the service, and only if it's being requested by different bundles.

In this scenario, you don't support the update of an existing Notification Broker service; hence, you raise a ConfigurationException if the PID is found in the brokers map. You also raise a ConfigurationException if no port property is found in the configuration properties.

> **NOTE** Contrary to the managed service case, the deletion of a configuration causes the deleted() method to be invoked in the managed service factory.

You're finished with the code changes. Reinstall the modified bundles and try it out; you should be able to see several NotificationBroker services in the OSGi service registry.

> **WARNING** Both the updated() and deleted() methods may be invoked asynchronously, so make sure you synchronize these methods as needed. In the last listing, you updated a non-concurrent map, so the method had to be synchronized.

It's also interesting to try out some erroneous scenarios. For instance, try creating a configuration object that doesn't have the `port` property. What happens? Well, somewhat disappointingly, nothing happens. It's true that no Notification Broker service is created, but you also don't get any indication of an exception anywhere, any log files, or any standard output messages.

Do you need a hint about the reason for this unexpected silence from the OSGi platform when an exception occurs? When we were looking for the Configuration Admin implementation in section 5.2.4, remember how the Felix implementation depends on the package `org.osgi.service.log`? As you've probably deduced by now, the Configuration Admin service uses the Log service to log all `Configuration-Exceptions`, which is the subject of the next section.

5.6 *When configuration update fails*

Managed services and managed service factories may throw configuration exceptions from within their `updated()` and `deleted()` callbacks to indicate that there's some problem with the configuration properties and that the target service can't be configured.

These configuration exceptions are caught by the Configuration Admin, which logs them using the OSGi Log service. The Configuration Admin then continues normally. That is, the configuring bundle gets no indication that the configuration has been rejected; neither is the configuration itself deleted from the Configuration Admin's persistent storage. If the target service is restarted, it will again receive the same set of configurations, even those that have been rejected in the past.

This behavior of the Configuration Admin can be somewhat frustrating. How can you inform the configuring bundle that the configuration object has been rejected? We'll look at three options for doing this.

The first option is to proactively provide better metadata about the configuration, so that the configuring bundle has a better chance of setting the correct data. We'll look at this option in detail in section 5.7.

The second option is to check in the OSGi service registry itself for the service that has been supposedly configured. In our case, the configuring bundle could use a service reference filter whereby it specifies the port configuration that was set. If the filter comes back with no references from the OSGi service registry, then it's a good indication that the configuration may have been invalid. There are a couple of caveats in this option. First, you need to be careful with the timing; the target service configuration is handled asynchronously, so there's a chance that the service is still being created. Second, the failure to find the service in the OSGi service registry may be due to some other unforeseen reason and may not be related to any problems in the configuration object itself.

The third option is to listen to the Log service for any log records that may be created by the Configuration Admin. This is the option described next. In the end, though, none of these three options is completely satisfactory.

Configuration listener

One suggestion for future versions of the Configuration Admin service is the inclusion of a `CM_FAILED` event state for the `ConfigurationEvent`, which should be used when a configuration update or delete fails due to a `ConfigurationException`. This event should allow configuring bundles to know whether their actions have failed.

5.6.1   *Log listener*

In order to listen to the Log service, you first need to make sure that there's a Log service implementation. If there's no Log service implementation, the Configuration Admin will just drop the exception. As usual, you can download an implementation from the OSGi Bundle Repository (OBR), such as the Apache Felix Log Service. Make sure you install it in Felix.

The next listing shows how you can read log records that have been logged using the OSGi Log service.

Listing 5.9   Log listener

```
public class LogListenerImpl implements BundleActivator, LogListener {

    public void stop(BundleContext context) throws Exception {
    }

    @SuppressWarnings("unchecked")
    public void start(BundleContext context) throws Exception {
        ServiceReference serviceReference =
            context.getServiceReference(                        ❶ Retrieve OSGi
                LogReaderService.class.getName());                Log service

        LogReaderService logReader =
            (LogReaderService) context.getService(serviceReference);

        logReader.addLogListener(this);
                                                    ❷ Add log listener
        // ...

    }

    public void logged(LogEntry entry) {
        if (entry.getException() instanceof               ❸ Log-created
            ConfigurationException) {                        callback
            ConfigurationException configExcep =
                (ConfigurationException) entry.getException();

            if (configExcep.getProperty().equals("port")) {
                // ...
            }
        }
    }
}
```

First, retrieve the `LogReader` service from the OSGi service registry ❶. Add the `LogListener` implementation to the `LogReader` service ❷. Make sure the object implements the `LogListener` interface. Finally, in the `logged()` method, check to see if the log record contains a `ConfigurationException` ❸. A `ConfigurationException` has a `getProperty()` method, which returns the name of the offending property.

5.6.2 Application logging

Logging is an important and useful feature. Should you use the OSGi Log service for logging application messages? Actually, you shouldn't. The OSGi Log service is simplistic and provides only the basic facilities for other services, like the Configuration Admin, that can't assume a better option, such as Log4J, is available.

You don't have this restriction when developing your own applications and application frameworks. For example, you can install Apache's Common Logging and use it in your bundles instead of the OSGi Log service. But the OSGi Log service has one keen advantage: it's started together with the framework, so it's always available and ready, even when a bundle tries to use it very early in the bootstrap process.

We'll look at this question of start level in chapter 10, but next we'll consider the important issue of automating configuration handling by means of management agents.

5.7 Management agents

Let's take a step back and look again into the configuring bundle that sets the port for the Notification Broker service. As we've discussed, the port is likely to be configured by some IT administrator, who's unlikely to want to write a Java application implementing the configuring bundle functionality. Furthermore, it seems like the configuring bundle is mostly boilerplate code that could be replaced by some generic code, right?

Yes, configuring bundles are often generic and are commonly referenced as management agents. Their purpose is to provide a simple high-level interface to the system administrator, like a GUI, a command-line interface (CLI), or even just an input XML file. Management agents collect all of the user input and use it to configure the backend system. Again, having the Configuration Admin as a mediator facilitates the creation of management agents, because you can develop a single management agent that interacts with several different target services through a single common interface—the interface of the Configuration Admin service.

Which management agent should you use to configure the Notification Broker service? For now, we'll ignore this issue and revisit it in chapter 11, where we'll discuss management in detail, particularly around the JMX technology.

But one interesting aspect of management agents with respect to configuration is the issue of metadata. How can the target service provide enough metadata to the management agent so that the agent has a better understanding of the configuration model without having to be hardcoded to work with a particular target service?

For example, when the management agent creates a configuration object that's the target of the Notification Broker service, how does it know that the only property

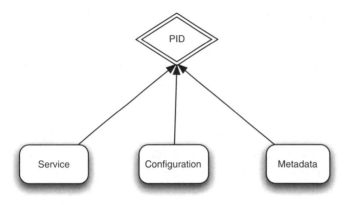

Figure 5.6
**Service, configuration, and
metadata objects are linked
through the service PID.**

supported is a port? Furthermore, how can we validate the property being set? For example, we'd like to reject a port value that's below 1000. This role of providing metadata is the responsibility of the OSGi Metatype service, which we'll discuss next.

5.7.1 *Validating configuration using a configuration model*

The OSGi Metatype service allows you to associate metadata with a service. This metadata includes a localizable description, graphic icons, and, most important, information about the attributes of the service, such as the name of the attribute, its cardinality, whether it's required or optional, its type, and a mechanism for validating values that are to be assigned to it. For instance, with the Metatype service, you can annotate the Notification Broker service stating that it has a single required attribute, named `port`, which is of type integer, and only accepts values ranging from 1000 to 10000.

The association between a metadata object and a service is done though a service PID. In other words, a metadata object points to a service PID. What this means is that not only can you associate the metadata with a service, but you can also associate it with a configuration object through the use of the managed service's PID, thus allowing a configuring bundle to retrieve the metadata and use it as the configuration model for the target service. In this role, the PID becomes the key that links together the service object, the configuration object, and the metadata object, as shown in figure 5.6.

5.7.2 *The metadata provider*

Following up with our example, let's change the `NotificationBrokerActivator` so that it provides metadata that can be used to validate the port configuration for the Notification Broker service, as shown in the following listing.

Listing 5.10   Metatype provider for the Notification Broker service

```
public class NotificationBrokerActivator implements BundleActivator,
    ManagedService, MetaTypeProvider {

    private ObjectClassDefinition configurationSchema;
    private ServiceRegistration registration;
```

**Implement
MetaTypeProvider
❶ interface**

```
private BundleContext context;
private NotificationBrokerImpl broker;
private ServiceRegistration brokerRegistration;

public void start(BundleContext bundleContext) throws Exception {
    this.context = bundleContext;

    initializeSchema();                          ⟵┐    Initialize validation
                                                 ❷    schema
    Dictionary<String, Object> properties =
        new Hashtable<String, Object>();

    properties.put(Constants.SERVICE_PID,
        "manning.osgi.notification.broker");

    registration = bundleContext.registerService(
            new String [] {ManagedService.class.getName(),
              MetaTypeProvider.class.getName()
            },
            this,
            properties
    );
}

public String[] getLocales() {
    return null;
}

public ObjectClassDefinition getObjectClassDefinition(String pid,
        String locale) {

    if (configurationSchema.getID().equals(pid)) {    ⟵┐    Return
        return configurationSchema;                   ❸    target PID
    } else {
        return null;
    }
}
```

You start by implementing the interface org.osgi.service.metatype.Meta-TypeProvider ❶. When registering the target service, you must also specify the MetaTypeProvider interface as part of your service interfaces. This is so that any consuming client can safely cast the service to the MetaTypeProvider interface.

The MetaTypeProvider interface defines two methods. The getObjectClass-Definition() method should return the metadata definition for the service object associated with the PID parameter. In this case, you return an ObjectClassDefinition object if the "manning.osgi.notification.broker" PID is used ❸. The initialization of this object is done at ❷, which is shown in listing 5.11. Finally, there's also a get-Locales() method, which should return the available locales for the metadata. Localization of metadata is important, because some of the information is related to descriptions and may be directly surfaced to the end users.

> **WARNING** Don't forget to import the package org.osgi.service.metatype in the bundle's MANIFEST.MF file to use the OSGi Metatype service.

Listing 5.11 ObjectClassDefinition for the Notification broker service

```
private void initializeSchema() {
    configurationSchema = new ObjectClassDefinition() {

        AttributeDefinition [] requiredAttrs = ...

        public AttributeDefinition[]
            getAttributeDefinitions(int filter) {
            return (filter == ObjectClassDefinition.ALL ||
                filter == ObjectClassDefinition.REQUIRED) ?
                    requiredAttrs : null;                     ◄──┐  Definitions used
        }                                                        ❶  for validation

        public String getDescription() {
            return "Configuration for Notification Broker service";
        }

        public String getID() {
            return "manning.osgi.notification.broker";   ◄──┐  Target PID
        }                                                    ❷  to be validated

        public InputStream getIcon(int arg0) throws IOException {
            return null;
        }

        public String getName() {
            return getID();
        }};
    }
```

As you've seen, an `ObjectClassDefinition` is associated with a PID. The method `getID()` should return this PID ❷. The `ObjectClassDefinition` provides a description and an icon, but the main information consists of its attribute definitions. Attributes may be required or optional. The `getAttributeDefinitions()` method returns the `AttributeDefinition` for this object class definition ❶, filtered by the following options: all attributes, only the required attributes, or only the optional attributes.

You can see how to initialize the required attributes for the Notification Broker service in the next listing.

Listing 5.12 AttributeDefinition for the Notification Broker service

```
AttributeDefinition [] requiredAttrs =
    new AttributeDefinition [] {
        new AttributeDefinition() {

            String [] defaultValues =
                new String[] {"8080"};

            public int getCardinality() {        ◄──┐  Configuration
                return 0;                            ❶  cardinality
            }
```

```java
public String[] getDefaultValue() {
    return defaultValues;
}
```
← ❷ **Configuration default values**

```java
public String getDescription() {
    return "Port for remote publishers.";
}

public String getID() {
    return "manning.osgi.notification.broker"
        + ".port";
}
```
← ❸ **Configuration PID**

```java
public String getName() {
    return "port";
}

public String[] getOptionLabels() {
    return null;
}

public String[] getOptionValues() {
    return null;
}

public int getType() {
    return AttributeDefinition.INTEGER;
}
```
← ❹ **Configuration type**

```java
public String validate(String value) {
    Integer portValue = null;

    try {
        portValue =
            Integer.valueOf(value);
    } catch (NumberFormatException e) {
        return "Not a valid integer.";
    }
```
❺ **Invalid configuration**

```java
    if (portValue < 1000 || portValue
        > 10000) {
```
← ❻ **Check configuration values**

```java
        return "Port must be set in the range [1000,
        ➥ 10000].";
    } else {
        return ""; // valid;
    }
```
← ❼ **Valid configuration**

```java
    }
  }
};
```

The notification broker object class has a single attribute definition, which is that of the port configuration. All attributes must have a unique ID, which generally is the object class ID appended with the attribute name ❸. You also need to specify the cardinality of the attribute, where 0 means a single value ❶, its type ❹, and if it has any default values ❷.

But likely the most important aspect of the `AttributeDefinition` class is the `validate()` method. This method takes as an argument the *stringified* value of the property and returns whether the value is valid. In this case, you first try to convert the string value that represents the port to a proper `Integer` ❺. If the conversion fails, you return a message indicating the failure ❻. Next, you check to see if the integer is within the allowed range. If it's within the range, you return an empty string, which indicates that the input value is valid ❼. If no validation is available for an attribute, the `validate()` method should return a `null` value.

Next, let's take a look at the configuring bundle, which is responsible for consuming this metadata.

5.7.3 *The metadata consumer*

At the configuring bundle, you retrieve the `MetaTypeProvider` interface and validate the configuration properties. You update the configuration object only if all the configuration properties are valid, as shown in the following listing.

Listing 5.13 Validating configuration

```
Dictionary<String, Object> configProperties =
    new Hashtable<String, Object>();

configProperties.put("port", 10);

ServiceReference [] serviceReferences =
    bundleContext.getServiceReferences(
            MetaTypeProvider.class.getName(),
            "(" + Constants.SERVICE_PID + "="
            + "manning.osgi.notification.broker" + ")");

MetaTypeProvider metaTypeProvider =
    (MetaTypeProvider)
        bundleContext.getService(serviceReferences[0]);        ◁──┐ Retrieve
                                                                   │ MetaTypeProvider
                                                                 ❶ service
ObjectClassDefinition ocd =
    metaTypeProvider.getObjectClassDefinition(
        "manning.osgi.notification.broker",
        null);

AttributeDefinition [] attrDefs =
    ocd.getAttributeDefinitions(
        ObjectClassDefinition.ALL);                          ◁──┐ Get attribute
                                                              ❷ definitions
for (AttributeDefinition attrDef : attrDefs) {
    Object configPropertyValue =
        configProperties.get(attrDef.getName());

    if (configPropertyValue != null) {
        String validationMessage =
            attrDef.validate(
```

```
                configPropertyValue.toString());              ◄─────┐  Validate each
                                                             ❸       attribute
          if (!validationMessage.equals("")) {
              throw new IllegalArgumentException(validationMessage);
          }
      }
  }
                                                        ❹  Update if all
configuration.update(configProperties);          ◄─────┘   are valid
```

You start by creating a dictionary that contains the configuration properties that need to be validated. Then you retrieve the `MetaTypeProvider` interface using the PID of the managed service representing the Notification Broker service ❶. Using the `MetaTypeProvider`, you retrieve the `ObjectClassDefinition`. Next, you retrieve the attribute definition for all the attributes ❷. For each attribute definition, you retrieve the corresponding configuration property value using the attribute definition name as the key. In this case, the only attribute definition you have is for the `port` property. You then convert the property value to a string and invoke the `validate()` method ❸. If the return isn't an empty string, which signifies that the input value is valid, you throw an illegal argument exception. If all properties are valid, you update the configuration property ❹.

> **NOTE** For the sake of simplicity, this example doesn't check to see if the configuration properties include all required attributes. We're also not checking to see if the configuration properties include any property that isn't defined as part of the metadata.

If this example is executed, you should get the following exception message:

```
java.lang.IllegalArgumentException: Port must be set in the range [1000, 10000].
```

Validating configuration at the Configuration Admin service

Were you surprised by the fact that you had to explicitly use the configuration metadata in the configuring bundle? I know I was when I first coded this; it seemed to me that this should have been one of the responsibilities of the Configuration Admin service. In other words, any time a consuming bundle updates a configuration object, the Configuration Admin should check to see if the target service provides any metadata, in which case it should use the metadata to validate the configuration before accepting it. If the configuration isn't valid, the admin could promptly raise an exception to the configuring bundle.

This suggested approach not would only avoid a lot of boilerplate code in the consuming bundle, but it would decrease the chance of persisting a configuration that's invalid, which is problematic to handle, as illustrated in section 5.5.

It's true that in some cases a management agent still needs to retrieve the configuration metadata to prepare a better interface for the end user, such as by using the icon information. Nevertheless, there are several simple cases where it makes sense to allow the Configuration Admin to validate the configuration properties before accepting them.

At this point, you understand how to develop a general-purpose configuring bundle and you are familiar with its advantages. But are there any disadvantages to having management agents? Considering that a management agent can arbitrarily configure bundles, one disadvantage is the lack of access control; how do you keep a client from configuring some target service if it doesn't have permission to do so? We'll briefly look into this aspect of security next, and we'll investigate it in detail in chapter 10.

5.7.4 *Protecting against malicious configuring bundles*

Another aspect of configuring bundles is access control. How can you prevent a malicious bundle from configuring some invalid port and thus shutting down the notification broker in the processor?

The first line of defense is that the OSGi API is local. For a malicious bundle to get hold of the Configuration Admin service and create an invalid configuration, it must first be installed in the OSGi framework, which means that the user who installed the bundle had enough credentials to do so.

In addition, the Configuration Admin service associates each configuration object with a single bundle through the association of a bundle location. Remember how we used the `getConfiguration(String)` method in section 5.2.2? This automatically associates the configuring bundle's location with the configuration object. Furthermore, you can invoke the method `ConfigurationAdmin.getConfiguration(String targetServicePID, String location)` to explicitly specify the location to be associated with the configuration object. Later, if any other bundle tries to update this same configuration object without using the same location, the operation will be denied with a security exception.

The result of this behavior is that only a single configuring bundle may handle a specific configuration object. This helps safeguard the managed services against improper setting of the configuration. But as it stands, this has been found to be too restrictive, and the newer version of the Configuration Admin specification is reconsidering this approach, which is likely to be relaxed.

5.7.5 *Achieving atomicity across configuration updates*

It's not uncommon that a management agent may need to update several target services as a unit. For example, suppose you'd like to update the configuration of a firewall service to open port 8080 for incoming connections and update the Notification Broker service to use this port. If the firewall service fails to update its configuration, then there's no point in updating the Notification Broker service. You want to perform a set of configuration object updates in a single atomic transaction, as shown in figure 5.7. Either all are successful or none should be executed.

This is a common requirement in systems where there are a lot of service dependencies, which tends to be the case in enterprise applications. Can we achieve this using the Configuration Admin service?

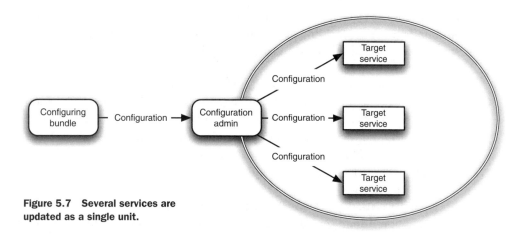

Figure 5.7 Several services are updated as a single unit.

Unfortunately, there's no direct support for any transactions in the Configuration Admin. To be able to implement this, the configuring bundle would have to be prepared to compensate for completed actions, a concept borrowed from workflow languages such as Web Services Business Process Execution Language (WS-BPEL). For example, first you could update the configuration for the firewall service and wait for its success. Then you could update the configuration for the notification broker and verify its result. If the latter fails, you'd need to undo, that is, *compensate for*, the configuration change done previously in the firewall service. Needless to say, this is an arduous process that can easily fail. Support for transactional updates is another feature that would be welcomed in the Configuration Admin.

5.8 Summary

Most applications need configuration data before they can service their end users. Configuration should be provided through a separate mechanism instead of being hardcoded into the service interfaces and service implementations.

The OSGi platform includes a Configuration Admin service, which allows configuring bundles to provide configuration objects to managed target services through an admin. The admin is responsible for persisting the configuration and managing its access control. In addition, the Configuration Admin decouples the producer from the consumer of the configuration, thus allowing a producer to provide configuration before the consumer is started.

The association of a configuration to a target service is done through a service PID. A target service must implement the `ManagedService` interface to be able to receive configuration objects. In addition, a target service may implement `ManagedService-Factory` in the case where each configuration object gets associated with a new service.

The Configuration Admin supports only Java simple types, and arrays or vectors of these, as configuration. In addition, it doesn't provide a facility for verifying that a configuration object has been successfully accepted and used by a target service. Another shortcoming of the Configuration Admin service is the lack of transactional support so that multiple services could be updated as a single unit, or none at all if any of them fails to update.

One way to decrease problems with configuration is to use the OSGi Metatype service to provide a configuration model, which can be used to validate the configuration prior to updates in a target service. The Metatype service allows a target service to describe each configuration attribute, indicating its type, a localizable description, default values, and its cardinality, and also to provide a validation method. Management agents, which are generic configuring bundles, tend to be heavy consumers of the Metatype service.

Finally, we used the OSGi Bundle Repository to find an implementation of the Configuration Admin service. Several implementations are provided, and we selected one from Eclipse Equinox instead of the one provided by Apache Felix to prove that the decoupling of service interfaces and service implementations indeed works.

In the next chapter, we'll look at another important OSGi service, the Event Admin.

A world of events

This chapter covers

- Publishing events using the Event Admin service
- Subscribing to events using the Event Admin service
- Trade-offs between publishing events in a blocked and unblocked manner
- Subscribing to specific events by using filtering
- Issues related to ordering of events and exception handling within event handlers
- Improving decoupling by exchanging events
- Subscribing to OSGi framework events
- The extender pattern

In this chapter you'll learn about the OSGi Event Admin service. The Event Admin provides a generic mechanism for handling events. Using the Event Admin service, you can not only receive events but also generate your own set of application events to be received by other applications. By employing the Event Admin service, you can create applications that communicate solely by exchanging events and thus take another important step toward building more scalable and flexible systems.

Why spend a full chapter on the subject of event handling? An application's ecosystem contains a plethora of events, including not only IT-related events but application events and even events generated by the OSGi framework itself, which you can leverage to implement what's known as the *extender pattern*. As you'll see, software systems are a world of events!

We'll start our investigation of the Event Admin service by exploring its underlying publish-subscribe model.

6.1   *The publish-subscribe model*

In this section, we'll explore two scenarios that are centered on the dispatching and handling of application events. The first one is a login auditor, and the second is a travel reservation system. Let's look at the details.

Consider a system that's hosting several web service applications. For example, one application allows a user to find the credit score of a client, and another allows a user to get pricing information for an item. As is customary, a user must first log into the web service application before being able to use it. Our goal is to audit the user logins. Note that we're not actually performing the authentication/authorization of the user login, but rather just auditing the granted or not-granted login access after it has happened.

One way of accomplishing this is to generate a login request every time a user attempts to log into one of the web service applications. Then we can define different auditor applications that receive the login request events and use them to perform their auditing. As an example, we could have two types of auditors; the first one simply logs the login request into a database for later auditing in case some discrepancy is found in any of the serving applications. A second auditor verifies in real time the number of unsuccessful login attempts and issues a warning if this number crosses some threshold. In this simple scenario, we'll call the web service applications that send login-request events *publishers*, and we'll consider the auditors who wish to receive login-request events as having subscribed to these events, or simply as *subscribers*. This is illustrated in figure 6.1.

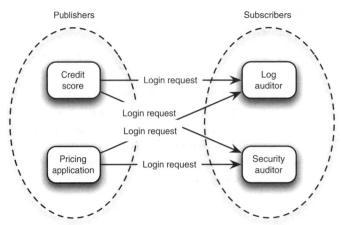

Figure 6.1   Web service applications publish login requests to multiple auditors.

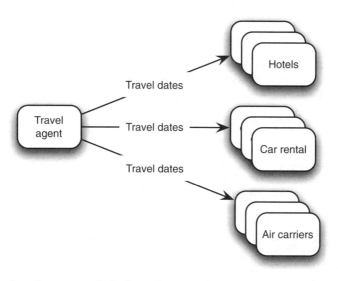

Figure 6.2 The travel agent publishes travel dates to multiple hotels, car rental companies, and air carriers.

Another example is that of a travel reservation (agent) application. In this case, a user inputs the travel dates, and the system tries to find the best provider of car rentals, hotels, and flights for the requested dates. As expected, the travel agent application is the publisher, and the car rental companies, hotels, and air carriers are the subscribers, as shown in figure 6.2.

Both of these examples share a set of common infrastructure requirements:

- *The publishers should not have direct knowledge of the subscribers.*

  For example, the credit score application doesn't know about the login-request auditors; likewise, the travel agent application doesn't need to know which air carriers are being evaluated (for example, American Airlines, United Airlines, British Airlines).

- *New publishers and subscribers may come and go dynamically without impacting the other components of the system.*

  For example, in the case of the travel arrangement application, initially we may only request quotes from a single car rental company (for example, Hertz) and later decide to add a second one (for example, Avis). The travel agent application doesn't need to change regardless of the number of car rental companies being evaluated.

- *Subscribers shouldn't block the publishers.*

  For example, even if no auditors are available, the web service applications are still able to do their work properly, without having to wait for a response from the auditors. In the case of the travel agent application, it's true that eventually the application will need a response from the subscribers, but it can continue doing other tasks until the response is received. For example, it can first request a quote from the car rental company and then immediately request a quote from the air carriers without waiting for the car rental response to arrive.

These infrastructure requirements are achieved by employing an event-driven architecture.

DEFINITION An event-driven architecture is one in which the components interact by exchanging events instead of communicating using the typical request-response paradigm.

Table 6.1 summarizes the differences between event-driven and request-response styles.

Table 6.1   Event-driven and request-response styles

Characteristics	Request-response	Event-driven
Granularity	One-to-one	Many-to-many
Flow control	Blocking	Asynchronous
Provider/consumer	Fixed	Varies dynamically
Response	Supported	Not supported

As you'll see next, the Event Admin service helps you to realize an event-driven architecture in OSGi.

6.2   *The Event Admin*

A mediator is needed so you can decouple the publishers from the subscribers. The OSGi Event Admin service is such a mediator. When you use this service, the publishers and subscribers are only aware of the Event Admin and not of each other, as shown in figure 6.3.

In our login auditor use case, the credit score and pricing applications send the login request event to the EventAdmin, which then takes care of publishing the event

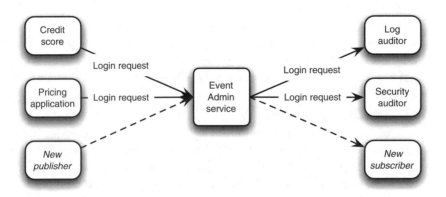

Figure 6.3   Event Admin mediates web service applications and auditors.

to all subscribed auditors. In the following listing, you can see the details of the subscribers, that is, the auditor applications.

Listing 6.1 Bundle activator for login-event subscriber

```
import java.util.Dictionary;
import java.util.Properties;

import org.osgi.framework.BundleActivator;
import org.osgi.framework.BundleContext;
import org.osgi.service.event.EventConstants;
import org.osgi.service.event.EventHandler;

public class SubscriberActivator implements BundleActivator {

    @SuppressWarnings("unchecked")
    public void start(BundleContext context) throws Exception {
        SimpleSubscriber subscriber = new SimpleSubscriber();

        Dictionary dict = new Properties();
        dict.put(EventConstants.EVENT_TOPIC,          ❶ Specify topic as
            "manning/osgi/LoginEvent");                   service property

        context.registerService(EventHandler.class.getName(),
                subscriber, dict);                    Register EventHandler
    }                                              ❷ service interface

    public void stop(BundleContext context) throws Exception {
        // ...
    }
}
```

When registering the `EventHandler` service, you need to specify the `EVENT_TOPIC` service property ❶. To act as a subscriber of events from the Event Admin service, it's enough to register a service object using the `EventHandler` service interface in the OSGi service registry ❷. This follows the whiteboard pattern, insofar as you don't need to retrieve the Event Admin service itself. Rather, you just register with the OSGi service registry (that is, the whiteboard), and let the Event Admin retrieve all event-handler services.

6.2.1 Topics

The Event Admin service works by defining separate delivery channels, or destinations, called topics, very much like the Java Messaging Service (JMS). A publisher sends events to a topic, and a subscriber receives events from a topic. This allows you to partition or segregate the events, thus permitting subscribers to select which types of events they wish to receive. As illustrated in figure 6.4, multiple publishers can publish to the same topic, and a single publisher can publish to multiple topics.

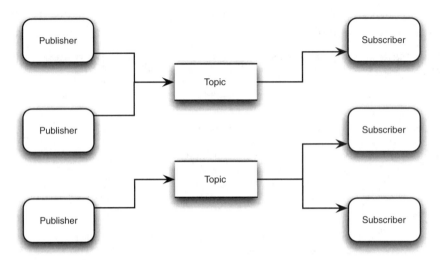

Figure 6.4   Topics are logical channels used to partition events.

This m-n granularity applies to
subscribers as well. A topic name is
specified using the syntax shown in
figure 6.5.

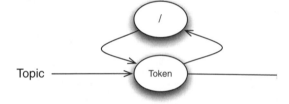

**Figure 6.5   Topic names are a collection
of slash-separated tokens.**

In our case, we'll define the following topic name:

```
"manning/osgi/LoginEvent"
```

In this example, the subscriber is stating that it wants to receive events of the type
Login.

> **NOTE**   It's customary to name the topic by using the Java class name that rep-
> resents the event, replacing the dot (.) with a forward slash (/).

Finally, let's look at the sample EventHandler implementation in the following listing.

Listing 6.2   EventHandler implementation

```
public class SimpleSubscriber implements EventHandler {

    public void handleEvent(Event event) {                          ❶ EventHandler
        System.out.println("Received event on topic = " +              callback
            event.getTopic());
        for (String propertyName :
          event.getPropertyNames()) {                               ❷ Returns all event
            System.out.println("\t" + propertyName + " = " +           properties
                event.getProperty(propertyName));
```

```
        }
    }
}
```

As expected, you need to implement the `EventHandler` interface, which gives you the `handleEvent(Event)` callback method ❶. All login events sent to our topic arrive through this callback as `org.osgi.service.event.Event` objects, which serve as containers of event properties ❷. In the next section, we'll look at the details of the `Event` object.

6.2.2 *Event object*

An `Event` object contains the topic name that it's associated with and a set of event properties, as illustrated in figure 6.6. An event property follows the same format as a service property. The rationale for this is explored in later sections.

You can't simply send any Java object through the Event Admin service; instead, you have to use the Event Admin's `Event` class. The reason for this is that it enforces the structure of an event as a set of event properties. This establishes a common contract between the subscribers and publishers without having them share a common Java interface, as you're used to when dealing with OSGi services.

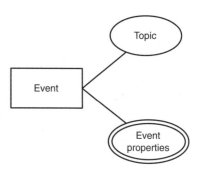

Figure 6.6 An event contains a topic name and event properties.

In this case, you can define a login event to contain two interesting event properties:

- `userid`—The user identification used to log in
- `timestamp`—The time at which the login request was attempted

Establishing these two properties allows any publisher to send an event to our auditor subscriber, provided they include these two properties.

The next listing shows a publisher of login events.

Listing 6.3 Bundle activator for login-event publisher

```
public class PublisherActivator implements BundleActivator {

    public void start(BundleContext context) throws Exception {
        LoginEventPublisher publisher =
            getPublisher(context);

        publisher.sendLoginEvent("anonymous");     ❶ Publish event for
                                                      anonymous user
    }

    private LoginEventPublisher getPublisher(BundleContext context) {
        ServiceReference ref =
            context.getServiceReference(EventAdmin.class.getName());

        LoginEventPublisher publisher = null;        Retrieve the
                                                   EventAdmin service ❷
```

```
        if (ref != null) {
            EventAdmin eventAdmin =
                (EventAdmin) context.getService(ref);
            publisher =
                new LoginEventPublisher(eventAdmin);        Use EventAdmin
        }                                              ❸  in publisher

        return publisher;
    }

    public void stop(BundleContext context) throws Exception {
        // ...
    }
}
```

Unlike the subscriber, the publisher must retrieve the EventAdmin service from the OSGi registry ❷. This is because the publisher must actively use it to send events. Subscribers passively wait for events to be pushed to them. Next, you instantiate the publisher object, pass it the EventAdmin service ❸, and use it to send login events for an anonymous user ❶.

The LoginEventPublisher is a simple wrapper on top of the EventAdmin:

Listing 6.4 Login-event publisher

```
public class LoginEventPublisher {

    private final EventAdmin admin;

    public LoginEventPublisher(EventAdmin admin) {
        this.admin = admin;
    }

    @SuppressWarnings("unchecked")
    public void sendLoginEvent(String userid) {

        Dictionary payload = new Properties();          ❶ Set the userid
        payload.put("userid", userid);                     event property
        payload.put("timestamp",
                System.currentTimeMillis());                  Set the timestamp
                                                         ❷  event property
        Event event =
            new Event("manning/osgi/LoginEvent",        ❸ Create event with topic
            payload);                                        and event properties

        admin.postEvent(event);                          Publish event
    }                                                ❹  asynchronously
}
```

The LoginEventPublisher is a simple wrapper on top of the EventAdmin. When asked to send a login event, the LoginEventPublisher creates a dictionary containing the two relevant event properties, userid ❶ and timestamp, the latter being retrieved from the

JVM's wall clock ❷. Next, it creates an `EventAdmin` event with the event properties ❸ and the destination topic of `"manning/osgi/LoginEvent"` and publishes it by calling the method `EventAdmin.postEvent(event)` ❹.

> **Event constants**
>
> You should avoid hardcoding the event properties and topic names; it's a good idea to define constants for these instead:
>
> ```
> public interface LoginEventConstants {
>    final static String TOPIC_NAME =
>     "manning/osgi/LoginEvent";
>    final static String USERID = "userid";
>    final static String TIMESTAMP = "timestamp";
> }
> ```
>
> But keep in mind that you don't need to and don't want to import this interface directly by the publishers; instead, you can use the interface as way of documenting the constants.

In this section, you learned how to publish and subscribe to events by using the Event Admin service. But for those used to other message-oriented middleware (MOM), such as JMS, so far the Event Admin seems lacking. In the next section, we'll remedy this by tackling the advanced features of the Event Admin, such as event filtering.

6.3   *Advanced event handling*

In this section, we'll look into more advanced scenarios, such as understanding the hierarchical nature of topic names, blocking the dispatch of events, and setting up filters on event subscriptions.

6.3.1   *Blocking dispatch and event-delivery guarantees*

So far in the login event auditor scenario, we've been working under the assumption that the web service applications that are publishing the login request events aren't concerned if the subscribed auditors fail to function.

For example, the credit score application could post the login event to the log auditor, and the system could crash before the auditor had a chance to log the login event, yet it crashes after the credit score application has already done some work on behalf of the logged-in user, as shown in figure 6.7. In this case, even though the user has been authenticated properly, the user's activities may go unaudited.

You can avoid this situation by using the blocking operation `EventAdmin.send-Event(Event)`. In the case of `sendEvent()`, the publisher is blocked; that is, its thread does no further work until all the available subscribers have returned from their

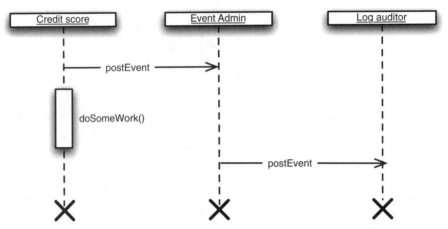

Figure 6.7 `postEvent()` publishes events asynchronously, allowing the publisher to proceed with work.

event-handling methods, as shown in figure 6.8. In our case, this means that the credit score application would only be able to continue processing after the log auditor has received the login event and properly logged it to some storage.

Generally, you should favor the nonblocking `postEvent()` method, because it allows the publishers to continue working concurrently with the subscribers. But you can use `sendEvent()` for those cases where you need to synchronize the publishers

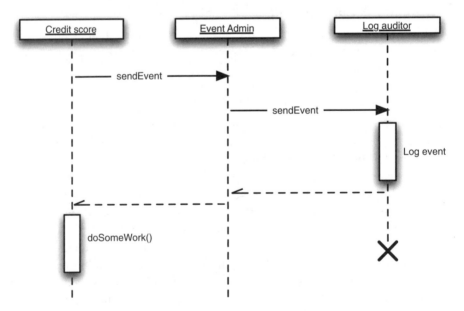

Figure 6.8 `sendEvent()` publishes events synchronously, blocking the publisher.

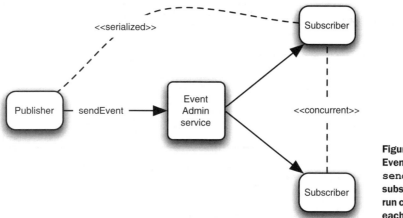

**Figure 6.9
Even in a blocking
sendEvent() call,
subscribers may still
run concurrently with
each other.**

and the subscribers, perhaps to avoid some race condition or to manage the flow of control.

> **WARNING** An EventHandler implementation should be careful to return as quickly as possible from its handleEvent() method; it could be blocking its publisher from proceeding if it is published using the postEvent() method.

What if the security auditor subscribed later; are there any guarantees that the log auditor would always receive the same event before the security auditor? No, the blocking sendEvent() method only guarantees synchronization between a publisher and its subscribers; it doesn't guarantee any synchronization between the subscribers themselves, which can, depending on the vendor's implementation, potentially run concurrently among themselves, as shown in figure 6.9.

Conversely, if a publisher sends multiple events using the same thread, the Event-Admin does guarantee that the order of the events will be kept for each of its subscribers. This same behavior is used for the nonblocking postEvent() method.

> **NOTE** The EventAdmin makes a copy of the available subscribers when an event is published, thus avoiding the situation where a new subscriber receives an event that was dispatched before the subscriber existed. Furthermore, before delivering the event to the subscriber, the EventAdmin makes sure that the subscriber is still registered to receive events, and that it hasn't removed itself from the EventAdmin service.

Continuing with our scenario, let's say that you want the log auditor to inform the credit score application when it fails to log the login request event, thus indicating that the credit score application should stop. To accomplish this, could the log auditor just raise an exception? No, an exception raised by a subscriber is caught by the EventAdmin, which may log it, but otherwise simply moves on to the next subscriber in the list, as shown in figure 6.10.

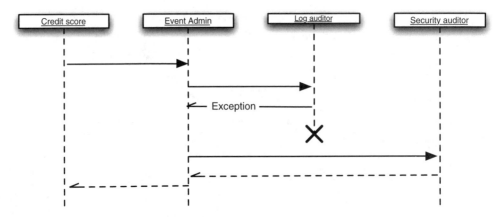

Figure 6.10   An exception from a subscriber doesn't stop the dispatching of events.

Even though you can block a publisher and have it wait for the subscribers to return, publishers and subscribers are still decoupled and have no mechanism by which they can respond to each other.

> **WARNING**   It's important to keep in mind that the decoupling between publisher and subscribers means that there's a bigger chance of deadlocks. For example, this would be the case if a publisher acquires a monitor (for example, a synchronized keyword) and then dispatches an event using the blocking call sendEvent() to a subscriber, which also needs the same monitor.

If you do need to wait for a response, then you should either switch to a request-response communication style or have the responder send an event back to the original requester, thus making an application both a publisher and a subscriber of events.

Table 6.2 summarizes the dispatching semantics for the EventAdmin for both postEvent() and sendEvent() methods.

Table 6.2   Event-dispatching semantics

Semantic	postEvent()	sendEvent()
Dispatch	Nonblocking	Blocking
Exception in subscriber	Continue to next	Continue to next
Ordering between subscribers	No guarantees	No guarantees
Ordering between events	Kept*	Kept*

* Ordering of events is kept if dispatched in the same thread

Next, we'll look into how to create better subscriptions by exploring the hierarchical nature of the topic names.

6.3.2 *Hierarchical topic names*

As you may recall from section 6.1, we defined a scenario where a travel agent sends an event containing the travel and return dates to car rental, hotel, and flight provider applications. These provider applications must respond to the travel agent with their quotes, so that the agent can select the best quote and finalize the booking. To send a quote to the travel agent, the provider applications can publish their quotes to another set of topics, and the travel agent, now acting as a subscriber, can subscribe to these new topics.

For example, you could define three topics, representing each type of event, as follows:

```
"manning/osgi/TravelAgent/CarEvent"
"manning/osgi/TravelAgent/HotelEvent"
"manning/osgi/TravelAgent/FlightEvent"
```

By doing so, you allow each booking application to send its quote to the proper topic. For example, the car rental application would send an event that contains the quote for booking a car during the requested travel dates to the topic `"manning/osgi/TravelAgent/car"`. At the end, the travel agent receives all the quotes from all the subscribers and selects the best ones to finalize the booking.

You can subscribe to multiple topics by using an array of `Strings` as the value of the `EVENT_TOPIC` property:

```
Dictionary dict = new Properties();
dict.put(EventConstants.EVENT_TOPIC,
    new String [] {"manning/osgi/TravelAgent/CarEvent",
    "manning/osgi/TravelAgent/HotelEvent",
    "manning/osgi/TravelAgent/FlightEvent"});
context.registerService(EventHandler.class.getName(),
    subscriber, dict);
```

> **NOTE** This approach is preferable to registering the same `EventHandler` instance multiple times, each using a different topic.

But rather than individually subscribing to each topic, you can instead subscribe to

```
"manning/osgi/TravelAgent/*"
```

This subscription receives events sent to any of the three topics presented previously (car, hotel, flight), simplifying the subscriber logic.

Matching topic names

The topic `"manning/osgi/TravelAgent/*"` wouldn't receive events sent to the following topics:

```
"manning/osgi/TravelAgent/HotelEvent/USA"
"manning/osgi/TravelAgent"
```

> **(continued)**
>
> In other words, the topic `"manning/osgi/TravelAgent/*"` relates to topics whose names have precisely four hierarchical levels. In the case of `"manning/osgi/Travel-Agent/HotelEvent/USA"`, there are five levels, and `"manning/osgi/TravelAgent"` has three levels, so neither match. Also, note that the topic names are not case-sensitive.

In essence, topics are the first line of filtering that a subscriber has. The ability to use the wildcard character (*) makes this even more powerful.

> **NOTE** An empty or nonexistent `EVENT_TOPIC` doesn't mean that the subscriber will receive all possible events; rather, it means that it won't receive any events at all. To receive all possible events, you can specify a sole * as the `EVENT_TOPIC`.

Does the Event Admin service define other ways of doing filtering? Yes, and this is the topic of the next section.

6.3.3   *Event filtering*

Looking back at the proposed solution in the previous section for the travel agent scenario, doesn't this setup of communicating through events seem excessively complicated? What does it buy you?

Consider the alternative of having the travel agent application directly invoke each of its vendors. Not only would you lose the flexibility of being able to add and remove vendors easily, but you'd also need to manually code the logic that selects the best quotes into the travel agent. One of the great advantages of using the `EventAdmin` service, or in fact any event-processing solution, is that you can associate complex filtering semantics with the subscriptions and thus implement some of the application logic in a declarative manner.

For example, let's say the travel agent is interested only in hotel quotes that are less than some specific value. This can be done using the predefined service property called `EVENT_FILTER`. An event filter is similar to the LDAP syntax-based service filters we studied at the beginning of this book, except that they act on event properties instead of service properties. Event properties follow the same rules as service properties.

In the case of the travel agent scenario, let's define an event property called `price` for the hotel quote event. Next, the hotel booking application must include this property in the hotel quote events it sends:

```
Dictionary payload = new Properties();
payload.put("price", 80);

Event event =
    new Event("manning/osgi/TravelAgent/HotelEvent", payload);

admin.postEvent(event);
```

Finally, the trade agent event handler can define the following event filter so that it receives only quotes that are less than $100:

```
Dictionary dict = new Properties();
dict.put(EventConstants.EVENT_TOPIC,
    "manning/osgi/TravelAgent/HotelEvent");
dict.put(EventConstants.EVENT_FILTER, "(price<100)");

context.registerService(EventHandler.class.getName(),
    travelAgentEventHandler, dict);
```

You can get arbitrarily complex with the event filter, adding several conjunctions and disjunctions. But it's still limited to Boolean predicates.

The constants EVENT_TOPIC and EVENT_FILTER are two of several constants defined by the Event Admin service. In the next section, we'll explore other predefined constants.

6.3.4 Predefined event properties

There are several standard event properties. Perhaps the most useful one is defined by the constant EventConstants.EVENT, whose value is the original event itself. The Event Admin service predefines several other event properties that may be used by publishers as a convention when deemed applicable. For example, the following code provides another way of retrieving the symbolic name of the installed bundle:

```
System.out.println("Bundle = " +
    event.getProperty(EventConstants.BUNDLE_SYMBOLICNAME));
```

Table 6.3 lists additional event properties. They're optional, so rely on them with caution as they may not be set by the vendor implementation.

Table 6.3 Event Admin standard event properties

Property name	Type
BUNDLE_SIGNER	String | Collection <String>
BUNDLE_VERSION	String
BUNDLE_SYMBOLICNAME	String
EVENT	Object
EXCEPTION	Throwable
EXCEPTION_MESSAGE	String
EXCEPTION_CLASS	String
MESSAGE	String
SERVICE	ServiceReference
SERVICE_ID	Long

Table 6.3 Event Admin standard event properties *(continued)*

Property name	Type
SERVICE_OBJECTCLASS	String [ ]
SERVICE_PID	String | Collection <String>
TIMESTAMP	Long

Most of these are self-explanatory. The BUNDLE_* properties contain information about the bundle that caused the event; the SERVICE_* properties can be used if the event is caused by a service or is related to a service change; the EXCEPTION_* properties are used if the event is caused by an exception; finally, the TIMESTAMP property can be used to annotate the creation time of the event.

Having gone through the advanced features of the Event Admin, you may still find it lacking in terms of messaging features. In the next section, we'll look at some of its major shortcomings.

6.4   *Event Admin shortcomings*

As you've seen, an event-driven architecture allows you to better decouple your applications. The Event Admin service provides you with a simple way to achieve this architecture, but there's a price to be paid for this simplicity. In this section, we'll explore several shortcomings of the Event Admin service. We'll look at ways of solving some of these problems if you're brave enough to extend or perhaps implement your own Event Admin service.

6.4.1   *Losing events*

Let's revisit our travel agent use case and consider the scenario where the machine crashes as the car rental application is processing the travel event posted by the travel agent application. When the machine comes back up, the whole process will have to commence again, as shown in figure 6.11. The original travel event was lost while it was being consumed, and a new event needs to be sent.

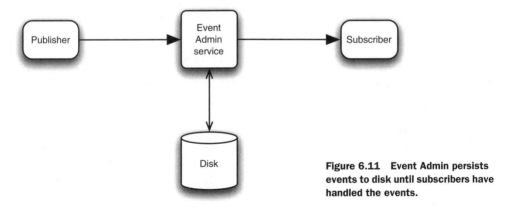

Figure 6.11 Event Admin persists events to disk until subscribers have handled the events.

Ideally, you'd like the original event to be redispatched to all subscribers that had not finished handling the event before the crash (or framework shutdown) happened. This could be achieved by having the Event Admin service implementation persist the events until their handling has been acknowledged. The persistence of an event could be configured as a property of the event itself or perhaps as an overall policy of the Event Admin service.

6.4.2 Feeble filtering

The second shortcoming is related to the filtering mechanism we used in section 6.3.3. Specifically, the travel agent application subscribed to receive only quote events whose `price` property is less than 100 (`price < 100`). But what if you wanted something more involved, such as the following?

- Receive only the quote event with the lowest price among the prices coming from all publishers (for example, car rentals).
- Receive events with the average price calculated from the price of all publishers.
- Add a travel agent's fee to the price.
- Disregard duplicate quote events.

Unfortunately, none of these are possible when using LDAP as the event-filtering mechanism.

The solution is to allow other filtering mechanisms to be plugged into the Event Admin service. If such extensibility was allowed, you'd be able to use other event-processing languages to perform what's commonly called complex event processing (CEP).

> ### CEP
> Complex event processing is an event-processing technology that allows the detection of complex relations between events, such as temporal constraints, For example, it could determine whether an event is followed by another event within a certain period of time.

Another issue related to filtering is that you can only filter *values* that are part of the event properties. For example, if you have an application event that contains 100 properties, and you want subscribers to be able to filter on any one of those 100 properties, you must copy and set these properties as event properties of the `org.osgi.services.event.Event` class. In other words, you must incur the overhead of creating an `EventAdmin`-based event representing the original application event and make sure that the new event contains a copy of all properties that can potentially be used for filtering. This can easily get out of hand on large systems.

One approach to solving this problem is to allow publishers to send Java objects directly to the Event Admin service and then map the manipulation of Java classes in the event-filtering language itself.

6.4.3   *Remote clients*

In the travel agent scenario, it may well be that some of the subscribers are located in remote OSGi framework instances. In such a case, how would you send events to remote event handlers?

The Event Admin service doesn't explicitly mention support for remote event handlers, but this is a conscious decision, because the remote invocation of a service is handled separately by the Remote Services specification and therefore is out of scope of this service (and of this chapter).

6.4.4   *Determinism*

The last issue we'll consider is the lack of determinism in the Event Admin service. How do you know which subscriber is notified first or the order of the dispatching of events when they're sent from different threads? All of these are underspecified and thus a problem when dealing with scenarios that need to have repeatable and deterministic behavior. For example, you may want the guarantee that the security auditor always runs before the log auditor in the login-event scenario, because the former has a higher priority in terms of importance.

In the end, despite its shortcomings, the Event Admin service provides enough functionality to support most common event-driven scenarios like those presented in this chapter. And even if you do need functionality that's currently not part of the Event Admin service, the underlying OSGi foundation on which it's based provides you with the flexibility to extend it as the need arises.

You've learned how to develop event-driven applications using the Event Admin. Let's take a step back and reconsider the advantages of using events.

6.5   *Decoupling using events*

In chapter 4, you learned that when two bundles interact through a service interface, they achieve implementation decoupling; you can change the implementation without impacting the bundles, but the bundles are still coupled to the interface of the service, as illustrated in figure 6.12. If the service interface changes, then so will the bundles.

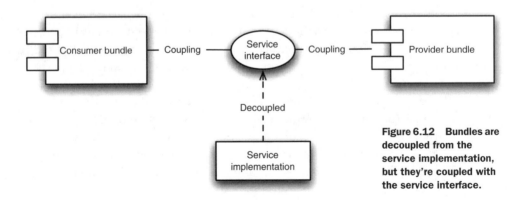

Figure 6.12 **Bundles are decoupled from the service implementation, but they're coupled with the service interface.**

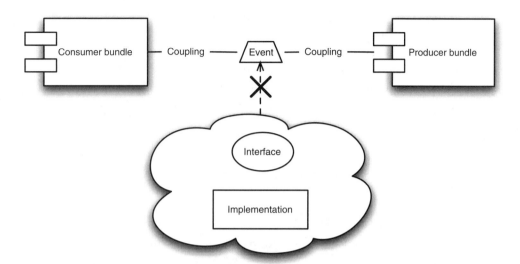

Figure 6.13 Bundles aren't tied to a service interface or its implementation. Instead, a bundle is coupled with the event data.

If two bundles interact by exchanging events, then you achieve a higher degree of decoupling, because an event doesn't define a contract for its usage. In other words, an event has a smaller surface area, as shown in figure 6.13.

For example, consider a Log service interface and a log event. The Log service interface is likely to define methods, such as `logError(String message)` and `log-Warning(String message)`. You're indicating that a consumer of this interface may either log an error or a warning message. In the case of a log event, which contains a severity and a message field, you only give the data to the consumer, and you don't tell the consumer what can be done with the data. The consumer could log the message or could just print it to the console. Coupling between a consumer and a producer of an event is solely on the data of the event and not on any interfaces.

Should you only use events then? Of course not; there are cases where you do want to establish a contract using a service interface, and there are cases where you do need the added flexibility achieved through the exchange of events. Let's consider a couple of examples of the latter case.

Say you have a restricted embedded environment and want to flag bundles that have large resources within them so that they may be examined later in detail. The developer is generally agnostic to the target environment and wouldn't want to be coupled to some interface where the (target) bundle would have to pass along its size for validation. Ideally, this validation should be performed without impacting the target bundles in any way.

As another example, suppose you want to support some form of domain-specific language (DSL). This is done by the Blueprint service. In this case, a client bundle is installed containing a special "application context" XML configuration file that's used to drive the classic dependency injection pattern as conceptualized by the popular Spring framework.

One of the advantages of dependency injection is that it avoids coupling the application to the hosting environment, like JEE, or for that matter OSGi. Hence, to have the client bundle use a Spring-DM service interface would be defeating the purpose. This is generally the case for any DSL. The goal of a DSL is to provide some declarative language at a higher level of abstraction than Java.

What event should you use for implementing these two examples? You could start off by using an event to tell you when a new bundle has been installed. It so happens that the OSGi framework provides a rich set of events. Next, we'll investigate the OSGi framework's events.

6.6   *OSGi framework events*

The OSGi framework generates events for the following situations:

- *Framework changes*—These events signal any changes to the framework itself, such as a change to the boot class path, the packages being refreshed, a framework exception, or the framework being stopped.
- *Bundle changes*—These events signal changes to bundles, such as the installation of a new bundle, the update of an existing bundle, or the uninstallation of a bundle.
- *Service changes*—These events signal changes to services, such as a new service being registered, the modification of an existing service, or the unregistration of a service.

You can get events for pretty much all OSGi-related changes.

How do you subscribe to these events? You can subscribe by registering listeners in the bundle context:

```
public void start(BundleContext bundleContext) throws Exception {

    BundleListener bundleListener = // ...

    bundleContext.addBundleListener(bundleListener);

    // ...
}
```

There are, as expected, three types of listeners: the FrameworkListener, the Bundle-Listener, and the ServiceListener, which are called back respectively with a FrameworkEvent when a framework change happens, a BundleEvent when a bundle change happens, and a ServiceEvent when a service change happens.

A FrameworkEvent contains three properties:

- The type of the event (for example, the framework is being stopped).
- An optional exception.

- The source bundle that caused the event. The source bundle is an instance of the class `org.osgi.framework.Bundle`. Generally, in the case of a framework change, the source bundle is the System bundle.

The System bundle

The System bundle is an OSGi bundle that represents the OSGi framework implementation. The reason for this is that it allows an operator to manage the framework as if it were any other regular bundle, thus providing the operator with a common and convenient interface. Among other things, the operator can upgrade the version of the framework implementation.

The `BundleEvent` likewise contains the following:

- The type of the event (for example, a bundle is installed)
- The source bundle

This is illustrated with the following code:

```
/* ... */ BundleEvent {

    int getType();

    Bundle getBundle();

}
```

Finally, the `ServiceEvent` contains these properties:

- The type of the event (for example, a service is registered)
- The service reference of the event source as an instance of the class `org.osgi.framework.ServiceReference`

The OSGi framework sends events to all registered listeners in the order in which they occurred. By and large, this is done asynchronously, although this is vendor specific; see figure 6.14.

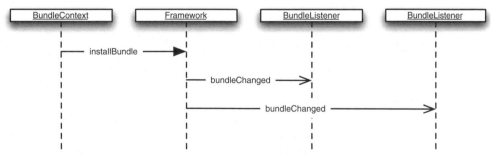

Figure 6.14   The invocation of `installBundle()` causes the asynchronous invocation of `bundleChanged()` for all registered listeners.

For example, consider that the following actions have occurred in this order:

1   `BundleListener` L1 is registered.
2   `BundleListener` L2 is registered.
3   Bundle B1 is installed.
4   `BundleListener` L3 is registered.
5   Bundle B1 is uninstalled.

Action 3 causes listeners L1 and L2 to receive the `BundleEvent` E1, whose type is set to `INSTALLED`.

```
import org.osgi.framework.BundleEvent;
import org.osgi.framework.BundleListener;

public class MyBundleListener implements BundleListener {

    public void bundleChanged(BundleEvent bundleEvent) {
        if (bundleEvent.getType() == BundleEvent.INSTALLED) {
            // ...
        }
    }
}
```

However, listener L3 doesn't receive event E1, even though by the time the framework has dispatched the event to L1 and L2, it could well have been that action 4 already had occurred. In other words, when E1 is created, the framework makes a copy of the available listeners and associates them with the event; this is done instead of referencing the available listeners when the event is dispatched.

Action 5 causes listeners L1, L2, and L3 to receive the `BundleEvent` E2, whose type is set to `UNINSTALLED`.

Even though the events are dispatched asynchronously, L1 and L2 are guaranteed to receive event E1 before receiving event E2. A consequence of this guarantee is that a listener can't be invoked concurrently with other listeners, even though it's invoked in a separate thread from that of the framework thread, which the OSGi framework uses when creating the framework events.

Finally, it's worth pointing out that L3 never receives event E1. This means that the events aren't persisted or kept in any way after they're dispatched.

Synchronous bundle listener

There's one other listener, the `SynchronousBundleListener`. As its self-describing name indicates, this listener receives `BundleEvent`s in a synchronous form. The framework is blocked from continuing until the bundle listener callback returns.

This is helpful when you want to perform some action before the situation that generated the event has finished. For example, in the case of an `UNINSTALL` event, the synchronous bundle listener could clean up some resources before the target bundle has been uninstalled.

You're now able to tell when a new bundle is installed. How do you examine its content?

6.6.1 Accessing a bundle's content

A `BundleEvent` contains an instance of the class `org.osgi.framework.Bundle`. The `Bundle` class provides several mechanisms for accessing a bundle's content:

- `Bundle.loadClass(String className): Class`

  This method loads any class that's part of the bundle's class space. As you saw in the previous chapter, a bundle's class space includes any classes that are defined in the bundle's internal class path, classes being imported by the bundle through the OSGi import-package mechanism, or even classes defined in any attached fragment. This method has the same visibility you'd get if you were trying to load a class directly from within the bundle.

  Because this method considers the complete class space of the bundle, the bundle must be able to resolve properly. If the bundle fails to resolve, then a `ClassNotFoundException` is raised and a `FrameworkEvent` containing the error is generated.

  NOTE If the framework hasn't attempted to resolve the bundle yet, then the `Bundle.loadClass()` method will trigger this action.

- `Bundle.getResource(String name): URL` and `Bundle.getResources(String name): Enumeration`

  Somewhat similar to the previous method, this method finds a resource in the bundle's class space. Hence, you're also able to access a resource that's being imported from another bundle. As expected, the bundle must be able to resolve if you're trying to access a resource exported by another bundle. But in this case, if the bundle doesn't resolve, then instead of raising an exception, this method will search only the resources within the bundle itself.

- `Bundle.findEntries(String path, String filePattern, boolean recurse): Enumeration`

  This method finds resources in the bundle space. The bundle space consists of the bundle JAR file itself and any attached fragments but doesn't include any imported packages from another bundle. Because the bundle class loader isn't used, the bundle doesn't need to resolve.

  For example, `bundleContext.findEntries("META-INF", "*.xml", true)` finds all XML files residing in the META-INF directory and its subdirectories in the bundle's JAR file and in any of its attached fragments.

- `Bundle.getEntry(String path): URL` and `Bundle.getEntryPaths(String path): Enumeration`

  This method finds resources located in the bundle's JAR file only. It won't search in any attached fragments or look in any imported packages. Again, because the bundle's class loader isn't used, the bundle doesn't need to resolve.

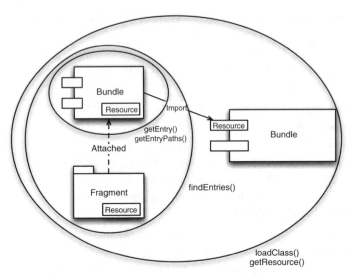

Figure 6.15   Visibility diagram for accessing a bundle's content. `loadClass()` and `getResource()` have the most visibility, and `getEntry()` and `getEntryPaths()` have the least.

Figure 6.15 demonstrates the visibility of the three approaches we've gone through. The methods `loadClass()` and `getResource()` have the largest visibility, whereas the method `getEntry()` has the smallest, and `findEntries()` is in the middle.

Now you know when a bundle is installed and you know how to access its content. Most important, you're able to do both without interfering with the original bundle, which has no knowledge of what you're doing. This approach allows you to freely extend the bundle, and it's commonly referred to as the *extender pattern*.

6.6.2   *The extender pattern*

In the extender pattern, an extender bundle, trigged by OSGi events, accesses a bundle's resources aiming to extend it with new functionality, without coupling the bundles through the sharing of any Java interfaces, as shown in figure 6.16.

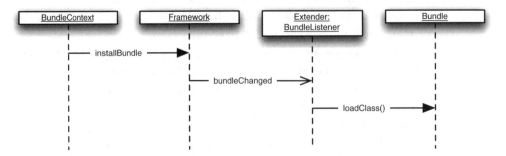

Figure 6.16   The extender receives an event indicating that a new bundle has been installed and then uses the bundle reference contained in the event to access its content.

The following listing implements an extender bundle that flags any resource within any installed bundle that's larger than 1 MB.

Listing 6.5 Size-checker extender bundle

```java
import static org.osgi.framework.BundleEvent.INSTALLED;

import java.io.IOException;
import java.io.InputStream;
import java.net.URL;
import java.util.Enumeration;

import org.osgi.framework.*;

public class SizeCheckerExtender                              ❶ Implement
implements BundleActivator, BundleListener {                    BundleListener
    private static final long MAX_SIZE_OF_1MB = 1024*1024;

    public void start(BundleContext bundleContext) throws Exception {
        bundleContext.addBundleListener(this);               ❷ Register listener
                                                               to context
        for (Bundle bundle :
            bundleContext.getBundles()) {                    ❸ Retrieve all
            if (bundle.getState()                              known bundles
              != Bundle.UNINSTALLED) {     ❹ Check size of
                checkSize(bundle);           uninstalled bundles
            }
        }
    }

    public void stop(BundleContext bundleContext) throws Exception {
        bundleContext.removeBundleListener(this);            ❺ Remove listener
    }                                                          when stopped

    public void bundleChanged(BundleEvent bundleEvent) {
        if (bundleEvent.getType() == INSTALLED) {   ❻ Check if a new bundle
            checkSize(bundleEvent.getBundle());       has been installed
        }
    }

    @SuppressWarnings("unchecked")
    private void checkSize(Bundle bundle) {
        Enumeration<URL> resources =                ❼ Retrieve all resources
            bundle.findEntries("/", "*", true);       within bundle

        if (resources != null) {
            while (resources.hasMoreElements()) {
                URL resource = resources.nextElement();

                InputStream inputStream = null;

                try {
                    inputStream =
                        resource.openStream();
```

```
            if (inputStream.skip(
                MAX_SIZE_OF_1MB)
        ==MAX_SIZE_OF_1MB) {
                System.out.println("Warning: resource "
                        + resource.toExternalForm() + " has at
                        least 1 MB in size.");
            }
        } catch (IOException e) {
            // log...
            e.printStackTrace();
        } finally {
            try {
                inputStream.close();
            } catch (IOException e) {
                // log...
                e.printStackTrace();
            }
        }
    }
  }
 }
}
```

Check if resource size
8 is at least 1 MB

You start the size checker extender class by implementing the `BundleListener` interface in addition to the usual `BundleActivator` **1**. When the extender is started, you use the bundle context to register the extender as a bundle listener **2**. Generally, you want to register the listener as soon as possible to avoid losing any events. Next, also using the bundle context, you retrieve all known bundles from the OSGi framework **3**. But you only want to check the resources of those bundles that are still installed—those that haven't been marked as uninstalled **4**. You'll check bundles that are in all other states, such as `INSTALLED`, `RESOLVED`, and `ACTIVE`. You invoke the method `checkSize()` for all of these bundles. Likewise, when a new bundle is installed, you're notified with a bundle event and again invoke the method `checkSize()` **6**.

The `checkSize()` method uses `Bundle.findEntries()` **7** to enumerate all of the resources within the bundle and within its fragments. Then, you open a stream to the resource and try to skip 1 MB of bytes **8**. If you're successful in skipping this amount of bytes, you flag the resource. Finally, you must remember to unregister the listener when the extender is stopped **5**.

Extender design pattern

Intent—Decouple client bundle from service-provider bundles.

Participants—Extender bundle, client bundle.

Structure—Extender bundle registers to receive OSGi events signaling the availability of a new client bundle. Next, the extender bundle introspects the client bundle's resources using `Bundle` instances retrieved from the OSGi events.

Consequences—The client bundle doesn't need to import packages from the service-provider bundle. Note that a contract between the extender bundle and the client bun-

> **(continued)**
>
> dle should still be established, generally through MANIFEST header entries, as you'll see in future chapters.
>
> *Known uses*—Blueprint service (chapter 13).
>
> *Related patterns*—Application-container design pattern (chapter 8).

The extender pattern is powerful and extremely flexible, but it has its own problems as well. The extended bundles have a brittle contract with the extender; hence, they could easily break the extender without realizing they've done so. For example, in the case of the Blueprint service, which you'll learn about in chapter 13, its configuration file must be placed under a /META-INF directory within the bundle's JAR file. This is an implicit contract; if the extended bundle inadvertently misspells the directory name, the Blueprint service extender could mistakenly consider that the bundle doesn't have a configuration file and silently ignore the bundle.

6.6.3 Subscribing to OSGi events using the Event Admin

As you've learned, you register instances of the classes `FrameworkListener`, `BundleListener`, and `ServiceListener` into the OSGi framework to receive OSGi-framework-related, bundle-related, and service-related events respectively. To avoid having to deal with two different subscription mechanisms, could you use the Event Admin service to also receive OSGi events?

Yes, you can use the Event Admin service to receive OSGi events. You do this by registering an `EventHandler` to a set of corresponding predefined topics. For `FrameworkEvents`, use the following topic,

```
org/osgi/framework/FrameworkEvent/<framework-event-type>
```

where `framework-event-type` maps to `STARTED`, `ERROR`, `PACKAGES_REFRESHED`, `STARTLEVEL_CHANGED`, `WARNING`, and `INFO`.

For `BundleEvents`, use the topic,

```
org/osgi/framework/BundleEvent/<bundle-event-type>
```

where `bundle-event-type` is `INSTALLED`, `STARTED`, `STOPPED`, `UPDATED`, `UNINSTALLED`, `RESOLVED`, and `UNRESOLVED`.

And finally, for `ServiceEvents`, use the topic

```
org/osgi/framework/ServiceEvent/<service-event-type>
```

The permitted values for `service-event-type` are `REGISTERED`, `UNREGISTERED`, and `UNREGISTERING`.

For example, the following code registers an event handler to receive a bundle event indicating that a new bundle has been installed:

```
Dictionary dict = new Properties();
dict.put(EventConstants.EVENT_TOPIC,
    new String [] {"org/osgi/framework/BundleEvent/INSTALLED"});
```

```
context.registerService(EventHandler.class.getName(),
    eventHandler, dict);
```

You can get details about the bundle itself by referencing its event properties:

```
public void handleEvent(Event event) {

    BundleEvent payload =
        (BundleEvent) event.getProperty(EventConstants.EVENT);

    System.out.println("Installed bundle = " +
            payload.getBundle().getSymbolicName());

}
```

By subscribing to OSGi events, the Event Admin becomes a useful tool for implementing the extender pattern, because it allows you to implement more complex event-handling scenarios, such as filtering.

6.7   *Summary*

Applications are part of a complex ecosystem. Applications are not only driven by external and environmental events but also on their own accord generate a deluge of application events. The Event Admin provides a systematic way of dealing with events.

Event-driven architectures are characterized by components that collaborate by exchanging events and are thus better decoupled, providing an ideal environment for scalability. The Event Admin service helps us to realize event-driven systems.

The Event Admin is a mediator service that allows publishers to send events to subscribers. A publisher can send an event by invoking the `EventAdmin.postEvent()` method to send an event asynchronously or the `EventAdmin.sendEvent()` method to send an event synchronously. A subscriber can receive events by registering the `EventHandler` interface in the OSGi registry. Publishers and subscribers exchange events on a common channel, or topic. A topic name is hierarchical, such as `"org/osgi/framework/BundleEvent/INSTALLED"`. Multiple publishers may send events to the same topic, and multiple subscribers can connect to the same topic.

Events are composed of a topic name and a set of event properties, which are name-value pairs. The subscribers can use event properties as a filtering mechanism, by having them register an LDAP filter in the `EventConstants.EVENT_FILTER` service property.

The Event Admin service is simple to use but lacks several important features, such as the persistence of unconsumed events and a more powerful filtering mechanism.

The OSGi framework likewise is a rich source of events and generates events for framework changes, bundle changes, and service changes. This can be used to extend bundles with new functionality without their prior knowledge. This pattern is commonly referred to as the extender pattern.

There are several mechanisms for accessing a bundle's content, ranging from accessing the complete bundle's class space, to the bundle space, and finally to the bundle JAR file only.

In this chapter, we looked into how to send and receive events. In the next chapter, we'll complement this by exploring how to access and write data to persistent storage.

The persistence bundle

7

This chapter covers

- Using the bundle's storage area to manipulate external data

- Reading and writing data to persistent storage using JDBC and JPA

- Registering new JDBC drivers

- Invoking external OSGi services through different transports

As you've learned, OSGi applications are part of a larger ecosystem and constantly need to engage with other applications and deal with external components. In the previous chapter, you learned how to interact with diverse components by publishing and subscribing to application and business events. In this chapter, we'll investigate other means of collaboration, specifically how to access external (business) data by reading and writing data to and from persistent storage.

The persistence of data is a common theme for most enterprise-grade applications because they must not lose data, particularly enterprise data, which may contain their client's transactions. For example, recall from section 6.4.1 that one of the issues of the Event Admin service is that it may lose events. One way to avoid this would be for the Event Admin implementation to store the events into some durable media as the events arrive.

In OSGi, there are different ways you can achieve the persistence of data. You'll first learn that the OSGi framework provides each bundle with its own bundle storage area, which can be used as persistent storage. Next, you'll learn how to use JDBC within OSGi by registering and retrieving JDBC data source factories. Finally, we'll take an abstraction leap, and you'll learn how to use object-relational approaches to automatically persist a bundle's Java objects. This is done using JPA, and, as you'll see, it has an interesting and somewhat involved setup within OSGi.

We'll start by looking at the bundle's storage area.

7.1   Bundle's storage area

The OSGi framework provides an isolated persistent storage area for each bundle. This area can be manipulated through the usual `java.io.File` abstraction. Through this interface, a bundle can read and write files and manipulate directories. In listing 7.1, you can see how to use the bundle's storage area to persist a `LoginEvent`, which was defined in the previous chapter. As you go through this listing, keep in mind that we'll look into simpler and more efficient ways of persisting data later on in this chapter.

Listing 7.1   Storing data using the bundle's storage area

```
int counter = 0;

File eventLog =
    bundleContext.getDataFile("event-"                    ❶ Retrive bundle's
        + (counter++) + ".dat");                            storage area

eventLog.createNewFile();
                                                          ❷ Instantiate
BufferedWriter writer =                                     file writer
    new BufferedWriter(new FileWriter(eventLog));

                                                          ❸ Persist each
                                                             event property
writer.write((String) event.getProperty("userid"));
writer.newLine();
writer.write((String) event.getProperty("timestamp"));    ❹ Separate properties
writer.newLine();                                            using newline

writer.close();
```

You can retrieve a reference to a file within a bundle's storage area by using the method `BundleContext.getDataFile()` ❶. In this example, you create a new file for each new event. You do this by encoding a counter in the filename and incrementing the counter for every event received—event-0.dat for the first event, event-1.dat for the second, and so on. Next, you instantiate a `FileWriter` class, using the reference to the new file ❷. Finally, you write each event property individually to the file ❸. The properties are separated using the newline character ❹.

> **NOTE** `bundleContext.getDataFile("")` returns a pointer to the base directory of the bundle's storage area.

To retrieve the information, you have to do the converse, as shown in the following listing.

Listing 7.2   Retrieving data using the bundle's storage area

```
File eventLog =
    bundleContext.getDataFile("event-0.dat");       ◁─────┐   Retrieve bundle's
                                                          ❶  storage area
BufferedReader reader =
    new BufferedReader(new FileReader(eventLog));   ◁─────┐   Create FileReader
                                                          ❷  to read file
String userId = reader.readLine();       ◁─────┐   Read each property
String timestamp = reader.readLine();    ❸      as separate line

reader.close();

Map<String, Object>
    properties = new HashMap<String, Object>();
                                                   ❹  Store properties
properties.put("userid", userId);       ◁─────     in Map
properties.put("timestamp", timestamp);

Event retrievedEvent =                   ❺  Create new event
    new Event("LoginEvent", properties);  ◁────    with properties
```

First, access the bundle's storage area ❶, open the corresponding file representing the event in question ❷, read each event property ❸, set it into a Map ❹, and finally create a new event using the Map of properties ❺.

At-least-once Event Admin

A simple algorithm for decreasing the chances of losing events in an Event Admin implementation is the following:

Receive the event from the publisher, and immediately write it into persistent storage. Only after it has been persisted, confirm the receiving of the event to the publisher. Having received the acknowledgement from the Event Admin, the publisher can now safely delete its copy of the event.

When publishing the event, the Event Admin first sends the event to all publishers, and only after the publishers confirm receiving the event should the Event Admin delete the event from its persistent storage.

This algorithm achieves at-least-once semantics for the delivery of events, even in the case of the system going down. But there's a chance of getting duplicate events. For example, if the system goes down after the Event Admin has sent the event to the subscribers but before it has had a chance to delete the event from persistent storage, the next time the Event Admin is brought up, it will try to deliver the same set of events again.

A bundle's storage area provides you with easy access to a bundle-isolated filesystem. But it's still up to the user to do all of the reading and writing of data, which can get cumbersome. For example, in the scenario we've been using so far of the Login-Event, how would you know the name of the files to open to retrieve the persisted events? You'd have to list all of the files in the directory and look for some particular pattern, such as event-?.dat, which isn't a resilient approach. In the next section, we'll look at how to improve our handling of data by using JDBC.

7.2   Using JDBC

The JDBC (Java Database Connectivity) standard provides us with a simpler and more powerful way of manipulating persistent data, by allowing us to directly interact with a Relational Database Management System (RDBMS), such as MySQL, Apache Derby, Oracle RDBMS, or Microsoft SQL Server.

JDBC is no stranger to JEE developers, and there are plenty of books and other documentation on the subject, but there are also some caveats that you need to be aware of when dealing with JDBC in an OSGi environment.

7.2.1   Bootstrapping JDBC drivers

In a regular Java application, the entry point for using JDBC is to instantiate a particular JDBC driver implementation through reflection; for example:

```
Class.forName("org.apache.derby.jdbc.EmbeddedDriver").newInstance();
```

This command creates a new driver for Apache Derby and registers it into a static `DriverManager` class. Having done so, a user can now retrieve a connection through this driver to the driver's database, as follows:

```
Connection connection =
    DriverManager.getConnection("jdbc:derby:derbyDB;create=true");
```

Can you follow the same pattern in an OSGi framework? No, this wouldn't work in OSGi for several reasons. First of all, you know that each bundle potentially could have its own class loader, so each `DriverManager` class, being static, would be scoped to a different bundle. Each bundle would have to instantiate a new driver and share neither the driver nor connections with each other, resulting in a nonscalable solution.

If you look into this carefully, you'll notice that the `DriverManager` class functions as a registry of JDBC connections. But in OSGi, the OSGi service factory already has this role of a registry. To address this mismatch, OSGi has come up with a different solution; it defines the `org.osgi.service.jdbc.DataSourceFactory` service, representing a factory of JDBC connections. This service is registered normally in the OSGi service registry and avoids the need for a `DriverManager` class, while still allowing JDBC drivers and connections to be shared across bundles and managed appropriately in an OSGi environment. In short, the `DataSourceFactory` service acts as a factory of `javax.sql.DataSource`.

7.2.2   *Providing OSGi-aware JDBC drivers*

Recall that a regular JDBC driver is registered when it gets instantiated, which generally is done through the use of reflection. But because in OSGi a driver has been abstracted as service, you can use the usual OSGi service registration mechanism, be it through a `BundleActivator` or through some declarative mechanism, such as Blueprint.

Furthermore, note how this service-oriented approach gives some additional benefits:

- You can dynamically add and remove new JDBC drivers.
- You can support multiple versions of the same driver.

OSGi defines two service properties to allow consumers to be selective of the particular driver they need:

- `OSGI_JDBC_DRIVER_CLASS`—The driver implementation class, such as `org.apache.derby.jdbc.EmbeddedDriver`
- `OSGI_JDBC_DRIVER_VERSION`—The driver version

In summary, a provider of JDBC drivers has to do the following to work in OSGi:

1 Package the driver implementation as a bundle.
2 Register a `DataSourceFactory` service in the OSGi service factory, which delegates to the driver implementation as needed.
3 Set the service properties `OSGI_JDBC_DRIVER_CLASS` and `OSGI_JDBC_DRIVER _VERSION`.

Next, let's look at how an application bundle can consume a JDBC driver.

7.2.3   *Consuming OSGi-aware JDBC drivers*

Because you're dealing with a standard OSGi service, you can employ the usual means to retrieve services. The following listing gives an example of how to retrieve a `Data-SourceFactory` for Apache Derby and then use it to persist a `LoginEvent`, improving upon the approach used in section 7.1.

> **Listing 7.3   Persisting a `LoginEvent` using a `DataSourceFactory` service**

```
ServiceReference [] serviceReferences =
    bundleContext.getServiceReferences(                              ❶ Use DataSourceFactory
            DataSourceFactory.class.toString(),          ←———┘          interface
            "(" + DataSourceFactory.OSGI_JDBC_DRIVER_CLASS +
            "=org.apache.derby.jdbc.EmbeddedDriver)");    ←———┐  Set
                                                                DRIVER_CLASS
if (serviceReferences != null) {                             ❷ property
    DataSourceFactory dsf = (DataSourceFactory)
        bundleContext.getService(serviceReferences[0]);

    Properties props = new Properties();
    props.put(DataSourceFactory.JDBC_URL,                   ←———┐  Set data
        "jdbc:derby:derbyDB;create=true");                  ❸  source URL
```

```
DataSource ds =
    dsf.createDataSource(props);                          Create data
                                                      4   source

Connection conn =
    ds.getConnection();

Statement stat =                          5   Create JDBC
    conn.createStatement();                   statement

stat.execute("INSERT INTO event-log VALUES (" +
        userId + ", " + timestamp + ")");       6   Insert LogEvent into
                                                    event-log table

stat.close();
conn.close();
}
```

First, you retrieve the `DataSourceFactory` service from OSGi ❶. You specify Derby's driver implementation ❷ to make sure you get the proper driver for Derby. Next, you set Derby's URL to the data source properties ❸ and use it to create a new data source for Derby ❹.

NOTE   If user authentication is enabled, you should also specify the user and password as part of the URL: jdbc:derby:derbyDB;create=true;user=alex; password=osgi.

Using the `DataSource` object, you establish a connection to Derby and create a new statement ❺. Finally, you insert the value of the `LoginEvent` properties as columns in an event-log table ❻ and close the connection.

Event-log table

In this approach, you rely on a database table defining two columns: `userid` and `timestamp`. This table can be created with the following SQL command:

`CREATE TABLE Event-Log (userid varchar(255), timestamp bigint)`

Each event is then stored as a new row in this table. As events are consumed, they're deleted from the table. Manipulating rows in a table is much easier than creating and deleting files in a directory.

The interaction between the driver bundle, the application bundle, and the actual RDBMS is presented in figure 7.1.

NOTE   Regardless of whether you're accessing a JDBC driver in a regular Java application or in an OSGi environment, the information needed remains the same. Specifically, a developer needs the driver class name, the driver version, the connection URL, and any other optional connection attributes, such as user and password.

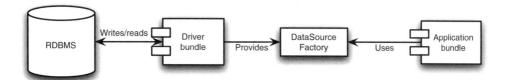

Figure 7.1 The application bundle uses the `DataSourceFactory` service, which is provided by the driver bundle.

As evident in listing 7.2, it's much easier to manipulate the data using JDBC than to write and read directly to a file. But one remaining drawback is that you still need to map the `LoginEvent` object into a relational model by explicitly creating an underlying table and assigning each object property to a table column. In the next section, we'll look at how you can automate this object-to-relational mapping.

7.3 Object-relation mapping through JPA

The Java Persistence API (JPA, http://jcp.org/en/jsr/summary?id=317) is a framework for automating the persistence of Java object instances into different storage mechanisms, most commonly to RDBMSs, in a manner that simplifies programming for the application developers.

In the following listing, you'll see how you can use JPA to simplify our scenario. Keep in mind that we're starting with a simple approach to illustrate the technology; we'll improve it as we move through the sections and in future chapters.

Listing 7.4 `LoginEvent` entity

```
package manning.enterpriseosgi;

import javax.persistence.*;
                                        Entity
                                        annotation
@Entity
public class LoginEvent {

    @Id                                 Annotation to
    @GeneratedValue                     specify key
    private int id;
                                        Login event
    private String userid;              properties
    private long timestamp;

    public int getId() {
        return this.id;
    }

    public String getUserid() {
        return this.userid;
    }

    public void setUserid(String userid) {
```

```
        this.userid = userid;
    }

    public long getTimestamp() {
        return this.timestamp;
    }

    public void setTimestamp(long timestamp) {
        this.timestamp = timestamp;
    }
}
```

The `LoginEvent` class looks like any other standard POJO (plain old Java object), with the addition of an `Entity` annotation, which marks this class for persistence as a stand-alone entity by JPA.

> **WARNING** Entity classes must also provide a no-argument public constructor and not be declared as final.

Furthermore, we've used the optional `Id` and `GeneratedValue` annotations to mark which Java field or property should be used as the primary key and to indicate that it should be generated by the underlying storage (for example, the RDBMS). Before we go any further, let's establish a couple of JPA concepts.

A JPA `Entity` class is responsible for persisting all of its attributes. An attribute may either be a *persistent field* or a *persistent property*.

> **DEFINITION** Persistent fields are Java class instance variables, that is, fields that are accessed directly.

Persistent fields must not be marked as transient.

> **DEFINITION** Persistent properties are properties inferred by the presence of Java class methods that follow the JavaBean conventions. That is, the methods have the appropriately named getters and setters.

The JPA provider checks the access type of an `Entity`, which may either be *field-based access* or *property-based access*, and then proceeds to manage either all persistent fields or all persistent methods of the `Entity` class respectively. The access type informs JPA whether it should be using the Java class fields or the Java class methods, but never both at the same time. This will be easier to understand when you look at an example later in this section.

How is the access type determined? It's determined by the presence of the JPA annotations in either the fields or methods of the Java class. If the annotations are placed on the fields, then it's a field-based access type. Otherwise, if the annotations are placed in the methods, then it's a property-based access type. It's an error to place (mapping) annotations in such a way that the access type becomes ambiguous and can't be determined.

Having established the access type of an `Entity` class, the JPA class `EntityManager` can then be used as the façade for applications to manage the persistence and retrieval of the Java objects.

This may all sound very confusing, but in reality it's generally trivial. For example, in listing 7.4 for the `LoginEvent` entity, we placed the `Id` annotation on the private `id` field; therefore it's a field-based access and the JPA provider will take care of persisting all fields—`id`, `userid`, and `timestamp`. Had we placed the annotation on the `getId()` method, then it would have transformed this entity into a property-based access type, and the JPA provider would have persisted it by invoking `getId()`/`setId()`, `get-Userid()`/`setUserid()`, and `getTimestamp()`/`setTimestamp()`. In most cases, this really won't matter much, but it's important to go through it, because some of the JPA annotations are dependent on this understanding.

Next, you must inform the JPA provider how you want the persistence to be achieved. This is done with an XML configuration file, as in the following listing.

Listing 7.5   Persistence XML configuration for `LoginEvent`

```
<persistence version="1.0" xmlns="http://java.sun.com/xml/ns/persistence"
    xmlns:xsi="http://www.w3.org/2001/XMLSchema-instance"
    xsi:schemaLocation="http://java.sun.com/xml/ns/persistence
http://java.sun.com/xml/ns/persistence/persistence_1_0.xsd">        ❶ Persistence
                                                                        unit name
    <persistence-unit name="LoginEvent">
        <class>manning.osgi.jpa.LoginEvent</class>    ❷ Class name
          <properties>
            <property name="javax.persistence.jdbc.driver"    ❸ JDBC driver
        value="org.apache.derby.jdbc.EmbeddedDriver"/>           class name
            <property name="javax.persistence.jdbc.url"
        value="jdbc:derby:derbyDB;create=true"/>
                                                      ❹ JDBC URL

        <!-- Other provider specific configuration -->

        </properties>
    </persistence-unit>
</persistence>
```

A JPA configuration, or persistence configuration, as it's called, is organized into persistence units (PU) ❶. Generally, a PU maps to an application or, as it is in our case, to a bundle, so it's advisable to use the bundle's symbolic name as the PU name. In addition, a PU configuration includes several specific directives on how to map each persistent entity, that is, a Java class ❷, into its target storage. In particular, two properties are needed—the JDBC driver class name ❸ and its corresponding URL ❹—which aligns quite nicely with OSGi's `DataSourceFactory` properties. This should come as no surprise. By specifying these two properties in the persistence configuration, you give the JPA provider all the information necessary to access a JDBC driver. This is similar to how we did it in section 7.2.3.

Where should you place the persistence configuration? In a general JEE environment, the XML file is located in META-INF/persistence.xml. But in OSGi you need to use a `Meta-Persistence` MANIFEST header entry, which serves to annotate the bundle as a persistence unit.

> **DEFINITION**   Bundles containing the `Meta-Persistence` header entry are known as *persistence bundles.*

The `Meta-Persistence` header specifies the location of the JPA configuration, as in the following example:

```
Meta-Persistence: META-INF/persistence.xml
Bundle-SymbolicName: manning.osgi.jpa
```

Which packages should we import in our `LoginEvent` bundle? So far, the only package needed is `javax.persistence`. In particular, we don't need to import any JDBC driver-related packages.

The next step is to make sure that all of the implementation bundles are in place. You need a JPA provider, and you need the JDBC driver that's being used by the persistence configuration. As you learned in the previous chapters, you can retrieve these dependencies from any common bundle repository, such as http://ebr.spring-source.com/repository/app/. Here are the bundles needed:

- `javax.persistence`
- `org.apache.derby`
- `org.eclipse.persistence`
- `org.eclipse.persistence.core`
- `org.eclipse.persistence.jpa`

With these in place, you're ready to take advantage of JPA. The following listing stores the `LoginEvent` class into the persistent storage using JPA's `EntityManager` class.

Listing 7.6   Persisting a `LoginEvent` using JPA

```
ServiceReference [] serviceReferences =
    bundleContext.getServiceReferences(              ❶ Retrieve
        EntityManagerFactory.class.toString(),         EntityManagerFactory
        "osgi.unit.name=LoginEvent");               ❷ Specify PU
                                                       name
if (serviceReferences != null) {
    EntityManagerFactory emf = (EntityManagerFactory)
        bundleContext.getService(serviceReferences[0]);

    EntityManager em = emf.createEntityManager();   ❸ Begin
                                                       transaction
    em.getTransaction().begin();

    em.persist(loginEvent);            ❹ Persist
                                          entity
    em.getTransaction().commit();              ❺ Commit
                                                  transaction
    em.close();
    emf.close();
}
```

The pattern for using JPA is similar to using a `DataSourceFactory` service. First, you retrieve the `EntityManagerFactory` service ❶ from the OSGi service factory, but you need to make sure you specify the persistence unit name using the `"osgi.unit.name"` service property ❷. Next, you create an `EntityManager` object and use it to begin a transaction ❸. The main value of JPA is that you can now persist an object simply by calling `persist()` ❹, without having to worry about the details of mapping this Java class to a relational model. Finally, you must commit the transaction ❺ and close the `EntityManager` and its factory.

Compare this implementation to the other two in sections 7.1 and 7.2.3. There's still some boilerplate code, but the actual persisting of the event is trivial.

The `EntityManager` class is the main JPA class, and it provides several easy-to-use methods for handling `Entities`, such as `persist`, `remove`, and `find`. For example, the following code retrieves a login event that has been persisted. In this case, we assume that the variable `id` contains the generated identification value of the login event to be retrieved:

```
LoginEvent loginEvent = em.find(LoginEvent.class, id);
```

If you're used to JEE and application servers in general, you may feel compelled to remember fondly the JEE's container-managed persistence (CMP), where all of this boilerplate code would have been avoided. In OSGi, there's still no standard CMP, partly because there are no application containers per se. Nonetheless, it should be easy to implement one. It's a question of time before we start seeing higher-level services that address these requirements.

Next, let's go through the most common JPA annotations for more advanced scenarios.

7.3.1 JPA annotations

Next, we'll look at the most common JPA annotations:

- `Access`—This annotation takes the value of either `field` or `property` and allows you to override the default behavior or mix and match both access types. For example, you can set a class with an `Access(Field)` annotation and then individually specify an `Access(Property)` on the Java methods you'd also like to be considered as persistent properties.

- `Cacheable`—Specifies whether the persistence provider may cache an entity. Here's an example:

```
Cacheable(false),
Entity
public class LoginEvent {}
```

- `Column`—This is used to specify the mapped column for an entity's property or field. For example, the following annotation states that the `userid` property should be mapped to a USER_ID column in the USERS table:

```
Column(name="USER_ID", table="USERS")
public String getUserid() {}
```

- If the name annotation element isn't specified, then it defaults to the property's name. Other optional annotation fields are columnDefinition, insertable, length, scale, nullable, precision, unique, and updatable.

- Embeddable/Embedded—The Embeddable annotation is used to specify a class as an intrinsic part of some entity. The owning entity uses the Embedded annotation to reference the embeddable class. An embeddable class shares the identity of this owning entity. Here's an example:

```
@Embeddable
public class UserDescr
{
    public long getId() {...};
    public String getName() {...};
}
@Entity
public class LoginEvent
{
    public String getTimestamp() {};
    @Embedded public UserDescr getUserDescription() {};
}
```

- Entity—Specifies that a class is a JPA entity and is therefore to be persisted.

- GeneratedValue—Specifies the strategy for generating the value of an entity's primary key. The available strategies are as follows:

  TABLE—An underlying table is used for generating the key.

  SEQUENCE—A table sequence is used for generating the key.

  IDENTITY—An identity column is used for generating the key.

  AUTO—The JPA provider selects the appropriate strategy.

  The default value is AUTO.

- Id—Annotates a property or field as a primary key.

- PrePersist, PostPersist—These and the following three sets of annotations (pre/post persist, pre/post update, pre/post remove, and post load) are used to specify methods on the Entity class to be called back when certain events happen. A method annotated with PrePersist is called back prior to the persisting of the entity, whereas the PostPersist annotated method is invoked after the entity has been persisted in the persistent store, that is, after a corresponding commit or flush.

- PreUpdate, PostUpdate—The PreUpdate annotated method is invoked when the EntityManager identifies an identity as modified, and the PostUpdate annotated method is likewise invoked after an entity is updated in the persistent store.

- PreRemove, PostRemove—The PreRemove annotated method is invoked prior to an entity being removed, and the PostRemove annotated method is likewise invoked after an entity is removed from the persistent store.

- PostLoad—The PostLoad annotated method is invoked on an entity after the entity has been loaded from the persistent store. This is the converse of the

PostPersist annotation, and it gives the application a chance to finalize the configuration of a class, similar in concept to the Spring Framework's after-PropertiesSet.

- Table—This annotation allows you to specify the primary table of an entity.
- Transient—You can use this annotation to set a field or property as transient and as therefore not to be persisted.

JPA is rich and has many other annotations, such as ones used to manipulate collections of elements, where you can even specify the multiplicity, be it one-to-many, many-to-many, and so on. There are whole books on the subject, and we defer to them for additional details.

7.3.2 Distilling JPA

From the application's perspective, persistence becomes easy enough. But the interaction between the implementation components isn't that simple, as illustrated in figure 7.2.

As you've learned, an application bundle defines the entities to be persisted by annotating them using classes from the javax.persistence API bundle. Next, the

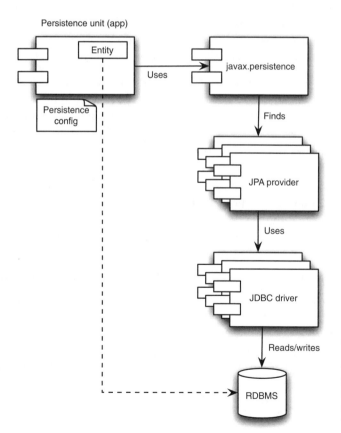

Figure 7.2 To persist an entity, an application uses **javax.persistence,** which finds the proper JPA provider and JDBC driver. Ultimately, the JDBC driver does the actual reading and writing to the RDBMS.

`javax.persistence` bundle functions as a framework and must find a proper JPA provider implementation that will be responsible for doing the actual work. The selected JPA provider bundle reads the application's persistence configuration and finds the proper JDBC driver.

Ultimately, the entities defined within the application bundle must be persisted in the RDBMS, which means that the JPA provider bundle must be able to *see* the entity's Java classes. But that would mean an upward dependency from the JPA provider bundle to application bundles, which are unknown to the JPA provider at install time. How is this achieved? The JPA provider bundle uses the extender design pattern, which you learned about in section 6.6.2. The algorithm that a JPA provider implements is as follows:

1 The JPA provider registers a `BundleListener` to the OSGi framework and listens for "install bundle" events.

2 Whenever a bundle is installed, the JPA provider receives the "install bundle" event and uses it to access the MANIFEST file of the installed bundle, checking whether the MANIFEST contains a `Meta-Persistence` header entry.

3 If it does, the provider again uses the bundle's class space to retrieve the Java classes of the entities to be persisted. Then the JPA provider uses the `Data-SourceFactory` service to retrieve the proper JDBC driver (that is, `DataSource`). With a reference to the application's class space and the correct JDBC driver, the JPA provider has all the pieces needed to persist the entities.

JPA providers participate in the JPA framework by registering a service implementing the interface `javax.persistence.spi.PersistenceProvider`. It should also include its provider class name in the `javax.persistence.provider` service property. The `javax.persistence` bundle is then responsible for selecting the proper `Persistence-Provider` service. Finally, the JPA provider is responsible for registering an appropriate `EntityManagerFactory` service into the OSGi service registry as application bundles containing persistence units are installed and their referenced JDBC drivers are available. Figure 7.3 highlights all of the different design patterns used to implement the interaction between the JPA components.

As you can see, this whole interaction is indeed complicated. But it does yield several advantages:

- You can dynamically add or remove different JPA providers, independently from one another.
- The JPA providers can use different JDBC drivers, which can be added or removed independently.
- The persistent unit applications need not import any packages from the JPA providers or from the JDBC drivers. The only dependency they have is with the `javax.persistence` API bundle.

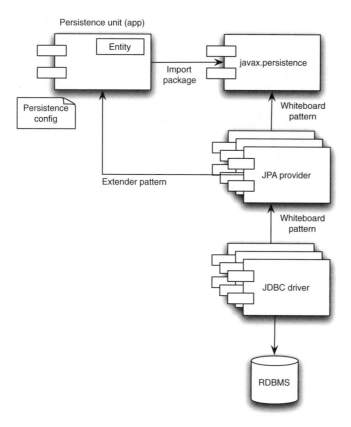

Figure 7.3
`javax.persistence` uses the whiteboard pattern to find the proper JPA provider, which likewise also uses the whiteboard pattern to find its JDBC driver. In addition, the JPA provider uses the extender pattern to introspect the details of the application entities to be persisted.

We've now looked into three different approaches for persisting data in OSGi. Table 7.1 summarizes these three approaches, highlighting their characteristics.

Table 7.1   Data persistence

Bundle's storage area	JDBC	JPA
No dependencies	JDBC drivers	JDBC drivers, JPA providers
File based	Relational	Object-relational
Marshaling is needed	Mapping is needed	Automapping from Java

As you've learned, the OSGi platform provides several options for persisting data, leveraging existing and proven technology, such as JDBC and JPA.

7.4   Summary

Enterprise applications seldom work in isolation. Instead, they constantly need to access external data.

OSGi provides several options for accessing external data. First, each bundle is given its own storage area, where you can read and write files to a filesystem. Second, an application can use JDBC through a `DataSourceFactory` service, which is registered by the different JDBC drivers hosted in the OSGi framework. When retrieving a `DataSourceFactory` service, the `OSGI_JDBC_DRIVER_CLASS` and `OSGI_JDBC_DRIVER_VERSION` service properties can be used to select the proper JDBC driver.

Finally, JPA is also supported. JPA allows an automatic mapping of Java classes, called entities, into some backend storage, such as an RDBMS. The mapping is driven by annotations and a persistence configuration file, which must exist within the application bundle and which is referenced by a `Meta-Persistence` header entry. The manipulation of entities is done through an `EntityManager` class. JPA providers register `ServiceProvider` services, and the JPA framework is responsible for creating `EntityManagerFactory` classes for all configured persistence units. Bundles defining persistent units are known as persisting bundles.

In the next chapter, we'll look into how you can extend the quality of an application's service beyond persistence to include atomicity.

8
Transactions and containers

This chapter covers

- The concepts of atomicity, consistency, isolation, and durability (ACID)
- The use of local transactions and global transactions
- How XA resources work to achieve consensus
- Handling exceptions in the context of a transaction
- Implementing container-managed transactions

In the previous chapter, we examined how to persist data, that is, make it durable. Yet, in several cases, this may not be enough. Not only do you need to make the enterprise data durable, but you may also need to make sure that either all of the data is persisted or none of the data is persisted. This all-or-nothing attribute is called *atomicity* and is achieved through the use of transactions.

Transactions are important to the enterprise, because enterprise applications generally involve several resources, and actions executed in these resources must

be done in an atomic fashion. We'll start our discussion by investigating a classic transaction use case where we need to transfer money between banking accounts.

8.1   *Undoing work*

Consider a banking application that transfers money from one account to another.
Each account is implemented as database tables in an RDBMS (relational database
management system). The banking application needs to debit one account and credit
the other account by executing SQL (Structured Query Language) statements.

In chapter 7, you learned that one way of doing this is to use JDBC, as shown in the
following listing.

Listing 8.1   Transferring money from one account to another

```
double currentA = 100.0;
double currentB = 0.0;
double amount = 50.0;
                                                    ❶ Retrieve JDBC
DataSource ds = ...                                    DataSource service

Connection conn =
    ds.getConnection();

Statement stmt =
    conn.createStatement();

stmt.execute("UPDATE account SET current = " + (currentA - amount)
    + " WHERE accountId = 001");              ❷ Debit first account

stmt.execute("UPDATE account SET current = " + (currentB + amount)
    + " WHERE accountId = 002");                   Credit second
                                            ❸      account
stmt.close();
conn.close();
```

First, you retrieve the JDBC `DataSource` service ❶. Next, you debit the first account
❷, withdrawing 50.0, and credit the second account with this same amount ❸, so that
the accounts start with 100.0 and 0.0 and finish with the values of 50.0 and 50.0,
respectively. Note how you start with the collective sum of 100.0 and finish with this
same collective sum.

> **DEFINITION**   Making sure that application invariants are always met is often
> referred to as consistency. In the banking example, *consistency* means that at
> any time you always have the same overall sum.

But what happens if for whatever reason the second execute ❸ fails? If that happens,
then the accounts will finish with 50.0 and 0.0, respectively; that is, 50.0 will have dis-
appeared and you would have lost the consistency of always keeping the collective sum
of 100.0. How do you cope with the fact that at any time any operation may fail? You
can solve this problem by making sure you compensate for the failures adequately.

One example of this compensation, or undoing of work, is demonstrated in the next listing.

Listing 8.2 Compensating for statement execution failure

```
stat.execute("UPDATE account SET current = " + (currentA - amount)
      + " WHERE accountId = 001");                    ◁─────┐
                                                      ❶ Do work

try {
    stat.execute("UPDATE account SET current = " + (currentB + amount)
      + " WHERE accountId = 002");
} catch (Throwable e) {
    stat.execute("UPDATE account SET current = " + (currentA + amount)
          + " WHERE accountId = 001");                 ◁─────┐
}
                                                      ❷ Undo work
```

You only need to compensate for the first statement ❶, and only if the second statement fails, by doing the opposite of what the first statement has done ❷. In this case, this would be to credit the same amount that was debited originally. Why don't you need to compensate for the second statement? The reason is that if the second statement is successful, then both statements were executed successfully and there's nothing to compensate for. Being able to either execute both statements successfully or execute neither is called *atomicity*.

> **DEFINITION** *Atomicity* guarantees that all of the actions of a task are executed successfully or none at all.

This compensation approach has two problems. First, what happens if the "compensation work" itself ❷ fails also? Then you wouldn't be able to undo the work and would therefore still lose consistency. Furthermore, consider if instead of 2 statements you had 10 statements; in this case, you'd have to code 9 compensating actions, as shown in figure 8.1.

Programming compensating actions isn't trivial, it's cumbersome, and it's prone to mistakes. Fortunately, there's a better way: the use of transactions, which you'll see in the next section.

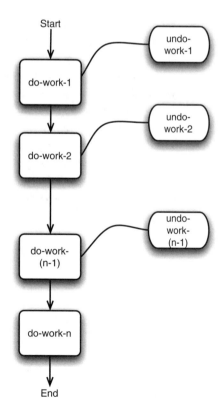

Figure 8.1 For each do-work, you need a corresponding undo-work, with the exception of the last one.

8.2   *Transactions*

Transactions are a programming abstraction representing a unit of work. A transaction may involve several actions, but it guarantees that either all of the actions are executed atomically or none are executed. A transaction also provides isolation, in the sense that from the outside a transaction is seen as an isolated single unit of work, even though internally it may encompass more than one activity. Finally, transactions are durable; that is, when they're terminated, their changes are guaranteed not to be lost.

> **DEFINITIONS**   *Isolation* allows actions to be performed independently without impacting each other. *Durability* guarantees that the results of these actions aren't lost.

Transactions are described by three main operations:

- `begin()`
- `commit()`
- `rollback()`

Intuitively, you start a transaction by invoking the `begin()` operation. Following that, you can do all the work that's involved as part of that transaction. Finally, when you've finished, you can invoke either `commit()` to end the transaction successfully or `rollback()` to discard the work that has been done since the call to `begin()`.

A transaction guarantees all four attributes we've discussed so far: atomicity, consistency, durability, and isolation. These are collectively known as ACID, as shown in figure 8.2.

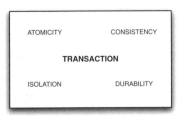

Figure 8.2   A transaction possesses the attributes of atomicity, consistency, isolation, and durability. These are commonly referenced collectively as ACID.

The following listing shows how you can use transactions to solve the atomicity problem described in the previous section.

Listing 8.3   JDBC local transactions

```
Connection conn =
    ds.getConnection();

conn.setAutoCommit(false);                                          ❶ Start
                                                                       transaction

Statement stat =
    conn.createStatement();

stat.execute("UPDATE account SET current = " + (currentA - amount)
    + " WHERE accountId = 001");                                    ❷ Do work

stat.execute("UPDATE account SET current = " + (currentB + amount)
    + " WHERE accountId = 002");
                                                                    ❸ End transaction
conn.commit();
```

By default, a JDBC connection commits for every statement executed. Setting the `AutoCommit` property to `false` ❶ changes this. This causes a new transaction to be started when a statement is created. Having started a transaction, you can now safely do all the work that needs to be done. In this case, you execute both debit and credit statements ❷. Finally, you commit ❸. The `commit` operation serves as a demarcation; it tells the transaction that all statements used so far must be executed atomically. What happens if the second statement fails to execute? If this happens, then the infrastructure will automatically make sure that the first statement is rolled back, that is, undone. A user may also explicitly call the `rollback` method and force the undoing of the whole transaction.

In our example, a single resource was involved, an RDBMS data source. Transactions that deal with a single resource are called local transactions. In the next section, let's consider a slightly more complicated scenario involving more than one resource.

8.2.1 Global transactions

Again, let's consider our banking application, but now let's investigate the case where each account is kept in a different RDBMS, as shown in the following listing.

Listing 8.4 Error-prone JDBC global transactions

```
DataSource ds1 = ...
DataSource ds2 = ...

Connection conn1 =
    ds1.getConnection();

Connection conn2 =                          ❶ Separate connections
    ds2.getConnection();                       for each RDBMS

conn1.setAutoCommit(false);
conn2.setAutoCommit(false);

Statement stat1 =
    conn1.createStatement();

Statement stat2 =
    conn2.createStatement();

stat1.execute("UPDATE account SET current = " + (currentA - amount)
    + " WHERE accountId = 001");

stat2.execute("UPDATE account SET current = " + (currentB + amount)
    + " WHERE accountId = 002");
                              ❸ End first            Do all
                                 transaction  ❹ End second  ❷ the work
conn1.commit();                                 transaction
conn2.commit();
```

When dealing with two RDBMSs, you retrieve two connections, one for each system ❶. Then you perform the update operations on each account ❷, one in each connection, and then commit both.

At first, this seems like it would work, but what happens if the application fails after the first commit ❸ but before the second commit ❹? If this unfortunate event happens, you'd be out of luck and would have decremented account 001 and never incremented adequately account 002.

When dealing with more than one resource, you need a mediator that coordinates the work across all resources. This is the role of the `TransactionManager`.

Things get a bit more involved in this case, as shown in the following listing.

Listing 8.5   JDBC global transactions

```
ServiceReference serviceReference =
    context.getServiceReference("javax.transaction.TransactionManager");

TransactionManager tm =                                    ❶ Retrieve
    (TransactionManager)                                     TransactionManager
        context.getService(serviceReference);              ← service

XADataSource ds1 = ...                        ←       Retrieve
XADataSource ds2 = ...                        ❷      XADataSource

XAConnection xaConn1 =
    ds1.getXAConnection();
                                              ←
XAConnection xaConn2 =                        ❸ Use XAConnection
    ds2.getXAConnection();

tm.begin();                                   ←       Begin
                                              ❹      transaction
Transaction transaction = tm.getTransaction();
transaction.enlistResource(xaConn1.getXAResource());  ←    Enlist all
transaction.enlistResource(xaConn2.getXAResource());  ❺    resources

Connection conn1 = xaConn1.getConnection();   ←
Connection conn2 = xaConn2.getConnection();   ❻  Do work

Statement stat1 =
    conn1.createStatement();

Statement stat2 =
    conn2.createStatement();

stat1.execute("UPDATE account SET current = " + (currentA - amount)
    + " WHERE accountId = 001");

stat2.execute("UPDATE account SET current = " + (currentB + amount)
    + " WHERE accountId = 002");
                                              ❼  Commit
                                                 transaction
tm.commit();                                  ←
```

You start by retrieving the `TransactionManager` service ❶, which can be done by using the OSGi service registry. Next, you retrieve a special kind of data source called `XADataSource` ❷. We'll discuss `XADataSources` later, but for the time being just assume these to be sources that are able to participate in global transactions. `XADataSources` can be accessed by the usual means of going through OSGi's `DataSourceFactory` or, more specifically, by calling `DataSourceFactory.createXADataSource()`. Next, you retrieve an `XAConnection` for each separate RDBMS ❸.

You're now ready to start the transaction, which you do by invoking the `TransactionManager.begin()` method ❹. Immediately, a transaction is commenced and associated with the current thread. This new transaction can be retrieved by calling `TransactionManager.getTransaction()`. Note, though, that you must call `getTransaction()` from the thread that initially started the transaction.

> **NOTE** A transaction must only be executed within the context of a single thread at a time. This makes sense because otherwise, if multiple threads were executing work for the same transaction, you wouldn't be able to determine the order of the actions.

Using the `Transaction` object, you can now enlist all resources that want to participate in this global transaction, which in this case are the RDBMSs represented by the variables xaConn1 and xaConn2 ❺. You're now ready to do the actual work of executing the update statements across the databases ❻. Finally, after both updates have been done successfully, you call `commit()` on the current global transaction to terminate ❼. It's noteworthy to mention that you call `commit()` only once, rather than having a commit for each separate resource, as was done in listing 8.4.

In the end, the main difference in the case of global transactions is that you have to use a `TransactionManager` to enlist and coordinate the transactional resources, which in this case were the two JDBC data sources.

What registers the `TransactionManager` service itself? That's the role of the Java Transaction API (JTA) provider, as you'll see in the next section.

8.2.2 *Transaction providers*

The JTA provider is responsible for registering the `TransactionManager` service and the `UserTransaction` service. You've seen the use of the former one already; the latter will be described in future sections. There can be at most one JTA provider in the OSGi framework, which means that there's only a single instance of the `Transaction-Manager` and `UserTransaction` services. Therefore, you can retrieve these services from the OSGi registry by using the service interface, such as `TransactionManager`.

Are there any available OSGi-based JTA provider implementations that you can leverage? As usual, let's check by browsing well-known bundle repositories. For example, you can check in SpringSource's repository: http://www.springsource.com/repository/app/. Type transaction manager in the input box, and as of this writing you'll get the following implementation: Java Open Transaction Manager 2.0.10. It's great to be able to reuse software, isn't it? You'll note that JOTM has several dependencies, such as the `javax.transaction` API itself, so don't forget to retrieve these as well.

As you've seen, one of the tasks of the `TransactionManager` is to coordinate resources, but what exactly are these, and how do they coordinate in a manner that we're able to accomplish atomicity across distributed resources? The answers to these questions are covered in the next section.

8.2.3   *The two-phase commit protocol*

To be able to reach an agreement across distributed resources, the Transaction-Manager uses what's known as a *consensus protocol.* As you've seen, the Transaction-Manager starts by having a list of all resources that wish to participate in the transaction. It then follows a two-step process:

1   The TransactionManager finds out if all resources are ready to commit. It does so by invoking the method prepare() on each resource.

2   If all resources acknowledge the prepare() method successfully, then the next step is to invoke the method commit() on each resource, informing the resource that it can commit its local part of the transaction. If at any point there's a failure, then the rollback() method is invoked on each resource, informing it to discard the changes.

Because of this two-phase approach, this protocol is also known as the *two-phase commit (2PC) protocol.* The Open Group organization specifies the 2PC protocol in the XA specification, so resources and connections that participate in the 2PC protocol are often called XA resources and XA connections. An example of this interaction between a TransactionManager and two XAResources is illustrated in figure 8.3.

As has become evident, dealing with global transactions can be daunting. We'll look into ways of simplifying this in the next section.

8.3   *Containers*

Dealing with all the details of resource managers, transaction managers, and XA protocols can be quite overwhelming. Consider again our simple bank application; at the

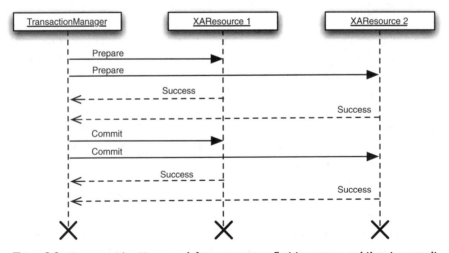

Figure 8.3   TransactionManager informs resources first to prepare and then to commit.

heart of it, we just want to debit one account and credit another one. In other words, our application logic shouldn't have to worry about enlisting resources and beginning and ending transactions. These activities are all potentially infrastructure work.

To simplify the development of transacted applications, we should refactor the transaction-handling code into some library or, more precisely, into the application container. Let's look at trivial example to illustrate the point. Suppose we define two Java annotations, @Resource and @Transaction, which respectively can be used to annotate methods that return XA resources and methods that perform work on these resources within the context of a transaction. These annotations can be implemented as follows:

```
@Retention(value = RetentionPolicy.RUNTIME)
public @interface Transaction {
}

@Retention(value = RetentionPolicy.RUNTIME)
public @interface Resource {
}
```

The following listing uses these annotations to implement our banking example.

Listing 8.6 Container-managed JDBC global transactions

```
public void start(BundleContext bundleContext) throws Exception {
    ServiceReference [] serviceReferences =
      bundleContext.getServiceReferences(
        DataSourceFactory.class.toString(),
        "(" + DataSourceFactory.OSGI_JDBC_DRIVER_CLASS +
        "=org.apache.derby.jdbc.EmbeddedDriver)");

  if (serviceReferences != null) {
     DataSourceFactory dsf =
        (DataSourceFactory)
        bundleContext.getService(serviceReferences[0]);

     Properties props = new Properties();
     props.put(DataSourceFactory.JDBC_URL,
   "jdbc:derby:derbyDB1;create=true");

     ds1 =
        dsf.createXADataSource(props);                   ❶ Create XADataSource
                                                            from factory

     props.put(DataSourceFactory.JDBC_URL,
        "jdbc:derby:derbyDB2;create=true");

     ds2 =
        dsf.createXADataSource(props);
  }
}
                                                         ❷ Enlist
                                                            XAConnection
@Resource
public XAConnection getAccountToBeDebited() throws SQLException {
```

```
        return ds1.getXAConnection();
}

@Resource
public XAConnection getAccountToBeCredited() throws SQLException {
        return ds2.getXAConnection();
}

@Transaction                                              ❸ Execute in context
public void doWork() throws SQLException {                   of a transaction
        Connection conn1 = getAccountToBeDebited().getConnection();
        Connection conn2 = getAccountToBeCredited().getConnection();

        Statement stat1 =
           conn1.createStatement();

        Statement stat2 =
           conn2.createStatement();

        stat1.execute("UPDATE account SET current = " + (currentA - amount)
           + " WHERE accountId = 001");

        stat2.execute("UPDATE account SET current = " + (currentB + amount)
           + " WHERE accountId = 002");
}
```

You start off by retrieving the DataSourceFactory from the OSGi service factory, which you use to create two XADataSources, one for each bank account ❶. You store these as field instances. Next, you annotate the methods getAccountToBeDebited() and getAccountToBeCredited() with the Resource annotation ❷, indicating that these methods are returning XA resources (or XA connections) that should be enlisted in the transactional work to be performed. As expected, these methods are returning the XAConnections created from the XADataSource retrieved previously. Finally, the method doWork() ❸ implements the actual application logic that's dealing with the bank account update. Note how the method includes no details related to transaction handling; not even a commit at the end is necessary.

> **NOTE** Application containers are powerful and useful. In this section, we're looking at a barebones example of how to implement a container that manages user transactions. We could have gone further and integrated the transaction handling with the persistence handling and avoided the user code having to deal with JDBC at all.

Next, you need to come up with a mechanism to inform the container that a particular bundle has transactional Java classes. To do this, follow a similar approach to that of JPA, which is the definition of a new manifest header entry, as follows:

```
Meta-Transaction: manning.osgi.TransactionalBankAcountTransfer
```

As expected, you can use the extender pattern to find the transactional Java classes and process them adequately. This is illustrated in the following listing.

Listing 8.7 Transactional container extender

```
public class TransactionalContainerActivator implements BundleActivator,
    BundleListener {

    TransactionManager tm;

    public void start(BundleContext context) throws Exception {

        tm = getTransactionManagerService(context);          ◁──── ❶ Retrieve
                                                                     TransactionManager

        context.addBundleListener(this);                     ◁──── ❷ Register
    }                                                                BundleListener

    public void bundleChanged(BundleEvent event) {
        if (event.getType() == BundleEvent.STARTED) {        ◁──── ❸ Check when
            try {                                                    bundle is started
                String transactionalClassName =
                    (String) event.getBundle().
                    getHeaders().get("Meta-Transaction");    ◁──── ❹ Retrieve
                                                                     Meta-Transaction
                                                                     header entry
                Class<?> transactionalClass =
                    event.getBundle().
                    loadClass(transactionalClassName);       ◁──── ❺ Load specified
                                                                     class
                Object transactionalObject =
                    transactionalClass.newInstance();

                List<XAResource> resourcesToEnlist =
                    new LinkedList<XAResource>();

                Method [] methods =
                    transactionalClass.getMethods();

                Method doWorkMethod = null;

                for (Method method : methods) {
                    if (method.getAnnotation(Resource.class)  ❻ Process Resource
                       != null) {                        ◁──────   annotation
                        Object obj =
                            method.invoke(transactionalObject, new Object[]{});

                        if (obj instanceof XAConnection) {
                            resourcesToEnlist.add(
                            ((XAConnection) obj).getXAResource());
                        } else if (obj instanceof XAResource) {
                            resourcesToEnlist.add((XAResource) obj);
                        } else {
                            throw new IllegalStateException("Missing Resource
                            ➥ annotation");
                        }
                    }

                    if (method.getAnnotation(Transaction.class)
                       != null) {                        ◁──────  Process Transaction
                        doWorkMethod = method;                ❼ annotation
                    }
                }
```

```
              doTransactionalWork(transactionalObject, resourcesToEnlisted,
                      doWorkMethod);                                       Execute
                                                                          transactional
          } catch (Exception e) {                                    ❽    work
              // Log
          }
      }

      // ...
  }
```

You start by retrieving the `TransactionManager` service ❶ and registering a bundle listener into the OSGi framework ❷. The `TransactionManager` service is kept as a field instance, because you'll use it later when processing the user's transactional class.

The `BundleListener` verifies whether a bundle that's being started ❸ contains the `Meta-Transaction` header entry ❹, in which case it loads the specified class using the client bundle ❺ to check the annotations it uses. If any of its methods declare a `Resource` annotation ❻, then you invoke such a method by instantiating a new object instance and storing the return value, which must be either an `XAResource` or an `XAConnection`. Likewise, you look for a method that's annotated with the `Transaction` annotation ❼. Finally, you gather all of these findings and invoke the method `doTransactionalWork()` ❽, which is explained in the next listing.

Listing 8.8 `doTransactionalWork` method

```
private void doTransactionalWork(Object transactionalObject,
        List<XAResource> resourcesToEnlist, Method doWorkMethod)
        throws Exception {
    if (doWorkMethod != null) {                              ❶  Begin
        tm.begin();                                              transaction

        javax.transaction.Transaction transaction =
tm.getTransaction();

        for (XAResource resource : resourcesToEnlist) {     ❷  Enlist all
            transaction.enlistResource(resource);               resources
        }

        doWorkMethod.invoke(transactionalObject,            ❸  Invoke client code
          new Object[]{});
                                                 ❹  Commit
        tm.commit();                                transaction
    } else {
        throw new IllegalStateException("Missing Transaction annotation");
    }
}
```

The `doTransactionWork()` method does the bulk of the work relating to handling the user's transaction. You start by commencing the transaction using the `Transaction-Manager` service ❶, and then you iterate through all the XA resources you retrieved from the methods that had been annotated with the `Resource` annotation and enlist each of them in the currently running `Transaction` object ❷. You're now ready to invoke the client's code ❸, which implements the application logic. But this application logic code can avoid becoming cluttered with the transaction-handling details, as in listing 8.6. Finally, after the client's code returns, you commit the transaction ❹.

In summary, note how the code in listing 8.5 is mostly refactored into an application piece, which is in listing 8.6, and a container (infrastructure) piece, which is in listings 8.7 and 8.8.

Distilling the extender pattern

Why do we need a `Meta-Transaction` header entry to begin with? Couldn't we just have our `TransactionalExtenderActivator` class blindly go through all the resources of all started bundles looking for those classes that have been tagged with our annotations?

In addition to the obvious performance downside, another reason to avoid this approach is that the extender class becomes tightly coupled with the client bundles. Instead, it's better to define an explicit contract between the extender and the clients, which is the role of the manifest header entry.

So there you have it; we've implemented our own naïve but functional container that provides managed transactions to our client bundles. Following are some ideas for improvements:

- Similarly to JPA, change the `Meta-Transaction` manifest header entry to point to an XML file rather than the Java class name.
- Integrate JPA into the container, so that it can provide not only managed transactions but also managed persistence.
- Similar to the JEE containers, you could support other transaction attributes, such as joining to some other running transaction, rather than always starting a new transaction for your transactional Java classes.

These are just some possible ideas. Now, let's take a step back and consider the interaction between the bundles involved. There's a client bundle, which contains the application logic, the container bundle, which manages the transaction on behalf of the client bundle, and the JTA provider bundle, which provides the implementation of the `TransactionManager` itself. Does this pattern of interactions, depicted in figure 8.4, remind you of anything?

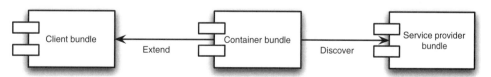

Figure 8.4 The client bundle is extended by the container bundle. The container bundle retrieves infrastructure service from the service provider bundle.

Yes, it's exactly how the JPA feature works. JPA similarly has a client bundle, the JPA bundle itself, and the JDBC driver bundle involved in doing the actual persistence. The JPA bundle acts as a mediator, simplifying the client's bundle usage of the JDBC driver to achieve persistence. This is the same role as our `TransactionalContainer-Activator` class; it hides the usage of the `TransactionManager` from the client bundle containing the application logic.

When well designed, application containers are just that: mediators between a client and an infrastructure service, which take care of abstracting the latter for the former. We can follow this same design pattern, which we'll denominate as the *application container design pattern*, for all types of infrastructure-related services, ranging from transactions and persistence to logging, security, and even domain-specific services, such as order processing and algorithmic trading.

Application container design pattern

Intent—Abstract application logic from having to know the details of infrastructure services, such as persistence and transactions.

Participants—Client bundle, container bundle, infrastructure-service provider bundle.

Structure—The container bundle mediates between the client bundle and the infrastructure-service provider bundle. This is done by having the mediator bundle reach out to the client bundle by means of the extender pattern and then using the registry design pattern to interact with the infrastructure-service provider bundle.

Consequences—The infrastructure-service provider bundles and client bundles are completely decoupled; the latter can use different programming models, such as annotations and declarative interfaces, without impacting the former and allowing the infrastructure services to evolve separately.

Known uses—JPA.

Related patterns—Extender design pattern, registry design pattern.

There's one final issue in the `TransactionalContainerActivator` class we've ignored so far, that of error handling. Next, we'll tackle this issue.

8.3.1 *Error handling*

Let's look at the core of the `doTransactionalWork()` method again:

```
tm.begin();

Transaction transaction = tm.getTransaction();

for (XAResource resource : resourcesToEnlist)
    transaction.enlistResource(resource);

doWorkMethod.invoke(transactionalObject, new Object[]{});

tm.commit();
```

What happens if the client code, which is invoked through the `doWorkMethod.`
`invoke()` method, fails and raises an exception? You would have started a transaction
but never invoked `commit`. The `TransactionManager` has no way of knowing about the
client's exception and would still think that the transaction is valid and that an outcome
is still coming. But eventually it would time out and realize something was wrong.

Instead of waiting for a timeout, the proper behavior for the container is to automatically roll back the current transaction in the case of a user error, as in the following listing:

Listing 8.9 Rolling back a transaction

```
tm.begin();
try {

    javax.transaction.Transaction transaction = tm.getTransaction();

    for (XAResource resource : resourcesToEnlist) {
        transaction.enlistResource(resource);
    }

    doWorkMethod.invoke(transactionalObject, new Object[]{});

    tm.commit();
} catch (Exception e) {
    tm.rollback();                              ◁────┐   Roll back if
    // re-throw, or consume...                       ❶  exception is raised
}
```

In this new version, you catch any exception that may have happened while the transaction is open and immediately roll back the transaction ❶. This is particularly important any time you're dealing with client code, because you have no control over what
the client application may be doing.

In this particular example, the client code raised an exception when things went
amiss. What if the client decided to abort the transaction, not because of an excep-
tional situation but because of the application's logic? Would you need to raise an
exception and cause it to be perhaps logged as an error, or is there a way of giving
back a bit of the control related to the transaction handling to the user? We'll investigate this question in the next section.

8.3.2 *User transactions*

Using container-managed transactions, clients get shielded from the grinding details
of the `TransactionManager` service, such as enlisting the XA resources. But there are
cases when the client needs to have some control over the transaction handling.

For example, you may need to explicitly start and end the transaction, perhaps
because you want to do some nontransactional work before getting into the transactional piece, as illustrated next:

```
nonTransactionalWork();

transactionalWork();

nonTransactionalWork();
```

Or, as you saw in the previous section, you may want to discard the transaction without having to raise an exception.

This is possible with the `UserTransaction` service. Similar to the `Transaction-Manager` service, the JTA provider registers the `UserTransaction` service, and you're guaranteed to have just one of it in the system. Using the `UserTransaction` service, a client can explicitly define the transaction boundaries by invoking the methods `begin()`, `commit()`, and even `rollback()`.

Let's look at an example of its usage. First, you retrieve the service as usual:

```
ServiceReference serviceReference =
    bundleContext.getServiceReference(
        UserTransaction.class.toString());

UserTransaction ut =
    (UserTransaction) bundleContext.getService(serviceReference);
```

Next, you change the `doWork()` method of listing 8.6 to validate whether the account has enough money to be withdrawn for the transfer, as shown in the following listing.

Listing 8.10   User transaction

```
public void doWork() throws Exception {
    Connection conn1 = getAccountToBeDebited().getConnection();
    Connection conn2 = getAccountToBeCredited().getConnection();

    conn1.setAutoCommit(false);
    conn2.setAutoCommit(false);

    Statement stat1 =
        conn1.createStatement();

    Statement stat2 =
        conn2.createStatement();

    stat2.execute("UPDATE account SET current = " + (currentB + amount)
        + " WHERE accountId = 002");

    if (currentA - amount < 0.0)                    ❶ Roll back current
        ut.rollback();                                transaction

    stat1.execute("UPDATE account SET current = " + (currentA - amount)
        + " WHERE accountId = 001");

}
```

If the account doesn't have enough money to be withdrawn for the transfer, you roll back the whole transaction ❶.

The OSGi framework provides us with one advantage that may have gone unnoticed here. In other platforms, the `UserTransaction` service would have been handled for the application by means of the container. In this case, the application has the flexibility of getting this service itself, when and if needed. Table 8.1 summarizes the different flavors of transaction handling we've discussed so far.

Table 8.1 Transaction-handling styles

Characteristics	Advantages	Disadvantages
Compensation handling	JTA provider not needed	Error prone; does not scale
TransactionManager	Most flexible	Client has to enlist resources and control transaction directly
UserTransaction	Some flexibility; user can determine demarcations	Client has to retrieve UserTransaction service
Container managed	Client is shielded from all complexity	Least flexible approach

Transactions are a powerful concept, because they provide a simple abstraction to deal with the complex problem of achieving atomicity across diverse actions, a common enough problem for most enterprise applications. Furthermore, OSGi improves this by allowing us to work with different transaction-handling approaches, varying from container-managed transactions to letting the client use the complete service.

8.4 Summary

It's not always enough to make a single action durable. There are cases, such as the transfer of money from one bank account to another, where several actions need to be made durable in an atomic fashion. That is, either all of them happen or none of them happen; otherwise, the application consistency may be lost.

There are several methods for achieving atomicity, one being the definition of an undo-work for each do-work. But this approach doesn't scale. Another approach is the use of transactions, which by definition are ACID (atomic, consistent, isolated, and durable).

Transactions provide three main operations: `begin`, `commit`, and `rollback`. Transactions can be local, if they involve a single resource, or global, if they involve several resources. When they're global, a `TransactionManager` is needed to coordinate consensus across all of the resources.

The JTA provider is responsible for registering a `TransactionManager` service and a `UserTransaction` service in the OSGi registry.

The `TransactionManager` service can be unyielding to use, so it's not uncommon for a container bundle to abstract it for a client bundle. The container bundle can extend the client bundle, for example, by providing annotations, and therefore prevent the client bundle from having to deal directly with the `TransactionManager` service. But if the client bundle needs additional flexibility, such as defining its own transaction demarcations, then it can interact directly with the `UserTransaction` service, which is simpler to use.

As you've seen, to support transactions it's often necessary to coordinate across distributed resources. But how do you find these resources to begin with? Finding resources in enterprise-wide *yellow pages* is the subject of our next chapter.

Blending OSGi and Java EE using JNDI

This chapter covers

- Sharing resources between Java EE and Java SE applications and OSGi bundles
- Exploring what JNDI is and how it's used
- Retrieving a JNDI object in an OSGi environment
- Performing object conversions
- Registering JNDI providers in an OSGi environment
- Embedding the OSGi framework on top of Java EE and Java SE applications

The OSGi technology and other Java platforms, such as Java EE, can commingle. You don't need to necessarily choose a single technology and stick to it. This is important, because it's unlikely that you'll be able to commit to a single technology anyway—there's always going to be the question of integrating and supporting legacy applications. This chapter describes mechanisms that allow for integration between OSGi and legacy Java EE and Java SE applications.

We'll start this chapter by addressing an issue that may have come to your mind when we went through the transaction-related examples of the last chapter. Specifically, how would you find a Java EE resource, such as `DataSource`?

9.1 Sharing resources

In the last chapter, you learned how to enlist resources together into a single transaction; this is needed to allow them to be executed atomically. But before you can utilize a resource, you must be able to find it. Finding resources in OSGi is simple enough; you use the OSGi service registry, because as the OSGi usage patterns observe, these resources have been registered as OSGi services. Unfortunately, this doesn't work in the case of Java EE resources, which are unaware of OSGi.

Is it common that you'd need to reach out to Java SE and Java EE applications to retrieve non-OSGi resources? Yes. In particular, Java EE applications are a rich provider of resources, such as these:

- EJB interfaces
- JDBC data sources and connection pools
- JMS factories and connections
- JCA adapters
- Business processes

What should you use to find and retrieve non-OSGi resources? As you'll see next, you need to use a yellow-pages service called JNDI.

9.2 Understanding Java's yellow pages

JNDI (Java Naming and Directory Interface) is a framework that allows Java clients to make use of naming and directory services. Different naming and directory service providers can plug into JNDI and by doing so provide a consistent naming and directory service API for their Java clients, as shown in figure 9.1.

Before we get into the details of JNDI, let's investigate the concepts behind naming and directory services.

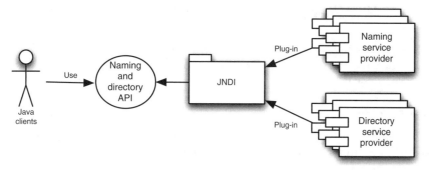

Figure 9.1 JNDI provides a common naming and directory service API that allows Java clients to make use of different providers.

A naming service is a service that can be used to associate a name with an object. Perhaps without realizing it, you've likely used this concept already. Anytime you type a web address, such as www.manning.com, into a browser, the browser is using a naming service called DNS (Domain Name System) to convert this URL string to an actual IP address. In this case, the URL is the name, and the IP address is the object bound to it. A naming service Name must support hierarchies. In the example shown in figure 9.2, the component "manning" is under the component "com", which is the root for commercial entities. In other words, a JNDI

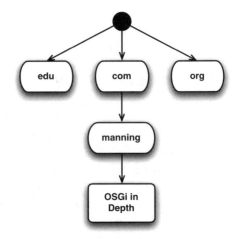

Figure 9.2   Hierarchical layout of a JNDI component name

name is made of individual components. An name that has more than a single component is called a compound name.

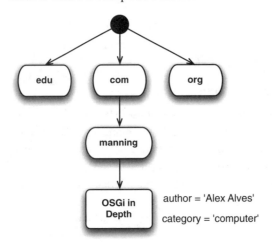

Figure 9.3   Attributes, such as author = 'Alex Alves', associated with objects

JNDI is also a directory service. A directory service allows the association of attributes to an object. One example of this is your phone service's yellow pages book. A yellow pages directory allows you to find a business address using different *attributes*, such as its profession or type of business. In figure 9.3, several attributes, such as author, are associated with the OSGi in Depth object.

LDAP (Lightweight Directory Access Protocol) is another example of a directory service.

Now that you understand the basic concepts, let's look at how you can retrieve an object using JNDI.

9.2.1 Looking up objects

The most basic operation of JNDI is to perform name-based lookups of objects that have been bound to it. The following example illustrates this:

```
InitialContext context = new InitialContext();

Context subContext =
    (Context) context.lookup("jdbc");
```

```
DataSource ds =
    (DataSource) subContext.lookup("AccountDS");
```

You start by creating an initial context, which establishes the root of the hierarchy of objects whose names exist in JNDI. We'll look into the details of creating the `Initial-Context` in later sections. Next, you need to invoke the `lookup()` method, specifying a name, which in this case is `"jdbc"`. The `lookup()` method returns the bound object. But in this case, it so happens that the object that has been bound to the `"jdbc"` name is yet another context, or rather a subcontext. Subcontexts function as directories within directories and allow you to create the hierarchical structure we discussed previously. Having gotten the `"jdbc"` subcontext, you use that to retrieve the actual `Data-Source` object bound to the name `"AccountDS"`.

> **NOTE**   A subcontext is a name component.

When looking up objects in JNDI, you don't always need to traverse the naming service in piecemeal steps. You can actually specify a compound name, as demonstrated next:

```
InitialContext context = new InitialContext();

DataSource ds =
    (DataSource) context.lookup("comp/env/jdbc/AccountDS");
```

As expected, you start by creating the initial context. Next, you invoke the `lookup()` method, specifying the compound name of `"comp/env/jdbc/AccountDS"`. In this case, you traverse through the subcontexts of `"comp"`, then `"en"`, and then finally `"jdbc"`, before getting to the actual `DataSource` object in which you're interested. Note that the name's literal value could have been anything, but it's a Java EE convention to place JDBC resources under the subcontexts of `"comp/env/jdbc"`. To be precise, you should also specify the namespace of `"java"`, transforming this compound name into a URL: java:comp/env/jdbc/AccoundDS. A URL is a special type of compound name and is treated differently by JNDI, as you'll see later in this chapter.

Let's contrast JNDI's lookup with the usual OSGi service retrieval you're now used to:

```
ServiceReference reference =
    context.getServiceReference("javax.sql.DataSource");

DataSource ds = (DataSource)
    context.getService(reference);
```

Note how, aside from the naming convention, there are many similarities between doing a lookup in JNDI and retrieving a service in the OSGi service registry. In the following listing, we'll look up an object using attributes.

Listing 9.1   Directory service lookup

```
InitialDirContext context = new InitialDirContext();

BasicAttributes attrs = new BasicAttributes();        ❶ Specify
attrs.put(new BasicAttribute("ver", "1.1"));              attribute
```

```
DataSource ds =
    (DataSource) context.search("java:comp/env/jdbc/AccountDS",
    attrs);
```

As usual, you start by establishing the root of the hierarchy, but in this case you use `InitialDirContext` instead of just `InitialContext`. Next, you specify the attribute that you're interested in using as the filtering criteria; in this example, we're looking for a data source whose version (that is, `ver`) is `"1.1"` ❶. Finally, you do the actual search.

You can also specify the attributes as a logical expression, instead of manipulating them programmatically as you did in listing 9.1. The following listing illustrates this.

Listing 9.2   Directory service lookup using logical expressions

```
InitialDirContext context = new InitialDirContext();

SearchControls control = new SearchControls();

DataSource ds =
    (DataSource) context.search("java:comp/env/jdbc/AccountDS",
        "(ver=1.1)", control);
```

To begin, you need to create an instance of a `SearchControls` class. This is used to set parameters for the search, such as the maximum number of entries to search for or the maximum amount of time to use. Next, you specify the logical expression to be used for filtering as `"(ver=1.1)"`. Note that for the purpose of this example, we're assuming that the `InitialDirContext` is being backed up by an LDAP directory service; therefore, the logical expression is the one defined by the LDAP recommendation.

Again, contrast this approach with OSGi:

```
ServiceReference [] references =
        context.getServiceReferences("javax.sql.DataSource","(ver=1.1)");
DataSource ds = (DataSource)
    context.getService(references[0]);
```

In the previous chapters, you learned that OSGi's service-filtering language is based on the LDAP syntax. As you can see, this isn't merely coincidental; the OSGi service registry can be considered an implementation of a directory service, albeit with some dissimilarities we'll discuss later.

So far, we've looked at how to retrieve objects. Next, let's look at how to get them into the directory, a process called *binding*.

9.2.2   Binding objects

Let's look how you bind an object to a name:

```
DataSource ds = ...
InitialContext context = new InitialContext();
context.bind("java:comp/env/jdbc/AccountDS", ds);
```

This is straightforward enough and still similar to OSGi's service registry:

```
context.registerService(DataSource.class.getName(), ds);
```

Finally, to bind a new subcontext, you can use the `createSubcontext()` method:

```
context.createSubcontext("jdbc");
```

We've discussed the similarities, but there are also meaningful differences. Most notably, JNDI is organized as a hierarchy, whereas OSGi's services are flat. For example, JNDI supports the listings of all objects under a context, through the `listBindings()` method. The following code lists all objects under the context of `"comp/env/jdbc"`:

```
NamingEnumeration<Binding> bindings =
    context.listBindings("java:comp/env/jdbc");

while (bindings.hasMore()) {
    Binding bd = (Binding) bindings.next();
    System.out.println("Name = " + bd.getName() + ", Object = " +
        bd.getObject());
}
```

Running this code should print out the relative name "AccountDS" and the actual data source object instance. The OSGi framework API has no such facility. That is, even though a service interface is defined as a hierarchical name, as in the case of `javax.sql.DataSource`, there's no mechanism for listing all services under `javax.sql`.

Another important differentiation is that JNDI natively supports federations, as you'll see in the next section.

9.2.3 *Naming federations*

A naming or directory service federation is a system that crosses over separate individual naming or directory services. This is better explained through an example.

Consider the following JNDI name of `"www.manning.com/Books/OSGi-InDepth.pdf"`. As you've seen, the initial part of `"www.manning.com"` maps into a manning subcontext related to a DNS naming service. But following that, the `"Books"` component represents a folder in a filesystem, and `"OSGiInDepth.pdf"` a file within that. In other words, we're crossing over from one naming convention to another. JNDI gracefully and transparently handles this by returning the appropriate `File` object when the name `"www.manning.com/Books/OSGiInDepth.pdf"` is looked up using the JNDI context. The JNDI provider accomplishes this by following a pointer object from one naming service to the next naming service. This pointer, or `Reference`, as it's called, is reached when the component name separator of / is found.

A JNDI name that includes components from more than one naming service or directory service is called a *composite name,* as opposed to a *compound name.* In other words, a composite name is federated, as illustrated in figure 9.4.

This concept of a reference is important for several reasons. It's not always possible to return the actual target object from a JNDI lookup. For example, the JNDI object might be pointing to a remote object instance that lives in a separate process or even a separate machine. Furthermore, there are cases when it may not even be ideal to store

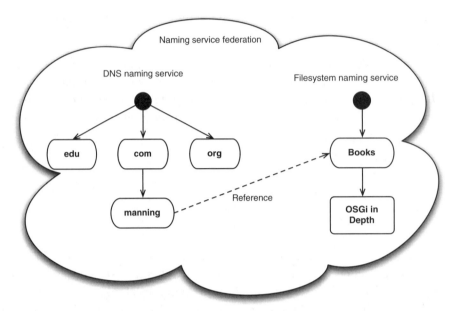

Figure 9.4   A composite name that crosses over a DNS naming service to a filesystem naming service

the object in the JNDI registry to begin with. One reason is that the object could be too large. In such cases, JNDI uses the concept of a `Reference`.

A `Reference` has information about the address of its target object, which is specified through the `RefAddr` class. One example of a `RefAddr` is a `URL`.

> **NOTE** A `Reference` may have several `RefAddr` classes; this is useful when you need to provide replicas of the object for the purpose of supporting fault tolerance. Application servers commonly use this approach for fault-tolerant RMI objects.

In addition, a `Reference` has metadata about the object itself, such as its Java class name. Finally, a `Reference` can provide for a factory, called the `ObjectFactory`, which is used to create a local copy of the object.

> **NOTE** `DirObjectFactory`, which extends `ObjectFactory`, can be used instead for directory service objects. `DirObjectFactory` takes one additional parameter, which is a set of directory service `Attributes`.

Continuing with our example, the following code binds a `Reference` to a JNDI lookup representing the external `"Books"` object:

```
manningContext.bind("Books", new Reference(Context.class.toString(),
    "com.manning.FSObjectFactory", null));
```

When a user looks up the `Object` that has been bound to the name `"Books"` under the context `"www.manning.com"`, JNDI uses the class `com.manning.FSObjectFactory` to create a new `Context` object that's located in the foreign filesystem-based naming service. Why not just bind the `File` object directly in JNDI? You can't bind it directly, because the `File` isn't a local file but rather a remote file that lives in the machine whose address (that is, IP address) has been bound to the parent context of `"www.manning.com"`. Thus, it's the role of the `FSObjectFactory` to convert the machine address combined with the `"Books"` name to a remote filesystem location. As you'll see, `ObjectFactory` objects are powerful and can also be used for the sole purpose of accomplishing object conversions, and not exclusively for federating naming and directory services, as we've done here. You'll see examples of this in the next section. To some extent, a JNDI `Reference` is comparable to an OSGi `ServiceReference`.

We've gone through the major concepts of JNDI, contrasting with the OSGi service registry when applicable. What you've learned so far is that these registries are similar in nature.

Let's take a step back. Our initial goal is to be able to access Java EE resources within an OSGi environment. As you've learned in this section, Java EE resources are bound to JNDI. Therefore, to fulfill our goal, we need to be able to use JNDI within a bundle. We'll look at how to accomplish that in the next section.

9.3 Establishing the initial context

In the previous section, we glossed over the creation of JNDI's `InitialContext`. The `InitialContext` not only establishes the root of the naming hierarchy but also works as a proxy to the actual naming and directory service provider.

Let's take another look at the creation of an `InitialContext`:

```
Hashtable env = new Hashtable();
    env.put(Context.INITIAL_CONTEXT_FACTORY,
        "com.sun.jndi.fscontext.RefFSContextFactory");
    InitialContext context = new InitialContext(env);
```

In reality, when creating the `InitialContext` you can pass along to its constructor a map of properties, containing the `INITIAL_CONTEXT_FACTORY` property. The value of this property must be the fully qualified name of a class that implements the `Initial-ContextFactory` interface and is responsible for creating the initial context instances that are backed up by a particular JNDI service provider, such as LDAP, or a filesystem-based one, as in the previous example.

> **NOTE** If the `INITIAL_CONTEXT_FACTORY` property isn't specified in the constructor, then an environment variable of the same name (`java.naming.factory.initial`) is used if available.

The interaction that happens within the JRE for making use of this factory isn't trivial. This interaction, illustrated in figure 9.5, is as follows:

1 The user instantiates an `InitialContext` object.
2 The `InitialContext`'s constructor invokes the static method `Naming-Manager.getInitialContext()`.

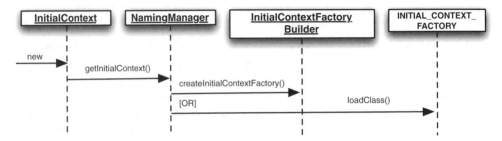

Figure 9.5 `InitialContext` **invokes the** `NamingManager`, **which invokes the** `InitialContexFactoryBuilder` **if set or loads the** `InitialContextFactory` **using the** `INITIAL_CONTEXT_FACTORY` **property.**

3   If `InitialContextFactoryBuilder` isn't set, then JNDI loads the class using the class name specified in the `INITIAL_CONTEXT_FACTORY` property. The class loader used in this case is the context class loader of the current thread (`Thread.currentThread().getContextClassLoader()`). A `NoInitialContext-Exception` is raised if this property wasn't set.

4   If `InitialContextFactoryBuilder` is set, then JNDI invokes `InitialContext-FactoryBuilder.createInitialContextFactory()`, which is responsible for interpreting the `INITIAL_CONTEXT_FACTORY` property as it wishes. Therefore, by calling `NamingManager.setInitialContextFactoryBuilder()`, a user can override the JRE's default policies. Note that in this case the `INITIAL_CONTEXT_FACTORY` property is optional.

5   Having retrieved an `InitialContextFactory`, JNDI finally invokes `Initial-ContextFactory.getInitialContext()`, which must return a non-null object that implements `Context`.

Unfortunately, this interaction has several problems when executed in the OSGi platform. First of all, because the thread's context class loader is used to load the `InitialContextFactory`, this forces the client bundle to import the JNDI provider implementation in the bundle's own class space. This breaks modularity. Ideally, we'd like to keep the JNDI provider implementation decoupled from the client bundle, as we've done for other services, such as JPA.

Furthermore, if a bundle were to instantiate an `InitialContext` object, then the fact that a static method is later invoked means that ultimately the JNDI implementation providing the `InitialContext` isn't able to keep track of the client dependencies. In other words, if the JNDI provider is implemented as an OSGi service and it dynamically changes, there's no way of letting the client know of the changes.

WARNING   Static method invocations break modularity.

Finally, this interaction prevents us from using OSGi as an extension framework to support the plug-ins of the different JNDI providers. In the next section, we'll look at how we can avoid all of these problems.

9.3.1 Initial contexts in OSGi

As you've seen, you need a different mechanism for getting access to the `Initial-Context` when running in an OSGi environment. It should come as no surprise that this new approach is to use an OSGi service. This is demonstrated in the next listing.

Listing 9.3 Using JNDI in a bundle

```
ServiceReference ref =
    bundleContext.getServiceReference(                    ➊ Retrieve
        JNDIContextManager.class.toString());    ⬅──┘       JNDIContextManager

JNDIContextManager ctxtMgr =
    (JNDIContextManager) bundleContext.getService(ref);

Hashtable env = new Hashtable();
env.put(Context.INITIAL_CONTEXT_FACTORY,              ➋ Set properties
"com.sun.jndi.fscontext.RefFSContextFactory");  ⬅──┘   as in Java EE

Context context =                          ➌ Create
    ctxtMgr.newInitialContext(env);  ⬅──┘    InitialContext

DataSource ds =
    (DataSource) context.                          ➍ Perform lookup of
        lookup("java:comp/env/jdbc/AccountDS");  ⬅──┘  Java EE resources
```

First, you retrieve the singleton service `JNDIContextManager` ➊. Next, as in the Java EE case, you need to set the same `INITIAL_CONTEXT_FACTORY` property with the name of the JNDI provider you wish to use ➋. You can now invoke the `newInitial-Context()` method in the `JNDIContextManager` service ➌, which returns the initial JNDI context. Using this context, you can finally look up the Java EE you want ➍.

> **NOTE** `newInitialContext()` returns an instance of `Context` and not of `InitialContext`. This is preferable because `Context` is defined as a Java interface and not as a Java class, which is the case for `InitialContext`.

If instead you need a reference to the initial directory context, you should invoke `JNDIContextManager.newInitialDirContext()`.

The `JNDIContextManager` service prevents you from having to go through a static method, as was the case with `NamingManager.getInitialContext()`. But you still have the problem of loading the class specified by the `INITIAL_CONTEXT_FACTORY` property, without using the thread's context class loader. This is naturally solved by the `JNDI-ContextManager` looking up the `InitialContextFactory` class in the OSGi registry as a standard OSGi service. In other words, for a JNDI provider to be used in an OSGi environment, it must be registered as an OSGi service. The OSGi service interface used must specify two Java classes: the `InitialContextFactory` interface, and the implementation class used in the `INITIAL_CONTEXT_FACTORY` property.

> **WARNING** During the lookup of the `InitialContextFactory`, the requesting bundle's context is used rather than the bundle context of the `JNDIContext-Manager` service. But the requesting bundle doesn't need to import the

package of the provider implementation class because the `JNDIContext-Manager` loads the provider implementation class.

For example, the following code registers a JNDI provider for the `RefFSContext-Factory` implementation that would be retrieved in the previous code listing:

```
bundleContext.registerService(
    new String [] {InitialContextFactory.class.toString(),
        "com.sun.jndi.fscontext.RefFSContextFactory"},
    refFSContextFactoryImpl,
    null);
```

How is the `InitialContextFactoryBuilder` handled in the OSGi case? As expected, the `InitialContextFactoryBuilder` must also be registered as an OSGi service in the service registry. But OSGi differentiates the cases when the `INITIAL_CONTEXT_FACTORY` property is being set or not. If it's being set, then the `InitialContextFactoryBuilder` is only used as a backup, should the appropriate `InitialContextFactory` service not be found in the OSGi registry. In other words, only if the `JNDIContextManager` can't find any `InitialContextFactory` services that implement the class being specified by the `INITIAL_CONTEXT_FACTORY` property would it then search for an `InitialContext-FactoryBuilder` service. If multiple builder services are found, then it tries each one in order of service ranking. It stops as soon as the first one returns a non-null value as a result of invoking the method `InitialContextFactoryBuilder.createInitial-ContextFactory()`.

But if the `INITIAL_CONTEXT_FACTORY` property isn't already set, then the roles are reversed. The `JNDIContextManager` retrieves all `InitialContextFactoryBuilder` services, and only if none of them return a non-null `InitialContextFactory` would it then try any `InitialContextFactory` services that may be registered. Likewise, considering the order of service rankings, it would try to create an `InitialContext` using the factories and stop when the first one returns a non-null value. This procedure is illustrated in figure 9.6.

As you can see, OSGi is used as the extension mechanism for plugging in different JNDI providers. But OSGi's dynamic nature allows JNDI providers to be dynamically added and removed. How do you cope with this potential change of providers as they're being used? You can handle this by having the `Context` object returned by the `JNDIContextManager` represent a proxy to the actual provider implementation, as shown in figure 9.7. This means that this `Context` object can be dynamically rebound to a different provider.

Complexity apart, what are the big takeaways you should learn in this section?

- A client bundle must go through the `JNDIContextManager` to use JNDI.
- A JNDI provider wishing to participate in an OSGI environment must register an `InitialContextFactory` service in the OSGi service registry.

With the proper OSGi-aware `InitialContext`, you're now able to look up Java EE resources in your client bundles. But sometimes looking up the resource isn't enough;

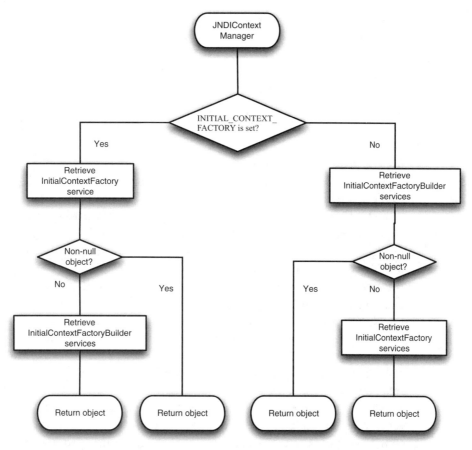

Figure 9.6 The `JNDIContextManager` retrieves `InitialContextFactoryBuilder` and `InitialContextFactory` services from the OSGi registry. The order depends on whether the `INITIAL_CONTEXT_FACTORY` is set.

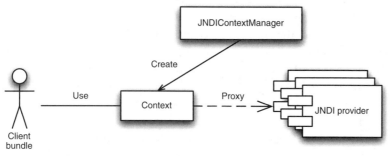

Figure 9.7 `JNDIContextManager` creates a `Context` functioning as a proxy to different JNDI providers, which may come and go due to OSGi's dynamic nature.

you may need to convert it before you can use it in OSGi. We'll look at this and the general problem of handling JNDI `References` within an OSGi environment in the next section.

9.4   *Handling object conversions*

As you've seen previously, JNDI allows a user to bind an object's Reference in the JNDI registry. During the process of lookup, JNDI attempts to convert the Reference to the target object. In fact, JNDI always checks to see if there are any ObjectFactory objects that may wish to convert the bound objects, regardless of whether they are References or not.

As you might expect, this conversion process isn't simple. Specifically, it consists of the following steps:

1   Invoke Context.lookup(name).

2   The lookup() method retrieves the object bound to the name parameter from its registry through some provider-specific mechanism. We'll call this object the bound object. Next, JNDI invokes the static method NamingManager.get-ObjectInstance() using the bound object as one of its arguments. In other words, even though JNDI has already retrieved the bound object, JNDI still needs to check to see if this object needs to be converted.

3   If an ObjectFactoryBuilder hasn't been set through the static method Nam-ingManager.getObjectFactoryBuilder(), then proceed to step 4. If a builder has been set, then you circumvent the whole process and use the builder to create an ObjectFactory. Note that it's an error for a builder to return a null ObjectFactory. Using this ObjectFactory, you invoke its get-ObjectInstance() method. If this method returns non-null, then its return value replaces the bound object and is returned to the caller of Context.lookup(). But if it does return null, then the original bound object is instead returned to the caller. Either way, you stop here.

4   If the object is *not* a Reference or a Referenceable, proceed to step 6.

5   If the object is a Reference or Referenceable, then JNDI verifies whether the Reference itself specifies an ObjectFactory class name (that is, the class name is an optional field of the Reference class).

6   If an ObjectFactory class name is present, then JNDI loads the factory class using the current thread's context class loader and invokes its getObject-Instance() method. If this method returns non-null, then its returned value replaces the bound object and is returned to the caller of Context.lookup(). But if the ObjectFactory.getObjectInstance() method returns null, then the original bound object is instead returned to the caller. Either way, you're finished.

7   If an ObjectFactory class name isn't present, then you proceed to step 6.

8   Finally, you check JNDI's environment for the property Context.OBJECT _FACTORIES. The value of this property is a list of class names. JNDI iterates through this list, loading each ObjectFactory class using the current thread's context class loader, and checks for the first factory whose getObject-Instance() method returns a non-null value. Note that if any factories throw

an exception, then the iteration stops immediately, and the exception is propagated to the caller. If no factories are specified, or all specified factories return `null` values, then no conversions are needed or available, and the original bound object retrieved in the second step is returned to the caller of the method `Context.lookup()`.

NOTE It's important to point out that JNDI always invokes `Naming-Manager.getObjectInstance()`, even if the bound object isn't a `Reference` (or `Referenceable`). The rationale is that even non-`References` may need to be converted. You'll see an example of this later on.

Figure 9.8 illustrates the `Context.lookup()` process, as described previously.

Unfortunately, not only is JNDI's lookup complicated, but it also carries the same problems as the initial context setup, which you saw in the previous section. In

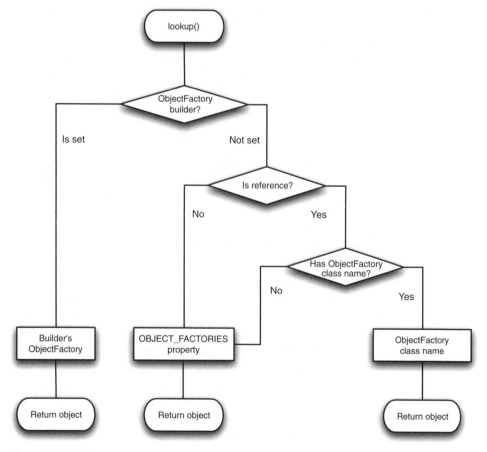

Figure 9.8 JNDI's lookup process results in either JNDI using an `ObjectFactory` created by a `Builder`, `ObjectFactory` objects specified by the `OBJECT_FACTORIES` property, or an `ObjectFactory` specified by a `Reference`.

particular, the fact that it goes through the static method `NamingManager.get-`
`ObjectInstance()` makes life unpleasant when executing on an OSGi platform.

> **NOTE** The process for handling URL names is slightly different than the one
> being presented here. Rather than complicating an already overly compli-
> cated process, we'll discuss URLs in general in a separate section 9.5.1.

Fortunately, the remedy to these problems is similar to the approach used for the
`JNDIContextManager` service. We'll look into this in the next section.

9.4.1 *Converting JNDI objects to be OSGi aware*

A JNDI provider implementation that's aware of the OSGi environment doesn't use the
static method `NamingManager.getObjectInstance()`; instead, it relies on the singleton OSGi service `JNDIProviderAdmin` to achieve `Object` conversions. In other words,
the implementation of `Context.lookup()`, which is provided by `JNDIContextManager`,
retrieves the `JNDIProviderAdmin` service from the OSGi registry and invokes its
method `JNDIProviderAdmin.getObjectInstance()`.

The handling of `ObjectFactory` objects in the `JNDIProviderAdmin` case is similar
but simpler than that of the `NamingManager`. As expected, it boils down to looking for
`ObjectFactory` and `ObjectFactoryBuilder` services in the OSGi registry that either
match the `Reference`'s object factory class name or that return non-`null` values when
their `ObjectFactory.getObjectInstance()` method is invoked. Let's look at the
details.

First, the `JNDIProviderAdmin` checks to see if the bound object is a `Reference` (or
a `Referenceable`) and that it specifies an `ObjectFactory` class name. If both conditions
are true, then it attempts to retrieve an `ObjectFactory` service in the OSGi service registry that also has been registered using the specified `ObjectFactory` class name. If such
a service is found, then it's used for the conversion, and the process stops there.

But if any of these conditions aren't met, that is, if the bound object doesn't specify
an `ObjectFactory` class name, or no registered `ObjectFactory` service is found, then
the `JNDIProviderAdmin` attempts the following:

1 The `JNDIProviderAdmin` retrieves all `ObjectFactoryBuilder` services registered in the OSGi registry. Next, it iterates over them in ranking order, and verifies whether any of them return a non-`null` `ObjectFactory` instance, which
  likewise must return a non-`null` `Object` when its `ObjectFactory.getObject-`
  `Instance()` method is invoked. This process stops when the first non-`null`
  `Object` is found; otherwise, it continues to the next step.
2 The `JNDIProviderAdmin` retrieves all `ObjectFactory` services registered in the
  OSGi registry and, iterating over them in ranking order, checks for the first factory that returns a non-`null` `Object`. Otherwise, if no factories are found that
  return a non-`null` `Object`, it returns the original bound object to the caller.

> **NOTE** The `JNDIProviderAdmin` uses its own bundle context when searching
> for `ObjectFactoryBuilder` and `ObjectFactory` services in the OSGi service
> registry.

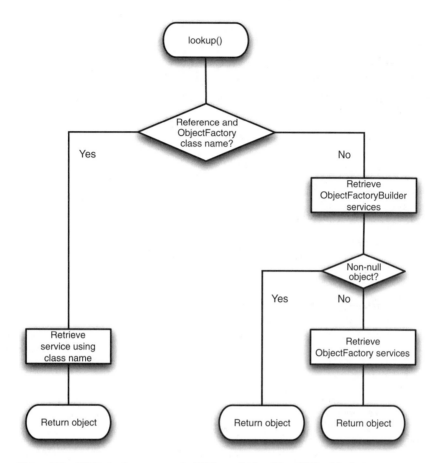

Figure 9.9 JNDI's lookup process in OSGi results in either JNDI retrieving an `ObjectFactory` **service using the** `Reference`**'s class name, or JNDI retrieving all** `ObjectFactoryBuilder` **services, and finally into JNDI retrieving all** `ObjectFactory` **services from the OSGi service registry.**

Figure 9.9 shows a flow chart that describes all possible outcomes of a JNDI lookup when implemented in an OSGi environment.

Even though the implementation of the JNDI lookup isn't trivial in either case, the new approach of using the `JNDIProviderAdmin` does address the class-loading issues we discussed in the past. Furthermore, it has an important advantage; it relies on OSGi as its extension mechanism, making it easy for a user to plug in new conversions by registering a new `ObjectFactory` service.

Next, let's look at an example of how an `ObjectFactory` service can be used to perform conversions. We'll do so by continuing our scenario illustrated in listing 9.4, where an OSGi bundle is looking up a `DataSource` that has been bound by a Java EE application into the JNDI registry. The goal is to set up an `ObjectFactory` that transparently configures the `DataSource`'s log writer to use OSGi's Log service instead of any native Java EE logger. A `DataSource` uses its log writer to print its log and trace messages.

Listing 9.4 DataSource `ObjectFactory`

```
public class DataSourceObjectFactory implements ObjectFactory,
    BundleActivator {

    private BundleContext bundleContext;
    private LogService logService;

    public void start(BundleContext context) throws Exception {
        bundleContext = context;

        retrieveLogService();                               ❶ Retrieve OSGi
                                                              Log service

        bundleContext.registerService(
            ObjectFactory.class.toString(),                 ❷ Register
            this, null);                                      ObjectFactory
    }

    public Object getObjectInstance(Object obj, Name name, Context nameCtx,
            Hashtable<?, ?> environment)
        throws Exception {                                  ❸ JNDI lookup
                                                              callback
        Object ret = null;

        if (nameCtx.getNameInNamespace().
          equals("comp/env/jdbc")) {                        ❹ Check parent
            if (obj instanceof DataSource) {                  context
                DataSource jeeDS = (DataSource) obj;

                if (logService != null)
                    jeeDS.setLogWriter(
                        createLogWriter());                 ❺ Set log writer
                                                              (conversion)
                ret = jeeDS;
            }
        }

        return ret;
    }

    private void retrieveLogService() {
        ServiceReference logServiceReference =
            bundleContext.getServiceReference(LogService.class.toString());
        logService = (LogService)
            bundleContext.getService(logServiceReference);
    }

    // ...
}
```

The `DataSourceObjectFactory` class implements the `ObjectFactory` interface as well as the `BundleActivator` interface. During its activation, you retrieve OSGi's Log service ❶ and most importantly register the ObjectFactory service in the OSGi registry ❷. Note how easy it has become to plug an extension into JNDI; it's just a matter of registering a new OSGi service. In particular, you don't need to worry about how the JNDIProviderAdmin works; this is a concern of the JNDI provider implementation. Eventually, when a JNDI lookup is realized in the OSGi environment, the getObject-Instance() method is called back ❸. Next, you check to see if it's appropriate to convert the Object ❹. You do this by making sure that the naming context used is the JDBC one of "comp/env/jdbc" and that the Object is an instance of the DataSource class.

> **WARNING** If the ObjectFactory shouldn't or can't convert the Object, then it must return null. This is necessary so that other ObjectFactory services get a chance to also try to convert the Object. If you return the original Object, even if unmodified, it will prevent other ObjectFactory objects from acting.

If these conditions are met, you proceed by setting a log writer in the DataSource object that delegates to the OSGi Log service ❺. The next listing shows how this delegate can be implemented.

Listing 9.5 Log service delegate

```
public PrintWriter createLogWriter() {
    return new PrintWriter(
        new LogServiceWrapper(logService), true);         ❶ Create PrintWriter with
}                                                             LogServiceWrapper

private class LogServiceWrapper extends StringWriter {     ❷ Extend a
                                                             StringWriter
    private LogService delegate;

    private LogServiceWrapper(LogService delegate) {
        this.delegate = delegate;
    }

    @Override
    public void close() throws IOException {              ❸ Override the
        delegate.log(LogService.LOG_INFO,                   close() method
            getBuffer().toString());
        super.close();
    }

    @Override                                            ❹ Override the
    public void flush() {                                  flush() method
        delegate.log(LogService.LOG_INFO, getBuffer().toString());
        super.flush();
    }
}
```

The DataSource.setLogWriter() takes a PrintWriter; therefore you create one, passing along to its constructor the LogServiceWrapper ❶. The LogServiceWrapper extends a StringWriter ❷, overriding its close() ❸ and flush() ❹ methods. You override these methods because whenever the `DataSource` decides to flush its log and trace message strings, you need to instead direct the `StringWriter`'s buffered `String` to the actual Log service as a log message.

As you can see, being able to transparently provide ad hoc conversions to objects is a powerful JNDI feature, which is compounded by OSGi's ease in supporting extensions through the OSGi service mechanism.

You've learned to retrieve and use a Java EE resource in an OSGi environment. But can you also do the reverse? For example, let's say you've created a `DataSource` service and registered it in the OSGi registry. How could a Java EE application, such as an enterprise application, use this `DataSource`? Allowing a Java EE application to retrieve an OSGi service is the topic of the next section.

9.5   *Exposing OSGi services in JNDI*

JNDI makes no distinction as to who binds and who looks up the objects, so one simple approach for sharing an OSGi service with a Java EE application is to have an OSGi bundle bind the (shareable) OSGi services into JNDI. But this would mean that the same service object would be bound to both JNDI and the OSGi registry, which not only is double the work but also raises potential problems with keeping these two registries in sync.

If both JNDI and OSGi are registries, couldn't you somehow just link them together? You could create a federation including both, but that would mean defining some subcontext `Reference` that contains the OSGi services, such as `"comp/env/services/javax.sql.DataSource/AccountDS"`, which is a non-intuitive way of naming OSGi services. Fortunately, JNDI provides another mechanism, that of *URL context factories*, which simplifies things.

A URL context factory allows a provider to register special `Context` objects to be used when a JNDI lookup specifies a particular URL scheme on an `InitialContext`.

> **NOTE** A URL scheme is the prefix before the colon (`:`) character. For example, the scheme for the URL http://localhost/index.xml is the string `"http"`.

For example, consider the case where you've created an `InitialContext` for LDAP. As you've learned, this `InitialContext` is a proxy; that is, it's being backed up by the proper LDAP provider. While working with LDAP names, suppose you sometimes also need to look up objects from some other registry, such as `myScheme`. Instead of creating a new `InitialContext`, specifying that a `myScheme` backed up `InitialContextFactory`, JNDI allows you to register a special `ObjectFactory`, called the URL context factory. The `InitialContext` invokes the URL context factory when a lookup is done using a URL. The `URLContextFactory` checks to see if the scheme of the URL is that of `myScheme`, and if it is, returns a JNDI `Context`. Then this `Context` is used to perform the actual lookup of the original `Name`. In other words, a URL context factory is an `ObjectFactory` that provides a `Context` to a different naming or directory service.

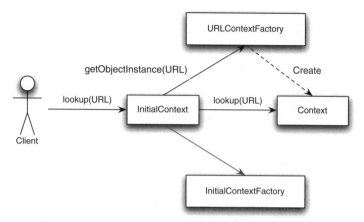

Figure 9.10   Lookup on a URL is serviced by a `URLContextFactory` instead of an `InitialContextFactory`.

Using this approach based on URLs, you're able to look up names from all the different providers starting from a single `InitialContext`, as shown in figure 9.10.

Considering this, OSGi has defined the following URL scheme, specified here using a programming language grammar notation, to allow JNDI clients to automatically access OSGi services:

```
service ::= "osgi:service/" interface ('/' filter )?
```

Let's walk through a couple of examples. The following code looks up the OSGi Data-Source service:

```
InitialContext context = new InitialContext();

DataSource ds =
    (DataSource) context.lookup("osgi:service/javax.sql.DataSource");
```

The URL osgi:service/javax.sql.DataSource is an intuitive way to retrieve an OSGi service whose interface is the `DataSource` one. This approach is similar to other JNDI URLs, such as ldap:/.

> **NOTE**   A URL lookup must be realized on the `InitialContext`. If realized on other `Contexts`, it will be handled by the backing provider and not by the URL context factory as observed.

Next is an example of a filter being used:

```
context.lookup("osgi:service/javax.sql.DataSource/(ver=1.1)");
```

As expected, the syntax of the filter is the usual LDAP-based one we used in the previous sections.

If multiple services are found, then the one with the highest service ranking is returned. If there's more than one service with the highest service ranking, then the one with lowest service ID (the `service.id` property) is returned. But you can retrieve multiple services using the `servicelist` path, as follows:

```
NamingEnumeration<Binding> bindings =
    context.listBindings("osgi:servicelist/javax.sql.DataSource");

while (bindings.hasMore()) {
    Binding bd = (Binding) bindings.next();
    System.out.println("Name = " + bd.getName() + "Class = " +
        bd.getClassName() + ", Object = " + bd.getObject());
}
```

When `servicelist` is used, a JNDI lookup returns a `Context` object. As usual, you can list the bindings of the `Context` object, and each binding represents an OSGi service. In particular, `Binding.getName()` returns the service ID (for example, 100), `Binding.getClassName()` returns the service interface (for example, `javax.sql.DataSource`), and `Binding.getObject()` returns the actual service object.

Finally, a new service property called `osgi.jndi.service.name` is provided. Using this property, a user can specify a JNDI name that can be used directly in the URL in place of the service interface, as in the following example:

```
props.put("osgi.jndi.service.name", "AccountDS");
bundleContext.registerService(DataSource.class.toString(),
    ds, props);

// ...

DataSource dataSource =
    (DataSource) context.lookup("osgi:service/AccountDS");
```

The OSGi URL scheme makes dealing with services very familiar to Java EE clients. But how is this implemented? For example, how can you register your own `URLContextFactory` in JNDI? We'll discuss these issues in the next section.

9.5.1 *Registering URL context factories*

In a non-OSGi environment, URL context factory classes are found by means of the property `Context.URL_PKG_PREFIXES`, which contains a colon-separated list of Java package prefixes.

For example, if this property is set to `com.manning` and a lookup is realized using the URL osgi:service/javax.sql.DataSource, then the `InitialContext` class looks for the following class:

```
com.manning.osgi.osgiURLContextFactory
```

In other words, it appends the package prefix to the scheme name (osgi) and the literal `URLContextFactory`. Specifically, it uses the following pattern: *package_prefix.scheme.scheme + URLContextFactory*. The `InitialContext` tries to load this class using the current thread's context class loader, and if successful invokes the `getObjectInstance()` method in the `URLContextFactory` object using the URL name as its first argument. If it returns a non-`null` value, this value must be a `Context` object, whose `lookup()` method is then invoked with the given URL name. Note that the `INITIAL_CONTEXT_FACTORY` property is ignored in this case. If the URL context factory returns `null`, then it tries to load the next one if one is available. If none return a non-`null` value, then the `InitialContext` class continues with the standard process as described in the previous sections, where it utilizes the `INITIAL_CONTEXT_FACTORY` property.

> **WARNING** If the `InitialContextFactoryBuilder` is set, then this default behavior of the `InitialContext` class is overridden, and the URL context factories aren't searched for in case of a URL lookup.

As you can see, the URL context factory allows a provider to interject a different `Context` than the one that would have been provided by the `InitialContextFactory`. Next, let's look at how this is done in an OSGi environment.

9.5.2 Registering URL context factories in OSGi

URL context factories implement the `ObjectFactory` interface, so OSGi treats them as such, and you can register your URL context factory as an `ObjectFactory` service in the OSGi registry. The one difference is that you should include the service property `osgi.jndi.url.scheme`, whose value must be set to the URL scheme. For example, to handle the URL osgi:service/javax.sql.DataSource, this property should be set to osgi.

During the `lookup()` process, the OSGi-aware JNDI context returned by JNDI-ContextManager verifies that the name is a URL and therefore looks for an Object-Factory service with the right `osgi.jndi.url.scheme` property.

StringRefAddrs

When a `Reference` is encountered containing a `StringRefAddrs` of the type URL, then JNDI will also attempt to find a proper URL context factory. In a non-OSGi environment, this is accomplished through the normal means of using the `URL_PKG_PREFIXES` property. In an OSGi environment, JNDI searches for `Object-Factory` services considering their `osgi.jndi.url.scheme` property value.

Let's take a step back and reconsider our scenarios. Our goal for this chapter is to allow resources and services to be shared back and forth between an OSGi environment and a non-OSGi environment, such as a Java EE application, or even a Java SE application for that matter. To accomplish this, you've learned how to use JNDI as a bridging registry. But there's one crucial issue that we haven't yet discussed: how you host these environments together in a single JVM process? We'll tackle this problem in the next section.

9.6   *Embedding OSGi*

There are two options for collocating the OSGi framework with Java EE or Java SE applications. The first option is to layer the Java EE platform or the Java SE application on top of the OSGi framework. The second option is the reverse, that is, to layer the OSGi framework on top of the Java EE platform or the Java SE application. This is commonly referred to as *embedding OSGi*. Because Java EE is the legacy and we have less control over it, the latter option is the most efficient and often-used approach, so it's the one we'll investigate further.

Quite simply, to embed OSGi, we just need to start the OSGi framework within a Java EE or Java SE application. This can be in the context of a running EJB, MDB, or other Java EE artifact, or in the case of Java SE, within the `main()` method. Fortunately, OSGi added a standard way of bootstrapping the framework, a process called *launching*. This is illustrated in the next listing.

Listing 9.6   Launching the OSGi framework

```java
import java.util.ServiceLoader;

import org.osgi.framework.BundleException;
import org.osgi.framework.launch.Framework;
import org.osgi.framework.launch.FrameworkFactory;

public class Launcher {

    public static void main(String[] args) throws BundleException,
            InterruptedException {

        ServiceLoader<FrameworkFactory> services =
            ServiceLoader.load(FrameworkFactory.class);    ◁——  ❶ Load
                                                                   FrameworkFactory
                                                                   service

        FrameworkFactory frameworkFactory =
            services.iterator().next();

        Framework osgiFrw =
            frameworkFactory.newFramework(null);    ◁——  ❷ Create OSGi
                                                           framework

        osgiFrw.start();    ◁——  ❸ Start system
                                    bundle

        //...

        osgiFrw.stop();    ◁——  ❹ Stop system
        osgiFrw.waitForStop(10000);       bundle
    }
}
```

You start by loading the Java SE service called `org.osgi.framework.launch.Framework` `Factory` ❶. The implementation of this service is provided by the OSGi framework implementation JAR and is specified by the resource `/META-INF/services/org.osgi.` `framework.launch.FrameworkFactory`. In our case, the Felix JAR file must be in the Java application's class path, and within its JAR file the cited resource specifies Felix's

FrameworkFactory Java class implementation. Using the FrameworkFactory, you create a Framework instance ❷, which is an extension of the Bundle interface and acts as the system bundle. Next, you start the system bundle ❸, and you're ready to use the OSGi framework. When you've finished, you stop the system bundle ❹. Stopping the system bundle is an asynchronous operation, so you wait for this operation to finish, giving it a timeout of 10 seconds. You'll learn more about launching and managing the OSGi framework in the next chapters.

The non-OSGi environment, that is, the code that's launching the OSGi framework, and the OSGi environment itself don't share Java packages, aside from the standard JRE java.* packages. This can cause class inconsistency between these two environments, as you'll see next.

9.6.1 Bridging JNDI

Let's go back to our scenario where we wish a Java EE or Java SE application to use an OSGi DataSource service. As you've learned, the launcher application can instantiate a JNDI InitialContext and perform a lookup using the URL osgi:service/javax.sql.DataSource. The lookup method returns a javax.sql.DataSource object. But the Java EE application's class loader would have loaded the javax.sql.Data-Source class from the JRE library, whereas the OSGi context would have its own class loader and therefore would have loaded a separate copy of this same DataSource class, likely from an OSGi javax.sql bundle. This situation is illegal and causes a class inconsistency exception to be raised, as shown in figure 9.11.

To solve this problem, you need to make sure that both the JNDI client and the OSGi context load this class from the same source. This can be accomplished by explicitly exporting this package from the class loader of the launcher code to the sys-

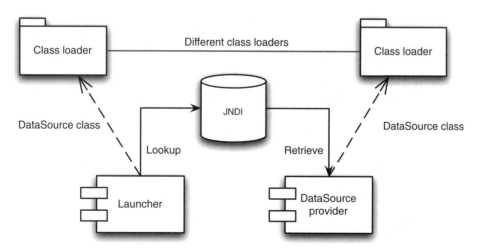

Figure 9.11 The launcher and the data source OSGi provider don't share the same class loader for the DataSource class, resulting in an inconsistent class space.

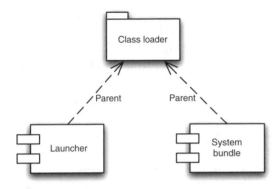

Figure 9.12   The launcher and the system bundle share the same parent class loader.

tem bundle's exported packages. In other words, the class loader of the launcher code becomes the parent class loader for the system bundle, as shown in figure 9.12.

The system bundle by default doesn't export any packages from its parent class loader, except for `java.*`. To change this, you can use the `Framework` property `org.osgi.framework.system.packages.extra`, as illustrated next:

```
Map properties = new HashMap();
properties.put("org.osgi.framework.system.packages.extra",
    "javax.sql");

Framework osgiFrw =
    frameworkFactory.newFramework(properties);
```

You're almost finished. You're now able to keep the class space consistent between the OSGi and non-OSGi environments.

System packages vs. boot delegation

Adding a package to `org.osgi.framework.system.packages.extra` has the same effect as exporting it with the `Export-Package` header entry. In other words, a consuming bundle still needs to import the package using the `Import-Package` header entry.

This is different than using the `org.osgi.framework.bootdelegation` launch property. Adding a property to the boot delegation means that the package is now part of the bundle's parent class loader and, similar to the `java.*` packages, is available to all bundles without them having to explicitly import the package using the `Import-Package` header entry. Generally, you should avoid using the boot delegation property.

One other difference that's a common source of error is that the syntax for the property `org.osgi.framework.system.packages.extra` is similar to that for `Export-Package` and doesn't allow for `*`, whereas the boot delegation property does allow for the specification of `*` in the package, such as in `javax.*`.

But when you create the `InitialContext` in the non-OSGi environment, the JNDI default implementation has no way of knowing about OSGi and therefore can't retrieve OSGi services or provide a `BundleContext` so that OSGi's URL context factory is able to do its work. You need to find a way of propagating the `BundleContext` from the `InitialContext` to the OSGi `Context`. This is done with the `osgi.service.jndi.bundleContext` property, which should contain a reference to a `BundleContext`. This is shown next.

Listing 9.7 Setting OSGi `InitialContextFactoryBuilder`

```
Framework osgiFrw =
    frameworkFactory.newFramework(properties);                    Instantiate
                                                              ❶ framework
osgiFrw.start();

Hashtable env = new Hashtable();
env.put("osgi.service.jndi.bundleContext",
  osgiFrw.getBundleContext());                                Set bundleContext
                                                              ❷ property
InitialContext ic = new InitialContext(env);

DataSource ds =
    (DataSource) ic.lookup(                          ❸ Perform lookup
      "osgi:service/javax.sql.DataSource");
```

You start by embedding the OSGi framework as you've done in the past ❶. Next, you get the system bundle's `BundleContext` and set it as the value for the `osgi.service.jndi.bundleContext` property ❷, which is used to set up the `InitialContext` object. You can now do a lookup using the OSGi schema to retrieve the `DataSource` service from the OSGi service registry ❸.

Finally, observe that you're using an `InitialContext` instead of the `JNDIContextManager`. This makes sense, because you're illustrating how a Java client that isn't aware of OSGi is able to still use OSGi services. But it also means that you need to register OSGi's URL context factory through the traditional mechanism of using the `Context.URL_PKG_PREFIXES` property. There's an alternative to this: you could register an `InitialContextFactoryBuilder` that overrides JNDI's default behavior and instead relies on the `JNDIContextManager`. This would allow you to plug in your URL context factory as an OSGi factory, but it also means that you wouldn't be using any of the default JNDI providers, such as LDAP, if the new `InitialContextFactoryBuilder` doesn't explicitly delegate to them.

JNDI is often overlooked, partly because of its complexity. But it's an elegant mechanism for bridging the existing world of enterprise applications with the new world of OSGi.

9.7   *Summary*

There's a need to share resources and services between non-OSGi applications, such as Java EE enterprise applications, with OSGi bundles. You can accomplish this with JNDI, Java's naming and directory interface. JNDI is a framework that allows different naming and directory service providers to plug in, providing a single interface to Java clients.

A naming service supports the association of a name to represent an object. The name may be hierarchical, in which case it's made up of components and called a compound name. One example of a naming service is DNS. A directory service adds attributes to the bound objects, therefore allowing the user to search for objects that possess certain criteria, such as their location, mode of operation, and the like. It works as a yellow pages service for finding resources. One example of a directory service is LDAP.

JNDI can be federated, spanning multiple naming and directory service providers. This is accomplished through the use of `References`. `References` are converted to objects using `ObjectFactory` services.

For a Java client to use JNDI, it must establish the `InitialContext`. In non-OSGi environments, this is done by instantiating an `InitialContext` class with the proper `INITIAL_CONTEXT_FACTORY` property. `InitialContext` delegates to the static method `NamingManager.getInitialContext()`. This approach causes several problems in an OSGi environment; therefore, an OSGi client bundle must instead use the `JNDI-ContextManager` singleton service to establish its initial context. `JNDIContextManager` retrieves `InitialContextFactory` services from the OSGi registry that implement the `INITIAL_CONTEXT_FACTORY` interface. Having established the initial context, a bundle is now able to access resources in JNDI that have been bound by Java EE and Java SE applications.

JNDI objects can be converted by means of `ObjectFactory` services. For example, when a bundle wishes to use a `DataSource` resource created by Java EE, you can use this facility to automatically change the `DataSource` to rely on OSGi's Log service instead of the native Java EE `logger`. For this purpose, OSGi provides the `JNDI-ProviderAdmin` singleton service, which is responsible for retrieving the proper `ObjectFactory` services from the OSGi service registry. This is achieved by having the `Context`, which is created by `JNDIContextManager`, delegate to `JNDIProviderAdmin` when a lookup is performed.

OSGi defines an OSGI URL to allow Java SE and Java EE applications to look up OSGi services using JNDI. For example, the URL osgi:service/javax.sql.DataSource looks up all OSGi services that implement the `DataSource` interface.

You can embed the OSGi framework within Java SE and Java EE applications by instantiating a `Framework` instance, which acts as the system bundle. This can be done through the `FrameworkFactory` Java SE service. OSGi framework implementations provide this service in their JAR files.

In this chapter, you learned how to share resources and services between OSGi and non-OSGi environments. Now that you're able to retrieve and use all the services you need, the next crucial issue is how to manage this complex environment. Managing the OSGi framework and its applications is the subject of the next chapter.

Remote services and the cloud

10

This chapter covers

- Importing and exporting a remote OSGi service
- Understanding distribution providers and their properties
- Selecting a specific service endpoint and negotiating endpoint policies
- Learning the semantics of dealing with remote entities
- Understanding cloud computing and how it relates to OSGi

In today's world, it's almost guaranteed that your machine is networked and the services you use are provided through the internet. Remote communication is essential, and OSGi supports it by means of the OSGi Remote Service specification, which is the subject of this chapter.

We'll start by examining how to export a service for remote access and conversely how to import a remote service for local consumption. Next, we'll investigate how

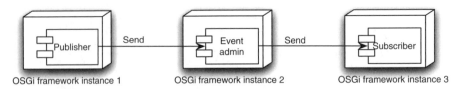

Figure 10.1 The publisher, subscriber, and Event Admin communicate remotely.

the actual transport is realized through the use of distribution providers, highlighting the fact that OSGi doesn't implement its own transport but rather allows existing transports to be plugged in. Finally, we'll look into how to negotiate common policies between the exporter and the importer of the remote services, for instance, to make sure that both sides agree on a common set of requirements, such as encryption.

Remote services opens up OSGi to be run in a remote server or, as is the tendency, in the cloud. We'll briefly discuss cloud computing and look at how the OSGi platform is an ideal platform for cloud computing. But before getting into cloud computing, we'll start the chapter by discussing remote service invocation.

10.1 Remote invocation

Recall from chapter 6 that one of the shortcomings of the Event Admin service is that it doesn't handle remote clients. Ideally, subscribers that have registered the `Event-Handler` interface should be invoked regardless of their location.

For example, you could have a scenario where the publisher, the actual Event Admin implementation, and the subscriber are hosted in three different OSGi framework instances, as depicted in figure 10.1.

This distributed configuration can be achieved using OSGi's Remote Service. In this setup, distribution providers are responsible for creating proxies that represent remote services, therefore achieving a distributed system. Let's investigate the pieces, starting with a remote `EventHandler` subscriber in the next section.

10.1.1 Exporting a remote service

A service is specified as remote by tagging it with the following service properties:

```
service.exported.interfaces
service.exported.configs
```

The former specifies which service interfaces are to be exported in a remote fashion, and the latter specifies how those interfaces are to be made remote. The following listing provides an example for this remote subscriber scenario.

> **Listing 10.1 Remote `EventHandler` service**

```
Dictionary props = new Hashtable();

props.put("service.exported.interfaces", "*");
props.put("service.exported.configs",
```

❶ Export EventHandler interface as remote

```
    "org.apache.cxf.ws");
```
◁――― **Select configuration**
❷ **type WS for transport**

```
props.put("org.apache.cxf.ws.address",
    "http://localhost:9090/eventhandler");
```
◁――― **Configure WS-specific**
❸ **configuration**

```
bundleContext.registerService(EventHandler.class.getName(),
    subscriber, props);
```

As usual, we need to register the `EventHandler` service. But here we've added the `service.exported.interfaces` property with a value of * ❶, stating that all of the service interfaces used for registration can be made remote, which in this case would include the `EventHandler` interface. Next, we need to specify which remote configuration type to use for the actual transport implementation. We selected the Web Services–based messaging provided by Apache's CXF project ❷.

> **NOTE** Some providers support a default configuration type, which is used when the `service.exported.configs` property isn't specified.

Finally, we need to add any configuration type–specific properties (for example, WS). In the case of CXF's Web Services stack, we have only one: the WS address to be used ❸.

> **WARNING** The OSGi Remote Services specification is recent, and there are still only a few implementations around and some rough edges to smooth out. One of the available implementations is Apache CXF (http://cxf.apache.org/distributed-osgi.html). But as of this writing, some of the properties and configuration being used in this open source product aren't fully compliant with version 4.3 of the OSGi Service Platform Core specification.

It's important to highlight that the actual service interface is invariant with regard to local or remote usage. This is noteworthy because it means that your service implementation likewise doesn't change. The only changes are constrained to the set of service properties used during registration.

As you've seen, the registration of a remote service is simple enough. Next, let's look at the consumer side.

10.1.2 Consuming a remote service

The consuming of a remote service is quite transparent; you just need to retrieve a service as usual, and the underlying framework takes care of proxying it accordingly, should it be remote. As an example, the following code retrieves our remote `Event-Handler`:

```
ServiceReference ref =
    context.getServiceReference(EventAdmin.class.getName());
```

There's no difference between the retrieval of a local or remote service. Similarly for the export case, the consumer is shielded from the fact that a service is local or remote. Again, this is to our benefit, but you should keep in mind that a remote service invocation might unexpectedly fail or yield a high latency because of problems with the underlying transport.

Is there a way of knowing if a service is remote? Yes, all remote services have the following service property:

```
service.imported
```

This property is useful for filtering. For example, the following expression filters out all remote services, making sure that only local services are used:

```
(!(service.imported=*))
```

Imported services are also set with the service property `service.imported.configs`, which specifies the configuration type used for the particular endpoint of the imported service. For example, in our case it would be set to `org.apache.cxf.ws`. We'll discuss configuration types in depth later.

Finally, keep in mind that imported services are *not* set with the `service.exported.*` properties, such as `service.exported.interfaces`.

Next, let's take a quick look at how things actually work under the covers.

10.2 *Distribution providers*

It's the role of distribution providers to implement the actual transport between the bundle that's exporting a remote service in one OSGi framework instance and the bundle that's importing the service in another framework instance. A distribution provider can support different transports, such as RMI (Remote Method Invocation), SOAP (Simple Object Access Protocol), and REST (Representational State Transfer). The transport to be used is determined by the configuration type specified in the `service.exported.configs` service property. An endpoint description is created for each remote service and a particular configuration type. Consuming bundles use the endpoint description to establish a connection to the remote service.

> **NOTE** The OSGi Remote Service specification is a framework for remote communication that supports different transports, such as RMI and SOAP. The specification itself doesn't specify which transports are supported. Further, it doesn't define any new transport protocols.

A remote service may have multiple endpoints. For example, a remote service may be exported with both an RMI and SOAP endpoint descriptions. Clients can then select the proper endpoint for invocation. This approach allows the support of different transports, in a manner agnostic to the remote service and its consumers. Figure 10.2 describes the interaction between distribution providers, their supported configuration types, and the endpoints created by each configuration type for each remote service.

As you can infer, a distribution provider is needed for both the consuming and the providing sides, as shown in figure 10.3. On the consuming side, the distribution provider takes care of importing the remote service by establishing a local proxy endpoint

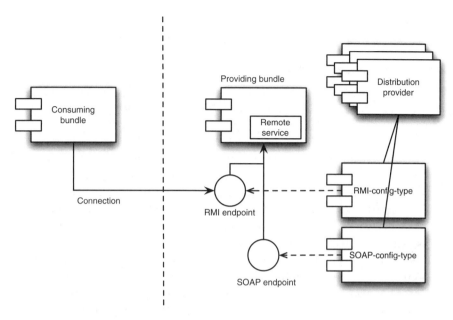

Figure 10.2 **Distribution providers support different configuration types, which create separate endpoints for each remote service. In this example, the provider supports RMI and SOAP transports. Each transport endpoint is associated with the remote service and is tied to the client when a connection is established.**

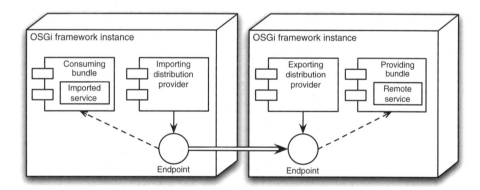

Figure 10.3 **There's a distribution provider in each distributed framework instance, each responsible for its local endpoint and connecting to a remote endpoint.**

and connecting it to the remote endpoint. We'll call it the *importing distribution provider*. On the providing side, the *exporting distribution provider* is responsible for establishing an endpoint that accepts connections and delegates to the proper service.

The distribution providers are also responsible for discovering and proxying the remote services as needed. That's why you don't need to explicitly mention the address of a remote service in the consuming bundle.

You've learned how a distribution provider works. In the next section, we'll look at how to handle multiple distribution providers and transports.

10.2.1 *Selecting the proper endpoint*

It's not uncommon for a system to support multiple transports. For example, RMI for general application communication, SOAP for web development, and perhaps some proprietary socket implementation (perhaps running on InfiniBand) when performance is essential.

When exporting a remote service, you should generally be as flexible as possible and therefore specify several or the entire set of supported configuration types. For example, we could export the `EventHandler` setting the `service.exported.configs` service property to `net.rmi`, `net.soap`, `net.socket`. If we did so, and the distribution provider supported all the aforementioned transports, then three distinct endpoints would be created, one for each transport.

But on the consuming side, we want to import the service using a single specific endpoint, as the situation demands. For example, if we wanted to use the event handler interface from a web application, then it's likely that we'd prefer to import the `EventHandler` service using the SOAP endpoint. This can be done using the `service.imported.configs` service property. The following code fragment retrieves an `EventAdmin` service that's tied to the SOAP endpoint:

```
ServiceReference ref =
    context.getServiceReference(EventAdmin.class.getName(),
        "(&(service.imported.configs=net.soap))");
```

Unlike the `service.exported.configs` property, the `service.imported.configs` property contains the single configuration type that's being used by the supporting endpoint, as shown in figure 10.4.

If the importing distribution provider in the OSGi framework supports all three transports we specified when exporting the remote service, then three endpoints are created and likewise three services are imported, each containing a different configuration type for its `service.imported.configs` property.

> **NOTE** The fact that endpoints for all configuration types are created may seem wasteful at first glance, but in reality a distribution provider implementation may do this on demand by using the OSGi service hooks.

But what happens if the importing distribution provider doesn't support the transport we specified? In other words, in the preceding example, how would we know there's a SOAP endpoint for us to depend upon? We can find the supported configuration types of a distribution provider by using the service property `remote.configs.` `supported`. The distribution providers register some anonymous service, setting this property to the list of supported configuration properties. In our case, should the importing distribution provider only support the configuration types of `net.rmi` and `net.soap`, then it would register a service whose `remote.configs.supported` service property is set to `net.rmi`, `net.soap`.

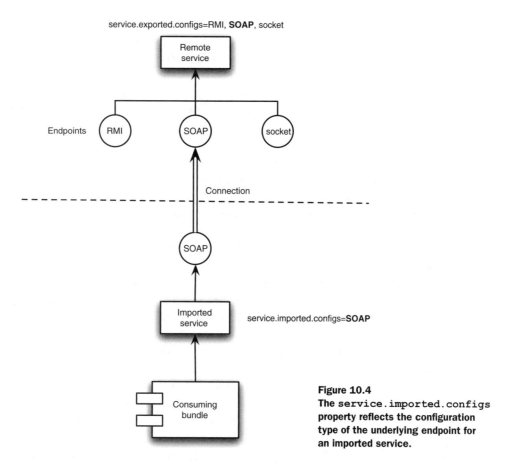

Figure 10.4
The `service.imported.configs`
property reflects the configuration
type of the underlying endpoint for
an imported service.

Knowing this, our consuming bundle should first find out if the `net.soap` configuration type is supported and only then retrieve the SOAP endpoint for the `EventHandler` service. We can find out if the `net.soap` configuration type is supported as follows:

```
ServiceReference ref =
    context.getServiceReference(null,
        "(&(remote.configs.supported=net.soap))");
```

Finding out the supported configuration types is useful, but sometimes you may need more information, such as whether a particular policy is supported. This is the subject of the next section.

10.2.2 *Negotiating policies*

There are cases when not only do you need a particular endpoint but you also need to certify that a policy from the remote service or distribution provider is being supported. It's sometimes even necessary to negotiate policies between the consuming and the providing systems and make sure that both sides of the equation agree on common vocabularies.

For example, let's say that our providing bundle wants to make sure that the (remote) service it is exporting is handled in a manner in which the invocations are kept in order. In other words, the underlying endpoint needs to keep the client invocations ordered, perhaps by using a transport-oriented protocol, such as TCP, instead of a message-oriented protocol, such as UDP. To relay this information, the remote service should be registered with the service property `service.exported.intents` set to the hypothetical value of `ordered`.

When the exporting distribution provider sees this service with the `ordered` intent, it must make sure it's able to support it with whatever configuration type it uses to establish the endpoint. If the exporting distribution provider isn't able to fulfill this requirement, then the remote service in question won't be exported. Next, the importing distribution provider goes through the same process. It realizes the presence of the `ordered` intent and likewise has to make sure it's able to fulfill this requirement. If it's successful in doing so, then the imported service is made available for consuming bundles with the service property `service.intents` set to `ordered`.

Therefore, client bundles can use the `service.intents` property to select the appropriate service endpoint in a manner similar to that of `service.imported.configs`. In our case, it would allow a consuming bundle to select an endpoint that keeps the remote method invocations ordered. In other words, on the importing side, the `service.intents` property specifies the capabilities of the remote service, as shown in figure 10.5.

The `service.exported.intents` property specifies requirements without which the remote service won't function properly. You can use the service property `service.exported.intents.extra` to specify additional requirements that may not always be present. For example, depending on the environment that's hosting the system, you may need to encrypt the messages being exchanged between the distribution providers. You can use the `service.exported.intents.extra` property to configure whether the service needs to be kept confidential or not, depending on whether the system is running within the intranet or outside it. You can do so by allowing this property to be configured through the Configuration Admin service. The distribution provider then merges `service.exported.intents` and `service.exported.intents.extra` together, after which their values are treated equally, as shown in figure 10.6.

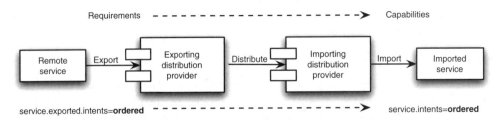

Figure 10.5   A remote service requirement is exported as an imported capability.

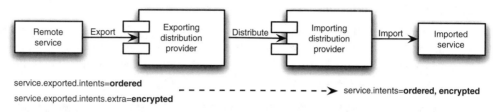

Figure 10.6   Exported intents are merged and treated equally by distribution providers.

Finally, let's say that the implementation of the remote service itself is able to fulfill the requirement. Continuing with our example, let's say that the implementation of our remote service could cope with unordered messages by reordering them internally through the use of monotonic IDs or timestamps. In this case, the remote service can be registered with the service property `service.intents` set to `ordered`. This tells the distribution provider that it doesn't need to support the requirement of keeping the invocations ordered because the remote service itself is doing it.

The distribution provider still propagates the ordered requirement downstream, eventually setting this value in the property `service.intents` of the imported service in the consuming OSGi framework instance. This allows clients to still filter on the ordered capability of the importing distribution provider endpoint. This makes sense, considering that from the point of view of the consuming bundle, it generally doesn't matter whether the capability is being served by the distribution provider or by the remote service implementation itself.

Nonetheless, for those cases where it does matter, the distribution provider also publishes an anonymous service containing the service property `remote.supported.intents`, which is used to specify the intents being supported by it. This follows the same pattern as the `remote.supported.configs` service property, as shown in figure 10.7.

Protocol negotiation is a common theme for most communication stacks, and the *intents* framework allows for a succinct and flexible, albeit somewhat complicated, approach for doing it. In the next section, we'll examine an approach to directly selecting an endpoint without having to rely on the use of service properties.

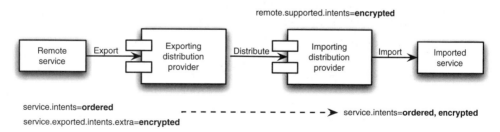

Figure 10.7   Remote services can implement their own requirements using the `service.intents` property.

10.2.3 *Endpoint descriptions*

In addition to the `service.imported.*` properties, a client can also explicitly select an endpoint. This is done using the MANIFEST.MF entry header `Remote-Service`, which should point to an endpoint description configuration file. The following listing describes our `EventHandler` endpoint.

Listing 10.2   `EventHandler` endpoint description

```
<endpoint-descriptions
    xmlns="http://www.osgi.org/xmlns/rsa/v1.0.0">
  <endpoint-description>
    <property name="objectClass"
      value="org.osgi.service.event.EventAdmin" />       ❶ Remote service
                                                            interface
    <property name="service.imported.configs"
      value="org.apache.cxf.ws" />                        ❷ Configuration type
    <property name="org.apache.cxf.ws.address"
      value=="http://localhost:9090/eventhandler" />      ❸ Configuration type-
  </endpoint-description>                                   specific properties
</endpoint-descriptions>
```

The endpoint description includes enough information to allow a client bundle to connect to a remote endpoint, particularly the service interface ❶, the configuration type ❷, and most important, the actual transport address ❸ for the selected configuration type.

For both OSGi Remote Service and OSGi data-access technologies, the usage pattern is quite common: the provider bundles use special service properties and the consuming bundles use special MANIFEST header entries that point to configuration files. This similarity is a good thing and is applicable to most OSGi services.

Now that you understand how to export and import remote services, in the next section we'll take a look at some caveats of using distributed services in general.

10.3   *Dealing with the semantics of distributed systems*

As you've seen, OSGi remote services let us deal with distribution in a transparent form. This simplifies application development, but it also hides some of the intrinsic issues of dealing with remote entities and transport protocols. Let's investigate a couple of scenarios where this is a problem.

First, consider a simple service, such as the following:

```
public interface CustomerRegistry { /* remote interface */

    public Customer findCustomer(String name);

}

public interface Customer {

    public String getName();

    public String getAddress();
```

```
        public void setAddress(String address);
}
```

Next, let's look at a client bundle that retrieves this service and updates the address of a customer:

```
ServiceReference servRef =
    bundleContext.getServiceReference(CustomerRegistry.class.toString());

if (servRef != null) {
    CustomerRegistry registry =
        (CustomerRegistry) bundleContext.getService(servRef);

    Customer customer =
        registry.findCustomer("Alex");

    if (customer != null) {
        customer.setAddress("Updated Address!");
    }
}
```

This works fine in a local setup, where changes to the Customer object instance would be reflected to any other client within the same JVM or, more precisely, that shares the same class space. But what happens if the CustomerRegistry is a remote service, and the client bundles that are updating the customer information reside in different OSGi framework instances? As you've guessed, updates to the Customer object instance wouldn't be reflected in other clients or even at the remote service itself. The reason is that remote services deal with call-by-value as opposed to call-by-reference, which means that the Customer object returned by the findCustomer() method is actually a new object instance that reflects the same value that's present in the exporting distribution provider.

Solving this problem becomes a matter of interface design. The remote service developer should be aware of the call-by-value semantic and design the interface accordingly to avoid the issue. For instance, the following interfaces do the trick:

```
public interface RemoteCustomerRegistry { /* remote interface */

    public Customer findCustomer(String name);

    public void updateCustomerAddress(String name, String address);

}

public interface Customer {

    public String getName();

    public String getAddress();
}
```

In other words, an update is done by invoking the remote service itself, passing the address information directly (as a value). Likewise, to avoid confusion, we remove the setAddress() method from the Customer object, which mostly becomes a structure of values. Because the consuming bundle generally wouldn't know it's dealing with a remote service, the onus of the interface design falls largely on the provider.

The next problem we'll look at is that a communication transport may go down for a variety of reasons at any arbitrary time. There isn't much we can do to deal with this in the provider, and instead we need to design for this possibility in the client itself. For instance, just before we invoke the updateCustomerAddress(), our wired or wireless network connection may be lost, and the importing distribution provider would lose connectivity to the exporting distribution provider. In this case, the imported service should raise the runtime exception ServiceException, and a consuming bundle should be ready to handle this exception.

A naïve exception-handling implementation for a ServiceException might wait a few seconds in case the network has simply run into some transient problem and try again, as demonstrated in the following code:

```
ServiceReference servRef =
    bundleContext.getServiceReference(RemoteCustomerRegistry.class.toString());

if (servRef != null) {
    RemoteCustomerRegistry registry =
        (RemoteCustomerRegistry) bundleContext.getService(servRef);

    try {
        registry.updateCustomerAddress("Alex", "Updated Address!");
    } catch (ServiceException e) {
        Thread.sleep(2000); // wait for two seconds and try again

        registry.updateCustomerAddress("Alex", "Updated Address!");
    }
}
```

One final issue to consider is the underlying communication stack being used. The different transports have different characteristics and limitations. For example, if CORBA is being used, there are restrictions on the Java types that can be referenced in the remote services. This is because CORBA IDL (Interface Definition Language) doesn't support the entire spectrum of the Java types.

Remote services, sometimes called Distributed OSGi, are a major foundation for the emerging cloud technology, which we'll investigate in the next section.

10.4   *Elasticity at the cloud*

Needless to say, cloud computing is a vast subject, and it's beyond the scope of this book. But as you'll see, OSGi has become an interesting technology for supporting the concept of Platform as a Service (PaaS). In the following sections, we'll make some assumptions and simplifications as we discuss why and how that is.

Let's begin by exploring a use case. Suppose we'd like to make the auction application, which was explained in chapter 3, a public service for a website. Somewhat similar to eBay, the goal is to support web clients making offers of items to sell and bidding

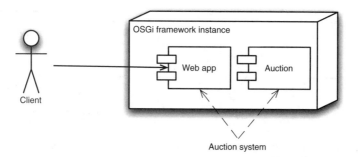

Figure 10.8 A single OSGi framework instance running the auction system

for these items. The first step toward achieving this is to create a web application that exposes a proper web page, where a customer makes offers and bids.

Simply put, the web application internals implement the `Participant` class and invoke the `Auction` class. And we are, in a naïve sense, finished. The web application is implemented as an OSGi bundle, and together with the auction application bundles and the bundle containing the web server (for example, Jetty), they're all installed in a single OSGi framework instance and hosted in a machine that's made accessible via the net. We'll refer to this whole environment as the *auction system*. That is, the auction system includes all the software components needed to run the auction application, such as the web server and any other supporting components, as shown in figure 10.8.

Life goes on; the auction system is running successfully and in fact is a major success—so much so that we get more customers than we expected, and because of that, performance degrades significantly. Whereas before buyers and sellers were able to bid and make offers instantly, it now takes several seconds, sometimes minutes if the item is very popular. The solution is to expand and acquire another machine. This trend continues, and we reach the point of having to manage a network of eight machines. This setup has become extremely expensive; not only do we need to buy several fully configured machines, but we also need to manage them. We decide to do some profiling to look for the bottleneckand find out what's causing the performance problems.

10.4.1 *Designing for the cloud*

As it turns out, the bottleneck occurs when correlating the offers and the bids in the `Auction` bundle implementation. Although we could try to improve the algorithm, this already tells us that the bottleneck isn't I/O bound and likewise isn't in the web application.

We decide to change our architecture. Rather then having eight instances of the OSGi framework each running the auction system, which consists of the web application, the auction application bundles, and the supporting infrastructure bundles, we change it to a two-tier architecture, as shown in figure 10.9. In our two-tier architecture, the first tier consists of the web application and the web server, which provides the client interface to the customers and then forwards the requests to the second tier,

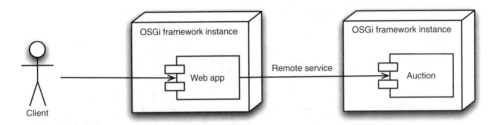

Figure 10.9 An auction system partitioned into two separate OSGi framework instances, communicating through an OSGi remote service

called the business tier. The business tier contains the auction bundles, because they perform the actual business-related code.

In this new setup, we host the web applications in only two machines, which communicate via REST with four other machines containing the auction application bundles. Because of the performance improvements, we're able to serve the same number of clients with only six machines, two fewer than before.

> **NOTE** In reality, we should have a three-tier architecture. The auction application would store its state in the third tier, the data tier. You'll see how to change the auction application to persist its data by using JPA in a future chapter. For the time being, we'll ignore this issue and focus on the communication aspect of the system rather than the persistence issues. But keep in mind that to function properly in the absence of a data tier, we'd need to make sure that all requests pertaining to an item are routed to a single auction bundle instance.

By doing this, we gain on several fronts:

- The machines are easier to manage. When a web server security patch is released, we only need to update the two machines of the client tier. Likewise, we only need to set up the firewall in these two machines. Further, had we been persisting the data, we'd only need to install the persistence storage, such as the RDBMS, in the machines of the data tier.
- The overall environment is less expensive, because we can customize the machines for their specific roles. For example, the machines in the client tier need better I/O but don't need particularly faster CPUs or disks. But the machines in the business tier should have fast CPUs, because we know from the profile that the auction application is CPU bound. By segregating the system into separate nodes, we can avoid having to buy a machine that has everything, such as fast I/O, fast CPUs, and fast disks. Instead, we can be smart and use cheaper machines without impacting the result.
- Performance improves, because we allow the machines that had the bottleneck to focus on just one thing, correlating the bids and offers, rather than also spending CPU cycles on the web application.

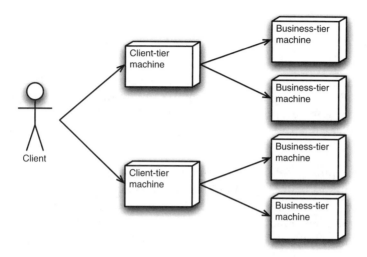

**Figure 10.10
Two-tier architecture
for the auction system**

- The system is overall more scalable, because we have a flexible setup, where we understand which components can be replicated and how best to partition the requests.

Surprisingly, it's quite easy to change our existing implementation to the new two-tier architecture. Instead of collocating all the bundles of the auction system in a single OSGi framework instance, we partition the system into several separate OSGi framework instances, placing the web application bundle in the OSGi framework instances hosted in the client tier machines and placing the auction application bundles in the business tier machines, as shown in figure 10.10. The main effort is in making sure that the web application bundle is able to locate and use the remote Auction service. This, as you've seen in this chapter, is done by using distribution providers and setting the proper service properties, such as `service.exported.configs`.

During this exercise, you've learned an important albeit subtle lesson. The reason we've been able to easily move from a local environment to a multiple-machine environment and finally to a two-tier multiple-machine environment is that our auction system is modular. Had we designed the whole system as a single monolithic (web) application, we wouldn't have been able to partition it when needed. As you'll see next, being able to partition our system is a prerequisite to running in the cloud.

Let's continue our story. We've been running our auction system successfully for several months now. During this period, we've noticed that business is very slow on some dates, like at the end of January, and business is very good in other cases, like near Valentine's Day. This burst-like behavior is difficult to manage and eventually becomes a problem. If the business continues doing well, we may have to double the number of machines we have for Christmas, only to have them sit idle in the months that follow. We need to be able to dynamically cope with this variation of demand. Coping with this dynamism is the exact proposition of cloud computing, as you'll see next.

10.4.2 *Cloud computing*

The National Institute of Standards and Technology (NIST) defines cloud computing as follows:

> **DEFINITION** Cloud computing is a model for enabling convenient, on-demand network access to a shared pool of configurable computing resources (e.g., networks, servers, storage, applications, and services) that can be rapidly provisioned and released with minimal management effort or service provider interaction.

To utilize cloud computing, we need to move our auction system from being hosted on our own machines to being hosted in machines managed by a cloud provider, as shown in figure 10.11. In fact, we don't even need to know the physical layout and characteristics of these machines; they're simply computing nodes performing their work. To do this, we create a virtual machine (VM) containing all of our software components—the operating system (OS), generally Linux, the OSGi framework distribution, and all of the application bundles and supporting libraries, like the Jetty web server. Our VM not only contains the binaries but also knows how to start them appropriately. For example, the VM should bootstrap the OSGi framework instance and make sure that our bundles have been installed and are activated. We can do this by setting up a shell script as an OS service. OS services are automatically started when the VM and thus the OS is booted.

Next, we give the VM to the cloud provider and tell the provider to assign six computing nodes to the VM. That is, our VM is deployed in six nodes somewhere in the cloud. As it gets close to Christmas, we ask the cloud provider to assign four additional

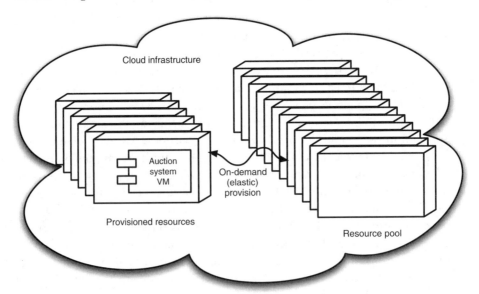

Figure 10.11 Auction system running in the cloud

nodes to our VM. After the holiday season ends, we ask the cloud provider to remove the four additional nodes; in fact, we ask it to keep only four nodes total running our VM. The cloud provider has a pool of resources, these being computing nodes, disks, and the like, which can be dynamically provisioned to run the customer's software.

> **DEFINITION**   The cloud is made up of a pool of resources that are provisioned dynamically on behalf of the customers.

In our particular case, we're assigning the nodes per calendar date, but we could even be more ambitious and monitor the utilization of the resources. For example, we could set up provisioning rules, as follows:

- If the CPU crosses an 80% utilization threshold, then automatically provision a new node for our VM.
- If the CPU utilization falls to below 20% for more than two days, then automatically shut down the node.

As you can see, cloud computing allows us to dynamically and efficiently change our environment based on demand. It also has other advantages, just like any other hosted service, such as us not having to manage our own machines and networks. But keep in mind that the main proposition for cloud computing is indeed its elasticity.

> **WARNING**   Cloud computing also has its drawbacks, one of the most serious being security. Because services from different customers are all sharing resources, there's always a higher likelihood of security breaches. Another disadvantage of cloud computing is the increased latency because services may hop several times between computing nodes before being fully served.

The question that remains to be answered is how OSGi relates to cloud computing. We'll address this question in the next section.

10.4.3   OSGi as the cloud platform

Let's say that to keep our business competitive, we need to fine-tune our auction algorithm frequently. Updating our auction system in the cloud isn't a trivial task; we need to change the auction bundle, re-create a new VM image, upload it to the cloud, shut down the VM instances, and finally replace them with the new image.

Generating VM images and the whole workflow process just described can be quite costly, especially if it must be done on a daily basis. Moreover, keep in mind that when generating a new VM image, we need to test all the components, and the time used for testing is proportional to the number of components being tested. By using OSGi, we can modularize our systems and therefore partition adequately, creating simpler and smaller VMs. You already saw an example of this when we partitioned the auction system into two tiers. The result is that we can have two separate VM images, one containing the components of the client tier and the second containing the components of the business tier. Managing smaller VMs is obviously better. For example, if we're updating just the auction bundle, it would prevent us from having to repackage and retest the web application and server. Potentially, we could also rent cheaper computing nodes for the client tier VM, which contains the less-demanding web application bundles.

> **WARNING** It's a common misconception that you don't need to design your system to run in the cloud. To fully utilize cloud computing, the system must be able to scale. Modular systems scale better; therefore, OSGi is a clear infrastructure choice, because it emphasizes and helps in the creation of modular applications.

That's not the complete story though. Suppose that instead of uploading and managing VMs in the cloud, we were allowed to manage OSGi framework instances and their bundles. If this were the case, we'd just need to inform the cloud provider to update our auction bundle. The auction application, being an OSGi application, already has to deal with the fact that dynamic changes and updates may happen, so the fact that it's happening when it's running in the cloud or running as a standalone local application is mostly immaterial. Thus, if our supposition were true, OSGi would give us two important advantages:

- OSGi would let us update our system quite easily and efficiently, without us having to get into the business of generating full VM images.
- It avoids lock-ins, because we can design and validate our applications using any OSGi implementation in a standalone environment before moving to the cloud.

We could even take it a step further. The cloud provider could give us access to an OSGi bundle repository (OBR), where we could install, update, and uninstall bundles as needed. Then, after having updated the auction bundle, we could select an OSGi framework instance and tell it to move forward and take the new versions of the bundles from the OBR. If there are any problems, we could always tell it to revert to the previous versions.

Let's take a step back and revise. We have several OSGi bundles that have been uploaded to the cloud's OBR. In addition, we've provisioned OSGi framework instances to computing nodes, as shown in figure 10.12. For example, we have two OSGi framework instances in the client tier; therefore, we could assign each to a different computing node. Next, we have the remaining eight OSGi instances, which we could likewise assign to a different computing node. Finally, we could install the web application in the OSGi instances of the client tier and the auction application bundles in the OSGi instances of the business tier. And, of course, we would need to make sure that the web application bundle could invoke remote services residing in the bundles of the business tier. In this environment, we can easily manage updates to our system by leveraging the OSGi framework. But there's still one problem to consider: we're having to explicitly provision the OSGi framework instances and target the bundles to specific framework instances.

A better scenario would be the following: we upload the bundles to the OBR in the cloud, and each bundle tells the cloud its requirements, so that the infrastructure can

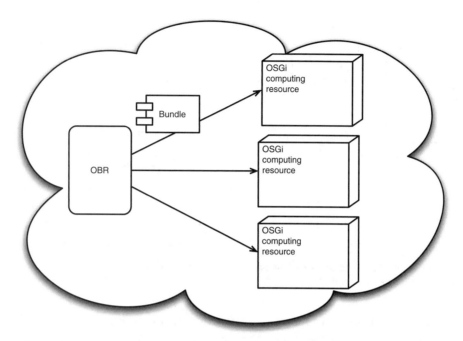

Figure 10.12 OBR and OSGi framework as a platform for cloud computing

dynamically provision the system. For example, the web application bundle could state that it depends on a web server and a cloud resource that has fast public access to the internet. Likewise, the auction bundles could state that they depend on a cloud resource where they get at least 80% CPU utilization.

The cloud infrastructure would consider all these requirements and assign the bundles to the correct OSGi framework instances that it provisions to its computing nodes. For example, the cloud infrastructure would spawn a new computing node that has internet access and install the web application bundle into it.

REQUIREMENTS AND CAPABILITIES

Does it seem far-fetched? Perhaps, but we already have most of the pieces. Dependencies between bundles can already be specified in OSGi using the regular `import-package` mechanism. Furthermore, starting in version 4.3 of the OSGi Service Platform, there's a generic mechanism for the specification of general requirements and capabilities. You can think of the `import-package` and `export-package` headers respectively as a particular case of a requirement and a capability specification.

For example, consider a bundle that specifies the following OSGi 4.3 `Require-Capability` MANIFEST header entry:

```
Require-Capability:
    com.cloudprovider;    filter:="(&(web-access)(cpu<90))"
```

This header is placed in the namespace of `com.cloudprovider`, which means that its interpretation is intended for some particular cloud provider. It states that this bundle

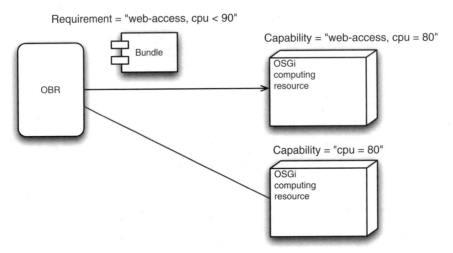

Figure 10.13   The cloud infrastructure matches a bundle's requirements with a resource node that's able to fulfill them.

requires the attribute `web-access` to be true and that the attribute `cpu`, which is a numeric value, must be less than 90 (percent).

On the opposite side, the cloud provider has to find an OSGi framework instance whose System bundle has been launched with the following property:

```
org.osgi.framework.system.capabilities.extra=
        "com.cloudprovider; web-access:Boolean=true; cpu:Long=80"
```

Essentially, the framework instance is telling us that it's capable of providing web access and it will monitor the CPU to make sure that it's never more than 80% busy. This is shown in figure 10.13.

There's still much to be collaborated before cloud computing is considered a mature technology. But the OSGi platform has three intrinsic qualities that make it ideal for supporting elasticity in the cloud:

- Application behavior dynamism provided by the OSGi framework API
- Transport abstraction through OSGi Remote Services
- Dependency management using the OSGi requirement/capability framework

In other words, cloud providers could expose the OSGi service platform as a service to their clients, so that they can manage their applications. In this environment, an OSGi bundle becomes the cloud's deployment unit, and OSGi the ideal Platform as a Service.

10.5   Summary

The OSGi Remote Service specification allows a consuming bundle to invoke a service that's provided by a bundle in a remote OSGi framework instance. You register a service using the service properties `service.exported.interfaces` and `service. exported.configs` to mark it as remote.

Distribution providers are responsible for transparently discovering and handling the remote services for the consuming bundles, and they support different transport protocols, as dictated by the `service.exported.configs` property. A remote service may be exported through different endpoints. A consuming bundle may optionally select a particular endpoint by filtering on the service property `service.imported.configs`.

It's not uncommon for the consumer and the provider of the remote services to negotiate policies, such as if encryption is necessary or based on the QoS of the transport itself. For this purpose, the provider can specify its requirements in the `service.exported.intents` property. The distribution providers must be able to fulfill these requirements, which are seen as capabilities in the consuming side in the service property `service.intents`.

Cloud computing is all about being able to efficiently meet the varying demand of customers by dynamically provisioning resources from a resource pool. The OSGi platform is an ideal Platform as a Service, because it has native support for the dynamic behavior of applications, remote services, and a generic requirements/capability framework for dependency resolution.

In the next chapter, we'll look into the crucial issue of how to manage this complex environment. Managing the OSGi framework and its applications is the subject of the next chapter.

Launching OSGi
using start levels

11

This chapter covers

- Managing bundles that are misbehaving by automatically uninstalling them
- Handling a large number of bundles without impacting startup time
- Enabling end users to interact with OSGi applications without learning the OSGi framework
- Creating an easy-to-use product installation kit for OSGi applications

---

So far we've created several OSGi applications. You've learned that OSGi applications are formed by a set of collaborating bundles and services, and you've learned how best to develop them, avoiding dependencies between services and therefore increasing their extensibility. In the process, you've learned how to configure your applications, handle events, persist data, participate in transactions, and share objects with other applications.

We're now ready to bootstrap and run the OSGi framework with our applications. To do so properly, you'll learn in this chapter how to launch the OSGi framework with a simpler custom interface, how to deploy your applications in a consistent manner, and finally how to keep the applications up to date and support live plug-ins of extensions.

We'll start the chapter by considering a common problem in OSGi: how do you handle the case where a user has installed a bundle that's behaving erratically and make sure that this problematic bundle doesn't disrupt the infrastructure or the other applications that are being hosted by the infrastructure? This is an especially important topic, considering that an OSGi application is likely to be composed of several independent bundles.

11.1 *Managing disorderly bundles*

One of the complexities of dealing with software frameworks is that they provide such a large surface area for their end users and vendor extensions that it's practically impossible to make sure that applications don't misbehave.

For example, an application developer could inadvertently never return from a bundle's `BundleActivator.start()` method. What would happen in this case? Let's try it out. To do this, code the following `BundleActivator`:

```
public class BlockerActivator implements BundleActivator {

    public void start(BundleContext context) throws Exception {
        System.out.println("Starting blocker");
        while (true);
    }

    public void stop(BundleContext context) throws Exception {
    }
}
```

Start Felix, install the bundle, say `blocker_1.0.0`, containing the `BlockerActivator` class, and start it:

```
g! install file:blocker_1.0.0.jar
Bundle ID: 18
g! start 18
Starting blocker
```

As expected, the `start` command never returns. This is less than ideal but somewhat obvious, because the command is waiting for the return from the `start` callback, which never happens.

What to do? As we've all learned from previous experience, when all else fails, reboot. In this case, shut down the OSGi framework and start it again. Because the shell is blocked, you can do this by pressing Ctrl-C or by invoking the `kill` command on a separate shell, should you be working in a UNIX environment.

What happens when you restart Felix? Initially, it may seem that you're OK; the shell isn't blocked. But on further investigation, you realize that the OSGi framework is still blocked, waiting for the start() method from the blocker bundle to return. The simplest way to verify this is to execute the lb command in the shell prompt:

```
g! lb
START LEVEL 1
   ID|State        |Level|Name
    0|Starting     |    0|System Bundle (3.0.6)
    1|Active       |    1|Apache Felix Bundle Repository (1.6.2)
    2|Active       |    1|Apache Felix Gogo Command (0.6.1)
    3|Active       |    1|Apache Felix Gogo Runtime (0.6.1)
    4|Active       |    1|Apache Felix Gogo Shell (0.6.1)
   18|Starting     |    1|blocker (1.0.0)
```

Note how both the state of the OSGi's system bundle and the blocker are set to Starting as opposed to Active, which should be the correct state.

There are other things amiss. For example, try to stop the blocker bundle, or, even more generally, try to start a new bundle. In the former case, the shell will again block, and you'll be back to the original situation. In the latter case, a new bundle does start correctly, but when you restart the framework, it won't start because the framework waits for the prior bundle, the blocker bundle, to return before moving on to start other bundles, such as the new bundle.

You may argue that a developer would never code a line such as while (true);, and although this may be true, there are several other reasons why the start() method may never return:

- The bundle enters some deadlock.
- The bundle performs a remote call for which there is no timeout or a very large timeout, such as one set in minutes.

How much of this behavior is implementation-specific? That is, would you run into similar problems in other OSGi frameworks? Although some of this is underspecified in the OSGi specifications, you'll certainly run into problems if a bundle doesn't return from its start() method in any framework implementation. The fundamental problem is that the framework must know the result of activating a bundle before proceeding.

How do you solve this problem? How can you resiliently deal with dysfunctional applications in an OSGi framework? First of all, let's see how we can fix the problem at hand. We've already tried stopping the blocker bundle and restarting Felix, and neither action helped. As you've guessed, trying to uninstall the bundle from the shell prompt won't do you any good either. What you'll have to do is shut down Felix and restart it without the offending bundle.

By default, Felix stores all of its persistent state in the felix-cache directory, present in its home directory. The easiest solution is to remove all of its cache by issuing the following command:

```
felix-framework-3.0.6$ rm -rf felix-cache/*
```

But a less drastic approach is to remove just the cache for the blocker bundle, which has the bundle ID number of 18 (as was indicated by the output of the lb command):

```
felix-framework-3.0.6$ rm -rf felix-cache/bundle18
```

Having done so, you'll be able to restart Felix without the blocker bundle and thus regain control of the framework.

> **TIP** In Equinox, you should delete the configuration/org.eclipse.osgi/bundles directory.

We've gotten ourselves out of the situation, but how can we avoid this problem altogether? You've learned that an OSGi application potentially comprises several bundles. Recall from chapter 3 how the auction application is made up of seven bundles! As you'll see next, you can protect your applications by creating management layers for the bundles.

11.2 Layered architecture to managing bundles

Before looking at the subject of bundle layering, you must first understand how the OSGi framework starts up, that is, bootstraps.

11.2.1 Bootstrapping the OSGi framework

The OSGi framework persists information for all bundles that have been installed and their current state. When booting, the framework makes sure that the state of the framework is as it was before the shutdown. In practice, this means the following:

1. All bundles that had been installed must be revived (reinstalled). Remember that a bundle must be kept installed in the OSGi framework until it's explicitly uninstalled.

2. The mechanism for reviving installed bundles into memory is vendor-specific, but the framework must again resolve all bundles that were previously resolved successfully. This means that the order of reviving the installed bundles is the same order in which they were installed or, more specifically, in ascending order of bundle IDs.

3. All bundles that had been started must be restarted. This is done by invoking a bundle's BundleActivator.start() method, should one be present. This step is actually a bit more complicated than that, but we'll leave it at this and discuss it in detail shortly.

4. After the framework has installed, resolved, and started all bundles so that it's in the same state as it was before the shutdown occurred, the state of the system bundle is set to Active and a FrameworkEvent.STARTED event is sent.

> **NOTE** Bundles that need to make sure that the framework is ready for use after a reboot has happened should listen for the STARTED event. This is generally the case for bundles acting as management agents.

The third step is the key to solving the problem of misbehaving bundles. You need a way of selectively starting the bundles during the boot process; that is, you want to start all bundles that you know can be trusted and only at a second step start those that have been provided as extensions by third parties or end users. This can be done through the Start-Level service.

11.2.2 *The Start-Level service*

All bundles have a *start level,* which is by default level 1. In conjunction with a bundle's start level, the OSGi framework itself is configured with an *active start level.*

When booting, the OSGi framework starts all bundles whose start level is equal to or lower than that of the framework's active start level. This is done in ascending order; that is, the framework starts all bundles whose start level is n, then $n+1$, $n+2$, ..., until n is equal to the framework's active start level. For example, if the active start level is 2, then first you'll start all bundles whose start level is 0, then those whose start level is 1, and then finally those whose start level is 2.

> **DEFINITIONS** *Bundle start level*—A number that indicates when a bundle should be started. A bundle is only started when the framework's active start level is equal to or greater than that of the bundle's start level. This can be changed dynamically.
>
> *Initial bundle start level*—The default start value assigned to a bundle when it's first installed. This default value can be changed dynamically, but the new value is applicable only to bundles installed after the change.
>
> *Active start level*—A number that indicates the OSGi framework's active start level. This can be changed dynamically and is applicable to all installed bundles; therefore, it may cause bundles to be stopped or started.
>
> *Beginning active start level*—The default active start level when the OSGi framework is launched. This is configured in some vendor-specific form and defaults to 1. This can't be changed dynamically.

By using start levels, you can create layers of bundles, where a layer is started before another layer, thus giving you some level of isolation between bundles and better ways of managing the bootstrap process of the OSGi framework.

Let's look at how this can be done for the blocker bundle. First, starting from a clean environment, install the blocker bundle into Felix. But rather than starting this bundle immediately, change its bundle start level to 2. This can be done using the shell commands shown in the following listing.

> **Listing 11.1 Setting the start level for the blocker bundle**

```
Welcome to Apache Felix Gogo

g! install file:blocker_1.0.0.jar
Bundle ID: 5
g! bundlelevel -s 2 5
```

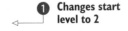 **1** Changes start level to 2

```
g! lb
START LEVEL 1
    ID|State       |Level|Name
     0|Starting    |    0|System Bundle (3.0.6)
     1|Active      |    1|Apache Felix Bundle Repository (1.6.2)
     2|Active      |    1|Apache Felix Gogo Command (0.6.1)
     3|Active      |    1|Apache Felix Gogo Runtime (0.6.1)
     4|Active      |    1|Apache Felix Gogo Shell (0.6.1)
     5|Installed   |    2|blocker (1.0.0)
```

Lists all ❷ **start levels**

The bundlelevel command ❶ changes the bundle whose ID is 5 to have a start level of 2. Execute the command lb ❷ to verify that the change was made. Note how the blocker bundle now has been configured with a start level equal to 2 in the bundle listing. This instance of the OSGi framework now has three layers:

- The first layer contains the framework core itself, which is the system bundle.
- The second layer contains Felix preinstalled services, such as the shell prompt.
- The third layer contains user-provided applications, such as the blocker bundle.

Finally, the bundle listing also shows the framework's active start level, which is by default always set to 1.

Next, try starting the blocker bundle as usual. You'll notice that nothing happens. The reason is that the active start level of the framework is lower than that of the blocker bundle. Hence the blocker bundle isn't started; instead, it's marked to start as soon as the framework's active start level allows it to by reaching the value of 2 or above.

NOTE Regardless of the blocker bundle not being activated because of its start level, it has been persistently marked as "to be started." This means that even if the framework is shut down and restarted, the framework will still start the bundle when its start level is reached.

Let's change the framework's active start level to 2.

Listing 11.2   Changing the active start level of the OSGi framework

```
g! lb
START LEVEL 1
    ID|State       |Level|Name
     0|Starting    |    0|System Bundle (3.0.6)
     1|Active      |    1|Apache Felix Bundle Repository (1.6.2)
     2|Active      |    1|Apache Felix Gogo Command (0.6.1)
     3|Active      |    1|Apache Felix Gogo Runtime (0.6.1)
     4|Active      |    1|Apache Felix Gogo Shell (0.6.1)
     5|Installed   |    2|blocker (1.0.0)
g! start 5
g! frameworklevel 2
Starting blocker

g! lb
START LEVEL 2
    ID|State       |Level|Name
     0|Starting    |    0|System Bundle (3.0.6)
```

Changes active ❶ **start level**

```
1|Active      |    1|Apache Felix Bundle Repository (1.6.2)
2|Active      |    1|Apache Felix Gogo Command (0.6.1)
3|Active      |    1|Apache Felix Gogo Runtime (0.6.1)
4|Active      |    1|Apache Felix Gogo Shell (0.6.1)
5|Starting    |    2|blocker (1.0.0)
```

2 **Misbehaving bundle still Starting**

This is done using the shell's `frameworklevel` command **1**. The blocker bundle starts as expected, but it doesn't block the shell. This is because the `frameworklevel` command is specified to run asynchronously; nonetheless, the `lb` command reveals that the blocker bundle is still misbehaving, because its state is set to `Starting` instead of `Active` **2**.

Shut down Felix and restart it as you did before. But observe how, unlike the previous case, the blocker bundle doesn't try to start:

```
g! ^C
felix-framework-3.0.6$ java -jar bin/felix.jar

g! lb
START LEVEL 1
   ID|State      |Level|Name
    0|Starting    |    0|System Bundle (3.0.6)
    1|Active      |    1|Apache Felix Bundle Repository (1.6.2)
    2|Active      |    1|Apache Felix Gogo Command (0.6.1)
    3|Active      |    1|Apache Felix Gogo Runtime (0.6.1)
    4|Active      |    1|Apache Felix Gogo Shell (0.6.1)
    5|Installed    |    2|blocker (1.0.0)
```

This gives you the opportunity to uninstall the blocker bundle and any other misbehaving bundles and then continue the startup of the remaining (well-behaved) user-provided bundles by again setting the active start level to 2:

```
g!
g! uninstall 4
g! lb
START LEVEL 1
   ID|State      |Level|Name
    0|Starting    |    0|System Bundle (3.0.6)
    1|Active      |    1|Apache Felix Bundle Repository (1.6.2)
    2|Active      |    1|Apache Felix Gogo Command (0.6.1)
    3|Active      |    1|Apache Felix Gogo Runtime (0.6.1)
    4|Active      |    1|Apache Felix Gogo Shell (0.6.1)
g! frameworklevel 2
g!
```

Why is it that Felix bootstrapped using the framework (active) start level of 1 instead of 2? All OSGi frameworks must by default start with the active start level of 1, which is called the beginning start level. In addition, implementations can provide a vendor-specific way of configuring the beginning start level.

> **NOTE** In Felix, you can change the beginning start level by editing the property `org.osgi.framework.startlevel.beginning` present in the file conf/config.properties in Felix's home directory.

By organizing the bundles into different layers, you can safeguard your applications by placing less-trustworthy user-provided bundles at a higher layer than that of more secure and tested bundles that make up part of the core.

> ## Start levels in Eclipse Equinox
>
> You can change a bundle's start level in Eclipse Equinox by using the command `setbsl` `<start-level>` `<bundle-id>`. For example, the command `setbsl 5 2` changes the start level of a bundle whose ID is 2 to 5.
>
> Using the command `setfwls <start-level>` changes the active framework start level.
>
> Finally, the initial bundle start level is changed using the command `setibsl <start-level>`.
>
> You can list all start levels by using the command `sl`.

The overall idea is to create a layered architecture, where the lower layers contain well-tested and known bundles. Enterprise-grade applications should have at least two layers in addition to the two layers that are already present in the OSGi framework, totaling four layers, as shown in figure 11.1. These are described next, starting from the lower core layers and moving up to the applications:

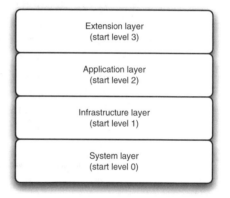

Figure 11.1 A four-layer architecture is suggested for better managing bundles in an application framework.

- *System layer*—This layer contains the implementation of the OSGi framework itself. This is done commonly using a single bundle called the *system bundle.*
- *Infrastructure layer*—This layer provides several out-of-the-box OSGi services, such as the Service Tracker service, the Start-Level service, and the Configuration Admin service. In addition, this layer may contain OSGi vendor-specific services, such as the shell console in the case of Felix, and other core bundles providing general application-agonistic functionality, such as a thread-pool implementation bundle. Bundles in this layer are sometimes referred to as the *infrastructure bundles.*
- *Application layer*—This layer contains the implementation of the application itself. These are trustworthy bundles developed and tested by you. Bundles hosted in this layer are commonly referred to as *application bundles.* These bundles can be further grouped into sets, forming enterprise application *features.*

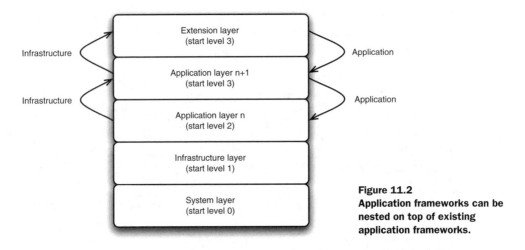

**Figure 11.2
Application frameworks can be
nested on top of existing
application frameworks.**

For example, an application can define a security feature, a transaction feature, and so on. Recalling the auction application from chapter 3, the bundles `auction.api`, `auction.spi`, and `auction.manager` are application bundles.

- *Extension layer*—This layer contains bundles installed by your service providers and end users, which use the services provided by the application layer. These are less trustworthy and need to be isolated in case they misbehave and need to be uninstalled or stopped. Bundles hosted in this layer are called *application extension bundles.* Again, in the auction application, these would be the bundles `auction.auctioneer.sealed`, `auction.auditor.sealed`, `auction.seller.simple`, and `auction.buyer.http`.

This layered architecture can be expanded to include several layers of application; that is, you can layer applications (or their frameworks) on top of applications, each time raising the abstraction level and further specializing the solution for a domain, as shown in figure 11.2.

For example, consider a bundle stack where you first place the Spring Framework (Spring DM) on top of Felix and only then place your application bundles on top of the Spring Framework bundles. In this case, the Spring Framework bundles act as infrastructure to the application bundles.

11.2.3 *Safe-mode boot*

This layered architecture allows us to implement a safe-mode boot of the application. For example, considering a system that has four layers as in figure 11.1, you can do this by providing a command-line option where the framework is booted using an active start level of 2; in other words, none of the extension bundles are started. Next, a management agent, which has a bundle start level of 2 and thus was started, goes through each extension and tries to verify if it's functioning correctly. The management agent can do this by asking the user. Those extension bundles found to be incorrect are uninstalled from the system. Finally, the framework is shut down and rebooted in normal mode, and it starts all the layers, including the extension layer, which now contains only application extensions known to work.

As you've seen, by using start levels, you're better able to manage the OSGi framework and its installed bundles, particularly when bootstrapping the OSGi framework itself. Are the start levels also applicable during the shutdown of the OSGi framework? Yes, as you'll see next.

11.2.4 *Shutting down the OSGi framework*

The shutdown process is, as expected, the inverse of its bootstrap:

1 First, the state of the system bundle is changed to `Stopping`.
2 All bundles that have been started successfully are stopped. This is done by invoking the bundle's `BundleActivator.stop()` method, should one be available.

> **IMPORTANT** Even though the bundles are stopped, their persisted state remains set to `Active`, which means that these bundles will be restarted when the OSGi framework boots up.

3 The bundles are stopped beginning at the active start level and proceeding down until 0 is reached. For example, bundles whose start level is set to n are stopped first, then bundles whose start level is set to n-1, n-2, ..., until 0.
4 The process exits.

Considering our example at hand, this means that the blocker bundle would stop first, then all of the Felix preinstalled bundles would be stopped, and finally the system bundle would be stopped. This process allows you to make sure that the applications are stopped before the OSGi framework attempts to stop any of the underlying services, which could still be in use by the applications.

> **WARNING** Start levels are useful only during the bootstrap and shutdown of the system, and their ordering shouldn't be relied on afterward. This is because bundles and services can come and go dynamically.

The Start-Level service gives you better manageability of the OSGi framework, allowing you to safeguard against applications that may misbehave, as well as other usages that may arise later. But what if you're starting a new bundle that you know can't be trusted? Can you take any additional precautions? Yes, you can start a bundle marking it as transient, as you'll see next.

11.2.5 *A transient start of a bundle*

When starting a bundle, you can specify the option `Bundle.START_TRANSIENT`. When `START_TRANSIENT` is used, the OSGi framework doesn't change the persisted state of the bundle. In other words, when the OSGi framework is restarted, the bundle still has the state it had prior to the call to start. In practice, this means that the OSGi framework won't attempt to start these bundles during a restart of the framework.

In our example, had you started the blocker bundle with the START_TRANSIENT option, then even if you didn't use start levels, the OSGi framework wouldn't have attempted to start the blocker bundle during a follow-up restart of the framework. This is because the persisted state of the blocker bundle would still have been set to RESOLVED and not STARTING or ACTIVE.

Unfortunately, at the time of this writing, the Felix shell prompt doesn't support this option. To start a bundle with the TRANSIENT option, you must use the programmatic Java interface:

```
Bundle bundle = //..
 bundle.start(Bundle.START_TRANSIENT);
```

A transient start of a bundle is invaluable when testing but not generally beneficial in a production environment; thus it's not commonly used. It's a pity that the shell prompt doesn't support this option, because it would be convenient in a test environment.

So far we've been dealing with the situation where one bundle is catastrophically misbehaving. In the next section, we'll look into a different problem, where rather than having one misbehaving bundle, the issue is handling too many bundles at a time.

11.2.6   *A lazy start of a bundle*

Consider the case where a bundle takes approximately 10 seconds to activate, that is, to return from its BundleActivator.start() callback. This may be because the bundle is caching some of its internal resources or because it may need to connect to an external site. Ten seconds isn't particularly excessive. But what if your application framework is hosting 10 or 50 applications at a time? Considering our start time of 10 seconds per bundle, such a framework containing 50 bundles would take roughly 8 minutes to start. As you saw previously, this means the OSGi bootstrap process would last for 8 minutes, only after which the framework would be considered ready to receive new commands. This would be too much; most users would have given up by then. How can we support a large number of applications in our application framework?

Obviously, one option is to improve the startup time of each bundle. This generally can be done by starting a new thread within the implementation of the Bundle-Activator.start() callback. But OSGi has a more holistic approach: you can configure a bundle to be activated lazily. A lazily activated bundle has its BundleActivator.start() callback invoked only when the bundle is first used by another bundle. A bundle uses another bundle when it loads a class from it, be it explicitly through the BundleContext.loadClass() method or implicitly by the OSGi framework when resolving the imported packages of a bundle.

For example, let's say you've installed bundle B1, which exports package P1. You can configure bundle B1 to be activated lazily by adding the following header entry to its MANIFEST:

```
Bundle-ActivationPolicy: lazy
```

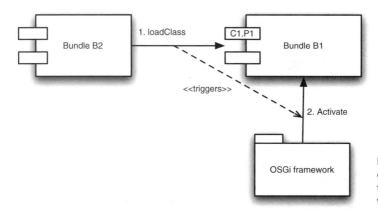

Figure 11.3 The loading of class C1 in bundle B1 triggers its activation by the OSGi framework.

And then you specify the following option in its `start` command:

```
Bundle bundle = //..
bundle.start(Bundle.START_ACTIVATION_POLICY);
```

Next, let's install bundle B2, which imports package P1. B2 instantiates the class C1, which is under the package P1, in its `BundleActivator.start()` method:

```
public void start(BundleContext context) throws Exception {
    C1 c1 = new C1();
    // ...
}
```

The loading of the class C1 from bundle B1 by B2 triggers the activation of B1, as shown in figure 11.3.

> **NOTE** How do you know if a lazily activated bundle has been started but not yet activated? In other words, if the `start` command has been invoked, but the bundle is not yet being used by another bundle, and hence its `Bundle-Activator.start()` callback hasn't been invoked yet? A lazily activated bundle that hasn't yet been activated has its state set to `STARTING`, whereas a bundle whose `start()` callback has already returned has its state set to `ACTIVATED`.

By setting bundles to be lazily activated, you can speed up the startup time of the OSGi framework and also save memory, because the bundles won't take up resources until they're actually needed.

Can you always do this? No, you need to be careful, because there are cases when there are no appropriate *triggers* that can be used. For example, still referencing the previous case, let's say that instead of exporting a package, bundle B1 is registering an OSGi service (S1) whose service interface, defined as the class C2, is being exported by some other bundle (B3). In this case, nothing would trigger the loading of a class from B1, because bundle B2 would load the service interface class C2 from B3 instead of B1 when retrieving the OSGi service S1, and hence B1 would never activate and have a chance to register its service to begin with! See figure 11.4.

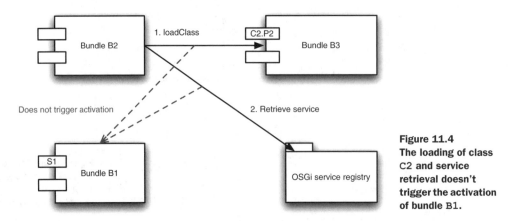

Figure 11.4
The loading of class C2 and service retrieval doesn't trigger the activation of bundle B1.

In the previous sections, we looked into how to identify and handle misbehaving bundles. In the next section, we'll look at how to deploy and update multiple bundles as a single cohesive application.

11.3   Deploying applications

As you've seen, an application in an OSGi framework may be implemented as a set of bundles, as we did for the auction application in chapter 3. If that's the case, you need a way of making sure all of these bundles are installed and started consistently and that none are forgotten or left out.

As it stands, all OSGi framework implementations provide some vendor-specific mechanism for configuring the bundles that are installed out of the box. In Felix, this is done by means of the file config.properties located in the conf directory. Within this file, locate the properties `felix.auto.deploy.action` and `felix.auto.deploy.dir`. The latter specifies the autoload directory, which by default is the bundle directory. When any files are placed in this directory, Felix will perform the actions established by the former property. By default, the `felix.auto.deploy.action` property is configured to `install` and `start`, which means all bundles placed in the bundle directory are installed and started automatically.

Let's list the current content of this directory for a fresh installation of Felix:

```
felix-framework-3.0.6$ cd bundle/
bundle$ ls
org.apache.felix.bundlerepository-1.6.2.jar
org.apache.felix.gogo.command-0.6.1.jar
org.apache.felix.gogo.runtime-0.6.1.jar
org.apache.felix.gogo.shell-0.6.1.jar
```

As expected, this reflects exactly the result you get when you issue the lb command:

```
g! lb
START LEVEL 1
   ID|State      |Level|Name
    0|Starting   |    0|System Bundle (3.0.6)
    1|Active     |    1|Apache Felix Bundle Repository (1.6.2)
```

```
2|Active      |     1|Apache Felix Gogo Command (0.6.1)
3|Active      |     1|Apache Felix Gogo Runtime (0.6.1)
4|Active      |     1|Apache Felix Gogo Shell (0.6.1)
```

In other words, a fresh install of Felix includes an OBR implementation and the Gogo shell. We used OBR briefly in chapter 5; we'll look at it again later in this chapter. Likewise, we're used to the Gogo shell.

A simple and consistent mechanism for installing and starting your OSGi applications when launching the framework is therefore to place the application's bundle files in the autodeploy directory. For example, to provide the auction application out of the box, you need to place the following files within the bundle directory:

```
bundle$ ls
auction.api_1.0.0.jar
auction.auctioneer.sealed_1.0.0.jar
auction.auditor.sealed_1.0.0.jar
auction.buyer.http_1.0.0.jar
auction.buyer.simple_1.0.0.jar
auction.core_1.0.0.jar
auction.seller.simple_1.0.0.jar
auction.spi_1.0.0.jar
```

Having installed your applications, the next step is to learn how to do live updates of individual application features, which generally would be a subset of an application's bundles. We'll do this in the next section.

11.3.1 Updating features

Even the best-implemented features need to be updated from time to time. For any moderately complex application, occasionally you'll need to update the bundles that compose the implementation of the application itself.

What's the best way of updating an application feature? Should you uninstall a running bundle and install a new version of the bundle, as we did in the initial chapters of this book? This works fine for testing, but in an actual production environment you need to be more comprehensive; for instance, you need to handle the following use cases:

- If the update of a new version of a bundle fails, you need to revert to the original version.
- You need to automate the process of updating, because otherwise the user will generally forget or ignore the need to update to new versions. This is not to say that the user shouldn't be notified of the update, but the actual downloading and updating of the bundle should be automated once confirmed by the user.

To handle the first requirement, you should use the `Bundle.update()` API. This method will attempt to stop the bundle if it's running by calling the `Bundle-Activator.stop()` callback. It will then install the new version of the bundle. If the bundle was originally running, it will start the new version of the bundle by calling the

`BundleActivator.start()` callback. If any of these steps fail, the OSGi framework restores the original bundle.

NOTE If any packages have been exported by the original bundle version, these packages remain exported until the OSGi framework is relaunched or the whole system is refreshed.

To handle the second requirement, you need to create a management agent that automates the update process. As you've seen, a management agent is a software component that manages the system in which it's being hosted, sometimes driven by a remote manager entity. For us, a management agent can simply be implemented as an application framework bundle.

NOTE Remember that in our layered architecture, a bundle can be either an infrastructure bundle, an application bundle, or an application extension bundle. A management agent is generally an infrastructure bundle.

Let's consider the trivial case of an agent that updates all application bundles every month. It does so every time the framework is started. This can be done with the following `BundleActivator` code.

Listing 11.3 Update management agent

```java
public class UpdateActivator implements BundleActivator {

    public void start(BundleContext context) throws Exception {
        Bundle [] bundles =
            context.getBundles();                      // ❶ List all installed
                                                       //    bundles

        for (Bundle bundle : bundles) {                // ❷ Select our
            if (bundle.getSymbolicName().              //    enterprise
              startsWith("com.myenterprise.myfeature")) {  //  bundles

                Date lastModifiedDate =
                    new Date(bundle.getLastModified());  // ❸ Check last
                                                         //    modification date
                Calendar targetDate = Calendar.getInstance();
                targetDate.add(Calendar.MONTH, -1);

                if (lastModifiedDate.before(targetDate.getTime())) {
                    try {
                        bundle.update();                 // ❹ Update
                    } catch (BundleException e) {        //    bundle bits
                        // log
                    }
                }
            }
        }
    }

    public void stop(BundleContext context) throws Exception {
        // ...
    }
}
```

First, you retrieve all installed bundles in the OSGi framework ❶. Next, you select only those bundles that are part of the actual application implementation ❷. In this particular case, you assume that all bundles whose symbolic name starts with some predefined value (for example, `com.myenterprise.myfeature`) are feature-related bundles. There are other more robust ways of doing this; for instance, you could check if the bundle location is within the product home directory, which is a good indication that the bundle is part of the framework implementation and not an application bundle:

```
bundle.getLocation().startsWith("file:bundle")
```

> **Bundle instances**
>
> When you install a new bundle, even if you're just changing the bundle version of an existing bundle, you'll always get a new `Bundle` object instance (for example, `org.osgi.framework.Bundle`). This is different than when you update a bundle, because it's guaranteed that the `Bundle` object instance will remain the same through the updates. This allows you to cache the bundle instances, further improving performance in scenarios where you need to manage a bundle repeatedly.

You should generally avoid updating the management agent bundle itself. You could do this by naming the bundle differently or adding another condition to the `if` statement:

```
if (bundle.getSymbolicName().startsWith(
  "com.myenterprise.myfeature") &&
  (bundle.getBundleId() != context.getBundle().getBundleId()))
```

Next, you retrieve the last time that the system bundle has been modified ❸. `Bundle.getLastModified()` returns the last time that a bundle has been installed, updated, or uninstalled. Then, you get the current date and subtract a month from it. For instance, if the current date of the system has been set to "30 of Oct of 2011," then after the subtraction, it would become "30 of Sep of 2011." Finally, you check to see if the last time the bundle was modified was prior to the subtracted date of one month ago, and if it was, you invoke the update method in the bundle ❹.

As we discussed previously, the bundle update can fail and throw a `Bundle-Exception`; if it does, you catch and log it and continue to handle the other infrastructure bundles.

One issue remains: where are the bits that contain the updated versions of the bundles located? There are three ways of specifying the location of the updated bits. First, if you don't do anything special, the framework assumes that the updated bits are located in the same location where the bundle was originally installed. That's the case here. For instance, let's install the updater bundle by invoking the following command in the Felix shell:

```
g! install file:updater_1.0.0.jar
Bundle ID: 5
```

In this case, when the method `Bundle.update()` is invoked for the bundle whose ID is 5, the OSGi framework will look for new bits for this bundle in the modules directory. One of the problems with this approach is that it assumes that someone has actually downloaded and updated the bits directly in the product home directory.

The second option is to specify an input stream to be used to retrieve the bits as an argument to the update call:

```
InputStream is = ...
bundle.update(is);
```

This option lets you use a different location than that of the install location, but it hardcodes the update location in the Java code of the management agent. Therefore, this isn't ideal.

The third option is to use the manifest header entry `Bundle-UpdateLocation`. For instance, consider the case of a bundle that has the following header in its MANIFEST.MF file:

```
Bundle-UpdateLocation: http://www.myenterprise.com/bundles/myfeature.jar
```

This means that if you invoke the method `Bundle.update()` without any arguments, the OSGi framework will attempt to retrieve the new bits using the URL http://www.myenterprise.com/bundles/myfeature.jar. This decouples the update location from the install location, avoids hardcoding the update location in the management agent, and still fulfills our second requirement of automatically handling the download of the new version bits.

Updated bits

When `Bundle.update()` is used, keep in mind that the bits for the new version of the bundle are directly installed into the OSGi framework, and it doesn't override the bits of the original bundle, whose location was specified when invoking the `install` command.

What this means is that if you uninstall the bundle and later decide to reinstall its latest version, you still need to get the latest bits from somewhere, because the original location still points to a previous version.

This behavior also explains why it's an understandable practice to include the bundle version number as part of the bundle's filename (for example, mybundle_1.0.0.0.jar); when this bundle is updated with a newer version, the file itself isn't changed, so the bundle filename is still valid.

It's striking how we're able to update a running system with so few lines of code. But you must keep in mind that this is possible only if you've correctly modularized your system in a way that updates to bundles and changes of services don't disrupt other bundles.

> ## Other provisioning mechanisms
>
> OSGi also defines the Initial Provisioning specification, which mostly deals with a standard form of installing management agents into the OSGi framework. This allows the basic bootstrap of the system to be standardized. The management agent is then responsible for installing the infrastructure bundles through some vendor-specific mechanism.
>
> The Eclipse Foundation also defines p2 (http://www.eclipse.org/equinox/p2/), which is a provisioning protocol for updating and installing Eclipse plug-ins.

In this section, we looked at how you can easily update bundles that implement your application and thus upgrade the features of your application seamlessly. What should you do regarding the application extensions themselves? Remember, application extensions are bundles that extend the behavior of the application, such as the different auditor in the auction application example of chapter 3. You could try to use the same approach to update the application extensions themselves, but this is less suitable, because generally extensions are updated directly by the end users or the managing IT person and not through an automated process. Let's look into how you can help users manage and update their application extensions.

11.3.2 Updating extensions

So far you've installed all of your bundles through the Felix shell, by using the `install` command. The Felix shell is a simple and effective way of using the OSGi framework APIs, but is this really the proper interface to provide to the application's IT personnel for management? More to the point, can you abstract the OSGi framework API so that IT people don't need to learn this API when managing the OSGi applications, such as when bootstrapping, shutting down an application, and installing vendor extensions?

Yes, you can create your own application management API. First, let's look at the details of installing an application's extension. When a user hosts an extension bundle in the OSGi framework, it essentially means that the bundle bits have been installed and started. We'll name this combination of actions *extension deployment*. Conversely, a user can stop and uninstall the extension; this we'll call *extension undeployment*. In summary, we've defined two management tasks: deployment and undeployment. Finally, a user should be able to list all extensions that are currently being hosted by the application; we'll call this *extension listing*. Different applications will have different application management tasks; for example, for some applications it may be worthwhile to separate the steps of installing and starting.

Our next job is to provide a user interface to execute the deployment, undeployment, and listing of tasks and to map these to the underlying OSGi commands, as shown in figure 11.5. The latter is actually trivial; deployment maps to the OSGi bundle `install` and `start` commands, and undeployment maps to the OSGi `uninstall`

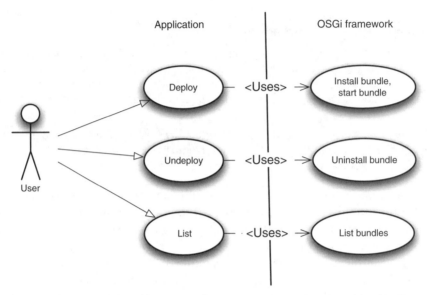

Figure 11.5   Application framework's management tasks and their mapping to OSGi commands

command (in this case, you don't need to stop it first). The list task maps to the retrieval of all application extension bundles. In other words, bundles installed by the user as extensions shouldn't include any of the system or infrastructure bundles.

With regard to the user interface, the first idea that comes to mind is to provide a web page for these tasks. This is generally the best approach. But because this isn't a book about web page development, we'll try to find another simpler option that still demonstrates the point. The simpler option is to use the filesystem itself as our user interface. When a user wants to deploy an extension, the user copies the extension's JAR file, which is defined as being an OSGi bundle, into a specific directory in the application's home directory. When the user wants to undeploy an extension, the user can then delete the extension JAR file from this directory. Finally, listings of all the extensions are done by listing the files contained in this directory. At first, this approach may seem somewhat clumsy, but it's actually quite flexible; not only does it shield the user from dealing with OSGi, but it's also easy to use and integrate into another tool, such as Ant.

Felix web management console

Felix also provides a web console (http://felix.apache.org/site/apache-felix-web-console.html) to manage the OSGi framework. This web console is very easy to use and complete; you can execute most of the OSGi framework APIs and also browse other things, such as bundle configurations.

But you should keep in mind that it doesn't hide OSGi in any form and thus is less appropriate for an end user.

So how do you implement this file-based management interface? As you've probably guessed, with an infrastructure bundle of your own. This bundle continuously polls a predefined directory, and whenever it finds a new file, it invokes the OSGi `install` command, passing along the file reference; it then starts this installed bundle. When it sees a file being deleted from the directory, it invokes the OSGi `uninstall` command on the missing file.

Fortunately enough, Felix already implements this with the Apache Felix File Install bundle. Let's install it and try it out.

11.3.3 *Deploying file install using OBR*

In section 5.2.4 of chapter 5, you learned how to use the OSGi Bundle Repository (OBR) to find and retrieve bundles from different providers. Interestingly enough, Felix also includes an OBR client as a service bundle, which can be used through its shell console. Let's look at it.

First, you can find out which repository your local instance of the Felix OBR client is using by reading Felix's configuration file and checking the `obr.repository.url` property:

```
obr.repository.url=http://felix.apache.org/obr/releases.xml
```

This URL points to Felix's own OBR repository. You can also add other repositories or delete existing repositories by adding or deleting other URLs to the configuration file.

Next, let's list all existing bundles available in this repository using the `obr:list` command:

```
g! obr:list
Apache Felix Bundle Repository (1.4.2, ...)
Apache Felix Configuration Admin Service (1.0.4, ...)
Apache Felix Declarative Services (1.0.8, ...)
Apache Felix EventAdmin (1.0.0)
Apache Felix File Install (2.0.0, ...)
```

The list goes on, but you've already seen a bundle that seems promising, the File Install bundle. Let's investigate its details:

```
g! obr:info "Apache Felix File Install"
------------------------
Apache Felix File Install
------------------------
description: A utility to automatically install bundles from a directory.
documentation: http://www.apache.org/
id: org.apache.felix.fileinstall/2.0.0
license: http://www.apache.org/licenses/LICENSE-2.0.txt
presentationname: Apache Felix File Install
size: 45481
symbolicname: org.apache.felix.fileinstall
url: http://repo1.maven.org/maven2/org/apache/felix/
     org.apache.felix.fileinstall/2.0.0/org.apache.felix.fileinstall-2.0.0.jar
version: 2.0.0
Requires:
```

```
    (&(package=org.apache.felix.fileinstall)(version>=2.0.0)(!(version>=3.0.0)))
    (&(package=org.osgi.framework)(version>=1.3.0)(!(version>=2.0.0)))
    (&(package=org.osgi.service.cm)(version>=1.2.0)(!(version>=2.0.0)))
    (&(package=org.osgi.service.log)(version>=1.3.0)(!(version>=2.0.0)))
    (&(package=org.osgi.service.packageadmin)(version>=1.2.0)(!(version>=2.0.0)))
    (&(package=org.osgi.service.startlevel)(version>=1.0.0)(!(version>=2.0.0)))
    (&(package=org.osgi.util.tracker)(version>=1.3.0)(!(version>=2.0.0)))
Capabilities:
    {manifestversion=2, presentationname=Apache Felix File Install,
      symbolicname=org.apache.felix.fileinstall, version=2.0.0}
    {package=org.apache.felix.fileinstall, version=2.0.0}
    {package=org.osgi.service.cm, uses=org.osgi.framework, version=1.2.0}
```

The description of the bundle confirms our suspicion: "A utility to automatically install bundles from a directory." You can check the dependencies of this bundle, which mostly comprise the Configuration Admin (CA) service and the OSGi Log service.

Next, let's download and install the File Install bundle. But first, make sure you have a clean install of Felix by removing all unneeded bundles; after the cleanup you should have only the following bundles:

```
g! lb
START LEVEL 1
   ID|State      |Level|Name
    0|Starting   |    0|System Bundle (3.0.6)
    1|Active     |    1|Apache Felix Bundle Repository (1.6.2)
    2|Active     |    1|Apache Felix Gogo Command (0.6.1)
    3|Active     |    1|Apache Felix Gogo Runtime (0.6.1)
    4|Active     |    1|Apache Felix Gogo Shell (0.6.1)
```

Now, let's deploy the File Install bundle:

```
g! obr:deploy "Apache Felix File Install"
Target resource(s):
-------------------
   Apache Felix File Install (2.0.0)

Optional resource(s):
---------------------
   OSGi R4 Compendium Bundle (4.0.0)

Deploying...done.
```

You can optionally specify the version of the bundle to be deployed. When none is specified, the OBR client will bring in the latest available one. The other great thing about the OBR is that it manages the dependencies. In this case, it will also install the compendium bundle, which includes the CA and logging interfaces. You can confirm this by listing all installed bundles:

```
g! lb
START LEVEL 1
   ID|State      |Level|Name
    0|Starting   |    0|System Bundle (3.0.6)
    1|Active     |    1|Apache Felix Bundle Repository (1.6.2)
    2|Active     |    1|Apache Felix Gogo Command (0.6.1)
```

```
3|Active    |    1|Apache Felix Gogo Runtime (0.6.1)
4|Active    |    1|Apache Felix Gogo Shell (0.6.1)
5|Installed |    1]Apache Felix File Install (2.0.0)
6|Installed |    1|OSGi R4 Compendium Bundle (4)
```

The OBR is a great tool for managing bundles. It has the following advantages:

- It allows an OBR client to find and retrieve bundles from different remote bundle repositories.
- It automatically manages dependencies between bundles.
- Different vendors can interoperate (because the OBR is defined as a standard service), thus allowing you to form large bundle repositories that span multiple enterprises.

From the perspective of an application developer, an OBR allows you to dynamically ship new application features to a running system. This can be done in different ways. One simple approach, shown in figure 11.6, is to set up an OBR server instance in the application developer's website containing all the new application features, and then let the user browse them and select the ones to install, much like what we've done with the File Install bundle.

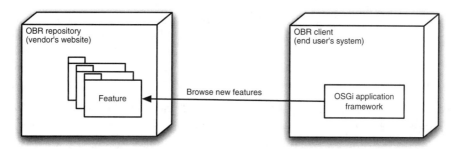

Figure 11.6 Application framework retrieving new features from an OBR repository

You're now ready to try our application management interface with the File Install bundle.

11.3.4 *The File Install service*

Having installed the File Install bundle in the previous step, you must not forget to start it:

```
g! start 6
g! {felix.fileinstall.poll (ms) = 2000, felix.fileinstall.dir =
/opt/felix-1.4.1/load, felix.fileinstall.debug = -1,
felix.fileinstall.bundles.new.start = true, felix.fileinstall.tmpdir =
./tmp, felix.fileinstall.filter = null}
```

Upon startup, the bundle will print its configuration. In particular, we're interested in the `felix.fileinstall.dir` property, which tells us the directory in which to place the bundles for deployment; this is generally a load directory in the home directory.

Leave Felix running, and copy a bundle to the load directory. You'll notice how it will get installed and started automatically. You can confirm this by issuing the ps command in the running instance of Felix.

Next, delete the bundle from the load directory, and it should be uninstalled.

NOTE Felix's File Install service is different than the autodeploy feature, because the latter is executed only when the framework first launches and not continuously as files are added to and removed from the autodeploy directory.

So far, you've learned how to handle individual offending bundles, and you've learned how to manage user applications as a whole, to the point of dynamically providing new application features. You've also learned how to deploy and manage extensions. Finally, we'll look into how to launch the OSGi framework in a user-friendly form.

11.4 *Simplifying launching of the framework*

Our first task toward going to production is to provide a custom and simple mechanism for the end user or IT personnel to bootstrap the OSGi framework implementation, a process called *launching*. We'll do this for the same reason we created an application management interface in the previous section—ease of use.

NOTE Instead of launching OSGi, we could have embedded the framework within some other application framework or platform, such an application server. In this case, the launching process would be controlled by the underlying platform. You saw an example of this in chapter 9 when integrating with JNDI.

We need to make sure that the launched OSGi framework instance contains all of our application bundles out of the box, so that the end user isn't bothered with the task of having to individually install our infrastructure bundles using the shell console or through some other custom form. After all, the application user, whether an IT person, an extension developer, or the end user, knows nothing about the implementation details of the application itself. Along the same lines, we want to remove any bundles that we deem not necessary for the purpose of executing our application. Let's investigate how we can achieve this.

First, let's assume that our application is implemented by a single infrastructure bundle, namely the file manning.osgi.mysystembundle_1.0.0.jar. For debugging and simplicity, let's further assume that it includes the following `BundleActivator`:

```
public class SystemBundleActivator implements BundleActivator {

    public void start(BundleContext context) throws Exception {
        System.out.println("My Application is ready.");

        // ...
    }

    public void stop(BundleContext context) throws Exception {
    }
}
```

We'd like to configure Felix so that when launched it automatically starts the bundle `manning.osgi.mysystembundle`. Should we just include this bundle in the load directory as we did in the previous section? We shouldn't, because if we place it in the load directory, this bundle would be considered an extension, and the user would be able to remove it from the OSGi framework by deleting the file from the load directory, which isn't what we want. In addition, we don't want Felix to start its standard shell console or the OBR implementation that's part of Felix out of the box. Finally, we do want to include the File Install bundle as part of our application. How do we configure which bundles should be installed and started out of the box in a fresh OSGi framework instance when it's launched for the first time?

The OSGi Initial Provisioning service can be used to manage the bootstrap of our application bundles, but it isn't simple to use, and it's also better suited for embedded use cases. And finally there are few implementations available. As it matures, you should hear more about the Initial Provisioning service, but for the time being there's a much simpler way to achieve our goal.

As you've learned, Felix has an autodeploy bundle directory. But instead of using it again, let's try something different. Open Felix's configuration file, and you'll notice the property `felix.auto.start.1`. This property defines which bundles are automatically started when Felix launches and reaches the start level of 1. It's empty out of the box, and you should set it to the following:

```
felix.auto.start.1= \
 file:modules/org.apache.felix.fileinstall-2.0.8.jar \
 file:modules/manning.osgi.mysystembundle_1.0.0.jar
```

The reason it's empty is that the out-of-the-box bundles, such as the Gogo shell, are placed in the bundle autodeploy directory. Because you don't need and don't want the shell in this case, you should delete any files residing in this directory. One advantage of using the `felix.auto.start` property instead of the `felix.auto.deploy.action` property is that the former allows you to implement the layered management model you learned in section 11.2.

Next, you need to copy the File Install JAR file and the mysystembundle JAR file to the just-mentioned modules directory in the Felix installation. This is the same directory that contains Felix's system bundle. Interestingly enough, even though you've installed the File Install bundle in Felix through the OBR, you don't have easy access to its actual JAR file. The reason is that Felix OBR installs the bundle without keeping a copy of the JAR file in the local filesystem. Actually, the OSGi install process itself will create a copy of the JAR file in the felix-cache directory, but this is internal to Felix's implementation and you shouldn't try to mess with it. What you should do is explicitly visit Felix's website and download the File Install bundle to the bundle directory as observed previously.

Finally, launch Felix. You usually do this by running the following command:

```
java -jar bin/felix.jar
```

You can abstract this for the benefit of the user of the application, who in principle doesn't need to know about the details of starting a Java application. There are several ways of doing this, but the simplest is to create a shell script. For example, you could create the script file launchMyApplication.sh:

```
!/bin/bash
$JAVA_HOME/bin/java -jar $APPLICATION_HOME/bin/felix.jar
```

This is what you get when you execute the launchMyApplication.sh shell script:

```
felix-framework-3.0.6$ ./launchMyApplication.sh
```

```
Welcome to Apache Felix Gogo

My Application is ready.
```

As expected, you don't get the prompt from the Felix shell.

> **WARNING** Because you're simulating a fresh start of Felix, remember to clear its cache by removing the directory felix-cache in the Felix installation.

Following this, users can place any extensions in the load directory, without having to worry about OSGi, Felix, or any other implementation details, and the extensions will get deployed into the running system.

The last step is to provide the actual bits of the application to your users. To keep it self-contained, the bits should include the Felix binary, the application bundles, and any other configuration files. You could even include the Java runtime, although this is generally a bit of overkill, because it's likely that the Java runtime is already present in the user's system. For example, here's a simple setup:

1 Clear the felix-cache and load directories.
2 Make sure that all infrastructure bundles are present in the modules directory (for example, mysystembundle_1.0.0.jar).
3 Configure Felix's conf/config.properties file adequately to load only your infrastructure bundles and any necessary OSGi service bundles, and set up the necessary start levels to establish the proper bundle management layers.
4 Zip all the content starting at the Felix installation directory. This zip file can be distributed to the users of the application framework as a standalone product install.

In summary, you can create a product installation of an OSGi application by zipping Felix's home directory and all the needed bundles. Take care not to forget to create a custom script to launch and shut down the application.

> **NOTE** Distributing zip files as product installs may seem a bit harsh, but it's simple enough and it works. Keep in mind that this is no different from how you'd install Eclipse for the first time in your system.

For example, in our previous scenario, the zip file would include the following files:

```
myaaplication-1.0.0/bin/felix.jar
myaaplication-1.0.0/modules/manning.osgi.mysystembundle_1.0.0.jar
myaaplication-1.0.0/modules/org.apache.felix.fileinstall-2.0.8.jar
myaaplication-1.0.0/conf/config.properties
myaaplication-1.0.0/launchMyApplication.sh
myaaplication-1.0.0/LICENSE
myaaplication-1.0.0/LICENSE.kxml2
myaaplication-1.0.0/load
myaaplication-1.0.0/NOTICE
```

One of the benefits of using the OSGi framework as the infrastructure of your applications is that OSGi, because of its inherent modular architecture, is greatly customizable, allowing you to simplify life for your end users, isolating them from the underlying technologies. We've done so in this section by creating a management interface and a simpler launch process.

You now have a running system that's capable of hosting your OSGi applications. The next issue becomes how to manage this running OSGi framework in production. This is the subject of the next chapter.

11.5 Summary

You need to manage your applications to keep them running correctly and efficiently. Among other tasks, you need to deal with the update of infrastructure bundles and the monitoring and automatic removal of misbehaving applications.

OSGi allows you to organize the bundles into layers and manage the activation of each layer sequentially. This is done using the OSGi Start-Level service. It's good practice to define at least four layers in an application framework implementation, where the topmost layer contains the user's application. By setting the initial active start level of the OSGi framework to be lower than that of the application layer, a management agent can implement a safe-boot mode. This is useful when application bundles are misbehaving.

The OSGi framework supports the lazy activation of bundles, where a bundle is activated only when it's needed. This can be used to speed up the start time of an application framework, particularly for those cases where the framework contains several applications.

Any moderately complex system needs to be maintained on a regular basis. You can maintain an application framework feature by updating its infrastructure bundles. An update of a bundle can be done through the `Bundle.update()` method.

A separate management interface other than that of the OSGi framework API itself should be used to allow end users to manage the applications and their extensions. This shields the user from the complexities of the underlying technologies. Two common options for this are a custom web console and a file-based deployment tool.

Each OSGi framework implementation provides a vendor-specific mechanism for specifying the bundles that are installed and started out of the box when the OSGi framework is first launched. This mechanism should be used to configure all service bundles and infrastructure bundles that are needed for the application framework to function properly, and you should remove those bundles that aren't needed.

In the next chapter, you'll learn how to manage the OSGi framework and the applications it's hosting in production, with an eye to keeping things simpler for the end users and IT personnel who will be managing your solution.

Managing with JMX

This chapter covers

- Using the Java Management Extension (JMX) API
- Remotely connecting to JMX agents
- Retrieving and changing the state of the OSGi framework while in production
- Managing OSGi services

When you're developing, you can manage the OSGi framework and its bundles and services by using the shell, as we've done in the previous chapters, or by installing custom management agent bundles. But this isn't the case when you're in production. In production, it's unlikely that you or the IT person has direct access to the OSGi framework. For example, it would be improbable that you'd be able to log in or telnet into the machine that's hosting the running OSGi framework instance. Among other reasons, this is a matter of security; the IT personnel wouldn't want you to inadvertently take up the CPU resources of a server by logging into it. This is magnified by the fact that increasingly these machines are being hosted in the cloud, that is, in some form of application grid.

This isn't an issue related exclusively to the OSGi framework; any other application in production would be kept under the same restraints. The question that arises then is how do you manage and monitor running Java applications? Fortunately, Java provides a standard mechanism for the management of running applications, namely, the Java Management Extension (JMX) API. Using JMX, you can dynamically install new applications, introspect exported packages, and even change the active start-level of bundles all in a running system.

We'll start by describing the basic concepts of JMX. Next, we'll walk through several management scenarios, starting with managing the bundles, then the services, then the packages, and finally the framework itself. Following that, we'll examine JMX notifications and how they can be used to keep management agents up to date. Finally, we'll explore common JMX usage patterns. Let's start with the basics.

12.1 *Java's management API*

JMX follows a similar model to other management technologies, such as SNMP (Simple Network Management Protocol). A special Java class called Managed Bean, or `MBean`, is defined for the resources that need to be managed. The MBeans act as a management façade for these resources and provide the metadata for management, which is sometimes referred to as the management information base (MIB).

You can reference an MBean by specifying its *object name.* An object name is defined by a namespace and a set of properties. For example, OSGi defines the following object name for the MBean that represents the OSGi framework:

```
osgi.core: type=framework,version=1.5
```

In this case, the namespace is `osgi.core`, and it has two properties, `type=framework` and `version=1.5`.

The MBeans are collectively contained within an MBean server. The MBean server works as a local agent running within each JVM that's to be managed, and it provides connectors to remote clients. The MBeans are organized in a hierarchical form within the MBean server by means of grouping their properties. Remote clients establish connections to an MBean server using different transport protocols, such as RMI. Having established the JMX connection, the client can manage the resources by invoking operations on the MBeans, as shown in figure 12.1.

Let's investigate JMX by going through a series of management scenarios. We'll begin by enabling the JVM hosting the OSGi framework for remote management. To do this, set the following system properties when starting the JVM:

```
java
-Dcom.sun.management.jmxremote.port=9999 \
-Dcom.sun.management.jmxremote.authenticate=false \
-Dcom.sun.management.jmxremote.ssl=false \
    -jar bin/felix.jar
```

The property `com.sun.management.jmxremote.port` tells the JVM to create a management agent and register it in the RMI registry using port 9999. Make sure that port

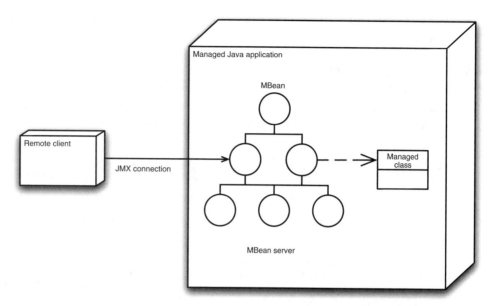

Figure 12.1   Remote client using JMX to connect to an MBean, which acts as a façade for managed Java classes

9999 is free, or choose a different port. The next two properties disable security. We're disabling security to keep things simple, but in a real environment you should keep these enabled.

> **NOTE** If you're using JDK 6.0 or higher, the management agent is automatically started and enabled for local access, that is, for a client running in the same machine. But should the client be remote (on a different machine), you'd still need to the set the `jmxremote` properties.

You can validate the connection by starting `jconsole`, the out-of-the-box management console provided in the JDK:

```
$JAVA_HOME/bin/jconsole localhost:port
```

We're now ready to manage the OSGi framework, which we'll do in the next sections by looking at each one of the major OSGi MBeans:

- `BundleStateMBean`
- `ServiceStateMBean`
- `PackageStateMBean`
- `FrameworkMBean`
- `ConfigurationAdminMBean`

> **WARNING** At the time of this writing, Apache Felix doesn't support the JMX OSGi MBeans. In fact, neither does Apache Aries nor Eclipse Equinox nor Gemini.

We'll start by looking at how to retrieve the state of the bundles of a running OSGi instance.

12.2 Managing bundles

Let's consider a simple management scenario, where we check to see if the OSGi framework has started and is ready for service. You can do this by verifying whether the state of the system bundle is set to active. This is demonstrated in the following listing.

Listing 12.1   Retrieving the state of the System bundle

```
public static void main(String []args) throws Exception {

    JMXServiceURL url =                                          ❶ JMX URL
        new
    ➥ JMXServiceURL("service:jmx:rmi:///jndi/rmi://localhost:9999/jmxrmi");
    JMXConnector connector = JMXConnectorFactory.connect(url, null);
    MBeanServerConnection msc = connector.getMBeanServerConnection();
                                                                ❷ BundleState
    ObjectName mbeanName = new                                    ObjectName
        ObjectName("osgi.core:type=bundleState,version=1.5");
                                                            ❸ Create BundleState
    BundleStateMBean bundleStateMBean =                          proxy
        JMX.newMBeanProxy(msc, mbeanName, BundleStateMBean.class);

    if (bundleStateMBean.getState(0).                       ❹ Get state for
        equals(BundleStateMBean.ACTIVE)) {                      bundle 0
        System.out.println("OSGi Framework is Ready for Service");
    }
}
```

Note how we've created a standalone Java application, with its own main() method. This application has no dependencies except for the OSGi MBeans API and can run in any remote machine that has access to the (managed) machine that's hosting the JVM process running the OSGi framework.

You start by specifying a URL for the remote MBean server of the JVM that's hosting the OSGi framework ❶. Replace the localhost with the name of your machine, and change the 9999 port to the appropriate values in your environment. With the JMX service URL, you can now establish a connection to the remote MBean server using the method JMXConnectorFactory.connect(). Next, you specify the name of the MBean that you'd like to use. In this case, it's the ObjectName for the BundleStateMBean ❷. Having specified the ObjectName, you can now create a local proxy to it. This is done using the method JMX.newMBeanProxy() ❸. This method takes the JMX connection, the ObjectName of the intended target, and a Java class to be implemented by the proxy, which in this case is the BundleStateMBean class.

The BundleStateMBean class allows you to find the complete state of all the installed bundles in OSGi, such as their imported packages, their headers, and even the services they've registered. In this example, you retrieve the bundle state for the

> ### Avoiding proxies
>
> In listing 12.1, you created an MBean proxy for the `BundleStateMBean`. Proxies make programming using MBeans easier, but it also means that the proxy classes, like the `BundleStateMBean` class, must be available for the remote client application.
>
> An alternative approach is to use the `MBeanServerConnection` class to generically handle an MBean's attributes and operations. For example, the following code retrieves the value of the `BundleStateMBean`'s attribute named `state`, similarly to invoking the method `BundleStateMBean.getState()`:
>
> ```
> String state =
>     (String) msc.getAttribute(mbeanName, "state");
> ```

bundle whose ID is 0 and verify whether it's equal to `ACTIVE` ❹. The method `BundleStateMBean.getState(long)` takes as input a `long` value, which represents the bundle ID, and returns this bundle's state. Which bundle always has ID equal to 0? The System bundle, which by definition is always the first bundle to be installed.

This is a bit of cheating, though, because generally you can't know beforehand the ID of a bundle from a remote client. We'll improve on this in the next listing, where you look for a bundle whose symbolic name is `mybundle`, and only then do you check its bundle state.

Listing 12.2 Searching for a bundle's symbolic name

```
TabularData bundlesTable =
    bundleStateMBean.listBundles();                          ◁─┐ List all
                                                            ❶   bundles
Collection<CompositeData> bundles =
    (Collection<CompositeData>) bundlesTable.values();

for (CompositeData bundleInfo : bundles) {
    if (bundleInfo.get(BundleStateMBean.SYMBOLIC_NAME).      ◁─┐ Get symbolic
            equals("mybundle")) {                            ❷   name
        System.out.println("Application state = " +
                bundleInfo.get(BundleStateMBean.STATE));
    }
}
```

In this case, you assume you've already created a proxy for `BundleStateMBean`, which can be done much like in the previous scenario. Next, you invoke the method `BundleStateMBean.listBundles()` ❶, which returns a special collection called `TabularData` containing the information for all installed bundles. What's tabular data? You can think of tabular data as a table containing rows of composite values, or `CompositeData` to be precise. `CompositeData` represents a structure, or in this case a bundle. You retrieve all the rows of the `TabularData` using the method `Tabular-Data.values()`. Next, you iterate through each `CompositeData`, and for each one you get the value of the column (item) named `SYMBOLIC_NAME` ❷. This is done using the method `CompositeData.get(BundleStateMBean.SYMBOL_NAME)`. Finally, you check to see if the composite data's symbolic name matches with your bundle name of `mybundle`, and if it does, you retrieve the bundle's state.

Open MBeans

`TabularData` and `CompositeData` are the mechanisms that JMX uses to represent a table-like collection of items in a generic way, without having to rely on user-defined Java classes. User-defined Java classes complicate matters for remote clients, because they would need to find a way to include these classes in their class path and make sure they're in sync with the server. To avoid all of these issues, MBeans should use only built-in types in their signatures, something known as open types.

`BundleStateMBean` has several other useful methods, such as `getBundleSymbolic-Name(long)`, `getHeaders(long)`, `getImportedPackages(long)`, `getLocation(long)`, and so on. Hopefully, the pattern of usage is clear: the `BundleStateMBean` works as a façade and thus isn't tied to a particular `Bundle` instance, as you may be inclined to think. Instead, you specify the bundle ID, and the MBean will take care of retrieving the corresponding bundle using the OSGi framework API. In other words, `BundleStateMBean` is stateless.

Why use the bundle ID instead of the more user-friendly bundle's symbolic name? For starters, the symbolic name alone doesn't uniquely identify a bundle; you'd have to compound it with the bundle's version. Furthermore, a `long` value is much easier to handle in an optimal form. Therefore, it's common for the management client to cache the bundle ID of the bundles it needs to manage regularly, as in the following example:

```
long myBundleId = -1;

for (CompositeData bundleInfo : bundles) {
    if (bundleInfo.get(BundleStateMBean.SYMBOLIC_NAME).
            equals("mybundle")) {
        myBundleId =
            (Long) bundleInfo.get(BundleStateMBean.IDENTIFIER);
    }
}
```

But keep in mind that a bundle ID is valid for only a particular instance of the OSGi framework; the value is no longer valid after a restart of the server.

WARNING A bundle ID is associated with a bundle when it is installed or reinstalled during the launching of the OSGi framework and potentially changes for every reinstall. If you remember from chapter 4, only the PID is persisted across launches of the OSGi framework.

You've learned how to retrieve the state of a bundle and, in particular, how to check if a bundle is active. Next, let's find the services being registered by the active bundle.

12.3 Managing services

The ServiceStateMBean can be used to retrieve information about all of the registered services in the OSGi service registry. As you'll see, it works similarly to the BundleStateMBean. Let's expand the previous example by finding all services that are being registered by the mybundle bundle, and then verify which bundles are using these services. This is illustrated in the next listing.

Listing 12.3 Retrieving registered services

```
long [] serviceIds =
    bundleStateMBean.getRegisteredServices(myBundleId);    ⬅┐  ❶ Get all registered
                                                                  services
mbeanName = new
    ObjectName
        ("osgi.core:type=ServiceState,version=1.5");    ⬅┐  ❷ ServiceState
                                                                MBean name
ServiceStateMBean serviceStateMBean =
    JMX.newMBeanProxy(msc, mbeanName, ServiceStateMBean.class);

for (long serviceId : serviceIds) {
    long [] bundleIds =                                      ❸ Get bundles
        serviceStateMBean.getUsingBundles(serviceId);    ⬅┘    using service

    System.out.println("The service '" +
            serviceStateMBean.getObjectClass(serviceId)    ⬅┐ Get service's
            + "' is being used by bundles :");                ❹ interface

    for (long bundleId : bundleIds) {
        System.out.println(
                bundleStateMBean.getSymbolicName(bundleId));
    }
}
```

You start with the BundleStateMBean and invoke the method getRegistered-Services() to retrieve all services registered by myBundleId ❶. This returns a list of long values, which represent service IDs. Next, you need to access the ServiceState-MBean, so you instantiate its ObjectName, which is osgi.core:type=Service-State,version=1.5 ❷, creating a proxy as usual. You retrieve all bundles that are using a particular service ID by invoking the method ServiceStateMBean.getUsing-Bundles() ❸. You also retrieve the service interface, aka its ObjectClass, by using the method getObjectClass(long) ❹. Finally, you iterate through the bundle IDs returned from the method getUsingBundles(), and use the BundleStateMBean to find their symbolic names.

Other methods of interest in the ServiceStateMBean are getProperties(long), which returns all the service properties of a particular service, and listServices(). The latter is particularly interesting, because it returns in tabular format all of the registered services in OSGi. Using listServices() in combination with ServiceState-MBean.getBundleIdentifier(long) allows you to find the owning bundle of all registered services in the framework.

Next, let's take a look at the one remaining aspect of a bundle: the packages it exports and imports.

12.4 *Managing import and export packages*

In the previous section, you discovered all bundles that use the services that the bundle mybundle registers. Let's follow up on this example and discover all bundles that are importing the packages that the bundle mybundle is exporting.

As you probably guessed, the pattern for doing this should be similar to what you did in the previous example. But there's one major difference: unlike bundles and services, packages aren't identified by a long ID, which complicates matters somewhat. Check this out in the next listing.

Listing 12.4 Retrieving exported packages

```
String [] packages =
    bundleStateMBean.getExportedPackages(myBundleId);          ❶ Get exported
                                                                  packages
mbeanName =
    new ObjectName
        ("osgi.core:type=PackageState,version=1.5");           ❷ PackageState
                                                                  MBean name
PackageStateMBean packageStateMBean =
    JMX.newMBeanProxy(msc, mbeanName, PackageStateMBean.class);

for (String osgiPackage: packages) {
    int sepIndex = osgiPackage.indexOf(";");                   ❸ Parse package
    String pkg = osgiPackage.substring(0, sepIndex);              and version
    String ver = osgiPackage.substring(sepIndex + 1);

    long [] bundleIds =
        packageStateMBean.getImportingBundles(pkg,
            ver, myAppId);                                      ❹ Importing
    System.out.println("The package '" + osgiPackage              bundles
        + "' is being used by bundles :");

    for (long bundleId : bundleIds) {
        System.out.println(
            bundleStateMBean.getSymbolicName(bundleId));
    }
}
```

As usual, you start with the BundleStateMBean, which you use to retrieve all packages exported by the bundle myBundleId ❶. Unlike before, though, you get back a String formatted as *package;version*. For example, if a bundle has the MANIFEST header entry Export-Package: manning.osgi;version=1.0.0.0, then you'd get the following return value: manning.osgi;1.0.0.0. You need to break this String into two values: one for the package and another for the actual version. You do this by looking for the semicolon (;) character ❸.

Next, you create a proxy for the PackageStateMBean ❷. Using the PackageStateMBean, you invoke its getImportingBundles() method, passing along the parsed package and version Strings. You also pass along the bundle ID of the exporting bundle ❹.

The first two arguments are obvious, but why do you also need the bundle ID of the exporting bundle? You need this because more than one bundle may be exporting the same version of a package, perhaps specifying different export attributes or use clauses.

You've now learned how to find the state of bundles, services, and packages. In the following section, we'll look into how you can change the state of the OSGi framework itself.

12.5 *Managing an OSGi framework instance*

Whereas the `BundleStateMBean` allows you to manage the state of an installed bundle, the `FrameworkMBean` allows you to manage the bundles themselves, that is, the installation, starting, stopping, updating, and uninstallation of bundles.

The following code installs the bundle `mybundle` into OSGi:

```
mbeanName = new ObjectName("osgi.core:type=Framework,version=1.5");

FrameworkMBean frameworkMBean =
    JMX.newMBeanProxy(msc, mbeanName, FrameworkMBean.class);

long bundleId =
    frameworkMBean.installBundle("bundle/mybundle.jar");
```

You start by specifying the `FrameworkMBean`'s `ObjectName`, which is `osgi.core:type=Framework,version=1.5`. This is used to create a proxy to the `FrameworkMBean`. Next, you invoke the method `installBundle()`, which takes as an argument the location of the bundle's JAR file. The method `installBundle()` returns the bundle ID of the newly installed bundle. Now that you have the bundle ID, you can use it with the other OSGi MBeans, for example, to get the bundle's state using the management operation `BundleStateMBean.getState(long)`.

> **NOTE** A bundle's install location is related to the current directory used to launch the OSGi framework. This is specified by the environment property `user.dir`.

What if you need to manage several bundles instead of just one? For example, it's not uncommon to install all the bundles located in a directory. In this case, should you invoke `installBundle()` multiple times? This would not only be unproductive, but it also would increase the network usage between the remote JMX client and the OSGi framework, a resource that may not be freely available when the OSGi framework is embedded on a device. Fortunately, the `FrameworkMBean` supports the batching of operations, as shown in the next listing.

Listing 12.5 Batch install of bundles

```
mbeanName = new ObjectName("osgi.core:type=Framework,version=1.5");

    FrameworkMBean frameworkMBean =
        JMX.newMBeanProxy(msc, mbeanName, FrameworkMBean.class);
```

```
String [] bundleLocations =
    {"bundle/bundleA.jar", "bundle/bundleB.jar",
    "bundle/bundleC.jar"};

CompositeData batchResult =
    frameworkMBean.installBundles(bundleLocations);
```
❶ **Batch install**

```
Long [] installedBundleIDs =
    (Long[]) batchResult.get(
        FrameworkMBean.COMPLETED);
```
❷ **Array of installed bundles**

```
for (int i = 0; i < installedBundleIDs.length; i++) {
    System.out.println("Bundle '" + bundleLocations[i] +
            "' was installed successfully and its ID is " +
installedBundleIDs[i]);
}
```

```
if (((Boolean) batchResult.get(FrameworkMBean.SUCCESS))
    == false) {
    String culpritBundleLocation =
        (String) batchResult.get(
            FrameworkMBean.BUNDLE_IN_ERROR);
```
❸ **Check if all were installed**

❹ **Culprit bundle**

```
    String reason =
        (String) batchResult.get(
            FrameworkMBean.ERROR);
```
❺ **Reason for error**

```
    System.out.println("Bundle '" + culpritBundleLocation +
            "' failed to install because of: " + reason);

    String [] remainingBundleLocations =
        (String []) batchResult.get(
            FrameworkMBean.REMAINING);
```
❻ **Remaining bundles to install**

```
    System.out.println("The remaining bundles still need to be
➥ installed: ");
    for (String remaingBundleLocation : remainingBundleLocations)
        System.out.println(remaingBundleLocation);
    }
}
```

A batch install is done using the method installBundles() ❶, which takes as an argument a String array of bundle locations. This isn't a transactional operation, where all bundles get installed or none get installed; instead, OSGi sequentially installs the bundles as specified in the bundle locations argument until all are installed or the first error is encountered. For example, in the previous listing you're trying to install bundles bundleA, bundleB, and bundleC. If bundleB has an error and doesn't install, then OSGi would have installed bundleA but would never attempt to install bundleC.

All bundles that installed successfully are returned in an array of longs representing their bundle IDs ❷. You can retrieve this information by getting the composite item FrameworkMBean.COMPLETED. This array contains the installed bundles in the same order that they were listed in the input bundle locations argument (bundleLocations).

Next, you check the result of the batch operation by getting the composite item FrameworkMBean.SUCCESS ❸. If there are no errors, then this is true; otherwise, it's false. If there's an error, you can find the bundle location that failed to install by getting the composite item FrameworkMBean.BUNDLE_IN_ERROR ❹. Because OSGi stops when it encounters the first error, this composite item returns a single String rather than an array, as was the case of the FrameworkMBean.COMPLETED item. You can get the reason for the error by using the composite item FrameworkMBean.ERROR ❺. Finally, you can get the locations of the bundles that remain to be installed by using the item FrameworkMBean.REMAINING ❻. In our case, this would be bundleC.

Batch operations may seem rather complex, but they yield better performance and provide information about their results. You can batch pretty much all other bundle-related operations, such as uninstall, start, stop, and update.

The FrameworkMBean also supports some other interesting operations. For example, you can manage start levels with the following methods:

- get/setFrameworkStartLevel()—These allow you to get and set the active start level of the OSGi framework. As you've seen previously, changing this value may cause bundles to be started or stopped.

- get/setInitialBundleStartLevel()—These allow you to get and set the initial start level assigned by default to an installed bundle. Changes to this value are only applicable to new bundles.

- get/setBundleStartLevel()—These allow you to get and set a bundle's start level. As you've seen, a bundle is started or stopped depending on whether its start level is lower or greater than that of the OSGi framework (active) start level.

You can also restart and shut down the OSGi framework itself using the methods restartFramework() and shutdownFramework(); therefore access to the Framework-MBean should be kept secured.

Next, suppose you want to develop a management tool that promptly shows all installed bundles and registered services. You can think of it as an OSGi browser, except that your tool is a standalone application instead of a web application, such as the Felix Web Management console. You could implement your OSGi browser by periodically invoking BundleStateMBean.listBundles() and ServiceStateMBean.list-Services(), but this approach not only wastes CPU resources but also won't guarantee that you have the latest updated state. Fortunately, JMX has a better solution, through the use of JMX notifications, which we'll examine next.

12.6 *Management notifications*

MBeans not only provide attributes and operations, but they can also emit notifications. Remote listeners can register to receive these notifications. In particular, the BundleStateMBean and the ServiceStateMBean MBeans emit notifications signaling changes to the state of a bundle, such as when a new bundle has been installed, and changes to the state of a service, such as when a new service is registered. In other words, these notifications reflect the OSGi bundle event (`org/osgi/framework/BundleEvent`) and the OSGi service event (`org/osgi/framework/ServiceEvent`), as explained in chapter 6.

Let's continue our previous example by looking at a JMX client that handles bundle events. First, you need to register a JMX notification listener, as in the following listing:

```
mbeanName = new ObjectName("osgi.core:type=bundleState,version=1.5");

BundleStateMBean bundleStateMBean =
    JMX.newMBeanProxy(msc, mbeanName, BundleStateMBean.class, true);

((NotificationEmitter) bundleStateMBean).addNotificationListener(
new BundleEventListener(), null, null);
```

As usual, you create a proxy to the `BundleStateMBean`, but in this case you need to invoke the overloaded method:

```
JMX.newMBeanProxy(MBeanServerConnection connection,
ObjectName objectName,
Class<T> interfaceClass,
boolean notificationBroadcaster)
```

This method has a fourth argument that must be set to `true` and indicates that the created proxy also implements the interface `NotificationEmitter`. Finally, you cast the proxy to the `NotificationEmitter` class and invoke the method `addNotificationListener()`, passing along the `BundleEventListener` implementation ❷, which is described in the next listing.

But before we look into the `BundleEventListener` implementation, let's examine the `addNotificationListener()` method. It takes three arguments: The first is the callback class that must implement the `NotificationListener` interface. The second argument is a notification filter; you can use this to filter the notifications that you're interested in. For example, you can specify a filter to receive notifications related only to a specific `ObjectName` or related to a particular MBean attribute. In our case, we haven't registered any filters; this is because we've registered our notification listener directly in the `BundleStateMBean` proxy, so we automatically receive notifications related only to this MBean. But had we invoked `MBeanServerConnection.addNotificationListener()`, then we'd receive notifications from all MBeans, and it would be appropriate to specify a notification filter, as in the following example:

```
MBeanServerNotificationFilter filter = new MBeanServerNotificationFilter();
filter.enableObjectName(
    new ObjectName("osgi.core:type=bundleState,version=1.5"));
```

Finally, the third argument to `NotificationEmitter.addNotificationListener()` is a hand-back object; that is, it's an opaque object that's handed back to the notification listener when it's called. This is useful if you need to pass any context from the code that's registering the listener to the listener itself.

Next, let's look at the `BundleEventListener` implementation, shown in the following listing.

Listing 12.6   The `BundleEventListener` class

```
public class BundleEventListener implements NotificationListener {

    public void handleNotification(                    ❶ Callback method
        Notification notification,
        Object handback) {

        CompositeData bundleEvent =                    ❷ Event is
            (CompositeData) notification.getUserData();    composite data

        String bundleSymbolicName =
            (String) bundleEvent.get(                  ❸ Bundle that raised
                BundleStateMBean.SYMBOLIC_NAME);          the event

        Integer bundleState =
            (Integer) bundleEvent.get(                 ❹ New bundle
                BundleStateMBean.EVENT);                  state

        if (bundleState == 1) // Installed
            System.out.println("Bundle '" + bundleSymbolicName
                + "' has been installed!");

        if (bundleState == 16) // Uninstalled
            System.out.println("Bundle '" + bundleSymbolicName
        + "' has been un-installed!");
    }
}
```

The method `handleNotification()` ❶ is invoked when a new `BundleEvent` is available. The `BundleEvent` is retrieved using the method `Notification.getUserData()` ❷. As usual, it's a `CompositeData` object.

JMX notification type

You know that the `BundleStateMBean` only emits `BundleEvent` notifications, so you can assume that `getUserData()` returns the appropriate `CompositeData` object. But in cases where the notification listener can't assume this, for example, because it may be the target of several `MBeans`, you can check the type of the object returned by `getUserData()` by using the method `Notification.getType()`. This returns a `String` naming the notification type. For example, in the case of the `BundleEvent`, it would return `org.osgi.jmx.framework.BUNDLE_EVENT_TYPE`, which is a reference to the `CompositeType` declared in `BundleStateMBean.BUNDLE_EVENT_TYPE`.

A `BundleEvent` informs you of the source bundle that generated the event and the type of the event. For example, if a new bundle, `bundleA`, is installed, then the source bundle is `bundleA` and the type of the event is `INSTALLED`. The `symbolicName` of the source bundle is retrieved using the composite item `BundleStateMBean.SYMBOLIC_ NAME` ❸. Similarly, you could retrieve the source bundle ID using the composite item

BundleStateMBean.IDENTIFIER. Finally, the type of the bundle change event is retrieved using the composite item BundleStateMBean.EVENT_ITEM ❹. It's an integer defined as follows:

- INSTALLED=1
- STARTED=2
- STOPPED=4
- UPDATED=8
- UNINSTALLED=16

NOTE Why does the BundleEvent use an integer to enumerate its stage change instead of a String? Mostly to save bandwidth; this is a general guideline when dealing with JMX notifications.

You've learned how to register a notification listener to handle bundle event changes. You can use the bundle event to promptly know when a new bundle gets installed or uninstalled. Next, let's see how you can do the same for service event changes.

First, you register a new notification listener in the ServiceStateMBean:

```
ServiceStateMBean serviceStateMBean =
    JMX.newMBeanProxy(msc, mbeanName, ServiceStateMBean.class);

((NotificationEmitter) serviceStateMBean).addNotificationListener(
    new ServiceEventListener(), null, null);
```

The following listing details the ServiceEventListener code.

Listing 12.7 The ServiceEventListener class

```
public class ServiceEventListener implements NotificationListener {

    public void handleNotification(Notification notification,
            Object handback) {

        CompositeData serviceEvent =
            (CompositeData) notification.getUserData();

        String [] serviceInterfaces =
            (String []) serviceEvent.get(          ❶ Service that
                ServiceStateMBean.OBJECT_CLASS);      raised event

        Integer serviceState =
            (Integer) serviceEvent.get(            ❷ New service
                ServiceStateMBean.EVENT);             state

        if (serviceState == 1) // Registered
            System.out.println("Service '" + serviceInterfaces[0]
                + "' has been registered!");

        if (serviceState == 16) // Unregistering
            System.out.println("Service '" + serviceInterfaces[0]
                + "' is being unregistered!");
    }
}
```

Handling a `ServiceEvent` isn't much different than handling `BundleEvents`. Like a `BundleEvent`, a `ServiceEvent` is `CompositeData` retrieved using the `Notification.getUserData()` method. You can discover the service interfaces of the service that changed its state by retrieving the composite item `ServiceStateMBean.OBJECT_CLASS` ❶. Likewise, you can find its service ID using the composite item `ServiceState-MBean.IDENTIFIER`. Finally, you can find the actual type of change of the service state by retrieving the composite item `ServiceStateMBean.EVENT_ITEM` ❷, which returns an `Integer` defining the following enumeration:

- `REGISTERED=1`
- `MODIFIED=2`
- `UNREGISTERING=3`

By subscribing to receive `BundleEvents` and `ServiceEvents`, you can implement real-time JMX applications that are constantly up to date.

So far, you've learned to how to manage the OSGi framework, as well as the state of the OSGi bundles and services. But you know that the OSGi framework itself is a small part of the overall OSGi Service Platform, which in addition includes several compendium and enterprise services. We've used several of these enterprise services, such as the Configuration Admin service, in the previous chapters, and you've learned how important they are toward contributing to a full-fledged platform for developing applications. In the next section, we'll look at how to manage some of the OSGi services.

12.7 Managing bundle configuration

In addition to the mandatory `FrameworkMBean`, `BundleStateMBean`, `ServiceState-MBean`, and `PackageStateMBean`, OSGi defines several other MBeans that a platform may optionally include in its MBean server. These are related to the management of OSGi services, such as the `ConfigurationAdminMBean`, the `PermissionAdminMBean`, the `ProvisioningServiceMBean`, and finally the `UserAdminMBean`.

As the Enterprise OSGi matures, you should see the proliferation of MBeans in the OSGi Service Platform, but at the time of writing only the aforementioned ones are specified as part of the Enterprise Specification Release 4.2.

In particular, the `ConfigurationAdminMBean` is very useful, because it's likely that a management tool may need to update the configuration of a running system. Let's say you'd like to remotely update the port of the Notification service using a JMX client application. This is shown in the next listing.

Listing 12.8 Updating the port property using `ConfigurationAdminMBean`

```
mbeanName = new ObjectName
    ("osgi.compendium:service=cm,version=1.3");          ◁──┐  ConfigAdmin
                                                          ❶  ObjectName
ConfigurationAdminMBean cmBean =
    JMX.newMBeanProxy(msc, mbeanName, ConfigurationAdminMBean.class);

TabularData properties =
```

```
new TabularDataSupport(
    JmxConstants.PROPERTIES_TYPE);
```
❷ **Table of props**

```
Map<String, Object> propertyValue = new HashMap<String, Object>();
propertyValue.put(JmxConstants.KEY, "port");
propertyValue.put(JmxConstants.VALUE, 9000);
propertyValue.put(JmxConstants.TYPE, JmxConstants.INTEGER);

CompositeData property =
    new CompositeDataSupport(JmxConstants.PROPERTY_TYPE,
        propertyValue);
properties.put(property);
```
❸ **Port property**

```
cmBean.update("manning.enterpriseosgi.notification.broker",
    properties);
```
❹ **Update ConfigAdmin**

As usual, you start by specifying the ObjectName for the ConfigurationAdminMBean ❶ and use it to create the proper MBean proxy. To update the configuration of a service using the ConfigurationAdminMBean, you need to create a TabularData, whose rows represent each property to be updated. To do this, you first create a TabularData-Support instance and specify its type as JmxConstants.PROPERTIES_TYPE ❷. Next, you create the actual property representing the port configuration. A configuration property, as defined by the CompositeType JmxConstants.PROPERTY_TYPE, consists of three items: the KEY, which you can think of as its name, its VALUE, and its TYPE. In our case, the key is port, the value is the integer 9000, and its type is Integer. You add these three items to a Map and use it to create a CompositeData ❸ whose CompositeType is JmxConstants.PROPERTY_TYPE. Finally, you can invoke the update() method ❹, passing along the configuration PID of manning.enterpriseosgi.notification.broker and the TabularData you created with the port property.

Having set the new value for the port property, you can check it with the following code:

```
TabularData newProperties =
    cmBean.getProperties("manning.enterpriseosgi.notification.broker");

CompositeData portProperty =
    newProperties.get(new String[] {"port"});

System.out.println("The value of the new port configuration is: " +
        portProperty.get(JmxConstants.VALUE));
```

ConfigurationAdminMBean.getProperties() returns all properties associated with a particular configuration PID in the format of a TabularData. Next, you retrieve the property whose key is port and print its value using the composite item Jmx-Constants.VALUE.

Using JMX in general and TabularData and CompositeData in particular isn't exactly trivial, mostly because JMX is designed as a generic mechanism to manage all types of resources. But hopefully by now you have noticed some coding patterns emerge. We'll explore these in the next section.

12.8 *OSGi JMX patterns*

Let's start by dissecting the `ObjectNames` used for the OSGi MBeans. Here are some of them:

- `osgi.core: type=framework, version=1.5`
- `osgi.core: type=bundleState, version=1.5`
- `osgi.compendium: service=cm, version=1.3`
- `osgi.compendium: service=useradmin, version=1.1`

The pattern is clear; there are two categories of OSGi MBeans: those pertaining to the OSGi framework itself (for example, the first two items in the previous list) and those pertaining to the OSGi compendium (enterprise) services (for example, the latter two items in the previous list).

The first category uses the JMX namespace of `osgi.core`, followed by two pre-defined properties: `type` and `version`. The `type` property is somewhat arbitrary and denotes the OSGi MBean's actual type, such as `framework`, `bundleState`, `service-State`, and `packageState`. The `version` property specifies the actual interface version of the targeted managed class. You can find this by looking at the `Export-Package` MANIFEST header entry of the intended Java package. For example, the package `org.osgi.framework` is being exported with version 1.5 by the OSGi Service Platform Specification Release 4.2.

The compendium service–related MBeans follow a similar pattern. Their namespace is defined as `osgi.compendium`, and they likewise use two predefined properties: `service` and `version`. The `version` property has the same semantic as in the previous case. The `service` property is used to identify the actual service and is inferred from the target service's package name. For example, the full class name of the Configuration Admin service is `org.osgi.service.cm.ConfigurationAdmin`; therefore the `service` property value is `cm`. The `service` property value is the local part after the `org.osgi.service`, not including the actual class name, as shown in figure 12.2.

Next, have you wondered how you can find out what types are returned from `TabularData` and `CompositeData`? To understand this, let's revisit listing 12.2, which uses the `BundleState.list-Bundles()` method. Listing 12.2 is duplicated here for your convenience:

org.osgi.service|cm|.ConfigurationAdmin

Figure 12.2 The `ObjectName`'s `service` property is the local part after the `org.osgi.service` namespace.

```
TabularData bundlesTable =
    bundleStateMBean.listBundles();

Collection<CompositeData> bundles =
    (Collection<CompositeData>) bundlesTable.values();

for (CompositeData bundleInfo : bundles) {
    if (bundleInfo.get(BundleStateMBean.SYMBOLIC_NAME).equals("mybundle")){
```

```
System.out.println("Application state = " +
        bundleInfo.get(BundleStateMBean.STATE));
    }
}
```

The method `listBundles()` returns a `TabularData`. The type of this `TabularData`, as defined by its Javadoc, is `BUNDLES_TYPE`:

```
Answer the bundle state of the system in tabular form. Each row of the
    returned table represents a single bundle. The Tabular Data consists of
    Composite Data that is type by BUNDLES_TYPE.
```

If you click `BUNDLES_TYPE` in the documentation, it takes you to the following definition:

```
TabularType BUNDLES_TYPE =
    Item.tabularType("BUNDLES", "A list of bundles", BUNDLE_TYPE,
        IDENTIFIER);
```

In other words, `BUNDLES_TYPE` is a table whose rows are of type `BUNDLE_TYPE`. Again, if you click `BUNDLE_TYPE`, you get

```
CompositeType BUNDLE_TYPE =
    Item.compositeType("BUNDLE", "This type encapsulates OSGi bundles",
        EXPORTED_PACKAGES_ITEM, FRAGMENT_ITEM, FRAGMENTS_ITEM,
        HEADERS_ITEM, HOSTS_ITEM, IDENTIFIER_ITEM, IMPORTED_PACKAGES_ITEM,
        LAST_MODIFIED_ITEM, LOCATION_ITEM, PERSISTENTLY_STARTED_ITEM,
        REGISTERED_SERVICES_ITEM, REMOVAL_PENDING_ITEM, REQUIRED_ITEM,
        REQUIRED_BUNDLES_ITEM, REQUIRING_BUNDLES_ITEM, START_LEVEL_ITEM,
        STATE_ITEM, SERVICES_IN_USE_ITEM, SYMBOLIC_NAME_ITEM, VERSION_ITEM);
```

This has the actual columns' types, defined as composite data `Items`, which is really what we're interested in. In listing 12.2, you use the `SYMBOLIC_NAME` item. Clicking the `BUNDLE_TYPE`'s `SYMBOLIC_NAME_ITEM`, you get its definition:

```
Item SYMBOLIC_NAME_ITEM = new Item(SYMBOLIC_NAME,
    "The symbolic name of the bundle", SimpleType.STRING);
```

This tells you that the symbolic name item can be retrieved using the key `BundleState.SYMBOLIC_NAME` and that it's of type `String`. That's all you need to know.

JMX is a well-understood and often-used model for managing Java systems, and no solution would be complete without it. OSGi's MBeans are complete, allowing you to manage most aspects of the OSGi framework and along the way establish the pattern for managing OSGi services.

12.9 *Summary*

JMX can be used to manage running OSGi frameworks, even when in production. JMX defines its management model based on MBeans, which act as façades to Java managed resources or classes. MBeans are named using an `ObjectName`, which includes a namespace and a set of properties. MBeans are organized within an MBean server, located within the JVM to be managed. Remote clients can establish connections to the MBean servers using different protocols, such as RMI.

OSGi defines several MBeans. The `BundleStateMBean` is used to retrieve the state of all installed bundles, such as a bundle's symbolic name, its location, and its headers.

The `ServiceStateMBean` is used to retrieve the state of all the available services in the OSGi framework. You can find out the service's properties, its `objectClass` (service interface), and the bundles that are using it.

The `PackageStateMBean` is used to retrieve information about all the packages that are being exported and imported in the OSGi framework.

The `FrameworkMBean` is used to manage the framework itself. It provides operations for shutting down the server, installing and uninstalling bundles, and even changing its start level.

Furthermore, OSGi also defines optional MBeans for the OSGi services, such as the `ConfigurationAdminMBean`, with which you can create, delete, and update configuration items.

Finally, both `BundleStateMBean` and `ServiceStateMBean` emit JMX notifications representing state changes to bundles and services, such as the installation of a new bundle or the registration of a new service.

In this chapter, you learned how to manage a running OSGi system, including both the framework and the deployed bundles that make up the OSGi applications. In the next chapter, we'll put together all of what you've learned so far for developing an OSGi application—configuration, transactions, data access, and management—by discussing OSGi's programming model.

Putting it all together by extending Blueprint

So far you've learned about and used several independent OSGi services, such as the Configuration Admin in chapter 5, the Event Admin in chapter 6, JPA in chapter 7, JTA in chapter 8, JNDI in chapter 9, remote services in chapter 10, Start-Levels in chapter 11, and finally JMX in chapter 12. The common pattern for using these services is to retrieve them from the OSGi service registry. This is done programmatically and generally leads to a lot of boilerplate code and decreases user productivity. Can we do better?

Fortunately, OSGi defines a declarative language for assembling applications together, applications that can use all sorts of different OSGi services. For example, as you'll see at the end of this chapter, we'll change the auction application developed in chapter 3 to use the Configuration Admin, the Event Admin, and JPA services. This is done using OSGi's Blueprint service, by specifying an XML document that *puts it all together.*

But before we get into Blueprint, we need to revisit a concept you learned about previously—the application container. In chapter 8, you learned how to annotate an application bundle in such a way as to allow its transactions to be managed by the infrastructure, that is, by some underlying container. We'll look into this first because Blueprint presents a better mechanism for implementing containers, by extending Blueprint with different namespaces.

But let's not get too far ahead of ourselves. We'll start by digging deeper into the idea of containers and application bundles.

13.1 Application bundles and their containers

As you've seen in the previous chapters, a common pattern for enabling a bundle with a new feature is to annotate the bundle's manifest file. For example, to enable a bundle to persist its Java classes, you can add the `Meta-Persistence` header entry to its MANIFEST.MF file. The following table summarizes some of the standard manifest header entries used to create *feature-specific powered bundles*, or, perhaps a bit more colorful, *bundle flavors.*

Table 13.1 Flavored bundles

Name	Description	Manifest header
WAB	Web application bundle	`Web-ContextPath`
Persistence bundle	Bundle with persistence units	`Meta-Persistence`
SCA config bundle	Bundle with SCA configuration	`SCA-Configuration`
Component bundle	Bundle with declarative components	`Service-Component`
Blueprint bundle	Bundle with Blueprint components	`Bundle-Blueprint`
Endpoint bundle	Bundle with endpoint descriptions	`Remote-Service`

Application bundles

Table 13.1 lists just a few examples of the different flavors of bundles that exist. Some of them have been discussed in previous chapters, but some of them are out of the scope of this book and aren't discussed; they've been included here for completeness.

New flavors are being created constantly. For instance, there's currently work on a resource adapter bundle (RAB), which contains configuration for Java EE connector-enabled resources.

In chapter 8, you created a transaction-enabled bundle by defining our own `Meta-Transaction` header entry. Let's expand on this to include other services and thus see how you can create high-level domain-specific bundles. These domain-specific bundles expose a simple programming model.

The feature we'll implement is that of a *subscriber application bundle*, or SAB for short. An SAB is a bundle that can be used to quickly and easily subscribe to events coming from the Event Admin. We'll look at the specification of the SAB in the next section.

13.1.1 *Subscriber application bundle*

An SAB is defined by using the `Meta-Subscriber` manifest header entry. Let's go through a couple of examples to demonstrate its use.

You can specify a Java class and an Event Admin topic in the `Meta-Subscriber` header entry, as in the following example:

```
Meta-Subscriber:
 manning.osgi.MySubscriber;org/osgi/framework/BundleEvent/*
```

This means that the bundle should contain a Java class named `manning.osgi.My-Subscriber`, which implements the `EventHandler` interface, as you saw in chapter 6, and a public default constructor. The SAB container instantiates this class and registers it as an event handler service to receive events from the topic `org/osgi/framework/BundleEvent/*` when the bundle is started and conversely unregisters it when the bundle is stopped.

In addition, you may specify multiple subscribers:

```
Meta-Subscriber:
 manning.osgi.Subscriber1;org/osgi/framework/BundleEvent/*,
 manning.osgi.Subscriber2;org/osgi/framework/ServiceEvent/*
```

In this case, `Subscriber1` receives `BundleEvents` and `Subscriber2` receives `ServiceEvents`.

The specification of an SAB is simple enough. Next, let's see how you can implement its container.

13.1.2 *Implementing the SAB container*

In chapter 8, you learned how to implement a container to manage user transactions. You follow a similar pattern for a SAB container.

We'll start by defining a proper extender class, as shown in the following listing.

Listing 13.1 The `SubscriberExtenderActivator`

```
public class SubscriberExtenderActivator implements
  BundleActivator, BundleListener {

  public void start(BundleContext context) throws Exception {
    context.addBundleListener(this);                        ← ❶ Register bundle
  }                                                              listener
```

```
@SuppressWarnings("unchecked")
public void bundleChanged(BundleEvent event) {
    try {
        if (event.getType() == BundleEvent.STARTED) {
            String subscriberClause = (String)
                event.getBundle().getHeaders().get("Meta-Subscriber");

            if (subscriberClause != null) {                      ◄───── ❷ Retrieve header's
                List<List<String>> subsInfo =                            value
                    parseSubscriberClause(subscriberClause);     ◄───── ❸ Parse header's
                                                                         value
                for (List<String> subInfo : subsInfo) {
                    Class<?> handlerClass =
                        event.getBundle().loadClass(subInfo.get(0));

                    Object handler =
                        handlerClass.newInstance();              ◄───── ❹ Create handler
                    assert handler instanceof EventHandler;              instance

                    Dictionary properties = new Hashtable();
                    properties.put(EventConstants.EVENT_TOPIC,
                        subInfo.get(1));

                    event.getBundle().getBundleContext().
                        registerService(
                            EventHandler.class.toString(), handler,
                            properties);                         ◄───── ❺ Register handler
                }                                                        service
            }
        }
    } catch (Exception e) {
        // Log
    }
}

public void stop(BundleContext context) throws Exception {
}

//
}
```

First, you create an activator that subscribes to bundle events ❶. When a bundle is started, you check to see if it contains a `Meta-Subscriber` header entry in its MANI-FEST.MF file ❷, and if it does, you parse its value ❸. For the time being, let's ignore how the parsing is done. Just know that it returns a list of subscribers, where each subscriber is defined as a list of two entries, the first item being its Java class name and the second being the topic it wishes to subscribe to. You iterate through each subscriber and use the Java class name to load the Java class and then instantiate a Java instance ❹. Next, for each subscriber, you register the instantiated Java instance as an `Event-Handler` service in the OSGi service registry, setting the topic in the `EVENT_TOPIC` service property ❺. Note that you use the bundle event's `bundleContext` to register the `EventHandler`. This associates the `EventHandler` with the SAB, which is the bundle that specifies the `Meta-Subscriber` header rather than the extender bundle itself. As a result, the `EventHandler` service is automatically unregistered when the SAB bundle is stopped or uninstalled, which is the appropriate behavior, and it allows you to leave the extender's `stop` method implementation empty.

> **NOTE** You could also have coded the SAB container extender's `stop` method to unregister all subscribers, but this seems largely unnecessary because the subscribers can stand on their own without the presence of the SAB container.

Next, let's check the details of the `parseSubscriberClause()` method in the following listing.

Listing 13.2   The `Meta-Subscriber` parsing method

```
List<List<String>> parseSubscriberClause(String clause) {
    List<List<String>> subs = new ArrayList<List<String>>();

    StringTokenizer tokenizer =
        new StringTokenizer(clause, ",");
    while (tokenizer.hasMoreTokens()) {                     ❶ Tokenize by ","
        String sub = tokenizer.nextToken();

        int index = sub.indexOf(";");
        assert index != -1;
                                                            ❷ Get class name
        String className = sub.substring(0, index);
        String topic = sub.substring(index + 1);
                                                            ❸ Get topic name
        List<String> subInfo = new ArrayList<String>();
        subInfo.add(className);
        subInfo.add(topic);

        subs.add(subInfo);
    }

    return subs;
}
```

As you'll recall from listing 13.1, this method takes as input the `Meta-Subscriber` header's value. For example,

```
manning.osgi.Subscriber1;org/osgi/framework/BundleEvent/*,
manning.osgi.Subscriber2;org/osgi/framework/ServiceEvent/*
```

First, you break this value into items separated by the comma character (,) ❶. The preceding example will yield as a first item the value `manning.osgi.Subscriber1;` `org/osgi/framework/BundleEvent/*`. Next, you further break each item into two tokens, separated by the semicolon character (;). The preceding example will now yield `manning.osgi.Subscriber1` ❷ and `org/osgi/framework/BundleEvent/*` ❸. Finally, you add this pair to a list, and then add the two-component list to a final list, which is returned to the caller.

You're finished with your SAB container implementation, and you can now test it. You should first install the SAB container (extender) bundle. This is because the extender, for simplicity's sake, doesn't check to see if the bundles that already have been started in the OSGi framework at the time the SAB container was activated are SAB bundles. Following this, you can install any client that implements the `Event-Handler` interface, as in the next example:

```
package manning.eosgi;

import org.osgi.service.event.Event;
import org.osgi.service.event.EventHandler;

public class SimpleEventHandler implements EventHandler {

    public void handleEvent(Event event) {
        // Application code...
    }
}
```

Here is its MANIFEST.MF file, which uses our newly defined header entry:

```
Manifest-Version: 1.0
Bundle-ManifestVersion: 2
Bundle-SymbolicName: SimpleEventHandler
Bundle-Description: SAB for a simple event handler
Bundle-Version: 1.0.0
Meta-Subscriber:
 manning.osgi.SimpleEventHandler;org/osgi/framework/BundleEvent/*
Import-Package: org.osgi.service.event
```

As you may have noticed, one advantage of an SAB is that it doesn't hardcode the client Java code with the `EventAdmin`'s topic name, which can now be easily changed by editing the manifest file.

But there are a few things that could be improved on. For starters, an SAB doesn't allow users any flexibility about how the `EventHandler` instance is created. In other words, the SAB container always performs a `handlerClass.newInstance()`, but what if the user wants to pass along some arguments to the `EventHandler` constructor, or wants to set some properties in the created object, or simply has to use some legacy object whose instantiation the user doesn't control?

Moreover, the current approach, albeit efficient, is inadequate for combining features. For example, how could you combine the use of the transaction container defined in chapter 8 with this subscriber container? It wouldn't be possible, because both containers *own the process* of instantiating the target's object instance. You could create a single container that supports both features, but then you'd be back to having a single monolithic container that does it all, as in the JEE era. There's great value in keeping the containers modularized and separate, because it allows different vendors to implement the features they know best, and, more important, it allows customers to selectively pick and choose an implementation from among several competing ones.

> **NOTE** OSGi provides a drastic change from the previous model where you selected an application server from a vendor and therefore were stuck using persistence, transactions, security, and the like from that one vendor. In the OSGi model, you can use persistence from one vendor and transactions from

another. Furthermore, in the OSGi model, there may be several bundles (implementations) competing to provide the same feature (such as TopLink JPA and Hibernate JPA). And as you know, competition is good.

Clearly, we need a different approach for mixing the bundle flavors. The solution is to use an extensible and declarative (nonprogrammatic) approach for assembling the pieces, as you'll see in the next section.

13.2   *Declarative assembly using Blueprint*

As a testament to OSGi's "let it compete" model, there are several declarative assembly mechanisms for the OSGi platform. We'll look into one of them, the Blueprint service. Blueprint provides an extension mechanism, which we'll use to provide an alternative non-extender-based implementation of the SAB container.

> **NOTE** Blueprint is a huge topic on its own, and describing it (or any other declarative assembly service, for that matter) isn't the main goal of this chapter. There are several other books that discuss this subject at length, such as Manning's *OSGi in Action*. Instead, I'll provide a quick introduction to Blueprint and then focus on how to extend it to provide bundle flavors.

A Blueprint-flavored bundle is a bundle that contains XML documents specified using Blueprint's schema that describe how components can be created and assembled together. *Component* is a rather loose term, but in the context of the OSGi platform a component is essentially either a Java object, an OSGi service, or an OSGi reference (to a service).

> **DEFINITION** The bundle that contains the Blueprint document is called the *Blueprint bundle,* and the code or abstraction that parses such a file is called the *Blueprint container.*

We'll start exploring Blueprint with a quick example. Recall from the beginning of this chapter how we created an `EventHandler` object instance and then registered it as a service in the OSGi service repository. Here's the code snippet for this:

```
Object handler = SimpleEventHandler.class.newInstance();
bundleContext.registerService("org.osgi.service.event.EventHandler",
    handler, null);
```

Relating back to our component model, this snippet defines two components: a Java component and an OSGi service component. An equivalent Blueprint document would likewise define two components, as follows:

```
<bean id="handler" class="manning.enterpriseosgi.SimpleEventHandler" />

<service ref="handler" interface="org.osgi.service.event.EventHandler" />
```

Intuitively, the `<bean>` tag instantiates an object using the Java class specified in the `class` attribute. The name of this component is defined by the `id` attribute, in this case, `handler`. The `<service>` tag registers an OSGi service, referencing the Java component named `handler` as the service object and using the service interface defined by the attribute `interface`. The full document must include the `<blueprint>` document element, as in his example:

```xml
<?xml version="1.0" encoding="UTF-8" standalone="no"?>
<blueprint xmlns="http://www.osgi.org/xmlns/blueprint/v1.0.0"
    xmlns:xsi="http://www.w3.org/2001/XMLSchema-instance"
    xsi:schemaLocation="
    http://www.osgi.org/xmlns/blueprint/v1.0.0
    http://www.osgi.org/xmlns/blueprint/v1.0.0/blueprint.xsd" >

    <bean id="handler" class="manning.enterpriseosgi.SimpleEventHandler" />

    <service ref="handler"
        interface="org.osgi.service.event.EventHandler" />
</blueprint>
```

Next, let's create an OSGi reference to the `EventAdmin` service:

```java
ServiceReference ref =
    bundleContext.getServiceReference("org.osgi.service.event.EventAdmin);
    EventAdmin eventAdmin =
        (EventAdmin) context.getService(ref);
```

The Blueprint equivalent is as follows:

```xml
<reference id="eventAdmin" interface="org.osgi.service.event.EventAdmin" />

<bean id="publisher" class="manning.enterpriseosgi.SimplePublisher" >
    <property name="eventAdmin" ref="eventAdmin" />
</bean>
```

The `<reference>` tag is intuitive and maps directly to the `getServiceReference()` call. But you may ask why we need a `<bean>` definition for `publisher`. Having retrieved the OSGi reference, we need to hand it back to Java, and this is done by setting it as a property of a new Java class component, namely the `publisher` object.

Here's the code for the `SimplePublisher` class:

```java
public class SimplePublisher {

    private EventAdmin eventAdmin;

    public void setEventAdmin(EventAdmin eventAdmin) {
        this.eventAdmin = eventAdmin;
    }

    // ...
}
```

The Blueprint container creates a Java object instance for the class `SimplePublisher` as a result of the definition `<bean id="publisher" />`. Next, it tries to set the previously retrieved `EventAdmin` service reference as a property of this object. This adheres to the JavaBean conventions, where a property `foo` is set by using a `setFoo()` method and retrieved by using a `getFoo()` method. Thus, the Blueprint container looks for a

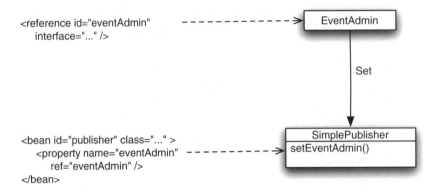

Figure 13.1 The EventAdmin reference is set in the SimplePublisher Java
component created by Blueprint.

method called setEventAdmin() in the SimplePublisher class. It finds one, which
takes EventAdmin as its argument, as shown in figure 13.1. At this point, it converts the
OSGi EventAdmin reference to an actual Java object, by internally invoking (Event-
Admin) BundleContext.getService(reference). Although this may seem a bit con-
voluted, the net result is quite simple; you can easily inject a service reference into any
of your existing Java classes.

How do you configure a Blueprint bundle? You simply use the Bundle-Blueprint
manifest header, setting it to a Blueprint XML document. Interestingly enough, the
Blueprint container itself is implemented using the extender pattern, which looks for
this particular manifest header entry in all activated bundles.

> **NOTE** As an alternative to the Bundle-Blueprint option, you may also place
> the Blueprint XML documents in the META-INF/blueprint directory.

You may ask, what happens if the service isn't found? Would the declarative assembly
fail? Not necessarily. This is one of the values of using a declarative approach; the low-
level details are hidden from the user. For example, Blueprint creates proxies for the
services and may wait until a service is actually used before retrieving the service from
the OSGi service registry.

Blueprint has several other advantages, some of which are enumerated here:

- Different mechanisms for instantiating Java components, such as factory meth-
  ods instead of constructors
- Facilities for populating the Java components with properties, following the
  JavaBean conventions
- Automatic type conversion, such as from an OSGi ServiceReference to the
  actual service object
- Lifecycle callbacks, such as init and destroy callback methods for the Java
  objects

- Different scoping rules for the Java components, such as singletons or prototypes
- Support for AOP (aspect-oriented programming)

Most important, Blueprint supports the concept of dependency injection.

> **Dependency injection**
>
> Dependency injection is a design pattern where dependencies between components are minimized by decoupling them from the program's code. This concept has been made popular by the Spring Framework.

But let's not stray too far from our original objective of implementing the SAB container by extending Blueprint, which is the subject of the next section.

13.3 *Extending Blueprint*

Choosing XML as the medium for specifying a Blueprint document wasn't accidental; XML is the perfect tool for extensibility. Keeping this in mind, let's see how you could author a Blueprint document that makes use of our SAB feature, as shown in the following listing.

Listing 13.3 The SAB Blueprint document

```xml
<?xml version="1.0" encoding="UTF-8" standalone="no"?>
<blueprint xmlns="http://www.osgi.org/xmlns/blueprint/v1.0.0"
  xmlns:xsi="http://www.w3.org/2001/XMLSchema-instance"
  xmlns:sab=
    "http://www.manning.com/xmlns/blueprint-sab/v1.0.0"      ① SAB namespace
  xsi:schemaLocation="
    http://www.osgi.org/xmlns/blueprint/v1.0.0 http://www.osgi.org/xmlns/
      blueprint/v1.0.0/blueprint.xsd
    http://www.manning.com/xmlns/blueprint-sab/v1.0.0 http://www.manning.com/
      xmlns/blueprint-sab/v1.0.0/sad.xsd" >

  <bean id="handler"                                          ② Standard
  class="manning.enterpriseosgi.SimpleEventHandler" />           EventHandler
                                                                 instance
  <sab:subscriber id="sub1"                   ③ SAB extension
    topic="org/osgi/framework/BundleEvent/*"     tag
    ref="handler" />
</blueprint>
```

You start by defining a new XML namespace and associating it with the sab prefix ①. All Blueprint extensions must be placed under a different namespace, which is a good design principle. Next, you define a standard Java component implementing the EventHandler interface ②, as you did in the previous example. Finally, you use our SAB <sab:subscriber> extension to annotate the handler Java component as a subscriber, and in the process you configure its topic ③. In other words, the <sab:subscriber> tag defines a new *event subscriber* component.

XML taxonomy

Consider the following XML:

```
<elementA xmlns="namespaceA" xmlns:pr1="namespaceB">
    <pr1:elementB attributeA="value" />
    <elementC pr1:attributeB="value" >
        <pr1:elementD/>
    </elementC>
</elementA>
```

Here is a simple taxonomy of the nodes involved in this example:

- XML elements—elementA, elementB, elementC, elementD
- XML attributes—attributeA, attributeB
- Namespaces—namespaceA, namespaceB
- Namespace prefix—pr1
- Default namespace—namespaceA
- Document element—elementA
- Top-level elements—elementB, elementC
- Nested elements—elementD
- Nodes under the namespace of namespaceA—elementA, elementC, attributeA
- Nodes under the namespace of namespaceB—elementB, attributeB, elementD

A document that contains XML is called an *XML document*. A schema may type an XML document. This schema definition is called *XSD* (XML Schema Definition).

The semantics of this component is similar to that of the Meta-Subscriber manifest header entry; that is, it registers an EventHandler service to receive events from the specified topic. But we've now blended the mechanism for defining a subscriber with that of defining a Java object through the fabric of Blueprint. This means that we can leverage Blueprint's features for creating Java objects together with that of creating subscribers.

For example, consider the following XML fragment:

```
<bean id="handler" class="manning.enterpriseosgi.SimpleEventHandler"
    scope="prototype" />

<sab:subscriber id="sub1" topic="org/osgi/framework/BundleEvent/*"
    ref="handler" />
<sab:subscriber id="sub2" topic="org/osgi/framework/ServiceEvent/*"
    ref="handler" />
```

In this case, we're defining the handler object with the scope of prototype. This means that each subscriber service gets a different object instance of the SimpleEventHandler class. Had we kept the default scope of singleton, both subscribers would have gotten the same EventHandler object instance. This example clearly shows how we've been able to decouple the SAB container from instantiating the `EventHandler`. If you recall from section 13.3, the extender-based implementation hardcodes the instantiating of the `EventHandler` instance.

Furthermore, consider the problem of combining both SAB and our transaction container implementation from chapter 8. A candidate solution for this using Blueprint is as follows:

```
<bean id="handler" class="manning.enterpriseosgi.SimpleEventHandler" >
    <tx:transaction method="handleEvent" value="Required" />
</bean>

<sab:subscriber id="sub1" topic="org/osgi/framework/BundleEvent/*"
    ref="handler" />
```

In fact, OSGi already defines a standard extension to Blueprint for specifying transaction demarcations, whose syntax we borrowed in the example.

Now that you understand how to define a SAB bundle, let's focus on how to implement a Blueprint-based SAB container.

13.3.1 Extending Blueprint with namespaces

The Blueprint container is extended by means of a Namespace Handler service. The extender registers a Namespace Handler service in the OSGi service registry, specifying the service property `osgi.service.blueprint.namespace`, which is set to the namespace URI value of the extension.

> **WARNING** Blueprint's Namespaces specification (RFC 155) is still being finalized, so some of the details presented here may eventually change. But the overall concept should be the same.

The following example creates a namespace handler for our SAB container:

```
<service interface="org.osgi.service.blueprint.namespace.NamespaceHandler">
    <service-properties>
        <entry key="osgi.service.blueprint.namespace"
            value="http://www.manning.com/xmlns/blueprint-sab/v1.0.0" />
    </service-properties>
    <bean class="manning.enterpriseosgi.sab.SabNamespaceHandler" />
</service>
```

First, note that we're using Blueprint itself to illustrate the example. This is merely to highlight Blueprint's usage, and we could have chosen to do this in a `Bundle-Activator`, as we did in previous chapters. We start by defining an OSGi service whose service interface is `org.osgi.service.blueprint.namespace.NamespaceHandler`, and with the service property `osgi.service.blueprint.namespace` set to `http://www.manning.com/xmlns/blueprint-sab/v1.0.0`. We then associate the Java component `<bean class="manning.enterpriseosgi.sab.SabNamespaceHandler" />` as the service object of the `NamespaceHandler` service, as shown in figure 13.2. The `osgi.service.blueprint.namespace` service property is very important, because it allows the `BlueprintContainer` to find the proper `NamespaceHandler` for a particular

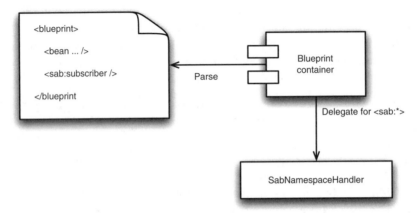

Figure 13.2 The Blueprint container parses the Blueprint documents and delegates to `SabNamespaceHandler` when `<sab:subscriber>` is found.

XML node. This follows the same pattern you've seen with the `DataSourceFactory` service and so many others.

Before we look at the `SabNamespaceHandler` class, note how we defined an anonymous Java component nested within the `<service>` tag in the previous XML example. This is another one of Blueprint's advantages—being able to succinctly nest anonymous components within components and avoid the verbosity and indirection of using `refs`.

Here's the implementation of the `SabNamespaceHandler`.

Listing 13.4 The `SabNamespaceHandler` class

```
public class SabNamespaceHandler implements NamespaceHandler {

    public SabNamespaceHandler() {
    }

    public URL getSchemaLocation(String schema) {               ❶ Return schema
        return this.getClass().getResource("schemas/blueprint-sab.xsd");
    }

    public ComponentMetadata decorate(Node node,
            ComponentMetadata component,                        ❷ Handle XML attributes
            ParserContext context) {
        return null;
    }

    public ComponentMetadata parse(Element element,            ❸ Handle XML elements
            ParserContext context){
        // Defined later...
    }
}
```

A `NamespaceHandler.getSchemaLocation` returns the location of the XSD file that defines its XML extensions ❶. We do this by loading a resource file within the SAB

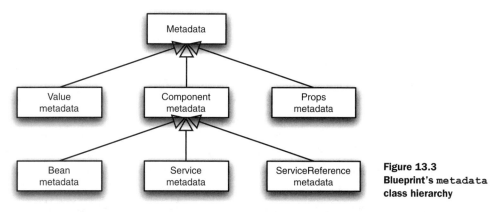

**Figure 13.3
Blueprint's metadata
class hierarchy**

container bundle itself, which we've placed under the schemas directory. We'll discuss this file later. Next, before getting into the details of the decorate() and parse() methods, you need to understand the overall design of a NamespaceHandler.

The way that Blueprint works is that the Blueprint container reads the Blueprint document and generates metadata information for all components that are being specified in the parsed document. For example, if there's a <bean> tag, then the container generates a BeanMetadata object, representing the Java component. The BeanMetadata class contains information for all the data being specified in the <bean> tag, such as the Java class name and the Java properties. Likewise, there's a ServiceMetadata class, which includes metadata defining the service interface and the service properties, and a ServiceReferenceMetadata class, which points to a BeanMetadata class representing the service object. The Blueprint metadata classes are shown in figure 13.3.

Component managers, or builders, use these collections of component metadata to build the appropriate component implementation. For example, the BeanManager uses the BeanMetadata to instantiate the appropriate Java class instances, as shown in figure 13.4.

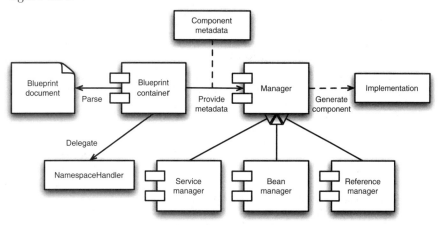

Figure 13.4   A Blueprint container parses document and generated metadata, which is used by managers to create the component implementation.

When the Blueprint container finds either an XML element or an attribute that's of a namespace it doesn't understand, it looks for a Namespace Handler service in the OSGi service registry whose `osgi.service.blueprint.namespace` property value matches that of the element's or attribute's namespace. Having found an appropriate handler, it delegates to the handler to create the correct metadata. This is done through the `parse()` and `decorate()` methods. The `parse()` method is used when a top-level XML element is seen, which represents a new component, and therefore new component metadata is needed. The `decorate()` method is used when an attribute or a nested element within some other namespace is seen, as in the case when the handler needs to decorate the metadata of an existing component.

Parse vs. decorate

The `parse()` and `decorate()` methods are invoked when parsing XML documents in different contexts.

For example, consider the following XML document:

```
<elementA xmlns="namespaceA" xmlns:pr1="namespaceB">
    <pr1:elementB attributeA="value" />
    <elementC pr1:attributeB="value" >
        <pr1:elementD/>
    </elementC>
</elementA>
```

`NamespaceHandler.parse()` is invoked (considering the default namespace to be that of Blueprint) for `elementB`.

`NamespaceHandler.decorate()` is invoked for `attributeB` and for `elementD`.

Back in listing 13.4, because we defined only a new top-level element, namely `<sab:subscriber>`, the `decorate()` method is never called and we can leave it empty ❷. As for the `parse()` method ❸, its implementation is in the next listing.

Listing 13.5 The `SabNamespaceHandler.parse()` method, part 1

```
public ComponentMetadata parse(Element element, ParserContext context) {
    if (element.getLocalName().equals("subscriber")) {        ❶ Check name
        final String id = element.getAttribute("id");
        final String topic = element.getAttribute("topic");    ❷ Get XML data
        final String ref = element.getAttribute("ref");

        MutableBeanMetadata factoryMetadata =                  ❸ Create metadata
            new MutableBeanMetadata();                            object

        factoryMetadata.setScope("singleton");                 ❹ Set metadata
        factoryMetadata.setClassName(SubscriberFactory.class.toString());  fields
        factoryMetadata.setInitMethod("init");
        factoryMetadata.setDestroyMethod("destroy");
```

```
        factoryMetadata.addProperty("id",                    ◁─────┐    Set metadata
                new ValueMetadata() {                          ❺    properties
                    public String getType() {
                        return String.class.toString();
                    }
                    public String getStringValue() {
                        return id;
                    }
                });

        factoryMetadata.addProperty("topic",
                new ValueMetadata() {
                    public String getType() {
                        return String.class.toString();
                    }
                    public String getStringValue() {
                        return topic;
                    }
                });

        // Defined Listing 13.7

        return factoryMetadata;

    } else
        throw new ComponentDefinitionException(
            "Illegal use of blueprint SAB namespace");
}
```

You start by making sure you're parsing the subscriber element ❶; if not, you should fail, because there are no other elements in this schema. Next, you retrieve all the data from the XML nodes that you need to use ❷, which are the element's id and the value of the topic and ref attributes.

You now need to set this data into an actual component metadata object. In general, you should be able to do this by asking the container to create an empty mutable metadata object. This would be done using the ParserContext object, received as an argument of the parse() method. But there's no standard way of doing this; each container implementation may provide different ways of setting metadata depending on the component managers it supports. For instance, a Blueprint container may decide to support additional components not initially defined by the Blueprint specification. Therefore, you take a simpler, albeit more cumbersome, approach of implementing the standard interfaces of the Metadata interface directly with your own utility classes.

With that in mind, you create a MutableBeanMetadata object ❸, which, as you'll see later, provides a way of setting the BeanMetadata interface. Next, you populate some of the standard BeanMetadata values ❹, such as its scope and, most important, the component's className, which is used to instantiate the component's actual Java implementation. In this case, this is the SubscriberFactory class. There's also metadata for an init and a destroy method. We'll talk about these methods and the className later on.

Finally, you set the XML data you retrieved as property metadata ❺, specifically the id property and the topic property, both of which are of type String.

There are two remaining properties to be set, which are described in the next listing.

Listing 13.6   The SabNamespaceHandler.parse() method, part 2

```
factoryMetadata.addProperty("target",
    new RefMetadata(){
        public String getComponentId() {
                return ref;
        }});
```
❶ RefMetadata implementation
❷ Ref XML data

```
factoryMetadata.addProperty("blueprintBundleContext",
    new RefMetadata(){
        public String getComponentId() {
                return "blueprintBundleContext";
        }});
```
❸ Predefined reference

The one remaining piece of XML data you haven't set yet is the ref attribute. Because ref is an actual reference to another component, you can't simply set it as a metadata value, as you did for id and topic. Instead, you create an anonymous class implementing the RefMetadata interface ❶ and populate it with the ref value ❷. When the BeanManager receives this RefMetadata object, it will automatically (in a magical wave of hands) replace the literal ref value with the actual Java component's object instance that represents the reference. This is possible because the BeanManager is responsible for creating the Java component's object instances and therefore knows about them in an internal registry.

You've set all the data you retrieved from the Blueprint document, so are you finished? Not actually. As you'll see next, the SubscriberFactory class needs to access the bundleContext of the SAB bundle. In another magical wave of hands, this is done using a predefined Blueprint reference called blueprintBundleContext ❸. In general terms, this isn't much different than what you did for the subscriber's ref attribute. The only difference is that instead of referencing a component defined by the Blueprint bundle itself, you're referencing a component predefined by the Blueprint container. In fact, the Blueprint container predefines several components:

- blueprintContainer—An org.osgi.service.blueprint.container.BlueprintContainer object instance that can be used to look up the Blueprint bundle's metadata and component instances.

- blueprintBundle—The Bundle object instance associated with the Blueprint bundle itself.

- blueprintBundleContext—The BundleContext object instance associated with the Blueprint bundle itself.

- blueprintConverter—An org.osgi.service.blueprint.container.Converter object instance that can be used to convert Blueprint components and properties.

Now that you understand the SabNamespaceHandler, let's look at the Subscriber-Factory class, which is the class being set in the BeanMetadata you return from the parse() method, as shown in the following listing.

Listing 13.7   The SubscriberFactory class

```
public class SubscriberFactory {

    private BundleContext bundleContext;
    private String topic;
    private String id;
    private Object target;
    private ServiceRegistration serviceReference;

    public void setId(String id) {
        this.id = id;
    }

    public void setBlueprintBundleContext(BundleContext
      blueprintBundleContext) {
        this.bundleContext = blueprintBundleContext;
    }

    public void setTopic(String topic) {
        this.topic = topic;
    }

    public void setTarget(Object target) {
        this.target = target;
    }

    @SuppressWarnings("unchecked")
    public void init() {
        Dictionary properties = new Hashtable();
        properties.put("COMPONENT_ID", id);
        properties.put(EventConstants.EVENT_TOPIC,
            topic);

        serviceReference =
            bundleContext.registerService(
                EventHandler.class.toString(), target, properties);
    }

    public void destroy() {
        if (serviceReference != null) {
            serviceReference.unregister();
        }
    }
}
```

❶ Set properties

❷ Set built-in reference

❸ Init method

❹ Set topic

❺ Destroy method

The BeanManager within the Blueprint container collects your BeanMetadata and uses its getClassName() method to instantiate a Java class for the subscriber component, which in this case yields a SubscriberFactory object. Next, it sets all the properties contained in the BeanMetadata in the SubscriberFactory object; these include its id ❶, topic, target, and the built-in blueprintBundleContext ❷.

After all the properties have been set, it checks to see if the BeanMetadata defines an init method. The init method is a callback method in the component implementation ❸ that's invoked by the Blueprint container after all the properties have been set. It gives you a chance to initialize the component, which in this case means registering an EventHandler instance in the OSGi registry. Specifically, you set the id and topic as service properties ❹ and then use the blueprintBundleContext to register the ref object as an EventHandler in the OSGi registry. By doing so, you can match the behavior of our extender-based implementation of the SAB bundle. Also note that every time the init method is invoked, you end up creating a new EventHandler service, which is the reason we called it a *subscriber factory*.

Finally, Blueprint also has a destroy method, which is invoked when the Blueprint bundle is stopped. In this case, you unregister the EventHandler ❺ when this happens.

> **NOTE** Recall that you use the blueprintBundleContext to register the Event-Handler service. Although this may not be obvious, this is the bundleContext of the Blueprint bundle, that is, of the application bundle that contains the Blueprint document and *not* the bundleContext of the Blueprint extender (implementation) bundle.

You're almost finished; you just need to close two open loops. First, let's go back and check the SAB's XSD file, as shown in the following listing.

Listing 13.8   The SAB XSD file

```xml
<?xml version="1.0" encoding="UTF-8"?>
<schema xmlns="http://www.w3.org/2001/XMLSchema"
    xmlns:tns="http://www.manning.com/xmlns/blueprint-sab/v1.0.0"
    targetNamespace="http://www.manning.com/xmlns/blueprint-sab/v1.0.0"
    xmlns:osgi="http://www.osgi.org/xmlns/blueprint/v1.0.0"
    xsi:schemaLocation="
        http://www.osgi.org/xmlns/blueprint/v1.0.0
        http://www.osgi.org/xmlns/blueprint/v1.0.0/blueprint.xsd" >

    <element name="subscriber">                          ◁─── ❶ Component name
        <complexType>
        <complexContent>
            <extension base="osgi:identifiedType">       ◁─── ❷ Implement identifiedType
            <attribute name="topic" type="string"
                    use="required" />
            <xsd:attribute name="ref" type="osgi:Tidref"
                use="required" />
            </extension>
        </complexContent>
        </complexType>
    </element>
</schema>
```

As expected, it defines an element named subscriber ❶ under the namespace of http://www.manning.com/xmlns/blueprint-sab/v1.0.0. All components must extend the Blueprint type of identifiedType ❷, which means they're identified by an id attribute. In addition, you include two attributes, one defining topic as a String and another defining ref as an ID reference.

The one remaining issue is implementing the MutableBeanMetadata class. After such a demanding section, you finish on a light task, because implementing Mutable-BeanMetadata is a matter of creating getters and setters for all properties defined by the BeanMetadata interface. The full code for this class is rather extensive; only the initial methods are shown here to highlight the idea:

```java
public class MutableBeanMetadata implements BeanMetadata {

    private List arguments;
    private String className;
    private String destroyMethod;
    private Target factoryComponent;
    private String factoryMethod;
    private String initMethod;
    private List properties;
    private String scope;
    private int activation;
    private List dependsOn;
    private String id;

    public List getArguments() {
        return this.arguments;
    }

    public void setArguments(List arguments) {
        this.arguments = arguments;
    }

    public String getClassName() {
        return this.className;
    }

    public void setClassName(String className) {
        this.className = className;
    }

    // ...
}
```

And there you have it; you've implemented a new Blueprint component that allows the definition of a subscriber that blends well with OSGi's declarative and extensive programming model.

To implement your SAB bundle, you've extended Blueprint by providing specific metadata to the BeanManager. That is, it was mostly a static extension. There are cases when this isn't enough. For example, in the case of our transaction container, where you need to add behavior to begin and end a transaction when certain methods are invoked, you need to be able to extend the runtime behavior of a component. This can be done with interceptors, which is the subject of our final section on Blueprint.

13.3.2 *Intercepting Blueprint*

Let's start by reconsidering the transaction extension in the Blueprint document we used previously:

```
<bean id="handler" class="manning.osgi.SimpleEventHandler" >
    <tx:transaction method="handleEvent" />
</bean>
```

In this example, you're informing the container that the method `SimpleEvent-Handler.handleEvent()` is required to run in the context of a transaction. The outcome of running this code should be equivalent to the following implementation:

```
public void handleEvent(Event event) {
    UserTransaction ut = getUserTransactionService();

    try {
        ut.begin();
        try {
            // User code to handle event

            ut.commit();
        } catch (Exception e) {
            ut.rollback();
        }
    } catch (Exception e) {
        // Handle TM exception...
    }
}
```

Assuming you've read chapter 8, there should be no surprises here; you retrieve the `UserTransaction` service, begin a transaction, and commit it if everything is successful in the user's code handling the event, or you roll it back if an exception is raised.

As in chapter 8, your objective in this section is to hide the transaction-handling infrastructure code within the container, but in this case we're going to do it by using Blueprint's interceptor mechanism.

> **WARNING** The Blueprint Interceptor specification (RPC 166) is still being finalized, so use it with care.

The process for registering Blueprint interceptors hasn't been fully standardized yet, so you can only do it using a rather vendor-specific API through the `Namespace-Handler`'s `ParserContext` object. Look at the code in the following listing.

Listing 13.9 The `TxNamespaceHandler` class

```
public class TxNamespaceHandler implements NamespaceHandler {

    private UserTransaction ut;

    public void setUserTransaction(UserTransaction ut) {
        this.ut = ut;
    }
```

```
public URL getSchemaLocation(String arg0) {
    return getClass().getResource("schemas/tx.xsd");
}

public ComponentMetadata decorate(Node node,
ComponentMetadata component, ParserContext context) {
    if (node.getLocalName().equals("transaction")) {        ❶ Check node
        TxInterceptor txInterceptor =                             name
            new TxInterceptor();                            ❷ Create
        txInterceptor.setUserTransaction(ut);                  interceptor
        txInterceptor.setMethod(((Element)node).            ❸ Set node
            getAttribute("method"));                             values

        context.getComponentDefinitionRegistry().          ❹ Register
            registerInterceptorWithComponent(component, txInterceptor);  interceptor
    }

    return null;
}

public Metadata parse(Element element, ParserContext context) {
    return null;
}
}
```

Recall from the Blueprint document used at the beginning of this section that the transaction element is a nested element within the Java component's <bean> element; therefore you use the decorate() method instead of the parse() method. In this example, you're intercepting the SimplerEventHandler object's invocations so that you can make them transaction-aware. You're not creating any new component metadata; rather, you're reusing the metadata provided by the Blueprint container for the Java component representing the SimplerEventHandler object.

The decorate() method implementation is simple. First, you check to see if it's indeed the target of the transaction element ❶; then you instantiate a TxInterceptor object ❷, which will be examined in the next listing. Next, you need to set the interceptor object with a reference to the UserTransaction service, and you need to set it with the value of the method attribute ❸, because it's the method name in the Simple-EventHandler class that you want to intercept, namely the handleEvent method.

Finally, you use the method parameter ParserContext to retrieve a registry of component metadata, and use it to register the interceptor object you just created ❹, associating it with the BeanMetadata for the SimplerEventHandler definition.

Apache Aries Blueprint

The ComponentDefinitionRegistry is an API specific to the Apache Aries Blueprint container implementation. This registry contains all component metadata for the Blueprint document being parsed and also allows interceptors to be associated with the metadata.

(continued)

At the time of writing, there is no standard approach for registering interceptors. It's possible that the Interceptor specification that is being worked on addresses this by using an approach based on the registration of an `Interceptor` service in the OSGi registry. In the meantime, we rely on Aries' `ParserContext`, with the understanding that this approach is not portable across containers.

Next, let's look at the `TxInterceptor` class, shown in the following listing.

Listing 13.10   The `TxInterceptor` class

```
public class TxInterceptor implements Interceptor {          Implement
                                                             Interceptor
    private UserTransaction ut;                          ❶  interface
    private String targetMethod;

    public void setUserTransaction(UserTransaction ut) {
        this.ut = ut;
    }

    public void setMethod(String methodName) {
        targetMethod = methodName;
    }

    public Object preCall(ComponentMetadata metadata, Method m,
        Object... args)                             Invoke prior
      throws Throwable {                         ❷  to method
        if (m.getName().equals(targetMethod)) {         Check method
            try {                                    ❸  name
                ut.begin();
            } catch (Exception e) {
                // Handle TM exception...
            }
        }

        return null;
    }

    public void postCallWithException(ComponentMetadata metadata, Method m,
        Throwable t, Object correlator)
          throws Throwable {                        Invoke after
        if (m.getName().equals(targetMethod)) {  ❹  method if error
            try {
                ut.rollback();
            } catch (Exception e) {
                // Handle TM exception...
            }
        }
    }

    public void postCallWithReturn(ComponentMetadata metadata, Method m,
        Object ret, Object correlator)
```

```
        throws Throwable {
    if (m.getName().equals(targetMethod)) {
        try {
            ut.commit();
        } catch (Exception e) {
            // Handle TM exception...
        }
    }
  }
}
```

Invoke after method
5 if no error

You start by implementing the org.osgi.service.blueprint.Interceptor interface
1. This interface defines three methods. The preCall() method **2** is invoked by the
container prior to the invocation of the actual component's method. For example, in
our case this method would be invoked before invoking the SimpleEventHandler.
handleEvent() method. In the preCall() implementation, you first check to see if the
method to be invoked is the one being annotated in the method attribute of the
<transaction> element **3**. If it is, you use the UserTransaction service set by the
NamespaceHandler to initiate a transaction by calling the UserTransaction.begin()
method.

The other two methods defined by the Interceptor interface are postCallWith-
Error() and postCallWithReturn(). These methods are invoked after the invocation
of SimpleEventHandler.handleEvent(), depending on whether handleEvent()
throws an exception or not. If it does, postCallWithError() is invoked, but if
handleEvent() returns successfully, postCallWithReturn() is invoked.

Multiple interceptors have been registered for a single component, so all preCall
methods are invoked first, then the actual Java method, and finally all postCall methods are invoked, as shown in figure 13.5. Supporting multiple interceptors for a single

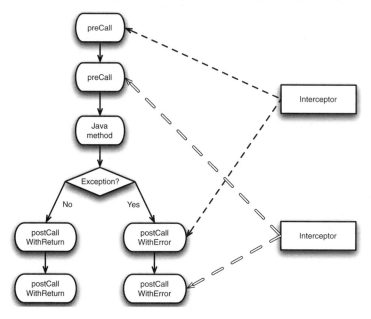

Figure 13.5
**A Java method
intercepted by multiple
interceptors, where all
preCall methods are
invoked, then the Java
method itself, and finally
the postCall methods,
depending on whether an
exception is raised or not**

component is fundamental, because separate namespace handlers, which know nothing about each other, may register the interceptors.

The implementation of both `postCallWithError()` and `postCallWithMethod()` is straightforward. The former ❹ rolls back the transaction by invoking `User-Transaction.rollback()`; this is if some error happened while executing the `handleEvent()` method, and you shouldn't commit the transaction. The latter ❺ commits the transaction, because the method `handleEvent()` finished successfully.

Correlating pre with post calls

The interceptor concept breaks the call to a single method into three stages: the `preCall()`, the actual method call, and the `postCall()`. This means that concurrent calls to a method may now cause race conditions. For example, if you call `methodA()` twice, the invocation to a `postCall()` could be either for the first thread that called `methodA()` or for the second thread. Because both would have the same component metadata, there's no way of differentiating between them.

The solution is that `preCall()` may return a correlating object, which is then passed as an argument to the corresponding `postCall()` method. This correlating object may be anything.

As you've noticed, you've propagated the `UserTransaction` service from the `TxNamespaceHandler` to the `TxInterceptor`, because the latter uses it to begin, commit, and roll back transactions. But how is the `UserTransaction` service retrieved? This is shown in the Blueprint document of the `TxNamespaceHandler` bundle, as follows:

```
<reference id="ut" interface="javax.transaction.UserTransaction" />

<bean id="txNsHandler" class="manning.osgi.TxNamespaceHandler" >
    <property name="UserTransaction" ref="ut" />
</bean>

<service interface="org.osgi.service.blueprint.namespace.NamespaceHandler"
    ref="txNsHandler" >
    <service-properties>
        <entry key="osgi.service.blueprint.namespace"
        value="http://www.manning.com/xmlns/blueprint-tx/v1.0.0" />
        </service-properties>
</service>
```

You retrieve a reference to the `UserTransaction` service using the `<reference>` tag and then set it in the `TxNamespaceHandler` bean. Then you register this bean as the service object of a Namespace Handler service, setting the `namespace` property, as you did for the SAB container implementation.

The only remaining piece is the definition of the transaction XSD itself, which we'll define now succinctly:

```
<?xml version="1.0" encoding="UTF-8"?>
<schema xmlns="http://www.w3.org/2001/XMLSchema"
```

```
xmlns:tns="http://www.manning.com/xmlns/blueprint-tx/v1.0.0"
targetNamespace="http://www.manning.com/xmlns/blueprint-tx/v1.0.0"
xmlns:osgi="http://www.osgi.org/xmlns/blueprint/v1.0.0"
xsi:schemaLocation="
    http://www.osgi.org/xmlns/blueprint/v1.0.0
    http://www.osgi.org/xmlns/blueprint/v1.0.0/blueprint.xsd" >

<element name="transaction">
    <complexType>
        <attribute name="method" type="string"/>
    </complexType>
</element>
</schema>
```

To keep things simple, a single transaction `element` defines a `method` attribute. Note that because this is meant to be used as a nested element within the `<bean>` tag, there's no need to make it extend `osgi:identifiedType`.

> **NOTE** Our transaction schema only roughly maps to that of the Blueprint Transaction (RFC 164) standard, which has options for declaring a document, a bean, or a method as transactional.

So far in this chapter, you've learned how to develop OSGi applications that implement several *container* features together, using a single declarative programming model. In particular, we've implemented a subscriber application bundle that not only receives events but also handles them in a transactional form. In the next section, we'll revisit the auction OSGi application developed in chapter 3 and change it to overcome its current shortcomings by using the diverse features you've learned so far in this book, such as persistence, event handling, and configuration. We'll do so by using Blueprint as our integration glue.

13.4 Revisiting the auction application

At this point, you may want to browse through chapter 3 to remind yourself about the auction application. With all you've learned in the chapters since chapter 3, it's evident that the auction application has a lot of room for improvement. But to keep things manageable, let's focus on the auction implementation, or more specifically, on the `auction.auctioneer.sealed_1.0.0` bundle. In the next section, we'll simplify the whole design of the auction application through events.

13.4.1 Using the Event Admin service

One of the complexities of the auction application is that we ended up having to develop an extensible mechanism for allowing auditors to know what's happening in the auctions. This was done by wrapping the `Auction` services with the `AuctionWrapper` class in the `auction.core` bundle. A more decoupled approach would have been for the `Auctions` to post events informing of the ask and bid activities and letting the auditors listen for them. You could even use the same approach to inform the sellers and buyers of the outcomes of their asks and bids, decoupling not only the auditors from the auctions but the participants as well.

Contrary to what you may be thinking, the implementation of this design change is simple and mostly consists of changes to the `SealedFirstPriceAuction.ask()` and `SealedFirstPriceAuction.bid()` methods, as follows.

Listing 13.11   An event-driven `ask()` implementation

```
public Float ask(String item, Float price, Participant seller)
        throws InvalidOfferException {
    if (price <= 0) {
        throw new InvalidOfferException("Ask must be greater than zero.");
    }

    Book book = openTransactions.get(item);

    if (book == null) {
        book = new Book();
        openTransactions.put(item, book);

    } else if (book.seller != null) {
        throw new InvalidOfferException("Item [" + item
+ "] has already being auctioned.");
    }

    book.ask = price;
    book.seller = seller;

    eventAdmin.postEvent(createAskEvent(item, price,               ◁──┐  Post ask
        seller.getName()));                                          ❶  event

    return price;
}

@SuppressWarnings("unchecked")
private Event createAskEvent(String item, Float price, String name) {
    Dictionary props = new Hashtable();
    props.put("AUCTION_ID", pid);                                  ◁──┐  Set ask
    props.put("ITEM", item);                                         ❷  properties
    props.put("PRICE", price);
    props.put("SELLER", name);

    Event event =
        new Event("manning/auction/ASKS", props);                  ◁──┐  Post to
    return event;                                                    ❸  ASKS topic
}
```

Most of the implementation remains the same, except that you post an event at the end, informing listeners that a new ask activity has been realized ❶. The event itself contains four properties: the auction id ❷, the `item` being sold, the asking `price`, and the seller's `name`. Note that you use the seller's `name` instead of the seller's `Participant` object instance, because the latter can't be set as an event property. Finally, you post this event to the `manning/auction/ASKS` topic ❸. This means that any interested bundle, not only auditors and participants, can subscribe and know about the items that are being auctioned.

This simple change has profound implications for the overall design of the system. For example, it allows bidders to listen for ask events before sending a bid, rather than sending bids first and hoping that a seller may come by eventually. For the time being, let's ignore how you retrieve the `EventAdmin` service and the `pid` value; we'll revisit these later. Next, let's take a look at the `bid()` method implementation, shown in the following listing.

Listing 13.12 An event-driven `bid()` implementation

```
public Float bid(String item, Float price, Participant buyer)
        throws InvalidOfferException {

    // No changes to the beginning, therefore omitted ...

    eventAdmin.postEvent(createBidEvent(item, price,
 ➥   buyer.getName()));                                        ◁─────┐ Post bid
                                                                    ❶ event

    if ((++book.numberOfBids) == maxAllowedBids) {
        if (book.seller != null) {
            if (book.highestBid >= book.ask) {
                eventAdmin.postEvent(                          ◁─────┐ Post accepted
                        createAcceptedEvent(item,                   ❷ event
                                book.getSeller(),
                                book.getHighestBid(),
                        book.getHighestBidder()));

            } else {
                eventAdmin.postEvent(                          ◁─────┐ Post rejected
                    createRejectedEvent(item,                       ❸ event
                    book.getSeller(), book.getHighestBid()));
            }
        } else {
            book.highestBidder.onRejected(this, item, book.highestBid);
        }

        openTransactions.remove(item);
    } else {
        System.out.println(buyer.getName() + " bidding for item "
                + item);
    }

    return null;
}
```

Again, the solution is to send a bid event ❶ when the bid is received. But you also send an accept event ❷ if there's a match of the bid with an ask, or a reject event otherwise ❸. Note that you no longer invoke the `Participant.onAccepted()` and `Participant.onRejected()` callback methods; instead, the sellers and buyers must listen for the accepted and rejected events. To understand this better, let's look at the create event methods:

```
@SuppressWarnings("unchecked")
private Event createBidEvent(String item, Float price, String name) {
```

```
        Dictionary props = new Hashtable();
        props.put("AUCTION_ID", pid);
        props.put("ITEM", item);
        props.put("PRICE", price);
        props.put("BUYER", name);

        Event event = new Event("manning/auction/BIDS", props);
        return event;
}


@SuppressWarnings("unchecked")
private Event createRejectedEvent(String item, String seller, float
    highestBid) {
        Dictionary props = new Hashtable();
        props.put("AUCTION_ID", pid);
        props.put("ITEM", item);
        props.put("HIGHEST_BID", highestBid);
        props.put("SELLER", seller);
        props.put("VERDICT", "rejected");

        Event event = new Event("manning/auction/" + item, props);
        return event;
}


@SuppressWarnings("unchecked")
private Event createAcceptedEvent(String item, String seller, float
    highestBid,
        String highestBidder) {
        Dictionary props = new Hashtable();
        props.put("AUCTION_ID", pid);
        props.put("ITEM", item);
        props.put("HIGHEST_BID", highestBid);
        props.put("SELLER", seller);
        props.put("BUYER", highestBidder);
        props.put("VERDICT", "accepted");

        Event event = new Event("manning/auction/" + item, props);
        return event;
}
```

These are similar to the creation of the ask event in the previous listing. The only noteworthy difference is that the accepted and rejected events are sent to a topic representing the item being sold. For example, if a book is being auctioned, then the topic used for the accepted and rejected events is manning/auction/book. This means that when a buyer makes a bid for a book, it needs to register to receive events from the topic manning/auction/book to know if the bid has been accepted or rejected. The buyer can even register an event filter matching the property buyer by name, therefore receiving only events targeted to that buyer. This interaction is shown in figure 13.6.

Likewise, an auditor registers to receive the bid and ask events and the accepted and rejected events for the auctions it wishes to audit. Instead of registering an Auditor service in the OSGi registry, an auditor would register an EventHandler

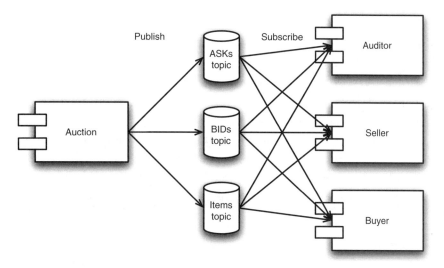

Figure 13.6 Auctions publish events to ASKs, BIDs, and items topics, which are subscribed by auditors, sellers, and buyers.

service. This may seem to involve the same effort at first, but keep in mind that the EventHandler service is more generic; therefore, it's easier to leverage tooling and libraries for it. For instance, you could actually implement an auditor using a SAB.

> ### Extending SAB
>
> Several features could be implemented to improve our SAB container. One idea is to extend the SAB container to support the proxying to any callback method, and not just to the handleEvent() method. This way you'd be able to leverage the existing SealedFirstPriceAuditor class as it is, replacing its activator with the SAB manifest header entry.

Overall, using the EventAdmin gives you several advantages:

- It decouples auctions, auditors, and participants by having them interact through events instead of services.
- It deems the auction.core bundle unnecessary, because you no longer need to wrap an auction to inform auditors of the bid and ask activities. This also means there is less state to manage, so you don't need to keep auditor references, which would be hard to persist.
- Other bundles, not initially envisioned, may participate in the collaboration.

In the next section, we'll look at how you can change the auction application to survive a restart of the OSGi framework without losing data. As you'll see, the fact that you no longer need to keep references to the participant's object instances helps you achieve this.

13.4.2 Using JPA

In the `SealedFirstPriceAuction` class, you keep all active auctioned items in a Map, defined as follows:

```
private Map<String, Book> openTransactions
```

Although the approach is simple enough, this information is lost when the system is shut down. You can easily improve upon this by using JPA.

The main change consists of using the `EntityManager` class and the methods `persist()` and `find()`, which replace the calls to `Map.put()` and `Map.get()`. But to do this, you need to change the `Book` class implementation, as follows.

Listing 13.13 The AuctionBook class

```
@Entity
class AuctionBook {                          ← ❶ JPA entity

    @Id
    private String item;                     ← ❷ Entity key
                                                  attribute
    private float ask;
    private int numberOfBids;
    private float highestBid;

    private String seller;                   ← ❸ Store name
    private String highestBidder;                 instead of
                                                  reference
    public void setItem(String item) {
        this.item = item;
    }

    public String getItem() {
        return item;
    }

    public float getAsk() {
        return this.ask;
    }

    public void setAsk(float ask) {
        this.ask = ask;
    }

    public String getSeller() {
        return this.seller;
    }

    public void setSeller(String seller) {
        this.seller = seller;
    }

    // Remaining getters/setters omitted...
}
```

First and foremost, you move the previously nested Book class to be a top-level class and rename it AuctionBook to make it more evident. The AuctionBook is persisted using the EntityManager; therefore, you need to annotate it as an Entity ❶. Next, to conform to JPA, you need to include its key within the class itself. The auction's key is the item being sold, which you add as another class field ❷. Finally, you can't persist the references of the seller and highest bidder, because these references aren't serializable. Therefore, you convert them to be the seller's and bidder's names ❸. This is acceptable because you're now using the Event Admin service and no longer need to invoke the participant's callback methods. Although it's not fully included in the listing, you provide getters and setters for all the fields, which is easy enough.

You can now change the SealedFirstPriceAuction class to use the Entity-Manager, replacing the openTransactions data structure. Let's look at the new implementation of the SealedFirstPriceAuction.ask() method using JPA.

Listing 13.14   The ask() method implemented using JPA

```
public Float ask(String item, Float price, Participant seller)
      throws InvalidOfferException {
   if (price <= 0) {
      throw new InvalidOfferException("Ask must be greater than zero.");
   }

   AuctionBook book = new AuctionBook();
   book.setItem(item);
   book.setAsk(price);                              ◄─── ❶ Set key
   book.setSeller(seller.getName());

   try {                                            ❷ Persist entity
       em.persist(book);                            ◄───
   } catch (EntityExistsException e) {
       throw new InvalidOfferException("Item [" + item
          + "] already being auctioned.");          ◄─── Entity already
   }                                                ❸ exists

   eventAdmin.postEvent(createAskEvent(item, price, seller.getName()));

   return price;
}
```

Because a buyer can now listen for ask events, you change the algorithm of the SealedFirstPriceAuction class to enforce that a seller must make known its desire to sell an item before buyers can place bids. Given this, the ask() method becomes straightforward. You create a new AuctionBook entity ❶ and make sure you set its item property, because it's the key. Next, you invoke the EntityManager.persist() method ❷. The persist() method raises an exception if another AuctionBook has already been persisted for the same item, in which case you simply rethrow it as an InvalidOfferException ❸. As you can see, the Map.put() call has essentially been replaced by the method EntityManager.persist().

Next, let's look at the new bid() implementation in the following listing.

Listing 13.15   The bid() method implemented using JPA

```
public Float bid(String item, Float price, Participant buyer)
        throws InvalidOfferException {
    if (price <= 0) {
        throw new InvalidOfferException("Bid must be greater than zero.");
    }

    AuctionBook book = em.find(AuctionBook.class, item);          ◄─── ❶ Retrieve existing entity

    if (book == null) {
        throw new InvalidOfferException("Item [" + item
                + "] is not being offered in this auction.");
    }

    if (price > book.getHighestBid()) {                          ❷ Update values ◄───
        book.setHighestBid(price);
        book.setHighestBidder(buyer.getName());
        book.incNumberOfBids();
    }

    eventAdmin.postEvent(createBidEvent(item, price, buyer.getName()));

    if ((book.getNumberOfBids()) == maxAllowedBids) {
        if (book.getHighestBid() >= book.getAsk()) {
            eventAdmin.postEvent(
                    createAcceptedEvent(item,
                            book.getSeller(),
                            book.getHighestBid(),
                            book.getHighestBidder()));
        } else {
            eventAdmin.postEvent(createRejectedEvent(item,
                    book.getSeller(), book.getHighestBid()));
        }
                                                    ❸ Remove entity
        em.remove(book);                         ◄───
    } else {
        em.refresh(book);                        ◄─── Persist updated ❹ values
    }

    return null;
}
```

You start by finding an AuctionBook entity using the item argument as the key ❶, and you throw an exception if no AuctionBook is found. Next, you check to see if it's a higher bid, updating the value of the entity ❷ if that's the case. Note that you don't need to create a new AuctionBook; you simply invoke the retrieved one's setter methods. Next, if the item is sold, you can safely remove the AuctionBook entity from persistence ❸. If it isn't sold, then you persist its updated value by invoking EntityManager.refresh() ❹ on the updated AuctionBook entity.

> **WARNING** Typically, you should also invoke EntityTransaction.commit() at the end, but I omitted this both for simplicity and because we can assume

that the underlying container would be managing the transactions, perhaps through the use of the Blueprint Transaction extension.

Finally, it remains to define the persistence JPA configuration:

```xml
<persistence version="1.0" xmlns="http://java.sun.com/xml/ns/persistence"
    xmlns:xsi="http://www.w3.org/2001/XMLSchema-instance"
    xsi:schemaLocation="http://java.sun.com/xml/ns/persistence
        http://java.sun.com/xml/ns/persistence/persistence_1_0.xsd">
    <persistence-unit name="AuctionBookPU">
        <class>manning.osgi.auction.auctioneer.AuctionBook</class>
          <properties>
            <property name="javax.persistence.jdbc.driver"
                value="org.apache.derby.jdbc.EmbeddedDriver"/>
            <property name="javax.persistence.jdbc.url"
                value="jdbc:derby:derbyDB;create=true"/>
          </properties>
    </persistence-unit>
</persistence>
```

By making these simple changes, you've achieved the durability of the auction application. You may now restart the OSGi framework, and any existing open auction items will still exist, and business can continue as usual. Persistence is commonly an essential aspect of any enterprise-grade solution.

In the previous listings, we omitted discussing how the `EventAdmin` and the `EntityManager` services were being retrieved. The assembly of these services, together with the configuration of the auctions, is the subject of the next section.

13.4.3 Using the Configuration Admin service and Blueprint

The `auction.auctioneer.sealed` bundle defines two main entities, the `SealedFirstPriceAuction` class and the `SealedFirstPriceAuctioneer` class. But the `Auctioneer` class essentially manages the creation of the auctions, keeping the auction's configuration data. For example, the `SealedFirstPriceAuctioneer` keeps the `duration` configuration of the `SealedFirstPriceAuction`. As you learned, you can use the Configuration Admin service to manage configuration, making it unnecessary to have an `Auctioneer` class.

Let's look at how you can do this, and along the way assemble the `SealedFirstPriceAuction` class with its needed services, as shown in the following listing.

> **Listing 13.16   Auction assembly and configuration**

```xml
<?xml version="1.0" encoding="UTF-8" standalone="no"?>
<blueprint xmlns="http://www.osgi.org/xmlns/blueprint/v1.0.0"
    xmlns:xsi="http://www.w3.org/2001/XMLSchema-instance"
    xmlns:cm="http://www.osgi.org/xmlns/blueprint-cm/v1.0.0">

    <reference id="eventAdmin"                                    ❶ Event Admin
        interface="org.osgi.service.event.EventAdmin" />  ◁───┘     reference

    <reference id="emf" interface="javax.persistence.EntityManagerFactory"
```

```
            filter="osgi.unit.name=AuctionBookPU" >
    </reference>

    <cm:managed-service-factory factory-pid="auction.sealed"      ❷  Managed
            auto-export="interfaces" >                               configuration
        <service-properties>                                    ❸  Use parent
            <cm:cm-properties persistent-id=""/>                    properties
        </service-properties>                                   ❹  Managed
        <cm:managed-component                                      component
            class="manning.osgi.auction.auctioneer.SealedFirstPriceAuction"
                init-method="init">
            <cm:managed-properties persistent-id=""
                    update-strategy="none" />
            <property name="type" value="Sealed-First-Price"/>
            <property name="eventAdmin"                          ❺  Inject
              ➡ ref="eventAdmin" />                                 service
            <property name="entityManagerFactory" ref="emf" />
        </cm:managed-component>
    </cm:managed-service-factory>
</blueprint>
```

This may seem daunting to begin with, but after we break it down, you'll see that there's nothing here that you haven't learned already. You start by retrieving OSGi references to the EventAdmin service ❶ and the EntityManagerFactory. In particular, for the latter, you specify the filter osgi.unit.name=AuctionBookPU, which guarantees that you retrieve the EntityManagerFactory for the AuctionBook persistence configuration. Both of these are later injected as properties of the SealedFirstPriceAuction class ❺.

Next, you specify the <managed-service-factory> tag ❷. This is provided by the Blueprint Configuration Admin extension under the namespace http://www.osgi.org/xmlns/blueprint-cm/v1.0.0. As its name clearly states, this represents a Configuration Admin's managed service factory, that is, a factory for managed services. You learned that a managed service is a service that handles configuration dictionaries (items). In this case, the SealedFirstPriceAuction is a managed service, because it needs to be configured with a duration configuration property. The role of the <managed-service-factory> element is to instantiate and register (managed) services defined by the <managed-component> element ❹. Specifically, it listens for configuration items related to its factory-pid attribute, which in this case is set to auction.sealed. When a new configuration is seen for this key (auction.sealed), it creates a new managed-component, similar to how it would have created a Java component, that is, by instantiating Java instances using the class attribute. Furthermore, it registers the Java component as a service in the OSGi registry, using the <managed-service-factory>'s interface attribute or the auto-export attribute. The latter is convenient; it tells Blueprint to inspect the Java component created and export the appropriate classes. When auto-export is set to interfaces, it means that only the Java interfaces being implemented by the Java component will be exported.

When exporting the managed component, you can configure its service properties by specifying the <service-properties> tag. In this particular case, you're telling Blueprint to use the configuration items of the parent, that is, the ones keyed by auction.sealed, as the service properties. This is done by setting the value of the persistent-id to an empty String ("") **❸**.

Finally, you can tell Blueprint to set the configuration items as properties within the managed component that was created. As shown in the listing, this is done using the following tag:

```
<cm:managed-properties persistent-id="" update-strategy="none" />
```

Blueprint looks for the configuration dictionary keyed by the persistent-id attribute and invokes the appropriate setter methods in the created Java component for each configuration property in the dictionary.

For example, the configuration dictionary for auction.sealed has a single property called duration, whose value is of type int. Therefore, the SealedFirstPrice-Auction class, which is being created as the managed component, must provide a public setDuration(int) method. This method is invoked when the configuration is first created. In addition, depending on the value of the attribute update-strategy attribute, the setters may be re-invoked if the configuration changes. In this case, because the SealedFirstPriceAuction is unable to handle changes to the duration property, you set update-strategy to none.

These few lines of Blueprint configuration are doing plenty for us, as shown in figure 13.7.

Here's a quick summary:

- The auction's duration configuration is being handled by the Configuration Admin service; therefore, we no longer need to manage it ourselves using the Auctioneer class, which can be removed. In addition, the duration configuration is injected into the SealedFirstPriceAuction class by Blueprint without us having to implement the ManagedService interface.

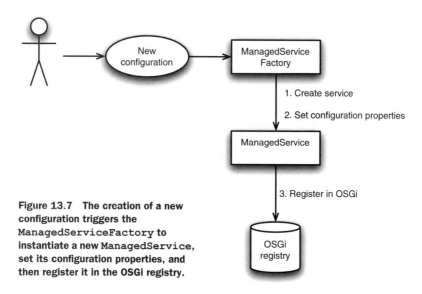

Figure 13.7 The creation of a new configuration triggers the ManagedServiceFactory to instantiate a new ManagedService, set its configuration properties, and then register it in the OSGi registry.

- The SealedFirstPriceAuction class is configured as a managed service of a managed service factory; thus, a configuration created for the PID auction. sealed results in the automatic creation of a new auction service and its registration in the OSGi service registry, with the configuration set as its service properties. This is a drastic change to the lifecycle of the auction application, which had a single auction service with a hardcoded duration configuration. With this new auction application, multiple auctions may exist at a time, and they're created by the triggering of a new configuration.
- Dependencies such as the EventAdmin and the EntityManager are easily retrieved and injected into the SealedFirstPriceAuction class.

What changes are needed to the SealedFirstPriceAuction class to support this Blueprint document? Mostly you just need to add the appropriate setters and getters for the new properties and managed properties, as follows:

```
public void setPersistentId(String pid) {
    this.pid = pid;
}

public String getPersistentId() {
    return pid;
}

public EventAdmin getEventAdmin() {
    return this.eventAdmin;
}

public void setEventAdmin(EventAdmin eventAdmin) {
    this.eventAdmin = eventAdmin;
}

public EntityManagerFactory getEntityManagerFactory() {
    return this.emf;
}

public void setEntityManagerFactory(EntityManagerFactory emf) {
    this.emf = emf;
}

public int getDuration() {
    return this.maxAllowedBids;
}

public void setDuration(int duration) {
    this.maxAllowedBids = duration;
}
```

Most of these are obvious, except for setPersistentId(). If you recall, all configuration dictionaries by default have the prebuilt property service.id, which you can access by including the appropriate setter/getter.

Finally, notice that we receive an `EntityManagerFactory`. Therefore, you need to create the `EntityManager` from it, which you do in the `init` method:

```
public void init() {
    em = emf.createEntityManager();
}
```

Like a Java component, you can configure the managed component with an `init` method to be called after all the properties have been set. This is done using the `init-method` attribute:

```
<cm:managed-component class="..." init-method="init">
```

We're finished with changes to the implementation, except for the changes that need to be made to the seller, buyer, and auditor classes to subscribe to the ask and bid events. You should find those changes straightforward to make. But to be able to test the new auction application, you still need to configure at least one auction managed service. You could do this programmatically, but a better option is to do it at runtime using JMX `ConfigurationAdminMBean`, as in the following example:

```
mbeanName = new ObjectName("osgi.compendium:service=cm,version=1.3");

ConfigurationAdminMBean cmBean =
    JMX.newMBeanProxy(msc, mbeanName, ConfigurationAdminMBean.class);

TabularData properties =
    new TabularDataSupport(JmxConstants.PROPERTIES_TYPE);

Map<String, Object> propertyValue = new HashMap<String, Object>();
propertyValue.put(JmxConstants.KEY, "duration");
propertyValue.put(JmxConstants.VALUE, 3);
propertyValue.put(JmxConstants.TYPE, JmxConstants.INTEGER);

CompositeData property =
    new CompositeDataSupport(JmxConstants.PROPERTY_TYPE, propertyValue);
properties.put(property);

String factoryPID =
    cmBean.createFactoryConfiguration(("auction.sealed");
cmBean.update(factoryPID, properties);
```

For managed service factories, you need to first invoke the `createFactory-Configuration()` method to create a new PID and then use it to set the configuration properties using the standard `update()` method, as we did in chapter 10.

So there you have it; we've been able to greatly improve our auction application by leveraging OSGi services as needed. Not only were the changes to use these services relatively simple to realize, but they were also implemented gradually, another testament to the power of modularity.

13.5 Summary

The OSGi Service Platform provides several bundle flavors, such as web application bundles (WAB), persistence bundles, and Blueprint bundles. We even created our own, the subscriber application bundle (SAB).

Flavors (features) can be combined into a single bundle by using a declarative non-programmatic approach for their assembly. OSGi defines several such approaches, Blueprint being the most popular.

Blueprint allows the specification of components and their dependencies. Blueprint supports Java components, OSGi service components, and OSGi reference components. In addition, it has several interesting features, such as support for dependency injection, lifecycle callbacks, and factory methods.

Blueprint also allows its extension, where an extender may contribute new components or decorate existing components with new features. This is done by using a Namespace Handler service, which is invoked when the extender's XML nodes are visited while parsing the Blueprint documents.

Furthermore, Blueprint allows the registration of interceptors, which intercept the runtime invocation of the method calls of the Java components. An interceptor defines `preCall()`, `postCallWithReturn()`, and `postCallWithError()` callbacks. These allow changes to the runtime behavior of components, such as beginning and committing transactions.

Finally, we revisited the auction application developed in chapter 3, changing it to support event handling, persistence, dynamic configuration, and its declarative assembly.

13.6 Epilogue

We started our journey by exploring why we need another development platform, in light of all the existing frameworks. As it turns out, OSGi's explicit handling of modularization and its service-oriented approach make the OSGi Service Platform unique.

You learned the basics of the OSGi framework, particularly the concepts of bundles and services, and developed the auction application, a system consisting of several individual bundles, broken into API, SPI, infrastructure bundles, extension bundles, and clients. Although not yet an enterprise-grade solution, the auction application was both modular as well as extensible. You also learned common patterns for developing robust OSGi solutions, including the directory service pattern, the whiteboard pattern, and the extender pattern.

Next, you learned how to properly configure bundles in a generic manner that decoupled the producers of the configuration from the consumers of the configuration. Along the way, you also learned how to make sure the configuration is valid, type-safe, and durable.

We examined the concept of an event-driven solution, particularly around the publish-subscribe model, and how to dispatch and handle business events asynchronously.

Hardly any software solution is complete without persistence, and you learned three different mechanisms for persisting application data, ranging from rudimentary to full-fledged object-relational systems. Yet, persistence without consistency isn't acceptable, so you learned about transactions, their properties, and how to leverage them within the framework. You also had your first exposure to the concept of a container, that is, a framework abstraction that takes care of an enterprise feature on behalf of the application, generally in a transparent manner.

Naming and directory services are a common solution pattern used by different technologies, such as LDAP. You learned their concepts and how you can leverage these services to share resources between the JEE world and the OSGi platform. This is increasingly important, because most real applications need to integrate with legacy solutions. Next, you learned that OSGi services are by default local and that transport endpoints need to be established and configured to allow for their remote use. You also found that remote services are among the prerequisites for using OSGi as a PaaS.

Once you understand the major features needed to develop robust applications, the next step is to be able to launch the OSGi framework appropriately, sometimes embedded within other platforms, deploy the bundles consistently as part of complete applications, and manage any offending bundles in the process. You learned how to manage the framework and its bundles at runtime using JMX technology, a useful and essential task in any production environment.

As an advanced OSGi developer, you learned how to implement containers of your own. Furthermore, you learned how to author OSGi applications, blending several container features in a declarative and intuitive form. To be able to participate in this ecosystem, you learned how to extend this declarative assembly by providing your own namespaces.

Finally, we revisited the auction application and changed it to make it a fully robust OSGi application. In the process, we were able to validate several of the services you learned about through the book.

At this point, you can now develop feature-rich Java applications. You have at your disposal a full spectrum of services, ranging from low-level infrastructure services to a complete Java EE environment. You may see yourself migrating your enterprise applications to OSGi, in the process providing a better modular architecture.

I hope you've enjoyed your journey and have understood the effort and the benefits of using the OSGi Service Platform. As is often the case with truly good things, the benefits are not immediately evident but rather come with time and are lasting.

appendix A
OSGi manifest headers

Manifest header entries are very significant in OSGi as they dictate behavior for several OSGi services and framework features. The following table includes all header entries used in the book. These are the most commonly used header entries in all existing OSGi specifications at the time of writing.

Header name	Description
Bundle-ActivationPolicy	Specifies how a bundle should be activated when started. This can be used for the lazy activation of a bundle, as explained in chapter 10. Example: `Bundle-ActivationPolicy: lazy`
Bundle-Activator	Specifies the Java class name of the bundle's activator. Example: `Bundle-Activator: com.manning.osgi.BundleActivator`
Bundle-Blueprint	Specifies the path of a Blueprint document to be used by the Blueprint container for assembling dependencies in a bundle. This is demonstrated in chapter 13. Example: `Bundle-Blueprint: META-INF/ blueprint.xml`
Bundle-Category	Specifies a comma-separated list of category names or tags. This can be used to describe a bundle. Example: `Bundle-Category: manning, auction-framework`
Bundle-ClassPath	Specifies paths within a bundle that are to be used as part of the bundle's class space. Example: `Bundle-ClassPath: /libs/app.jar`

(continued)

Header name	Description
Bundle-ContactAddress	Specifies the contact address of the vendor. Example: `Bundle-ContactAddress: 123 My Road, CA, my@email.com`
Bundle-Copyright	Specifies the copyright information of the bundle. Example: `Bundle-Copyright: Manning© 2011`
Bundle-Description	Specifies a user-friendly short description for the bundle. Example: `Bundle-Description: Manning's OSGi in Depth Auction Application`
Bundle-DocURL	Specifies a URL pointing to a bundle's documentation. Example: `Bundle-DocURL: http://www.manning.com/alves`
Bundle-Icon	Specifies a URL within the bundle's JAR file for an image file, useful for a pictorial representation of the bundle. Example: `Bundle-Icon: /images/bundle.jpg;size=64`
Bundle-License	Specifies license information that can be used to validate the bundle's usage terms. This can be in some internal format or even a URL. Example: `Bundle-License: http://www.manning.com/validate-license.php`
Bundle-Localization	Specifies the location within the bundle where localization files reside. Example: `Bundle-Localization: OSGi-INF/l10n/bundle`
Bundle-ManifestVersion	Specifies the OSGi specification to be used. For our purposes, it should be set to 2. Example: `Bundle-ManifestVersion: 2`
Bundle-Name	Specifies a user-friendly readable name for the bundle. Example: `Bundle-Name: auction application`
Bundle-NativeCode	Specifies the native code libraries contained within the bundle. Example: `Bundle-NativeCode: /lib/io.dll; osname = Linux`
Bundle-Required-ExecutionEnvironment	Specifies a comma-separated list of execution environments demanded by the bundle. This header has been deprecated in version 4.3 of the OSGi specification. Example: `Bundle-RequiredExecutionEnvironment: CDC-1.0/Foundation-1.0`

(continued)

Header name	Description
Bundle-SymbolicName	Specifies the non-localizable identity of the bundle. This header together with the bundle version uniquely identify a bundle. Example: `Bundle-SymbolicName:` `com.manning.osgi.auction`
Bundle-UpdateLocation	Specifies a URL where updates for this bundle can be retrieved. An example of how this can be used is in chapter 10. Example: `Bundle-UpdateLocation:` `http://www.manning.com/alves/auction.jar`
Bundle-Vendor	Specifies a user-friendly description of the bundle's vendor. Example: `Bundle-Vendor: manning`
Bundle-Version	Specifies the version of the bundle. This header together with the symbolic name uniquely identify a bundle. Example: `Bundle-Version: 1.0.0.1`
DynamicImport-Package	Specifies a comma-separated list of package names that are imported when needed. This is explained in chapter 4. Example: `DynamicImport-Package:` `com.manning.osgi.*`
Export-Package	Specifies the exported packages of the bundle. Example: `Export-Package: com.manning.osgi`

Fragment-Host	Specifies the host bundle of this fragment.
	Example: `Fragment-Host:`
	`com.manning.osgi.auction;`
	`bundle-version="1.0.0.1"`

Import-Package	Specifies the imported packages for this bundle. Example: `Import-Package: com.manning.osgi`
Provide-Capability	New header in OSGi version 4.3 used to specify a generic capability. Example: `Provide-Capability: com.cloudprovider;` `web-access:Boolean=true; cpu:Long=80`
Meta-Persistence	Specifies the path to the persistence unit configuration of a JPA persistence bundle. Chapter 7 explains how JPA is used. Example: `Meta-Persistence: META-INF/auction-jpa.xml`
Meta-Transaction	Specifies Java classes to be run in a transactional context. This is part of an example explained in chapter 8. Example: `Meta-Transaction:` `com.manning.osgi.MyTransactionalClass`
Remote-Service	Specifies the endpoint description of a remote service. This is explained in chapter 7. Example: `Remote-Service: META-INF/endpoint.xml`

(continued)

Header name	Description
`Require-Bundle`	Specifies dependency to another bundle. As explained in chapter 4, this should be avoided. Example: `Require-Bundle:` `com.manning.osgi.auction`
`Require-Capability`	New header in OSGi version 4.3 used to specify a dependency on a provided capability. Example: `Require-Capability: com.cloudprovider;` `filter:="(&(web-access)(cpu<90))"`

All manifest header constants can be found on the OSGi website at http://www.osgi.org/javadoc/r4v43/org/osgi/framework/Constants.html.

index